AS
UK Government & Politics

Philip Lynch
Paul Fairclough

Editor: Eric Magee

Philip Allan, an imprint of Hodder Education, an Hachette UK company, Market Place, Deddington, Oxfordshire OX15 0SE

Orders
Bookpoint Ltd, 130 Milton Park, Abingdon, Oxfordshire, OX14 4SB
tel: 01235 827827
fax: 01235 400454
e-mail: uk.orders@bookpoint.co.uk

Lines are open 9.00 a.m.–5.00 p.m., Monday to Saturday, with a 24-hour message answering service. You can also order through the Philip Allan website: www.philipallan.co.uk

© Philip Lynch, Paul Fairclough and Eric Magee 2004, 2005, 2010, 2013
ISBN 978-1-4441-8352-8

First published 2004
Second edition 2005
Third edition 2010
Fourth edition 2013

Impression number   5   4   3
Year   2017   2016   2015   2014

The Publishers would like to thank the following for permission to reproduce copyright photos:

p.17 Tony Foggon/Alamy; **p.62** Mark Sykes/Alamy; **p.103** The Conservative Party/Hulton Archive/Getty Images; **p.129** Philip Lewis/Alamy; **p.149** Jan Madsen Photography/Fotolia; **p.166** c/Fotolia; **p.176** Maurice Savage/Alamy; **p.297** Roger Pilkington/Fotolia; **p.298** Chris Howes/Wild Places Photography/Alamy; **p.309** Josemaria Toscano/Fotolia; **p.339** Jean-Christophe/AFP/Getty Images

All other photographs are reproduced by permission of TopFoto.

In all cases we have attempted to trace and credit copyright owners of material used.

Typeset by Integra Software Services Pvt., Ltd., Pondicherry, India
Printed in Dubai

Environmental information
Hachette UK's policy is to use papers that are natural, renewable and recyclable products and made from wood grown in sustainable forests. The logging and manufacturing processes are expected to conform to the environmental regulations of the country of origin.

P2220

Contents

Introduction

About this book

This textbook is designed to meet the needs of AS students of government and politics. It provides comprehensive, accessible and up-to-date coverage of all the key topics on the AQA, Edexcel and OCR specifications (see the exam specifications grid at the end of this introduction). Our aim is that you should need few other resources when studying the subject. However, politics is, by its nature, ever-changing. You should therefore enhance your understanding and keep up to date by following the news in the mainstream media and by reading subject-specific magazines such as *Politics Review*.

Each of the 11 chapters in this book provides comprehensive coverage of the topic under consideration. You don't have to read the chapters in order, but can start reading wherever you or your teacher(s) decide to begin the course. To enable you to make connections between topics, there are references in the chapters to the other places in the book where a particular issue is discussed in more detail. In addition, you can use the detailed contents pages and the index (at the back of the book) to lead you to the section containing the information you require.

Online resources

 PowerPoints summarising key knowledge and arguments for each chapter, and extension tasks and up-to-date weblinks to help you revise and consolidate your knowledge for each chapter are available online. Go to **www.hodderplus.co.uk/philipallan**.

Features to help you succeed

Each chapter begins with a series of **key questions** which will be answered during that chapter. These can be used as a revision tool to check your knowledge before the exam. At the end of each chapter you will find a **what you need to know** summary of the main points and a **further reading** section to extend your reading. Throughout, the **UK/US comparison** explains the differences between the UK and the USA in a given area to enhance your knowledge of the topic.

This new edition also benefits from a number of special features designed to focus your attention on the ideas, issues and debates that really matter at AS:

 Key concept
> Key concepts, as identified in the specifications, are explained on the page where they appear.

 Key term
> Clear, concise definitions of essential key terms are provided where they appear.

Summaries

Distinguish between

➤ These clarify the differences between similar or commonly confused political concepts or features.

Links to follow up

Useful weblinks providing opportunities for further research to extend your knowledge.

Case study

Examples for you to use in your essays.

Viewpoint

● Both sides of a controversial question set out.

**Stretch and challenge**

Activities designed to develop your skills of analysis and evaluation.

Exam focus

Questions of varying length at the end of each chapter to test your knowledge and understanding. These will help you prepare for the kinds of questions that appear on your exam papers.

What is politics?

Before starting to study UK government and politics it is helpful to define our subject matter. A student of English literature or chemistry may have little difficulty in offering a 'definition' of their chosen subject, but it is less easy to explain precisely what politics is. This is hardly surprising, given the range of definitions and interpretations in common usage.

Definitions of politics

One of the most memorable and effective definitions of politics is found in the title of American political scientist Howard Lasswell's 1935 book *Politics: Who Gets What, When and How*. Politics is, in essence, the process by which individuals and groups with divergent interests and values make collective decisions. It is present because of two key features of human societies:

➤ **Scarcity of resources.** Certain goods, from material wealth to knowledge and influence, are in short supply so disputes arise over their distribution.
➤ **Competing interests and values.** In complex societies, we find competing interests, needs and wants as well as different views on how resources should be distributed.

Power and conciliation

There are two broad perspectives on the conduct of politics:

➤ **Politics is about power.** Power is the ability to achieve a favoured outcome, whether through coercion or the exercise of authority (see Key concepts below). The study of politics thus focuses on the distribution of power within a society: who makes the rules, and where does their authority come from?

> **Politics is about conciliation.** Here the focus is on conflict resolution, negotiation and compromise. Politics can be a force for good, a way of reaching decisions in divided societies without resorting to force.

Key concepts

Power is the ability to do something or to make something happen. It can be sub-divided into four forms:

> **Absolute power** is the unlimited ability to do as one wishes and this exists only in theory.
> **Persuasive power** is the ability to persuade others that a course of action is the right one.
> **Legitimate power** involves others accepting an individual's right to make decisions, perhaps as a result of an election.
> **Coercive power** means pressing others into complying using laws and penalties.

In a democracy, governments exercise legitimate power, with elements of persuasive and coercive power.

Authority is the right to take a particular course of action. The German sociologist Max Weber (1864–1920) identified three sources of authority:

> **Traditional authority** based on established traditions and customs.
> **Charismatic authority** based on the characteristics of leaders.
> **Legal-rational authority** granted by a formal process such as an election.

In the UK only parliament has the authority to make and unmake laws. This legal-rational authority is legitimised through free and fair elections.

Authority and power may be held independently of one another: a bomb-wielding terrorist may have power without authority; a teacher might have authority without genuine power; and a police officer in a tactical firearms unit may have power and authority.

Where do we find politics?

Politics is found in various spheres of human activity:

> **The state.** The most common perspective on politics sees it as taking place primarily within the state — that is, the set of institutions that exercise authority over a political community within a territory. Here, the focus is on those formal institutions such as government and parliament that play a central role in decision making.
> **Civil society.** Politics is also found in civil society — that is, the realm of autonomous groups and associations found between the state and the individual. Civil society thus includes pressure groups, businesses, trade unions, churches and community groups.
> **All collective social action.** In *What is Politics? The Activity and its Study* (2004), Adrian Leftwich argues that politics is present in all collective social activity, whether formal and informal, and in all human groups and societies. This perspective rejects the notion of a public-private divide in which politics is only present in the public sphere. Although the focus is still on power and conciliation, it shows how politics pervades our everyday lives — for example, 'who gets what, when and how' in the family.

Continuity and change in British politics

The British political system has not undergone the upheavals — revolution, invasion, new constitutions — experienced by most other European states. Pre-democratic features, such as an uncodified constitution, a constitutional monarchy and an upper house of parliament that contains hereditary peers, survive in twenty-first century Britain. To the casual observer, key features of the British political system appear relatively unchanged.

However, closer inspection reveals important challenges to the traditional 'Westminster model' of British politics. Parliamentary sovereignty is the guiding principle of the British constitution, but it is challenged by developments such as devolution, judicial review and membership of the European Union. The United Kingdom was once viewed as the classic example of a centralised unitary state, but much domestic policy in Scotland, Wales and Northern Ireland is now determined by the devolved institutions. Debates in the study of British politics have also evolved. When examining where power lies in the core executive, many political scientists no longer ask whether cabinet government has been replaced by prime ministerial government, but whether the office of prime minister has become more presidential.

The 2010 general election provided further evidence of change. What we thought we knew about politics in the UK may no longer be accurate. The following traditional perspectives need to be reassessed:

➢ **The 'first-past-the-post' electoral system produces a clear outcome.** The 2010 general election produced a hung parliament in which no single party won a majority of seats in the House of Commons.

➢ **Coalition government is not found in Britain.** A Conservative–Liberal Democrat coalition took office following the 2010 election, and coalition governments have often been formed in the devolved administrations.

➢ **Britain has a two-party system.** The Conservatives and Labour together won a postwar low of 67% of the vote in 2010. The Liberal Democrats entered government, the Greens won their first Westminster seat and UKIP polled almost a million votes. Beyond Westminster, the Scottish National Party and Plaid Cymru have held office in the devolved administrations.

Looking ahead, we can identify potential sources of change. A 'yes' vote in the referendum on Scottish independence on 18 September 2014 would bring fundamental change in the government and politics of the UK. The Fixed-term Parliaments Act (2011) sets the date of the next general election as 7 May 2015. Should the Conservative–Liberal Democrat coalition collapse and no alternative government be formed, the election could be held before then. But regardless of its timing, the next general election could be one of the most interesting of recent times. Will it bring a return to single-party government, or will coalition government (perhaps with different coalition partners) become the new norm?

Former prime minister Harold Wilson remarked that 'a week is a long time in politics'. For students of politics, this is why it is both an interesting and challenging subject.

Exam specifications

The table below shows you how you can use this book in conjunction with the specifications of the three main UK awarding bodies: AQA, Edexcel and OCR.

Chapter	AQA	Edexcel	OCR
1 Democracy and participation	**AS Unit 1 (GOVP1)** Participation and voting behaviour	**AS Unit 1 (6GP01)** Democracy and political participation	**AS Unit 1 (F851)** [Implicit throughout unit but not as a core 'topic']
2 Elections and voting	**AS Unit 1 (GOVP1)** Participation and voting behaviour Electoral systems	**AS Unit 1 (6GP01)** Elections	**AS Unit 1 (F851)** Electoral systems and referenda UK parliamentary elections Voting behaviour in the UK
3 Political parties: structure	**AS Unit 1 (GOVP1)** Political parties	**AS Unit 1 (6GP01)** Party policies and ideas	**AS Unit 1 (F851)** Political parties (mandatory topic)
4 Political parties: policies and ideas	**AS Unit 1 (GOVP1)** Political parties	**AS Unit 1 (6GP01)** Party policies and ideas	**AS Unit 1 (F851)** Political parties (mandatory topic)
5 Pressure groups	**AS Unit 1 (GOVP1)** Pressure groups and protest movements	**AS Unit 1 (6GP01)** Pressure groups	**AS Unit 1 (F851)** Pressure groups (mandatory topic)
6 The constitution	**AS Unit 2 (GOVP2)** The British constitution	**AS Unit 2 (6GP02)** The constitution	**AS Unit 2 (F852)** The constitution
7 Parliament	**AS Unit 2 (GOVP2)** Parliament	**AS Unit 2 (6GP02)** Parliament	**AS Unit 2 (F852)** The legislature (mandatory topic)
8 The prime minister and the core executive	**AS Unit 2 (GOVP2)** The core executive	**AS Unit 2 (6GP02)** The prime minister and cabinet	**AS Unit 2 (F852)** The executive (mandatory topic)
9 Judges and civil liberties	**AS Unit 2 (GOVP2)** The British constitution	**AS Unit 2 (6GP02)** Judges and civil liberties	**AS Unit 2 (F852)** The judiciary
10 Devolution and local government	**AS Unit 2 (GOVP2)** Multi-level governance	**AS Unit 2 (6GP02)** The constitution	**AS Unit 2 (F852)** The constitution
11 The European Union	**AS Unit 2 (GOVP2)** Multi-level governance	**AS Unit 2 (6GP02)** The constitution	**AS Unit 2 (F852)** The European Union

Acknowledgements

We would like to thank Nick Gallop for writing the Exam focus sections at the end of each chapter and David O'Dell for his helpful review of the online resources.

Chapter

Democracy and participation

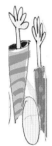

Key questions answered in this chapter

➢ What is democracy and what forms can it take?

➢ What is the difference between direct democracy and representative (or indirect) democracy?

➢ How effectively do citizens participate in politics in the UK?

➢ How democratic is the UK?

➢ What attempts have been made to enhance democracy and participation in the UK and how successful have they proven?

What is democracy?

Democracy is 'rule by the people' or 'people power'. The term has its origins in the Greek word *dēmokratia* — a union of *dēmos* (meaning 'the people') and *kratos* (meaning 'power'). Put simply, democratic systems of government give citizens a say in choosing the politicians, and in some cases even the policies, that will shape their everyday life.

However, this broad definition of democracy can cause problems, for while it is often used when referring to political systems such as those operating in the UK and the USA, it might also be said to apply to countries where the power of the people is channelled in a manner that some might consider to be 'undemocratic': for example, in 'single-party states' such as the former East Germany (German Democratic Republic) and North Korea (Democratic People's Republic of Korea). A further problem with the term 'democracy' is that the word *demos* could just as easily be translated as 'the mob', leaving democracy as little more than 'mobocracy', 'mob rule' or 'anarchy' (literally, 'no government').

Such confusion over the precise meaning and application of the term 'democracy' has resulted in a situation where it is now common to use the word not in isolation but rather prefixed with a 'qualifier' that serves to describe both the style of democracy in operation and the way in which it operates in practice (see Box 1.1). Thus we commonly refer to the UK not simply as a 'democracy', but as a **liberal democracy** or a **representative democracy**.

Key terms

➢ **Democracy** Rule by the people or 'people power'.
➢ **Representative democracy** Where citizens elect representatives to formulate legislation and take other decisions on their behalf.

Key concepts

➢ **Liberal democracy** Liberal democracy is a style of democracy incorporating free and fair elections with a belief in the importance of certain key rights and responsibilities. Liberal democracies extend the right to vote (the franchise) widely among citizens. They guarantee freedom of speech and allow the people to assemble and petition for the redress of grievances.

Box 1.1 Other types of democracy

➢ **Totalitarian democracy:** where citizens of a given state are granted the right to vote but are unable to choose between candidates representing parties other than the one in power. Totalitarian democracies are 'top-down'; citizens are not allowed any real input into the policy-making process.
➢ **Majoritarian democracy:** where the government is based on the majority support of those who inhabit a given territory. This form of democracy has the potential to see minorities marginalised and excluded from the policy-making process.
➢ **Consensual democracy:** where there is a conscious effort to reach out in a more inclusive way to all groups within a given territory as opposed to simply seeking to carry the support of a majority.
➢ **Parliamentary democracy:** where the executive part of government is drawn from the elected legislature and is, in turn, accountable to it.
➢ **Consultative or participatory democracy:** where a more conventional representative democracy incorporates elements of direct democracy — such as public inquiries, referendums, citizens assemblies or elements of e-democracy — with a view to engaging the broader citizenry in the policy-making process.
➢ **Pluralist democracy:** a system of government that encourages participation and allows for free and fair competition between competing interests.

Direct democracy and representative democracy

Direct democracy

Direct democracy is said to have its origins in classical Athens (*c.* 500 BC), where the city-state's 40,000 free men had the right to attend assembly meetings at which certain policies or actions could be approved or rejected. Attendance at such meetings was not compulsory, though a quorum of around 6,000 citizens was required on certain key votes.

Key term

➢ **Direct democracy** Where citizens are given a direct input into the decision-making process.

Voting at the assembly is often said to have involved those present casting coloured stones into a clay urn in order to indicate their preference, with the vessel being broken apart and the stones counted at the end of the process. However, in reality most votes would have been conducted through a simple show of hands.

New England 'town hall meetings'

A more contemporary example of direct democracy in action would be the 'town hall meetings' still held in New England states such as Maine and Massachusetts in the USA. As was the case in ancient Athens, however, modern town hall democracy commonly operates on a small scale with hundreds or thousands involved as opposed to tens of thousands.

Representative democracy

It is clear that direct democracy in it purest sense is simply not practical in a modern state comprising millions of citizens. Even the Athenian model presented a problem for those counting hands at assembly meetings, and the form of direct democracy practised at New England town hall meetings is commonly limited to areas with eligible populations of under 10,000. As a result, most modern democracies practise an 'indirect' or representative form of democracy.

Edmund Burke summed up what many see as the essence of representative democracy in Britain in a speech he made to his Bristol constituents in 1774: 'Your representative owes you not his industry only but his judgement,' Burke argued, 'and he betrays you if he sacrifices it to your opinion.'

The Burkean view, therefore, is that citizens elect individuals to represent them in a legislature and that such individuals are expected to represent the interests of their constituents until the following election. Crucially, however, they are not simply delegates sent with specific instructions or orders to follow. As a result, our elected representatives might at times make decisions that are contrary to our wishes.

Viewpoint	Is direct democracy compatible with representative democracy?

YES

- Elected representatives often enjoy lengthy terms in office (up to 5 years in the case of UK MPs). Referendums and recalls make them more directly accountable between elections, thereby enhancing representative democracy.
- Many MPs simply toe the party line and do as the whips tell them, rather than thinking for themselves and/or representing the interests of their constituents. Incorporating elements of direct democracy would remind representatives of who they were elected to serve.
- Conventional representative democracy limits the opportunities for meaningful participation between elections. It is also said to contribute to political apathy. Wider use of referendums and other more 'direct' tools may stimulate participation and public debate; thus reinvigorating representative democracy.
- Traditional representative democracy has a tendency towards elitism, where those returned to the legislature are drawn from a narrow range of social backgrounds and those from different backgrounds or with less centrist views are not properly heard. Direct democracy has the potential to allow people to participate on a level playing field.

NO

- Those elected to office are given a mandate to act on behalf of voters, along the lines set out in their election manifestos. Representatives should not feel pressured into going back to the people in order to seek approval for specific policies.
- Elected representatives are often better informed than the general public. They have access to relevant research and are able to educate themselves on the merits and demerits of a particular course of action before casting their vote in parliament. It is nonsensical to leave key decisions to the broader public.
- Representative democracy allows parliament to implement policies that are necessary but unpopular — the kinds of things that would not secure support if put to a public ballot.
- Representative government also allows for 'joined-up government' where individual policies are decided not in isolation but with full consideration of potential knock-on effects for other areas of policy. Wider use of referendums would undermine joined-up government.

Referendums

While direct democracy in its purest form is impossible to achieve on a large scale in a modern democratic state, orthodox representative democracy can all too easily become remote and unresponsive to the needs of citizens. This paradox has led many democratic states to employ elements of direct democracy, while holding to the representative model.

The classic modern tool of direct democracy is the **referendum**. Outside of the UK, referendums are used to resolve a wide range of issues. In Eire, for example, a 1995 referendum legalised divorce, whereas in Switzerland, where they average around four referendums per year, the people rejected a proposal to guarantee all workers 6 weeks annual leave by 66.5% to 33.5% in 2012.

Key term

➤ **Referendum** A vote on a single issue put to a public ballot by the government of the day. Referendums offer a degree of direct democracy. They are generally framed in the form of a simple 'yes/no' question.

The UK experience

In the 1940s, the incumbent prime minister Clement Attlee described referendums as 'a tool of demagogues and dictators', concluding that the referendum was 'a device so alien to all our traditions'.

'A tool of dictators and demagogues'

Attlee's first criticism was clearly 'of its time'. He had seen how totalitarian leaders such as Adolf Hitler employed such devices as a means of legitimising courses of action that (a) had already been determined and (b) were clearly not democratic. But even in the modern era, critics of referendums argue that they can result in a kind of tyranny of the majority — and that the majority in question are often ill-equipped to understand precisely what is being asked of them.

Referendums and initiatives

Referendums

➤ Ordinary referendums are called by those in power either when they want to legitimise a certain course of action or where they are constitutionally required to hold a referendum due to the nature of the proposed changes. In a referendum, matters such as the question which is to be put to the public ballot are left largely in the hands of elected politicians.

Initiatives

➤ Initiatives give ordinary citizens the opportunity to call a public ballot on a question of their own choosing, often by collecting a predetermined number of signatures on a petition and thereby triggering a referendum. Many US states allow such ballot initiatives, and although not all of these measures pass into law, many do. For example, California's Proposition 8 (2008) banned same-sex marriage and an initiative proposed in 2012 aimed to abolish the death penalty in the state (see case study). Many other countries have similar provisions in their constitutions. In New Zealand, for example, the Citizen's Initiated Referenda Act (1993) required support of only 10% of the electorate for a non-binding referendum to be initiated.

Case study   The initiative process in California

In order to qualify for a public vote on changing a regular law in California, petitions must secure a number of signatures equal to at least 5% of the total number of votes cast for state governor at the previous election. In 2012 the target was 504,760 signatures (with a higher target of 807,615 applying to any initiative proposing an amendment to the California State Constitution).

In 2012, a ballot initiative proposing the abolition of the death penalty in the state of California gained enough signatures to qualify it for the November ballot as 'Proposition 34'.

This proposal, which grew out of the 'Savings, Accountability, and Full Enforcement for California Act' (or 'SAFE California Act'), aimed to replace the death penalty with a life sentence without the opportunity for parole. The proposition also provided for an extra $100 million per annum to be spent investigating cases of rape and homicide within the state. This additional spend was to be funded from the monies saved in no longer having to administer the death penalty and the appeals process associated with it — estimated to have cost some $4 billion since the death penalty was restored in the state under Proposition 7 (1978). Proposition 34 was narrowly defeated (53% : 47%) in November 2012.

'A device so alien to all our traditions'

Taken literally, Attlee's second criticism was simply a statement of reality — referendums were not a feature of the UK political landscape when he was writing. However, the comment also hints at a deeper meaning: that the UK is essentially a 'representative democracy'.

When are referendums used in the UK?

Most other countries either have codified constitutions that clearly set out the circumstances in which a referendum must be held — or leave the decision to a supreme court. Although the UK, in contrast, still has no formal list of circumstances in which referendums are legally required, it has long been accepted that referendums can provide a way of legitimising major constitutional changes. In the nineteenth century, A. V. Dicey referred to the referendum as a kind of 'people's veto' and modern UK leaders such as the former prime minister Tony Blair have largely accepted this premise: 'in the case of major constitutional change,' Blair remarked in 1995, 'there is clearly a case for that decision to be taken by the British people'.

Although the public reaction to the increased prevalence of referendums in recent years has been largely positive, the UK experience of referendums thus far has highlighted a number of problems. They are divided here into five broad categories: topic; wording; timing; funding; and turnout.

Topic

At the time of writing in 2013, there had only been two UK-wide referendums: the ballot held on continued membership of the EEC (now the European Union) in 1975, and the offer of the alternative vote (AV) system for use in elections to the Westminster Parliament in 2011. Whereas referendums in other parts of the world have been held on issues ranging from the legal status of marijuana to the rights of aborigines, ten of the eleven referendums sanctioned by the UK Parliament between 1973 and 2012 (see Table 1.1) related directly to the distribution of power between supranational, national and subnational institutions. Moreover, there is a sense that governments are inclined to offer referendums only when they are relatively certain of securing the outcome they desire — or where they have a direct interest in going to the people. This was certainly a criticism levelled at Harold Wilson's decision to hold a ballot over continued membership of the EEC in 1975, an issue on which his Labour administration was deeply divided. The future prime minister Margaret Thatcher saw that poll as serving only to 'sacrifice parliamentary sovereignty to political expediency'.

Table 1.1 UK referendums, 1973–2012

Date	Who voted	Question (paraphrased)	% yes	% no	% turnout
1973 (Mar.)	N Ireland	Should NI stay in the UK?	98.9	1.1	58.1*
1975 (June)	UK	Should UK stay in the EEC?	67.2	32.8	63.2
1979 (Mar.)	Scotland	Should there be a Scottish Parliament?	51.6	48.4	63.8
1979 (Mar.)	Wales	Should there be a Welsh Parliament?	20.3	79.7	58.3
1997 (Sept.)	Scotland	Should there be a Scottish Parliament?	74.3	25.7	60.4
		With tax-varying powers?	63.5	36.5	
1997 (Sept.)	Wales	Should there be a Welsh Assembly?	50.3	49.7	50.1
1998 (May)	London	A London mayor and London Assembly?	72.0	28.0	34.0
1998 (May)	N Ireland	Approval for the Good Friday Agreement	71.1	28.9	81.0
2004 (Nov.)	North East	A regional assembly for the North East?	22.0	78.0	48.0
2011 (Mar.)	Wales	Primary legislative powers for the Welsh Assembly in 20 policy areas?	63.5	36.5	35.6
2011 (May)	UK	Should AV replace FPTP for elections to the House of Commons?	32.1	67.9	42.2

*This referendum was boycotted by nationalists.

Wording

The wording of the 1975 referendum on whether or not the UK should remain in the EEC was said to have been phrased in such a way as to encourage a positive response — a criticism that was also levelled at the SNP's preferred wording for the 2014 referendum on Scottish independence: 'Do you agree that Scotland should be an independent country?' Although the Electoral Commission was granted the authority to comment on the intelligibility of questions posed in all future referendums under the 2000 Political Parties, Elections and Referendums Act (see Box 1.2), the then deputy prime minister, John Prescott, was quick to confirm that the government (through its control of parliament) would retain the final say.

Box 1.2 — The Electoral Commission's Question Assessment Guidelines

➤ The question should prompt an immediate response.
➤ Words and phrases used in the question should not have positive or negative connotations.
➤ Words and phrases used in the question should not lead voters in a particular direction.
➤ Words and phrases used in the question should not be loaded.
➤ The question should not contain 'jargon'.
➤ The language used in the question should be consistent.
➤ Words and phrases used in the question should reflect the language used and understood by the voter.
➤ The question should not provide more information than is necessary to answer the question meaningfully.
➤ The question should not be longer than necessary.
➤ The question should be well structured.

Source: Electoral Commission.

Timing

Even when referendums are offered — and they are offered rarely in the UK — those scheduling them routinely delay until such a time as they think they are most likely to secure their desired outcome. This criticism could certainly be applied to the SNP's decision to delay the referendum on Scottish independence until 2014.

Funding

At the time of the 1975 referendum on EEC membership, the 'yes' camp was said to have outspent the 'no' camp by a ratio of 3 to 1. Under the Political Parties, Elections and Referendums Act (PPERA 2000), referendums in the UK were to be state funded, with the 'yes' and 'no' campaigns each receiving a £600,000 public grant. However, funding remained an issue at the 2011 AV referendum.

Turnout

The paradox of referendums is that, while such devices are championed as a means of encouraging political participation and enhancing legitimacy, turnout at UK referendums is

⟨⟩ Stretch and challenge

Funding the 2011 AV referendum

Although the PPERA (2000) resulted in the introduction of publicly funded grants for lead campaign groups at UK referendums, it did not ban private funding of such campaigns. Instead, those campaigners wishing to spend more than £10,000 at a referendum were simply required to:

- register with the Electoral Commission
- report details of their income and expenditure to the Commission
- keep to the overall spending limits imposed by the Commission

Whereas the 'yes' campaign revealed the names of its major donors early in the campaign, the 'no' campaign proved less forthcoming ahead of the key vote. It was not until 2 May 2011 that the *Guardian* was able to reveal that 42 of the 53 largest donors to the 'no' campaign were known Conservative Party donors.

Table 1.2 Spending (£5 million limit for designated lead campaigner)

	Total spend by designated lead campaigner	Expenditure by other registered campaigners	Total campaign spend
'Yes'	£2,139,741	£70,007	£2,209,748
'No'	£2,598,194	£874,019	£3,472,213

Table 1.3 Published donations received by each campaign

'Yes'	£2,228,114
'No'	£2,731,533

Table 1.4 Publicly funded grant received (£380,000 limit for designated lead campaigner)

'Yes'	£140,457
'No'	£146,432

Source: Electoral Commission (2012)

Questions

1. Why does the relative funding of the 'yes' and 'no' campaigns at referendums matter?
2. Why did the 'No to AV' campaign's failure to disclose the identities of its major backers until so late in the campaign provoke such criticism?

often very low, bringing into question both stated goals. Though the latter problem can be addressed by incorporating thresholds (i.e. requiring a fixed percentage of the electorate to give a 'yes' vote, as opposed to a majority of those turning out), such artificial hurdles can create problems of their own; as seen in the Scottish devolution referendum in 1979. The reality is stark. Turnout at the eleven referendums called by the Westminster Parliament between 1973 and 2011 averaged just 54.1%. Moreover, while low turnout at referendums is disappointing in itself, the problem is made worse still when the results in such referendums are marginal. The Welsh devolution referendum of September 1997 is a case in point — only 50.3% of the 50.1% who turned out favoured the establishment of the National Assembly of Wales.

Local referendums

While attention naturally focuses on the eleven major referendums called by the Westminster Parliament between 1973 and 2011, we should not ignore the increasing use of such devices at local level since the 1990s, both in approving structural changes to the local government in some areas and in seeking to authorise policies such as the congestion charge.

Establishing directly elected mayors

The Greater London Authority, comprising a directly elected mayor of London and a 25-member assembly, was established following a regional referendum in the capital in 1998. Since then there have been around 50 separate referendums on the question of whether or not to establish directly elected local mayors in places as distant as the Isle of Wight and Hartlepool (see case study).

Case study | The rise and fall of the Mayor of Hartlepool

The election of the Hartlepool FC mascot, H'Angus the Monkey (otherwise known as Stuart Drummond) as mayor of Hartlepool in 2002 brought widespread criticism. How, it was argued, could an individual initially campaigning on a platform of giving free bananas to schoolchildren be placed in charge of a £106 million municipal budget? Drummond's performance in office and subsequent re-election in 2005 and 2009 led many to reconsider their position. However, a second referendum held in Hartlepool in November 2012 saw voters approving the abolition of the post of Mayor of Hartlepool, with effect from May 2013.

H'Angus the Monkey, otherwise known as Stuart Drummond

May 2012 saw referendums in the 10 largest English cities that had neither balloted residents previously, nor introduced directly elected mayors by some other means — in line with a pledge made in 2010 Conservative Party manifesto. However, only in Bristol did voters deliver a 'yes' vote (see Table 1.5).

Although turnout at some of the local mayoral referendums held since 1997 — ranging between 10% and 64% — has given cause for concern, the widespread use of such public polls has clearly added to the sense that referendums are now part of the UK's democratic architecture.

Table 1.5 May 2012 mayoral referendum results

City	Outcome	'Yes'	'No'	Turnout	Electorate
Birmingham	'No'	88,085 (42.2%)	120,611 (57.8%)	27.7%	754,765
Bradford	'No'	53,949 (44.9%)	66,283 (55.1%)	35.2%	341,126
Bristol	'Yes'	41,032 (53.3%)	35,880 (46.7%)	24.1%	318,893
Coventry	'No'	22,619 (36.4%)	39,483 (63.6%)	26.2%	236,818
Leeds	'No'	62,440 (36.7%)	107,910 (63.3%)	30.3%	562,598
Manchester	'No'	42,677 (46.8%)	48,593 (53.2%)	24.7%	369,376
Newcastle-Upon-Tyne	'No'	24,630 (38.1%)	40,089 (61.9%)	32.0%	202,527
Nottingham	'No'	20,943 (42.5%)	28,320 (57.5%)	23.8%	206,555
Sheffield	'No'	44,571 (35.0%)	82,890 (65.0%)	32.1%	397,510
Wakefield	'No'	27,610 (37.8%)	45,357 (62.2%)	28.3%	257,530

Source: adapted from Sear, C. and Parry, K. (2012) *Directly Elected Mayors*, House of Commons SN/PC/5000.

Congestion charges

The congestion charge initiative originated with central government, but it was largely left to local authorities to adopt and implement. Whereas the first mayor of London, Ken Livingstone, used his considerable executive powers over London transport to introduce the charge in the capital, efforts to do so in Edinburgh (2005) and in Manchester (2008) involved seeking public approval for the introduction of such charges through a local referendum (see Table 1.6).

Table 1.6 Congestion charge referendums

Year	Place	Turnout	'Yes'	'No'
2005	Edinburgh	61.7%	25.6%	74.4%
2008	Manchester	53.2%	21.2%	78.8%

While some regard the holding of these referendums and the resounding 'no' votes that resulted as a welcome exercise of 'pure democracy' or 'people power', others have been more circumspect. In the case of Edinburgh, the cost of developing the proposals rejected in the referendum was estimated at £9 million — a considerable sum of money simply to write-off on the basis of what may well have been a knee-jerk reaction to the prospect of paying a new 'tax'. The rejection of charges in Manchester appeared to have been prompted by similar concerns — particularly an unwillingness to pay the charge before the public transport infrastructure was in place.

In both Edinburgh and Manchester, the 'no' votes effectively prevented the improvements in transport infrastructure that those on all sides of the funding argument accepted were necessary. In the case of Manchester, the 'no' vote was particularly significant as the transport secretary Geoff Hoon had already conceded that there was 'no Plan B' for improving transport infrastructure in the city. As Lord Peter Smith, chairman of the Greater Manchester Authorities, commented to the *Manchester Evening News*, the result was 'very clear...this is not just a vote "no" for congestion charging, it is a vote "no" to improvements on the trams, railways and buses and there will now be no improvements'.

Should the UK use more referendums or provide for initiatives?

Despite the promise of a number of referendums in recent years, the vast majority of those English people under the age of 50 in 2010 — the year before the nationwide AV referendum — had never had the opportunity to vote in a major UK referendum. The eleven referendums called by the Westminster Parliament between 1973 and 2011 focused on an extraordinarily narrow range of issues. The way in which such ballots have been conducted and the low levels of turnout witnessed have raised issues of legitimacy that go beyond simply questioning whether or not such devices are compatible with our representative democracy.

However, while there is no great clamour for the adoption of the kind of **initiative** process seen in many US states and in some European countries, public support for the wider use of referendums appears to be increasing. This greater public acceptance of referendums, allied to the prospect of further constitutional reform, makes it likely that such devices will be used, or at least offered, a good deal more in the coming years.

Should the UK allow recalls of elected officials?

A **recall** election is a procedure that allows registered voters to petition for a public vote to remove an elected official from office before the end of his or her term. In most cases, recalls are permitted only where there is evidence of corruption, negligence or, in some cases, incompetence. Although recalls have not traditionally been available to voters in the UK, the 2009 MPs' expenses scandal led to calls for the introduction of such a system. The 2010 general election manifestos of all three main UK parties proposed introducing the power of recall, though little progress had been made towards this goal by the time of writing in October 2012 (see stretch and challenge activity).

Key terms

➤ **Initiative** A process by which citizens can call a referendum, normally by collecting a predetermined number of signatures on a petition.
➤ **Recall** A device that allows citizens to unseat an elected official before the end of their term in office.

Problems with recalls

Although the recall process can make politicians more accountable to voters, it also undermines the principle of representative democracy. For example, when the 'Recall Gray Davies' campaign was launched in California in February 2003, the Democrat governor was only weeks into his second term in office, having been convincingly re-elected the previous November. There was even evidence that the campaign had been organised and funded by Republicans unhappy at his re-election.

⟷ Stretch and challenge

Recall of MPs in the UK

The coalition agreement promised legislation that would allow constituents to force a by-election if their MP was found guilty of serious wrongdoing. In December 2011 the government published both a White Paper and the draft Recall of MPs bill. The proposals set out a three-stage process for recalling MPs:

- **Stage 1: Triggering a petition for recall.** A petition could be triggered either by an MP receiving a custodial sentence of 12 months or less (those sentenced for longer are already disqualified) or where the House of Commons passes a resolution.
- **Stage 2: Petition.** Once triggered, a petition would be available for the MP's constituents to sign. A by-election would be triggered if 10% of those on the electoral register signed the petition.
- **Stage 3: By-election.** In either case, a petition would then be opened for the MP's constituents to sign; if 10% of those on the electoral register signed, a by-election would be called.

In June 2012, the Commons Political and Constitutional Reform Committee published its report on the draft bill. It was critical of the proposals, arguing that the petitions would most likely be triggered 'seldom, if ever' and that the House of Commons already has sufficient disciplinary powers. Despite making specific proposals for improving the bill, the committee recommended that the government 'abandon its plans to introduce a power of recall and use the parliamentary time this would free up to better effect'.

Source: adapted from Monitor 52, Constitution Unit Newsletter, October 2012.

Questions

1 How do the proposals outlined in the draft Recall of MPs bill differ from the kind of recall process in place in many US states?

2 What criticisms could be made of these proposals?

Political culture and participation

What is political culture?

The nature of political participation within a given state will be influenced, in part, by the prevailing **political culture**.

Political culture and participation in the UK

UK political culture was traditionally said to be defined by three characteristics:

Key concept

➤ **Political culture** The ideas, beliefs and attitudes that shape political behaviour within a given area. It describes the way in which citizens collectively view the political system and their status and role within it.

- ➤ **Homogeneity** — the belief that citizens shared a common heritage and identity; a sense of togetherness that transcended what divided them.
- ➤ **Consensus** — where UK citizens accepted the basic 'rules of the game'. These rules include the need for toleration, pragmatism, peaceful negotiation and compromise.

➤ **Deference** — the idea that people deferred to an elite that was regarded as being 'born to rule', that there was a natural willingness to accept an ingrained, class-based inequality and a rigid social hierarchy.

Such defining features were said to favour certain, perhaps more passive, forms of political participation. For example, one would hardly expect to see high levels of direct action in a society where most citizens shared a common view of what was needed, accepted the rules of the game and were deferential towards those holding positions of authority.

In the second half of the twentieth century, however, UK political culture underwent something of a transformation. Successive waves of immigration, the rise of Scottish and Welsh nationalism, and the decline of the Church of England all played their part in creating a situation in which the UK was increasingly said to be characterised more by multiculturalism than by homogeneity. At the same time, the postwar consensus broke down in the 1970s with the rise of politicians such as Margaret Thatcher. In recent years, this decline in consensus has been reflected in the proliferation of single-issue campaigns, the rise of direct action and increased support for nationalist parties. It is probably also fair to say that the UK has become a less deferential society. Where the power of the ruling elite was once perpetuated by the veil of secrecy and mystery that surrounded it, the rise of modern, less deferential media has done much to demystify such individuals and institutions. Unthinking deference towards the ruling elite has, as a result, declined significantly.

Political participation in the UK

Political participation can be broadly categorised into its electoral and non-electoral forms.

Electoral participation

Those who are eligible and registered to vote in a given election are referred to collectively as the electorate. Under the Representation of the People Act (1969), the **franchise** was extended to virtually all citizens aged 18 or over. The effect of this Act and other changes dating back to the Great Reform Act (1832) was significantly to increase the number of individuals eligible to vote.

> **Key terms**
>
> ➤ **Political participation**
>   Collectively refers to the range of ways in which citizens can involve themselves in the political process.
> ➤ **Franchise** The franchise is the right to vote as established by parliamentary statute. The vast majority of adult UK citizens have the right to vote.

➤ In 1831, only 5% of adults were able to vote. This represented 450,000 individuals from a population of around 25 million.
➤ By 1969, 99% of adults were able to vote. This represented around 40 million individuals from a population of 58 million.

In the UK, voters are legally required to register to vote. Voter registration averaged around 95% of the voting age population (VAP) in the second half of the twentieth century but it is said to have declined to around 90% in recent years, perhaps as a result of a more mobile population. Although British citizens living abroad retain the right to vote, not all of the UK VAP is eligible. For example, you cannot vote in parliamentary elections if you are:

➤ a European Union citizen from an EU country other than the UK or Ireland, although European citizens can vote in European Parliament elections and local elections in any EU country in which they are living

➤ a member of the House of Lords

➤ a convicted criminal serving a custodial sentence (a prohibition currently under review in the wake of a number of cases in the European Court of Human Rights)

➤ convicted of a corrupt or illegal electoral practice

➤ suffering from a severe mental illness

Turnout

One of the most obvious ways in which an individual can participate in a political system is to vote. Levels of **turnout** are, therefore, one important measure of political participation (see Table 1.7).

Key term

➤ **Turnout** The percentage of registered voters who cast a ballot in a given election.

Table 1.7 General election turnout, 1945–2010

Year	%	Year	%	Year	%	Year	%
1945	72.8	1964	77.1	1979	76.0	2001	59.4
1950	83.9	1966	75.8	1983	72.7	2005	61.4
1951	82.6	1970	72.0	1987	75.3	2010	65.1
1955	76.8	1974 (Feb.)	78.8	1992	77.7		
1959	78.7	1974 (Oct.)	72.8	1997	71.4		

Low turnout is a problem because it brings into question the government's **legitimacy** and the strength of its electoral **mandate**. In 2005, for example, the Labour Party secured a Commons majority of 65 with the support of only 35.2% of the 61.4% of eligible voters who turned out to vote. This was equivalent to just 21.6% of the electorate.

Key concepts

Legitimacy The legal right or authority to exercise power. A government claims legitimacy as a result of the mandate it secures at a general election.

Mandate The right of the governing party to pursue the policies it sets out in its general election manifesto.

➤ The doctrine of the mandate gives the governing party the authority to pursue its stated policies but does not require it to do so or prevent it from introducing proposals not included in its manifesto.

➤ In its 1997 general election manifesto, New Labour promised both to remove the rights of hereditary peers to sit and vote in the House of Lords and to move towards a more democratic and more representative second chamber. It largely delivered on the first of these pledges with the House of Lords Act (1999).

Key concept

Differential turnout Where the national turnout figure recorded at a given election masks differences in turnout by constituency or by region. A number of factors might account for differential turnout:

➤ how marginal an individual seat or election is (is there a chance to make a real change?)

➤ the electoral system in operation (do people think that their vote will count?)

➤ local or national issues and controversies

➤ the 'intensity' of the campaign

➤ media attention (lesser or greater media activity in one constituency or in a given election may affect turnout)

When considering turnout one should, however, remember three things. First, the national turnout figure masks massive regional variations. For example, although the national turnout in 2010 was 65.1%, there was a significant gulf between the highest constituency turnout (77.3% in East Renfrewshire) and the lowest (44.3% in Manchester Central). This variation is referred to as **differential turnout**.

Second, turnout varies considerably according to variables such as age, gender, social class and ethnicity. Older voters, women, those in higher social classes and Caucasian voters are statistically more likely to turn out and vote. For example, only 44% of eligible voters in the 18–24 age category cast a ballot at the 2010 general election, compared to the 76% turnout figure recorded for the over-65s. At the same election, just 57% of those in the DE social classes cast a ballot, compared to a 76% turnout in the AB categories.

Third, turnout varies significantly between different types of election. So-called 'second order' elections such as local elections and elections to the European Parliament often witness far lower levels of turnout than general elections (see Table 1.8).

Table 1.8 Turnout at selected UK elections, 1994–2012 (%)

	1997	2001	2005	2010
General	71.4	59.4	61.4	65.1

	1994	1999	2004	2009
European Parliament	36.5	24.0	38.5	34.5

	1999	2003	2007	2011
Northern Ireland Assembly**	70.0	64.0	62.3	54.7
Scottish Parliament*	58.8	49.4	51.7	50.4
Welsh Assembly*	44.6	38.2	43.5	41.5

	2000	2004	2008	2012
London Assembly*	31.2	34.7	44.3	37.4
London mayor**	33.7	35.9	44.5	37.4

	2002	2006	2008	2012
English local	33.3	36.5	35.0	31.1

*Turnout shown for constituency contests
**Turnout shown for first preferences
Source: adapted in part from data in McGuiness, F., *UK Election Statistics: 1918–2012*, House of Commons Research Paper 12/43, August 2012.

What factors might account for variable turnout?

➢ **Type of election.** Voters are more likely to turn out to vote when they value the institutions to which individuals are seeking to be elected. This may account for the relatively low levels of turnout witnessed at local elections.

➢ **Political apathy or disengagement.** The POWER Report suggested that increasing numbers of voters were coming to the conclusion that elections made little difference, particularly where the main UK political parties were seen to be converging ideologically.

➢ **'Hapathy'.** A proportion of those who abstain do so because they are happy with the status quo and do not, therefore, feel the need to cast a ballot.

➢ **The relative value of a vote.** Those living in safe seats may feel that there is little point in their voting because the result is already a foregone conclusion. Those in marginal seats may be more likely to turn out and cast a ballot.

➢ **The electoral system in operation.** Some voters may be more inclined to cast a ballot where they think that their vote will be counted. Some argue that turnout would be higher at UK general elections if they were contested under a proportional electoral system as opposed to a 'winner-takes-all' system such as first-past-the-post.

➢ **The role of the mass media.** Intense media coverage can have the effect of stimulating turnout in a particular election or constituency, particularly where polling published in the media appears to suggest that the contest is close and every vote might matter.

Distinguish between

Political apathy and 'hapathy'

Political apathy

➢ A state of passivity or indifference towards political institutions and their associated processes — linked to a decline in political participation. Although passivity need not necessarily carry negative connotations, apathy is generally seen as something that can have a corrosive effect on democracy.

'Hapathy'

➢ Hapathy is the idea that voters may abstain from voting as a result of happiness with (as opposed to indifference towards) the way in which they are being governed. Research conducted on behalf of the Electoral Commission in 2005 showed that 29% of those who described themselves as 'satisfied with democracy' did not cast a vote at the 2005 general election whereas 59% who were 'dissatisfied with democracy' still turned out.

Links to follow up

'General Election 2005' (RP05/33) 17 May 2005, **www.parliament.uk** — a research paper on the 2005 general election, including evidence on political participation: turnout, candidacy, etc.

'General Election 2010' (RP10/36) 2 February 2011, **www.parliament.uk** — a similar research paper on the 2010 general election.

Non-electoral participation

Studies of political participation often focus on electoral participation defined in narrow terms: that is, electoral turnout. If we adopt a more inclusive definition of electoral participation, we might include other activities: for example,

> **Canvassing and leafleting.** Large numbers of volunteers are mobilised at grassroots level in support of each party's election campaign. While some of these individuals are paid-up members of the party they are working for, many are not.

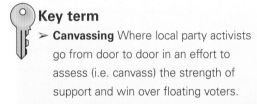

Key term

> **Canvassing** Where local party activists go from door to door in an effort to assess (i.e. canvass) the strength of support and win over floating voters.

> **Organising election events and fundraising activities.** Most election campaigns are funded locally, the major exception being those in marginal constituencies at general elections. Although the Political Parties, Elections and Referendums Act (PPERA 2000) imposed a £30,000 per-constituency spending limit on candidates at general elections, it is generally up to local activists to raise the funds needed by collecting donations from local party backers and organising fundraising events in support of their chosen candidate.

> **Staffing campaign offices.** Every candidate is required to name an election agent (or 'official agent'). This individual acts as 'campaign manager', liaising with the returning officer in the constituency and managing the official records of campaign revenue and expenditure. The major parties often employ professional election agents, whereas independent candidates and those representing smaller parties tend to rely on a volunteer to perform this role, or even act as their own agent. The agent manages the candidate's campaign team — those who staff the campaign office in the run-up to the campaign and perform specific roles on election day. This team includes counting agents and party 'tellers' who stand outside polling stations in an effort to gauge support for their chosen party on the day of the election, thereby allowing their preferred candidate to target their 'get-out-the-vote' strategies.

It is also important to remember that there are many forms of non-electoral participation: for example,

> **Writing to one's elected representatives or meeting with them in person.** MPs are expected to work as advocates for constituents facing particular difficulties. Constituents may write to their MP asking for advice or support in relation to a particular problem, or seek to meet the MP in person. Although many MPs do not live in the constituencies they represent in parliament, most take the time to hold surgeries at their constituency offices.

For example, although the Respect MP for Bethnal Green and Bow, George Galloway, was widely criticised for spending several weeks in the Big Brother House in 2006, he routinely held a weekly surgery at his constituency office in London.

> **Having an ongoing membership of and/or involvement in a political party.** While the memberships of the main UK political parties have fallen significantly in recent years (see Table 1.9), such organisations still provide a significant avenue for political participation. Even those who are not themselves a member of a political party may attend meetings organised by a party, and some parties actively seek to involve non-members when selecting their parliamentary candidates. This was seen with the Conservatives' use of an open primary in Totnes in 2009 and their use of open selection meetings in many other constituencies ahead of the 2010 general election.

> **Engaging in political protest or organised pressure group activity.** As party memberships have fallen, so involvement in pressure group activity of all shades has risen. There has been a particular increase in less formal, protest activity and in ethical, consumer-based campaigns.

> **Engaging with, discussing or debating political issues.** The act of discussing political issues with friends or family might be seen as a low-level form of political participation. Engaging with political issues by watching relevant television programmes (e.g. the televised debates between the leaders of the three main parties at the time of the 2010 general election) — whether alone or with others — might also be seen as a form of political participation.

Is there a participation crisis in the UK?

There has been a great deal of debate about the alleged **participation crisis** in the UK since the historically low levels of turnout at the 2001, 2005 and 2010 general elections. Some commentators have highlighted other areas where political participation has declined, such as falling party membership.

The POWER Report

Although it was criticised at the time for the fact that its conclusions did not appear to be based squarely on empirical evidence, the 2006 **POWER inquiry** probably still offers us the most accessible recent snapshot of political participation in the UK. The report's main

Key terms

> **Participation crisis** The view that declining levels of political participation in the UK threaten to undermine its democratic systems.

> **POWER inquiry** An inquiry into the state of political participation in the UK initiated by the Joseph Rowntree Trust. The inquiry resulted in the publication of the POWER Report: *Power to the People: The Report of POWER — An Independent Inquiry into Britain's Democracy.*

conclusion was that the popular disillusionment with democratic institutions and the main political parties demanded immediate attention.

The changing nature of political participation

Recent years have witnessed a move away from traditional forms of participation, such as voting and party membership, towards membership of mainstream pressure groups and involvement in protest movements, consumer campaigns and direct action.

Links to follow up

'Power to the People' (SN/PC/3948), 14 March 2006, **www.parliament.uk** — a short set of briefing notes on the POWER inquiry.

The POWER Report, **www.jrrt.org.uk** — click on 'Publications' to find a pdf of the full report from the POWER inquiry.

Although such changes in participation were already well under way by 2000, they gathered pace after this, with low turnouts in the 2001, 2005 and 2010 general elections and a rise in 'the politics of protest' over fuel duty, fox hunting, globalisation, the war in Iraq and government spending plans.

Declining party membership

The sharp decline in individual party membership in the last 30 years has been matched by the steep rise in pressure group membership. In 2012, for example, the Royal Society for the Protection of Birds (RSPB) had more than twice as many members as the three main UK political parties combined (see Table 1.9 and the case study on the RSPB). Indeed, whereas membership of the main UK parties continued to spiral downwards during the first decade of the twenty-first century, the RSPB's membership increased steadily. Thus, as Noreena Hertz

Case study — **The Royal Society for the Protection of Birds**

➢ Over a million members.

➢ A staff of over 1,300 and almost 18,000 volunteers.

➢ In 2010 resources available for charitable purposes totalled £94.7 million.

➢ A UK headquarters, three national offices and nine regional offices.

➢ A local network of 175 local groups and more than 110 youth groups.

➢ At least 9 volunteers for every paid member of staff.

Table 1.9 Individual party membership (000s)

Year	Conservative	Labour	Liberal Democrat
1951	2,900	876	–
1983	1,200	295	145*
1987	1,000	289	138*
1992	500	280	101
1997	400	405	87
2001	311	272	73
2005	300	198	73
2008	250	166	60
2010	177	193	65
2011	c130-170	193	49

*SDP–Liberal Alliance.
Source: Feargal McGuinness, *Membership of UK Political Parties*, House of Commons Library, 2012.

remarked in the *Independent* back in 2001, 'It's not about apathy': 'while voting is waning, alternative forms of political expression…are all on the rise.'

In his 2009 book, *Trust: How We Lost it and How to Get it Back*, Blair's biographer Anthony Seldon made the link between declining levels of public trust in formal politics and this decline in party membership. While it is difficult to prove that such a causal link exists, this line of reasoning appears plausible in light of the anecdotal evidence compiled by the POWER inquiry. It might also be argued that the loss of trust identified by Seldon is one aspect of the declining deference identified earlier in this chapter.

The rise of consumer campaigns

As well as the growth in more conventional pressure group activity, in the last two decades there has also been a significant increase in the number of individuals involved in politically motivated consumer boycotts, social movements and other kinds of less formal political participation. For example, research has demonstrated that the percentage of individuals who have boycotted products for ethical reasons rose from 4% in 1984 to 31% in 2000 — with 28% also admitting to having bought certain goods for political ethical or environmental reasons in 2000.

Does political participation matter?

On a simple level, participation clearly matters because low levels of political participation undermine the legitimacy of political institutions and processes. In the case of low electoral turnout, it brings the governing party's mandate into question. In a similar vein, low levels of turnout at referendums undermine all the main arguments commonly advanced in favour of their wider use.

However, there is evidence to suggest that the damage done by low levels of political participation may extend beyond the theoretical, impacting not only on the legitimacy of government, but also on its quality and effectiveness. In an article in *Politics Review* in 2009, Paul Whiteley highlighted the link between political participation and government effectiveness in 37 countries. The evidence (see Figure 1.1) would appear to suggest that countries with high levels of political participation are more likely to enjoy effective government. Note that each diamond on the graph represents a single country.

Worrying also is the fact that those in the social classes C2 and DE appear to be far less likely to participate directly in more conventional forms of political activity than those in classes AB and C1 (see Figure 1.2).

Addressing the participation crisis

Efforts to address falling levels of participation in formal politics have generally fallen into two broad categories:

➢ those that attempt to deal with the problem of electoral turnout head-on, generally by making it easier to vote
➢ those that try to get to the root of the problem by considering some deeper problems affecting democracy in the UK

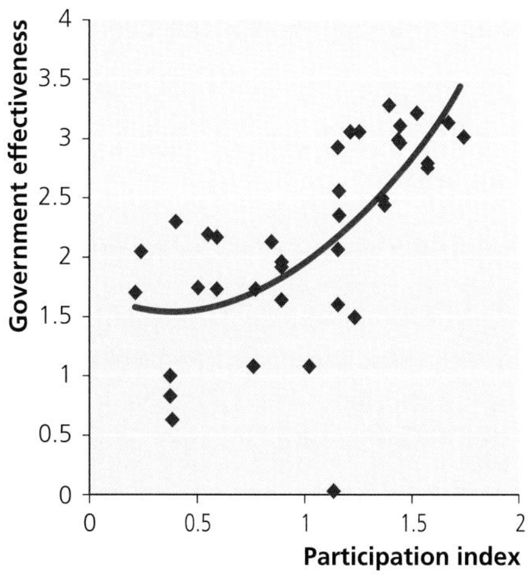

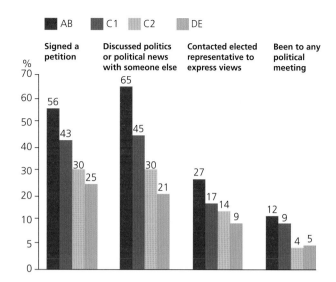

Source: Whiteley, P. (2009) 'Democracy and participation: is there a participation crisis?', *Politics Review*, Vol. 19, No. 1.

Figure 1.1 The relationship between political participation and government effectiveness in 37 countries, 2004

Source: Wilks-Heeg, S., Blick, A., and Crone, S. (2012) *How Democratic is the UK? The 2012 Audit* (Fig.6), Liverpool: Democratic Audit.

Figure 1.2 Political participation by social class

Tackling the issue of low turnout

Two initiatives have already been trialled with a view to tackling the issue of low voter turnout 'head-on':

➢ encouraging a greater take-up of postal voting

➢ experimenting with SMS text voting and web-based voting

Such initiatives have brought mixed results. Although the extension of postal voting has certainly increased turnout, particularly at local elections, it has also led to allegations of voter fraud and intimidation, particularly where a significant number of voters are registered at a single address. In a sense, therefore, what has been gained in terms of turnout (i.e. the 'size' of the vote) has been lost in terms of the 'quality' of the vote, with the principle of a secret ballot being brought into question.

Trials of SMS text voting and web-based voting between 2000 and 2007 faced similar criticisms, the result being that such trials are now unlikely to be extended more widely.

A number of other proposals have also been made, most notably:

➢ making voting compulsory for those eligible, as in Australia

➢ lowering the minimum voting age from 18 to 16

Compulsory voting

Many countries require eligible voters not only to register to vote (as is the case in the UK) but also to cast a ballot on election day. In Australia, this requirement is included in the Commonwealth Electoral Act (1918), which was amended in 1924 to make voting at federal elections compulsory. The Act states that 'it shall be the duty of every elector to vote at each

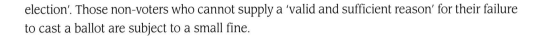

election'. Those non-voters who cannot supply a 'valid and sufficient reason' for their failure to cast a ballot are subject to a small fine.

Case study — Compulsory voting in Australia

The introduction of compulsory voting in Australia had an immediate and significant effect on electoral turnout. Australia had experienced sharply falling turnouts at the start of the 1920s, with only 59.4% casting a ballot in the 1922 elections to the House of Representatives (compared to 71.6% in 1919). Turnout at the first election held after the introduction of compulsory voting, in 1925, rose to 91.4%. Whereas only 65.1% of registered voters cast a ballot in the 2010 UK general election, the 2010 elections to the Australian House of Representatives saw a turnout of 93.2%.

Critics of compulsory voting in Australia and elsewhere argue that forcing those who do not want to vote to cast a ballot results in high levels of 'donkey voting' and 'informal voting':

➤ Donkey votes: under a preferential voting system, votes which are simply numbered 1, 2, 3, 4, etc. in order vertically down the list of available candidates. A 'reverse donkey' is one where candidates are numbered up the ballot paper.

➤ Informal votes: ballots which are completed incorrectly (intentionally or otherwise) or left blank under a system of compulsory voting — thus rendering them void. In the 2010 Australian elections 5.65% of ballots were classified as 'informal' (up from 3.95% in 2007).

Despite the obvious benefits it brings in terms of electoral turnout, compulsory voting is criticised by some civil liberties groups, which argue that the right not to cast a ballot should be protected. Forcing eligible citizens to vote runs the risk of repeating problems seen with postal voting: specifically, that while the numbers of ballots will increase, the quality of the vote will not. Some people will be voting simply because of their desire to avoid a fine, as opposed to participating more purposefully in the democratic process.

Links to follow up

www.aec.gov.au — click on 'Voting' then 'Voting overview', and scroll down to 'Compulsory voting' to access the relevant page from the Australian Electoral Commission website.

Reducing the voting age

The idea of reducing the voting age from 18 to 16 found some favour with the Labour prime minister Gordon Brown and was also discussed widely in the press following the decision in October 2012 to give 16 and 17 year olds in Scotland the opportunity to vote in the 2014 independence referendum. However, such a move seems unlikely to improve the national turnout figure.

Younger voters are statistically less likely to cast a ballot than those who are older. For example, only 44% of eligible voters in the 18–24 age category cast a ballot at the 2010 general election, compared to the 76% turnout figure recorded for over-65s. Reducing the voting age from 18 to 16 would increase the number of voters, but the percentage turnout figure would almost certainly fall. This move would also raise the issue of whether those who are in many cases still not eligible to pay certain taxes should have a say in the make-up of the government that would set them.

Viewpoint Should voting be made compulsory?

YES
- Voting is a civic duty comparable to other duties that citizens perform (e.g. paying taxes, attending school, completing jury service).
- It teaches the benefits of political participation.
- Parliament reflects more accurately the 'will of the electorate'.
- Governments must consider the total electorate in policy formulation and management, rather than simply focusing on those who are likely to turn out.
- Candidates can concentrate their campaigning energies on issues, rather than encouraging voters to attend the poll through 'get out the vote' activities.
- The voter is not actually compelled to vote for any single candidate because voting is by secret ballot. They can choose to leave their ballot paper blank or spoil their ballot.

NO
- It is undemocratic to force people to vote (i.e. an infringement of liberty).
- The ill informed and those with little interest in politics are forced to the polls.
- It may increase the number of donkey votes when used alongside a preferential voting system.
- It may increase the number of informal votes.
- It can serve to increase the number of safe, single-member constituencies — encouraging political parties to concentrate on the more marginal seats.
- It takes time and money to determine whether or not those who have failed to cast a ballot have done so for a valid reason or reasons.

Source: Australian Electoral Commission.

Links to follow up

www.votesat16.org — the site of the Votes at 16 campaign.

Addressing perceived flaws in UK democracy

The second broad approach to tackling low levels of participation in formal politics has been to find ways of enhancing the UK's democratic institutions and processes as a means of reigniting public interest in them.

This approach is the one advocated by the POWER Report, among others (see Box 1.3), and also provides the focus for the last section of this chapter.

Box 1.3 Recommendations of the POWER inquiry

- ➤ A rebalancing of power away from the executive and unaccountable bodies towards parliament and local government.
- ➤ The introduction of greater responsiveness and choice into the electoral and party systems.
- ➤ Allowing citizens a much more direct and focused say over political decisions and policies.

Source: *Power to the People: The Report of POWER — An Independent Inquiry into Britain's Democracy*, 2006 (executive summary).

Is the UK democratic?

Assessing the UK's democratic credentials is made hard by the fact that there are so many different perspectives on precisely what democracy should be. Few would argue that the UK perfectly fits the definition of a **pluralist democracy**. It makes more sense, therefore, for us to use the model of a liberal democracy for the purposes of our discussion here.

Key concept
Pluralist democracy

A system of government that encourages participation and allows for free and fair competition between competing interests.

In a pluralist democracy:
➢ there will be a diverse range of competing interests
➢ there will be numerous access points — points of leverage where pressure groups can exert influence
➢ no single group will be able to exclude any other from the political process

Some argue that the UK is a pluralist democracy. Others, however, maintain that the UK system of government is in fact dominated by elites: that members of a particular social class, those of a particular educational background, or those who move in particular social circles (virtuous circles) dominate the higher levels of government, industry and the media. Although the range of available access points has been increased both by UK membership of the EU and as a result of devolution, the term 'pluralist democracy' still appears more applicable to the USA than to the UK.

The main features of UK democracy

UK democracy has the following features:
➢ multi-level government where policies can, in theory at least, be developed and implemented by those best placed to understand the needs of the people (i.e. **subsidiarity**)

Key term

➢ **Subsidiarity** The principle that decisions should be taken at the lowest tier of government possible.

➢ a system of free and fair elections, incorporating a wide franchise and operating under a secret ballot
➢ the protection of basic rights and liberties under the rule of law
➢ the existence of a wide range of political parties and pressure groups, providing numerous avenues for political participation and representation

A critique of UK democracy

Critics of the UK system are also able to point to a number of deficiencies in our democratic arrangements and practice:
➢ the use of the first-past-the-post system at general elections
➢ the failure properly to reform parliament

➤ low levels of voter turnout and widespread disillusionment with other traditional forms of participation, such as membership of political parties and mainstream pressure groups

➤ the rise of (often extreme) single-issue pressure groups, and groups that seek to destabilise or even overthrow the state

➤ the absence of a complete separation of powers and the tendency towards executive dominance (or 'elective dictatorship')

➤ the transfer of government power away from elected bodies, particularly local government, towards unelected quangos and free-standing agencies

➤ the absence of a properly drafted bill of rights incorporated within a codified and entrenched constitution

Has the UK become more democratic since 1997?

Although the reforms introduced by New Labour in the wake of its landslide victory at the 1997 general election have gone some way towards addressing those concerns identified, there is still considerable debate over precisely how much progress has been made.

On the positive side

➤ All but 92 of the 759 hereditary peers who had held the right to sit and vote in the upper Chamber prior to the House of Lords Act (1999) have been removed.

➤ A better separation of powers has resulted from changes to the role of Lord Chancellor and the creation of the UK Supreme Court under the Constitutional Reform Act (2005).

➤ The passage of the Human Rights Act (1998) and Freedom of Information Act (2000) have provided a clearer outline of the rights available to citizens.

➤ Devolution and the introduction of directly elected local mayors in many areas have brought government closer to the people, enhancing local democracy and local accountability.

➤ The increased use of referendums from 1997 is said to have enhanced democracy by giving those changes approved greater legitimacy.

On the negative side

➤ The first-past-the-post system remains in place for elections to the Westminster Parliament, in the wake of the decisive 'no' vote in the 2011 AV referendum.

➤ The UK experienced historically low levels of turnout at the 2001, 2005 and 2010 general elections.

➤ Lords reform stalled after 1999 and significant reforms to the House of Commons have failed to materialise.

➤ There has been an erosion of civil liberties since the attacks in the USA on 9/11 (2001) and London on 7/7 (2005) — see Chapter 9.

Democratic Audit (2012)

The Democratic Audit (2012) looked to recognise the progress that had been made in some areas, while at the same time identifying others where there was still significant room for improvement. Comparisons with the Nordic democracies, also included in the report, were particularly telling (see Table 1.10).

Table 1.10 UK and Nordic democracies compared

	United Kingdom	Nordic average*
Turnout in parliamentary elections (average, 2000s)	60%	79%
Proportion of the electorate who are members of political parties (late 2000s)**	1%	5%
Proportion of MPs who are women (2010)	22%	41%
Global ranking for levels of press freedom (2011; Freedom House index)	26th	2nd
Global ranking for absence of corruption (2010; Transparency International index)	20th	4th
Compliance with human rights (2010; score out of 22 on CIRI Human Rights index)	19	21
Full-time employees earning < 2/3 of median gross annual earnings (2006)**	21.6%	7.9%
Proportion of the labour force who are members of trade unions (2010)	26.5%	69.2%
Proportion of tax revenue raised by sub-national government (2009)	5.3%	25.4%
Overseas aid as a proportion of national income (average, 2000s)	0.4%	0.8%

* The Nordic average is for Denmark, Finland, Iceland, Norway and Sweden.
**In these cases, the Nordic average is for Denmark, Finland and Sweden only.
Source: Wilks-Heeg, S., Blick, A., and Crone, S. (2012) *How Democratic is the UK? The 2012 Audit* (Fig. 3), Liverpool: Democratic Audit.

Enhancing future UK democracy

In many cases, future changes to the way in which democracy operates in the UK will build upon the successes and failures outlined above under 'positive' and 'negative'.

Some of these ideas — for example, the possibility of making greater use of referendums, initiatives or recalls — have already been dealt with in this chapter. Others — for example, devolving power to the English regions — will be discussed in their proper context in later chapters. However, it is worth focusing on two areas that do not receive a great deal of coverage elsewhere in this book, namely:

➢ the extension of experiments in e-democracy
➢ greater use of citizens' juries and citizens' assemblies (or 'citizens' conventions') as a way of engaging citizens and enhancing the legitimacy of the policy-making process

Embracing e-democracy

The term **e-democracy** refers to the greater use of the internet, mobile phones and other electronic media as a means of enhancing the operation of existing political institutions and processes. It seeks to address the decline in some forms of political participation by making it far easier for citizens to engage with decision-makers and shape the political agenda. While the term is commonly used when referring to initiatives taken by central government, e-democracy also refers to initiatives started by citizens and pressure groups. Although there appears to be little prospect of the 2000–07 trials in e-voting being rolled out more widely, e-democracy can be seen in a number of other initiatives, some government led and others citizen led (see stretch and challenge activity).

Key term

➤ **e-democracy** The greater use of the internet, mobile phones and other electronic media as a means of enhancing the operation of existing political institutions and processes, and encouraging greater political participation.

Stretch and challenge

What is e-democracy?

There is no single definition for e-democracy: it can broadly be described as the use of new information and communication technologies (ICT) to increase and enhance citizens' engagement in democratic processes. Traditionally, initiatives have been categorised as follows, although the boundaries are becoming increasingly blurred:

- **top-down:** initiatives by the government, or local authorities, often with the goals of lowered costs, or increased efficiency, transparency and convenience
- **bottom-up:** initiated by citizens and activists at the grassroots level. These generally aim to increase transparency, accountability or convenience as well as to inform, educate and campaign.

In each category activities can be either:

- **one-way processes:** such as dissemination of information from the government to citizen
- **two-way processes:** such as public opinion polls, or consultation on draft bills. Such two-way, interactive forms of web-based e-democracy are often referred to as Web 2.0 applications.

Examples of e-democracy in the UK

- **www.parliamentlive.tv** (top-down, one-way). This website carries live and archived coverage of all public proceedings in parliament.
- **http://theyworkforyou.com** (bottom-up, two-way). This website provides a searchable, annotatable version of what is said in parliament. Used by over 100,000 visitors a month, it provides information on a range of different measures of activities by MPs, such as parliamentary appearances and voting patterns.
- **http://epetitions.direct.gov.uk** (bottom-up, two-way). This website allows members of the public to petition the government about whatever issues they see fit. One of the most popular petitions, on road pricing, received over 1.8 million signatures.
- **www.mysociety.org** (bottom-up, two-way). This is a hub that provides links to many of the sites above — but also a group providing support to other individuals hoping to establish similar citizen-led web initiatives.

Source: adapted from Postnote No. 321, 'E-democracy', Parliamentary Office of Science and Technology, 2009.

Questions

1 Why might the UK government be so keen to experiment with e-democracy?
2 What are the limitations of e-democracy as a form of political participation?

Links to follow up

'E-democracy' (Postnote 321) 1 January 2009, **www.parliament.uk** — a four-page briefing paper from the Parliamentary Office of Science and Technology, which addresses the issue of e-democracy.

Citizens' juries and citizens' assemblies

A citizens' jury is a panel of citizens convened to hear evidence and deliver their verdict on a government proposal or a specific policy area. Citizens' juries are used widely outside the UK, most notably in the USA and Germany, and were championed by the prime minister Gordon Brown in 2007 as a means of enhancing political participation. Crucially, such juries do not have final say on a given policy. Their feedback is considered by a panel of specialists and, ultimately, those politicians serving in government posts, who make the final decision over policy.

Links to follow up

'Citizens' Juries' (SN/PC/04546) 14 December 2007, **www.parliament.uk** — a research briefing from the House of Commons Library on the subject of citizens' juries.

Gordon Brown taking part in the first citizens' jury event in Bristol, September 2007

A citizens' assembly (or 'citizens' convention') is similar to a citizens' jury in the sense that it looks to involve a representative cross-section of the population in the policy-making process, in a way that is more meaningful than the kind of consultation routinely undertaken at the Green Paper stage of a legislative proposal. Where assemblies differ from juries is, first, that they involve a lot more people (hundreds or thousands as opposed to tens) and, secondly, that they are often given more power to decide upon a particular course of action, which can subsequently be put to a public vote through a referendum. This means that politicians are, in a sense, absenting themselves from the decision-making process.

It is likely that such citizens' assemblies would be used to provide the kind of 'public conversation' that the leaders of the three main UK parties have advocated ahead of the next wave of constitutional reform.

Box 1.4 What makes a good citizens' assembly?

➢ Citizens' assemblies have been successful where it has been established from the outset that their findings will be put straight to a referendum, without amendment or modification by government.

➢ In these cases the assembly was seen to be independent and consequently the public and media bought into the process.

➢ Where it is not clear what the outcome will be or the assembly merely reports to Parliament as in the Netherlands, the assembly is dismissed as yet another consultation exercise that is unlikely to lead to change.

➢ Deliberative techniques on their own are not enough, the assembly has to be seen to be independent and have the power to propose change.

Source: A. Runswick, *A Guide to Involving Citizens in Constitutional Reform*, Unlock Democracy, 2007.

Links to follow up

'A Guide to Involving Citizens in Constitutional Reform', 03 July 2007, **http://unlockdemocracy.org.uk** — a briefing paper on citizens' assemblies from the pressure group Unlock Democracy.

'Citizens' assemblies' (SN/PC/04482) 25 November 2009, **www.parliament.uk** — a research briefing from the House of Commons Library on the subject of citizens' assemblies.

What you should know

❯ Democracy is 'rule by the people' or 'people power', but this can mean different things to different people. Consequently, it has become common practice to prefix the term 'democracy' with another word as a way of affording it greater meaning. Thus the UK is said to be a liberal democracy because it incorporates free and fair elections with a commitment to the protection of certain key liberties and freedoms.

❯ Liberal democracies such as the UK and the USA tend to operate under a representative (or 'indirect') form of democracy, where the citizens elect politicians to make decisions on their behalf. This is a result of the fact that direct democracy (where citizens have a direct input into decision making) is regarded as impractical in a modern democracy with a large population and a wide franchise. However, the increasing use of referendums in the UK is an example of the way in which elements of direct democracy can operate alongside the representative model. A purer form of direct democracy operates in the form of the town hall meetings held in small towns in several New England states in the USA.

❱ The term 'political participation' refers collectively to the various ways in which citizens can involve themselves in the political process. Political participation covers all manner of activities, from voting at an election or joining a political party, to taking part in pressure group activity or boycotting certain products on ethical grounds. In recent years the UK has witnessed a decline in the more formal (or traditional) aspects of political participation, such as voting, and a rise in less formal, more spontaneous activity such as direct action.

❱ Many commentators regard this participatory shift as a major threat to UK democracy and have therefore looked for ways to halt and reverse the trend. The more notable proposals have included the introduction of compulsory voting, the lowering of the voting age and the extension of experiments in e-democracy (or 'digital democracy').

❱ In some respects the UK has become more democratic in recent years as a result of the removal of the right of most hereditary peers to sit and vote in the House of Lords, and the passage of the Human Rights Act (1998) and the Freedom of Information Act (2000). However, in other areas there is still significant room for improvement: parliamentary reform is incomplete; the inequities of the first-past-the-post system suggest the need for reform; and scrutiny of the executive needs to be enhanced.

UK/US comparison

Democracy and participation in the USA

➤ Whereas UK political culture was traditionally said to be characterised by homogeneity, deference and consensus, US political culture is based on principles such as individualism, liberty and a belief in limited government.

➤ The USA is far more diverse than the UK. It comprises 50 states covering six different time zones. The US population of over 300 million individuals encompasses all races and religions. This multi-variance is key to any understanding of US political culture.

➤ Like the UK, the USA is said to be a liberal democracy, but it is also widely seen as a pluralist democracy. This is due both to the availability of numerous access points and to the expectation of open competition between competing interests.

➤ Political power in the USA is fragmented 'vertically', under the federal system, and 'horizontally', through the entrenched separation of powers and the system of checks and balances. This fragmented system provides numerous access points, allowing greater political participation and providing for greater government accountability. This contrasts with the UK's unitary system and its partial fusion of powers.

➤ Whereas the fusion of powers present in the UK system is said to favour executive dominance (or 'elective dictatorship'), the US system is far more prone to gridlock — particularly where there is divided government: that is, where one of the two main parties controls the White House and the other controls all or part of the bicameral Congress.

➤ The US system has a long-established rights culture rooted not only in the Bill of Rights but also in subsequent constitutional amendments such as the Fourteenth Amendment (guaranteeing equal protection under the law). The rights of US citizens are also protected in regular congressional statutes (e.g. the 1964 Civil Rights Act) and through the rulings of the US Supreme Court. The UK was traditionally said to operate under a system of negative rights, but the passing of the Human Rights Act (1998) and other measures is said to have enhanced the protection of civil liberties.

➤ While both the UK and the USA are seen as operating under the representative model of democracy, many US citizens also have the opportunity to get involved more directly in policy making. While the US Constitution does not provide for US-wide direct democracy, the majority of states hold referendums and many also allow initiatives and recalls. Small towns in some US states also operate a more primitive form of direct democracy in the form of New England town hall meetings.

➤ Although electoral turnout is often lower in the USA than in the UK, this is partly explained by the fact that US turnout is commonly calculated as a percentage of the voting age population, as opposed to a percentage of registered voters — the measure used in the UK.

➤ The USA is widely seen as a participatory democracy with far higher levels of pressure group membership and involvement in grassroots activities such as campaigning, canvassing and 'get out the vote' campaigns than are seen in the UK.

Further reading

Batchelor, A. (2012) 'Referendums: without a consensus, the answer is no', *Politics Review*, Vol. 21, No. 3.

Bodganor, V. (2011) *The Coalition and the Constitution*, Hart Publishing.

Fairclough, P. (2004) 'Direct democracy in the USA: referendums, initiatives and recalls', *Politics Review*, Vol. 13, No. 4.

Lynch, P. (2010) 'Democracy in the UK: the 2010 general election', *Politics Review*, Vol. 20, No. 2.

Lynch, P. (2010) 'UK update: recall of MPs', *Politics Review*, Vol. 19, No. 3.

Stoten, D. W. (2011) 'The coalition government and constitutional reform', *Politics Review*, Vol. 20, No. 3.

Whiteley, P. (2009) 'Democracy and participation: is there a participation crisis in the UK?', *Politics Review*, Vol. 19, No. 1.

Whiteley, P. (2010) 'Enhancing democracy: how might participation be improved?', *Politics Review*, Vol. 19, No. 3.

Wilks-Heeg, S. (2012) 'How democratic is the UK? The 2012 audit', *Political Insight*, Vol. 3, No. 2.

Wilks-Heeg, S., Blick, A., and Crone, S. (2012) *How Democratic is the UK? The 2012 Audit*, Liverpool: Democratic Audit.

Exam focus

Short response questions (around 5–6 minutes each)

1 Define direct democracy.
2 What is a referendum?
3 Define representative democracy.
4 Give three examples of how political participation has fallen in the UK.
5 What is e-democracy?

Mid-length response questions (around 10–12 minutes each)

1 Distinguish between direct and representative democracy.
2 Identify and explain *three* ways in which people can participate in the political process.
3 Discuss the view that voting should be made compulsory in the UK.
4 Outline and explain the circumstances in which referendums are held in the UK.
5 Using examples outline the strengths and limitations of e-democracy in the UK.

Mini-essay questions (around 25–30 minutes each)

1 'Referendums should be used more widely in the UK.' Discuss.
2 Why and to what extent can the UK be considered 'undemocratic'?
3 To what extent is there a 'participation crisis' in the UK?
4 Discuss the view that the UK has become more democratic in recent years.

Extra resources to help you revise and consolidate your knowledge for this chapter are provided online at **www.hodderplus.co.uk/philipallan**. These include a revision PowerPoint, extension tasks and up-to-date weblinks.

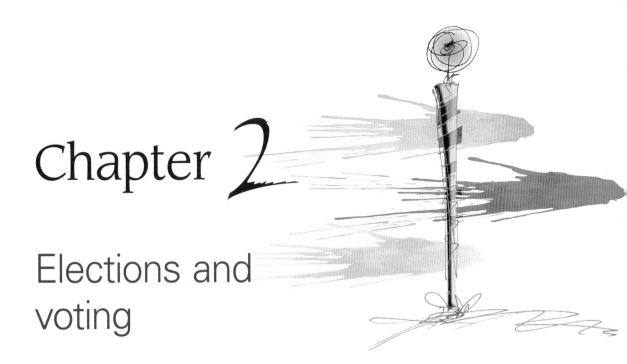

Chapter 2

Elections and voting

Key questions answered in this chapter

➢ What are the functions of elections?

➢ What are the advantages and disadvantages of the first-past-the-post system?

➢ How do the other electoral systems used in the UK operate?

➢ How important is social class in determining voting behaviour?

➢ How significant are issues, leaders and election campaigns?

Elections are at the heart of the democratic process. Voting in an election is the main form of political activity for many people. Through the electoral process, governments are chosen and held accountable. Political parties issue **manifestos** outlining the policies they would introduce in government. The victorious party is expected to deliver those pledges in government and claims a **mandate** to do so.

Key term

➢ **Manifesto** A document in which a political party sets out its policy programme at an election.

Key concepts

➢ **Election** A competitive process in which a designated group of people, known as the electorate, select individuals who will fill particular posts. Elections to public office are a central feature of the democratic process. The electorate consists of almost all of the adult population. Members of legislatures, and the executive in presidential systems, are chosen in elections.

➢ **Mandate** A mandate is an authoritative instruction or command. The doctrine of the mandate gives the winning party the authority to press ahead with the programme it presented to the electorate. An election manifesto is seen as a promise of future legislative action, or a contract between a party and those who voted for it. The mandate also implies that a government should not introduce a major policy change unless it has been presented to the electorate.

Functions of elections

Elections have a number of functions:

➢ **Representation.** In a representative democracy, elections enable a large group (the electorate) to select a smaller group (representatives) to act on their behalf. In a direct democracy, by contrast, all eligible citizens take part in decision making.

➢ **Choosing a government.** In the UK parliamentary system, general elections determine the composition of the House of Commons rather than the executive. However, because the majority party in the Commons forms the government, general elections normally determine which party takes power. When no party won a parliamentary majority at the 2010 general election, a government only emerged when the Conservatives and Liberal Democrats agreed to form a coalition.

Key term

➢ **Turnout** The proportion of the electorate that votes in an election.

➢ **Participation.** Voting is the key act of political participation for most citizens. **Turnout** in recent elections has been lower than the postwar average.

Distinguish between

Elections and referendums

Elections

➢ These are required by law and must take place within a specified period.
➢ They are a feature of representative democracy — citizens choose representatives to make decisions on their behalf.
➢ They determine who holds political office and, in the case of a general election, who forms the government.
➢ Citizens vote for candidates in single-member, or multi-member, constituencies, with most candidates standing for a political party.
➢ An election campaign will cover many issues of public policy.

Referendums

➢ A referendum is a one-off vote on a specific issue of public policy.
➢ The choice offered to voters is normally a simple 'yes' or 'no' to a proposal.
➢ The decision to hold a referendum in the UK is taken by the government, although referendums are required on some issues by statute (e.g. the European Union Act 2011) or convention.
➢ Referendums are an example of direct democracy — citizens make the decisions themselves.

➢ **Influence over policy.** In theory, elections allow citizens to have their policy preferences heard, but in reality, they have limited scope to influence decisions. Election defeat can, however, force a party to rethink unpopular policies (e.g. Labour's 1983 policy of unilateral disarmament was subsequently jettisoned).

➢ **Accountability.** Facing the electorate every 5 years is one of the ways by which the government is held accountable for its performance in office. Individual MPs may also be held accountable for their record. Following the 2009 expenses scandal, many MPs stood down rather than face the verdict of voters.

➢ **Citizen education.** Election campaigns provide citizens with information on major political issues and the policies of the main parties. In theory, this enables citizens to make an informed decision on how to vote, but in practice the information provided is imperfect.

> **Legitimacy.** Elections give **legitimacy** to the winning party and to the political system as a whole. By voting, even for a losing party, citizens give their consent to the system. The government can claim to be acting on the will of the people.

> **Elite recruitment.** Political parties nominate candidates for election, provide them with campaign resources — and expect loyalty from them if they become MPs.

Democratic theorists prioritise the role of the people in the political process. They focus on 'bottom-up' functions such as policy influence, participation and accountability. In a representative democracy, the government should act in accordance with the wishes of the people.

For elite theorists, elections provide authority and stability for the political system, allowing elites to get on with the task of governing, with only limited recourse to the expressed wishes of the people. They highlight 'top-down' functions such as legitimacy and elite recruitment. In a representative democracy, the political elite decides what is in the best interests of the people.

Key concept

> **Legitimacy** A contested concept, usually equated with rightfulness. A political system is legitimate when it is based on the consent of the people — winning an election gives a government legitimacy. Political actions are also legitimate if they follow from agreed laws and procedures. Citizens in a liberal democracy accept the legitimacy of a government, even if they did not vote for it, if it acts within its lawful powers.

⟷ Stretch and challenge

Elections and coalition government

Coalition government raises a number of questions about the functions of elections:

- **The mandate.** Can a coalition government claim the same democratic mandate as a party that wins a parliamentary majority in a general election? Although the Conservatives and Liberal Democrats together have a majority of seats, no one voted for a coalition between the two parties at the 2010 election. Both parties dropped manifesto pledges in coalition negotiations and the coalition agreement included policy commitments (e.g. to hold a referendum on the alternative vote electoral system) that did not appear in the manifestos of either party. The House of Commons Political and Constitutional Reform Committee (2011) found that a policy commitment in a coalition agreement does not have the same mandate as a manifesto pledge, unless it featured in the manifestos of both coalition parties. Coalition policies not included in their manifestos only have the same authority as policies of a majority government that did not originate in a manifesto pledge.

- **Policy influence.** If government policies emerge in negotiations between coalition parties, can electors know how their vote will influence future policy? If coalition government becomes the norm, manifestos may no longer offer reliable guides to what parties will do in government. This would be addressed if parties reached pre-election agreements, or indicated who they might enter coalition with and on what terms.

● **Electoral accountability.** If policies are developed by a coalition, how can voters identify which party should be held responsible for them at the next election? Identifying the party responsible for a policy may be especially difficult if it emerged as a result of significant compromises by the coalition partners, or had not featured in the manifestos of either party. The Conservatives and Liberal Democrats have individually claimed credit for popular policies and blamed their coalition partner for unpopular decisions.

Questions

1 Can the Conservative–Liberal Democrat coalition claim a mandate for its programme?

2 Which of the coalition government's policies are particularly associated with (a) the Conservatives and (b) the Liberal Democrats?

Elections and democracy

In a liberal democracy, elections should be competitive, free and fair. A competitive election requires that voters have a meaningful choice between different political parties. Free elections require basic civil liberties such as freedom of speech and association, the right to join and stand for a party of one's choice, and a free press. The maxim 'one person, one vote, one value' is a key criterion for a fair election: each citizen should have one vote that is of the same worth as everyone else's. Electoral law should be free from bias and overseen by an impartial judiciary. The electoral system should also translate votes cast into seats won in the legislature in a reasonably accurate manner.

Links to follow up

www.electoralcommission.org.uk — the Electoral Commission website which provides information on the conduct of elections in the UK.

Representation

Choosing a **representative** is an important function of elections. But there are competing perspectives on **representation**:

➤ delegate model
➤ trustee model
➤ constituency representation
➤ party representation
➤ descriptive or functional representation

Key terms

➤ **Representative** (a) *noun:* an individual who acts on behalf of a larger group but is free to exercise their own judgement; (b) *adjective:* exhibiting a likeness or being typical.

➤ **Representation** The process by which an individual or individuals act on behalf of a larger group.

Delegate model

A **delegate** is an individual selected to act on behalf of others on the basis of clear instructions. They should not depart from these instructions in order to follow their own judgement or preferences. Examples include trade union delegates who cast votes according to an earlier decision of union leaders or members. However, MPs are not expected to act as delegates, slavishly bound by the instructions of voters. There is unlikely to be a consensus among voters in a constituency on complex issues, while ascertaining the views of the majority on every issue would be difficult.

Trustee model

Edmund Burke MP (1729–97) proposed the **trustee** model. MPs are responsible for representing the interests of their constituents in parliament. Once elected, they are free to decide how to vote based on their own independent judgement of the merits of an issue. Burke's perspective had a strong elitist undercurrent. It assumed that MPs knew best because they had greater understanding of affairs of state.

Key terms
- **Delegate** An individual authorised to act on behalf of others but who is bound by clear instructions.
- **Trustee** An individual who has formal responsibility for the interests of another (in law, this will often be property).

Delegates and trustees

Distinguish between

Delegates
- Delegates are given clear instructions on how they are to act on behalf of the people they represent.
- They must follow these instructions in full and must not adapt them based on their own judgement of the issues.
- They must not vote on the basis of their personal views or conscience.

Trustees
- Trustees should take account of the interests and values of the group they represent, but they are not bound by strict instructions from them.
- They are free to exercise their own judgement on issues and to vote accordingly.
- They may vote according to their conscience.

Constituency representation

MPs are expected to protect and advance the collective interests of the **constituency** they represent, and to represent the interests of individual constituents. They may lobby the government about developments in the

Key term
- **Constituency**
  A geographical territory for which representatives are chosen in an election.

constituency (e.g. the site of a wind farm). MPs receive numerous requests for help from constituents by post and e-mail, and in person at constituency surgeries. They may then take up individual cases (e.g. on housing) with the relevant authorities and raise them in parliament.

The relationship between an MP and his or her constituents is often seen as important for a healthy democracy. It may also bring an active MP a 'personal vote' at a general election. However, relatively few MPs defy their party whip in their pursuit of constituency interests.

Party representation

Political parties dominate elections. Almost all successful general election candidates are elected not for their personal beliefs and qualities, but because they represent a political party. Parties also provide candidates with campaign funding. In return, MPs owe loyalty to their party in parliament. This perspective also sees parties as representative of the interests of particular groups in society.

Descriptive representation

A final perspective, known as descriptive or functional representation, suggests that parliament should mirror the society it represents. Representation is equated with resemblance. Parliament should be a microcosm of the larger body: all major social groups should be present in numbers roughly proportional to their size in the electorate.

The underlying assumption is that people with similar social characteristics (e.g. gender, ethnicity and social class) can best identify with and represent the interests of particular groups. So, women understand motherhood better than men, and members of ethnic minorities have more experience of racism. Critics argue that individuals need not have suffered disadvantage or discrimination to regard these as reprehensible and demand reform. It is also problematic to assume that people belong to only one social group, and that groups are homogeneous.

The House of Commons does not resemble British society (see Chapter 7). Most MPs are middle class. A growing number are career politicians with little work experience outside politics. Women and ethnic minorities are also under-represented. In 2010, 22% of MPs were women and only 4% had a black and minority ethnic background.

Links to follow up

www.fawcettsociety.org.uk — the website of the Fawcett Society which campaigns for greater representation of women in parliament.

Elections in the UK

Elections take place at different levels in UK politics:

➤ **General elections.** These elect all 650 MPs who make up the House of Commons. The Fixed-term Parliaments Act 2011 introduced fixed-term elections for the House of Commons. The next general election will be on 7 May 2015, with subsequent general elections held on the first Thursday in May in the fifth calendar year after the previous contest. Parliament can still be dissolved before its full term if (i) the government is defeated on a motion of no confidence, as happened in 1979, or (ii) a motion calling for an early general election is supported by two-thirds of MPs. Prior to this Act, the prime minister could call an election at a time of his or her choosing within the 5-year term.

➤ **European Parliament elections.** The UK elects 73 Members of the European Parliament at elections held at fixed-term intervals of 5 years.

➤ **Elections to the devolved assemblies.** Elections to the Scottish Parliament, Welsh Assembly and Northern Ireland Assembly are held at fixed 4-year intervals. The next elections to the Scottish Parliament and Welsh Assembly have, however, been moved to 2016 to avoid a clash with the next general election.

➤ **Local elections.** Local councillors are elected for fixed 4-year terms. In some local authorities, all councillors face the electorate at the same time; in others, only a proportion of members (normally a quarter) are elected each year. Some towns and cities also have directly elected mayors. In London, there is an elected mayor and London Assembly. Police and crime commissioners have been elected since 2012.

➤ **By-elections.** If a constituency seat in the House of Commons, devolved assembly or English local authority becomes vacant because of the death or resignation of an elected member, a by-election is held to choose a new representative.

Significant parts of the UK polity are not elected:
➤ the head of state — the hereditary monarch
➤ the second chamber of the legislature — the House of Lords
➤ the judiciary

Electoral systems

Electoral systems translate votes cast by citizens into seats in an assembly or a political office. There are four main types of electoral system:
➤ majoritarian (e.g. the alternative vote)
➤ plurality (e.g. simple plurality)
➤ proportional (e.g. the list system)
➤ mixed or hybrid (e.g. the additional member system)

Majoritarian system

A **majoritarian system** is one in which the winning candidate must secure an absolute majority of the vote (i.e. 50% + 1 vote). Candidates are usually elected in single-member constituencies. The first-past-the-post system used for UK general elections is often described as a majoritarian system. This is not strictly accurate because the term is being used to reflect a system output, when it should describe its mechanics.

Key term

➤ **Majoritarian system** An electoral system in which the winning candidate must achieve an absolute majority of votes cast in a single-member constituency.

Plurality system

First-past-the-post is, in fact, a **simple plurality system** in which the winner needs only a plurality of votes cast (i.e. one more than their closest rival), not an absolute majority. Plurality systems share characteristics of majoritarian systems. MPs are elected in single-member constituencies and both systems are non-proportional. Large parties tend to get a higher proportion of seats than their vote merits, while smaller parties whose support is thinly spread are under-represented.

Proportional representation

The term **proportional representation** (PR) covers many systems with similar features. They produce a close fit between votes and seats, although no system can deliver perfect proportionality. The **district magnitude** (i.e. the number of legislative seats per constituency) is a crucial factor — the larger the constituency, the more proportional the result. In the European Parliament elections in Great Britain, using the regional list system, a smaller party is more likely to win a seat in the southeast region (which elects 10 MEPs) than the northeast (3 MEPs).

PR systems use multi-member constituencies and electoral formulas. Some (e.g. the single transferable vote) allow electors to vote for as many candidates as they wish in order of preference, but others (e.g. the regional list system) permit only a single vote.

Mixed system

A **mixed system** (sometimes referred to as a hybrid system) such as the additional member system (AMS), combines elements of the plurality or majoritarian systems and proportional representation. Some MPs are elected in single-member constituencies. The remainder are elected by proportional representation in multi-member constituencies. These list seats produce 'additional members' that are allocated to parties on corrective lines.

Some people believe that the most important tasks of an electoral system are to produce a clear winner and a strong government, and to maintain a link between MPs and geographical constituencies. Majoritarian or plurality systems are appropriate in this case. Others argue that an electoral system should provide maximum choice for voters and reflect accurately the diversity of opinion among the electorate. PR systems fit the bill here.

Key terms

➢ **Simple plurality system** An electoral system in which the candidate with the most votes in a single-member constituency wins.

➢ **Proportional representation** An electoral system using multi-member constituencies in which an electoral formula is used to match the percentage of seats won by each party to the percentage of votes they won.

➢ **District magnitude** The number of representatives elected from a particular constituency.

➢ **Mixed system** An electoral system where a proportion of representatives are elected under a majoritarian/plurality system in single-member constituencies, and the others are elected as 'additional members' using a proportional system in multi-member constituencies.

Links to follow up

www.politicsresources.net/election.htm — a gateway providing links to information on electoral systems and elections across the world.

Majoritarian and proportional representation systems

Distinguish between

Majoritarian systems

➤ In a majoritarian system, a candidate must secure an absolute majority of the vote to win; in a plurality system, they need only win more votes than the second-placed candidate.
➤ Candidates are elected in single-member constituencies.
➤ The outcome is not proportional — large parties take a higher proportion of seats than their share of the vote merits, while smaller parties are often under-represented.
➤ They tend to produce single-party governments with working parliamentary majorities.

Proportional representation systems

➤ Candidates are elected in multi-member constituencies.
➤ Electoral formulas are used to allocate seats in the legislative assembly.
➤ The outcome is proportional — there is a close fit between the share of the vote won by a party and the share of seats it is allocated.
➤ They tend to produce coalition governments, as no single party wins a majority of seats.

Electoral systems in the UK

Five different electoral systems are currently in use in the UK:

➤ first-past-the post — a plurality system used for general elections
➤ supplementary vote — a majoritarian system used to choose directly elected mayors and police and crime commissioners
➤ additional member system — a mixed system used for elections to the Scottish Parliament, Welsh Assembly and London Assembly
➤ regional list — a proportional system used for elections to the European Parliament
➤ single transferable vote — a proportional system used in Northern Ireland for elections to the Northern Ireland Assembly, local authorities and the European Parliament, and for local elections in Scotland

The adoption of the alternative vote for general elections was rejected in a referendum in 2011.

First-past-the-post

The first-past-the post system (FPTP), also known as simple plurality, is the most significant electoral system in the UK because it is used for general elections. A variant of it, known as the block vote — in which constituencies elect more than one candidate — is used in local elections in England and Wales. FPTP operates as follows:

➤ A candidate requires a plurality of votes to win: that is, one more vote than the second-placed candidate. There is no requirement to obtain a majority of the votes cast. In contests involving three or more candidates, the winner may fall well short of an overall majority.

Case study   Simple plurality

In FPTP elections, the winning candidate requires a plurality rather than a majority of votes cast. In close contests, the victorious candidate may win with a relatively low share of the vote. Table 2.1 shows the 2010 general election result in Hampstead and Kilburn, a three-way marginal seat won by the Labour candidate, Glenda Jackson, with under one-third of the votes cast.

Glenda Jackson and Gordon Brown at a party meeting in Kilburn before the May 2010 general election

Table 2.1 Result in Hampstead and Kilburn, 2010 general election

Candidate	Party	Vote	% vote
Glenda Jackson	Labour	17,332	32.8
Chris Philp	Conservative	17,290	32.7
Edward Fordham	Liberal Democrat	16,491	31.2
Bea Campbell	Green	759	1.4
Magnus Nielsen	UKIP	408	0.8
Victoria Moore	BNP	328	0.6
Tamsin Omond	The Commons	123	0.2
Gene Alcantara	Independent	91	0.2

➤ Electors cast a single vote by placing a cross (an 'X') on the ballot paper next to the name of their favoured candidate.

➤ MPs are elected in single-member constituencies. Each of the 650 constituencies in the UK elects one representative to the House of Commons.

➤ Constituencies are of roughly equal size (70,000 electors). Constituency boundaries are determined by independent boundary commissions which review the size of the electorate in each constituency every 8–12 years. Differences in the size of constituencies are permitted if there are significant geographical factors. The most populous constituency, the Isle of Wight, has an electorate five times larger than the smallest constituency, Na h-Eileanan an Iar (formerly the Western Isles). Constituencies in Scotland have fewer voters on average than those in England, but the over-representation was reduced when the number of Scottish constituencies was cut from 72 to 59 for the 2005 general election. The coalition government's plans to reduce the number of MPs to 600 by 2015 and equalise the size of constituencies collapsed when the Liberal Democrats withdrew their support for the required boundary changes.

Characteristic features or outcomes of FPTP elections are:
- a two-party system
- a winner's bonus
- bias to the Labour Party
- discrimination against third parties and small parties
- single-party government

Two-party system

FPTP tends to foster a two-**party system**. It favours major parties with strong nationwide support, giving them a good chance of securing a parliamentary majority. But it disadvantages smaller parties whose support is spread thinly. There is little incentive for a faction within one of the main parties to break away and form a new party because small parties find it very difficult to win seats. The Social Democratic Party (SDP) was formed by disaffected Labour MPs in 1981. It fought the 1983 general election in an alliance with the Liberals, winning 25% of the vote but only 23 seats.

Key concept

- **Party system** The set of political parties in a political system and the relationships between them. In a two-party system, only two main parties have a realistic chance of taking power. They will secure most votes and seats, and alternate in office as majority governments. In a two-and-a-half-party system, a smaller party exists alongside two major parties but is far from their equal. In a multi-party system, several parties are politically relevant — they win seats in the legislative assembly and are potential coalition partners. Coalition or minority government is the norm.

The UK's two-party system is in failing health. Support for the two main parties fell to 65% of the electorate in 2010 as the Liberal Democrats won 23% of the vote and smaller parties polled a combined vote share of 12%. FPTP acts as a life support machine for the two-party system and disguises the advance of multi-party politics. But the Liberal Democrats entered government as part of a coalition with the Conservatives after the 2010 election delivered a hung parliament.

Winner's bonus

FPTP tends to exaggerate the performance of the most popular party, producing a winner's bonus or landslide effect. A relatively small lead over the second-placed party is often translated into a substantial lead in seats in parliament. The Conservatives won landslide victories in 1983 and 1987, with Labour doing likewise in 1997 and 2001 (see Table 2.2).

Table 2.2 UK general election results, 1945–2010

Year	Con vote %	Con seats	Lab vote %	Lab seats	Lib Dem vote %	Lib Dem seats	Others votes %	Others seats	Turnout %
1945	39.6	210	48.0	393	9.0	12	3.4	25	72.8
1950	43.4	298	46.1	315	9.1	9	1.4	3	83.9
1951	48.0	321	48.8	295	2.6	6	0.6	3	82.6
1955	49.7	345	46.4	277	2.7	6	1.2	2	76.8
1959	49.4	365	43.8	258	5.9	6	0.9	1	78.7
1964	43.4	304	44.1	317	11.2	9	1.3	0	77.1
1966	41.9	253	48.0	364	8.6	12	1.5	1	75.8
1970	46.4	330	43.1	288	7.5	6	3.0	6	72.0
1974 (Feb.)	37.9	297	37.2	301	19.3	14	5.6	23	78.8
1974 (Oct.)	35.8	277	39.2	319	18.3	13	6.7	26	72.8
1979	43.9	339	36.9	269	13.8	11	5.4	16	76.0
1983	42.4	397	27.6	209	25.4	23	4.6	21	72.7
1987	42.3	376	30.8	229	22.5	22	4.4	23	75.3
1992	41.8	336	34.2	271	17.9	20	6.1	24	77.7
1997	30.7	165	43.4	419	16.8	46	9.3	29	71.5
2001	31.7	166	40.7	413	18.3	52	9.3	28	59.4
2005	32.3	197	35.2	355	22.1	62	10.4	31	61.4
2010	36.1	307	29.0	258	23.0	57	11.9	28	65.1

Note: Liberal Democrats includes Liberals (1945–79) and SDP/Liberal Alliance (1983–87).
Northern Ireland MPs are included as 'Others' from 1974.

Bias to Labour

Rather than simply favouring the winning party, FPTP has become biased in favour of Labour. Labour won a 167-seat majority in 2001 on a smaller share of the vote than the Conservatives managed in 1992, when a record 14 million votes delivered a 21-seat majority. The Conservatives fell 19 seats of an overall majority when winning 36% of the vote in 2010, whereas Labour had a majority of 66 in 2005 on a 35% vote share. There are a number of reasons for the bias towards Labour:

➤ **Differences in constituency size.** The electorate in constituencies won by Labour in 2010 was on average 3,800 lower than in those won by the Conservatives. This is largely because of population movement from inner-city constituencies to suburban and rural ones.

➤ **Differential turnout.** Turnout is lower in Labour-held seats — 61% in 2010, compared to 68% in seats won by the Conservatives. Labour wins seats with lower turnouts, while the Conservatives pile up wasted votes in safe seats.

➤ **Tactical voting.** Labour's total of seats was boosted by anti-Conservative tactical voting in 1997, 2001 and 2005.

The overall effect is that Labour's vote is more efficiently distributed — it needs fewer votes to win seats.

Discrimination against smaller parties

FPTP discriminates against third parties and smaller parties whose support is not concentrated in particular regions. There are no rewards for coming second or third; winning a plurality of votes in single-member constituencies is what counts. The Liberal Democrats have been consistent losers from FPTP, although they have increased their tally of seats through effective local campaigning. Small parties whose support is concentrated in a particular region — notably the Scottish Nationalist Party (SNP) and Plaid Cymru — fare better in terms of matching seats to share of the vote. The grip that the two main parties have had over seats at Westminster has been loosened to some extent, with the Liberal Democrats and smaller parties winning more seats in 2005 and 2010 than in other postwar elections. Their combined 85 MPs in 2010 made up 13% of the total, but this was still poor reward for 35% of the vote.

Single-party government

FPTP tends to produce single-party governments with working parliamentary majorities. Coalition governments and minority governments are relatively rare at Westminster. Only the February 1974 and 2010 general elections did not deliver a majority of seats for one party. A minority Labour government took office after the former, while the 2010 Conservative–Liberal Democrat coalition was the first coalition government since the Second World War. However, four of the seven general elections held between 1910 and 1929 — when Britain had a three-party system — failed to produce a majority government, and a National Government of four and then three parties held power from 1931 to 1939.

Advantages of FPTP

Supporters of the first-past-the-post system point to a number of advantages.

Simplicity

FPTP is easy to understand and operate. The ballot paper is simple, electors only vote once and counting the votes is straightforward. Voters are familiar with the current system and, for the most part, view it as legitimate and effective.

Clear outcome

FPTP elections normally produce a clear winner. Even if no party secures a majority of the votes cast, the party securing the largest number of votes often achieves a majority of seats in the House of Commons.

Strong and stable government

By favouring the main parties and giving the winning party an additional bonus of seats, FPTP produces strong government. Single-party governments with working majorities exercise significant control over the legislative process. They can fulfil their mandate by enacting the policy commitments they made in their manifestos, and act decisively in times of crisis.

Responsible government

Voters are given a clear choice between the governing party, which is held responsible for its record in office, and a potential alternative government. The doctrine of the mandate obliges the winning party to put its proposals into effect.

Effective representation

Single-member constituencies provide a clear link between voters and their elected representative, with one MP responsible for representing the interests of the area.

Disadvantages of FPTP

Critics of FPTP respond by noting its disadvantages.

Disproportional outcomes

The number of parliamentary seats won by parties at a general election does not reflect accurately the share of the vote they achieved. A number of points can be mentioned here:

- The two main parties tend to win more seats than their vote merits, with the lead party given an additional winner's bonus.
- Third parties and small parties whose votes are spread thinly rather than concentrated in particular areas are under-represented.
- FPTP creates 'electoral deserts', or parts of the country where a party has little or no representation. The Conservatives won 17% of the vote in Scotland in 2010, but only one seat. Labour won only two of 58 seats in eastern England on almost 20% of the vote, and the Liberal Democrats polled 21% in the East Midlands but did not win a seat.
- A party can, on occasion, win the most votes but receive fewer seats than its main rival. Twice in postwar politics, the party coming second in the popular vote gained more seats than its opponent. The Conservatives won more seats than Labour in 1951 despite trailing it in votes, and the roles were reversed in February 1974 when Labour got more seats despite the Conservatives outpolling them (see Table 2.2).

Plurality rather than majority support

Victorious candidates do not need to secure a majority of the votes cast. Two-thirds of MPs elected in 2010 did not achieve a majority in their constituency. Low turnout meant that a majority of MPs were supported by less than one in three of the electorate. Most voters are represented by an MP who is not from their chosen party. The general election of 1935 was the last time that a party won a majority of the popular vote. In 2010 the Conservatives and Liberal Democrats, who formed a coalition, won a combined 59% of the vote.

Votes are of unequal value

FPTP does not meet the 'one person, one vote, one value' principle. Disparities in constituency size mean that votes are of different value. A vote cast in a small constituency is more likely to influence the outcome than one in a larger constituency. Many votes are wasted because they do not help to elect an MP. A **wasted vote** is:

➢ any vote for a losing candidate — 53% of all votes cast in 2010

➢ a vote for a winning candidate that was not required for him or her to win — 18% of votes in 2010

Limited choice

Voters are denied an effective choice because only one candidate stands on behalf of each party. They cannot choose between different candidates from the same party. Furthermore, many constituencies are **safe seats** in which one party has a substantial lead over its rivals that is unlikely to be overturned. Supporters of other parties have little prospect of seeing their candidate win. Voters whose favoured party is unlikely to win might engage in **tactical voting**. A tactical vote is one cast not for the voter's first-choice candidate, but for the candidate best placed to prevent a party they dislike from winning the seat.

Divisive politics

In the 1960s and 1970s, critics argued that FPTP brought **adversarial politics**. Small shifts in voting produced frequent changes of government. Parties were able to overturn policies introduced by their rivals, producing instability. From 1979 to 2010, FPTP contributed to long periods of one-party rule, first by the Conservatives then by Labour, without them winning majority support.

Key terms

➢ **Wasted vote** A vote for a losing candidate in a single-member constituency, or a vote for a winning candidate that was surplus to the plurality required for victory.

➢ **Safe seat** A constituency that normally elects an MP from the same political party at every election.

➢ **Tactical voting** Voting for the candidate most likely to defeat the voter's least favoured candidate.

➢ **Adversarial politics** A situation often found in two-party systems in which the governing party is confronted by an opposition party that offers a different policy programme, and which is outwardly hostile towards the government even when in broad agreement with it.

Links to follow up

www.electoral-reform.org.uk — follow the links under 'Research and information' for the Electoral Reform Society's critique of first-past-the-post.

 Stretch and challenge

Is FPTP becoming less effective?

John Curtice (2010) shows that FPTP is becoming less effective at delivering alternating single-party government with a bonus of seats for the winning party. He identifies a number of reasons for this:

- FPTP is less effective in persuading electors not to vote for smaller parties who stand little chance of winning a seat. Labour and the Conservatives together polled a postwar low of 65% of the vote in 2010, the Liberal Democrats won their highest vote share since 1923 and 'Others' a record total.
- The number of seats won by the Liberal Democrats has increased — reaching a postwar high of 62 in 2005 before falling back to 57 in 2010 — as its vote becomes geographically less evenly spread.
- The number of marginal seats has declined as support for Labour and the Conservatives becomes concentrated in particular regions, with fewer seats changing hands at general elections.
- The electoral system is biased towards Labour. A seven-point lead over Labour did not bring the Conservatives a parliamentary majority in 2010 — they needed a lead of 11 points to achieve a bare majority.

Questions

1 Visit the Electoral Calculus website at **www.electoralcalculus.co.uk**. Based on its prediction for the general election, how effectively might the electoral system translate votes into seats?

2 Using the website's 'Make your prediction' function, what percentage of the vote will (a) Labour and (b) the Conservatives need to win a parliamentary majority (i.e. 326 seats)?

Other electoral systems

The Blair governments undertook a major programme of electoral reform beyond, but not for, Westminster. A range of electoral systems are used in the UK — majoritarian, proportional representation and mixed systems (see Table 2.3).

Alternative vote

In a referendum in 2011, voters rejected the introduction of the alternative vote (AV) for general elections. AV is used to elect Australia's lower house, the House of Representatives. In the UK, it is used in Labour Party and Liberal Democrat leadership elections.

It has the following features:

➤ Representatives are elected in single-member constituencies.

➤ The winning candidate has to achieve an overall majority of the votes cast.

➤ Voters indicate their preferences by writing '1' beside the name of their first choice, '2' next to their second choice, and so on.

➤ If no candidate secures an absolute majority of first preferences, the lowest-placed candidate is eliminated, and the second preferences of his or her voters are transferred to the remaining candidates.

➤ The process continues until one candidate reaches the 50% + 1 vote threshold.

Table 2.3 Electoral systems in the UK

Electoral system	Use in UK	Key features
First-past-the-post	General elections to the House of Commons	Simple plurality system; single-member constituencies; disproportional outcome.
Supplementary vote	Mayor of London and directly elected mayors, police and crime commissioners	Majoritarian system; used to elect individuals; voters record two preferences; winning candidate has a majority.
Closed regional list	European Parliament elections in Great Britain	Proportional representation system; electors vote for a party in multi-member regions; proportional outcome.
Single transferable vote	Assembly, local and European Parliament elections in Northern Ireland Local government in Scotland	Proportional representation system; electors rank candidates in multi-member constituencies; proportional outcome.
Additional member system	Scottish Parliament Welsh Assembly London Assembly	Mixed electoral system; electors cast two votes — one for a constituency candidate elected by FPTP, one for a regional list candidate elected by PR; list candidates are allocated to parties on a corrective basis to produce a proportional outcome.

Advantages of AV

The advantages of AV are:

➤ Representatives are elected by majorities in their constituencies.

➤ The winning candidate must achieve broad support.

➤ The link between representatives and their constituencies is retained.

Disadvantages of AV

The disadvantages of AV are:

➤ It is not a proportional system, and can produce less proportional outcomes than FPTP. If used for the 1997 general election, AV would have given Labour an even larger majority and the Liberal Democrats more seats than the Conservatives.

➤ The candidate who secures most votes may not be elected when second preferences have been distributed — the least unpopular rather than most popular candidate may be elected.

➤ The second preferences of electors who voted for small extremist parties are taken into account.

Supplementary vote

The supplementary vote (SV) is a variant of AV. It is used to elect the mayor of London (see Table 2.4) and directly elected mayors in other towns and cities. In 2012 it was used to elect police and crime commissioners (except in contests with only two candidates, where simple plurality was used). Its key features are:

➤ The elector has one vote and records only his or her first and second preferences on the ballot paper.

Table 2.4 Election of mayor of London, 2012

Candidate	Party	First preference (%)	Second preference (%)	Final (%)
Boris Johnson	Conservative	44.0	44.7	51.5
Ken Livingstone	Labour	40.3	55.3	48.5
Jenny Jones	Green	4.5		
Brian Paddick	Liberal Democrat	4.2		
Siobhan Benita	Independent	3.8		
Lawrence Webb	UKIP/Fresh Choice for London	2.0		
Carlos Cortiglia	BNP	1.3		

➤ If no candidate wins a majority of first preferences, all but the top two candidates are eliminated, and the second preference votes for the remaining two eligible candidates are added to their first preference votes.
➤ The candidate with the highest total is elected.

Advantages of SV

The advantages of SV are:

➤ The winning candidate must achieve broad support.
➤ The second preferences of voters who supported minor parties are not counted.

Disadvantages of SV

The disadvantages of SV are:

➤ The winning candidate does not need to get a majority of first preference votes.
➤ If used for general elections, it would not deliver a proportional outcome.

Regional list

The regional list system of proportional representation has been used for elections to the European Parliament in England, Scotland and Wales (but not Northern Ireland) since 1999. Its key features are:

The mayor of London, Boris Johnson

➤ Representatives are elected in large multi-member regions. For European Parliament elections, there are 11 regions in Great Britain electing between three and ten MEPs.
➤ Political parties draw up a list of candidates, in the order in which they will be elected.
➤ Electors cast a single vote for a political party or independent. In the 'closed list' system used in Britain, electors can only vote for a party or for an independent candidate. They cannot choose between candidates representing the same political party. This gives

political parties greater control over the electoral process, as they can position their favoured candidates at the top of the list. In an 'open list' system, voters can choose between candidates from the same party.

➢ Seats are allocated according to the proportion of votes won by each political party in the region.

Advantages of regional list

The advantages of the regional list system are:

➢ There is a high degree of proportionality. The size of the region (the 'district magnitude') matters — results are more proportional in regions electing a high number of representatives, but smaller parties are less likely to win seats in regions electing a small number of representatives.

➢ Political parties have used their lists to increase the number of women and ethnic minority candidates.

Disadvantages of regional list

The disadvantages of the regional list system are:

➢ In closed list systems, voters cannot choose between candidates from the same party.

➢ Parties control the order in which candidates appear on the list and can favour candidates who support the leadership.

➢ The link between representatives and constituents is weakened in large multi-member constituencies.

Case study   The European Parliament elections, 2009

Table 2.5 shows that the outcome of the 2009 European Parliament elections in Great Britain was largely proportional. However, the share of seats won by the four leading parties was higher than their share of the vote. The Greens won the same number of seats as the SNP despite polling more votes. The relatively small size of some regions makes it difficult for a party whose vote is evenly distributed to win seats.

Table 2.5 Elections to the European Parliament, 2009 (GB only)

Party	Share of vote	Seats (share of seats)
Conservative	27.7	25 (36%)
UKIP	16.5	13 (19%)
Labour	15.7	13 (19%)
Liberal Democrat	13.7	11 (16%)
Green	8.6	2 (3%)
BNP	6.2	2 (3%)
SNP	2.1	2 (3%)
Plaid Cymru	0.8	1 (1%)
Others	8.5	0 (0%)

Single transferable vote

The single transferable vote (STV) is used in Northern Ireland for elections to the Assembly, local government and the European Parliament. It is also used for local elections in Scotland — and for general elections in the Republic of Ireland. The main features of STV are:

➤ Representatives are elected in large multi-member constituencies. In elections to the Northern Ireland Assembly, 17 constituencies each elect six members.

➤ Voting is preferential — electors indicate their preferences by writing '1' besides the name of their first preference, '2' next to the name of their second choice and so on.

➤ Voting is also ordinal — electors can vote for as many or as few candidates as they like.

➤ A candidate must achieve a quota, known as the Droop quota, to be elected. Any votes in excess of this quota are redistributed on the basis of second preferences. The quota is calculated as follows:

$$\left(\frac{\text{total valid poll}}{(\text{seats} + 1)} \right) + 1$$

If no candidate reaches the quota on the first count, the lowest-placed candidate is eliminated and their second preferences are transferred. This process of elimination and redistribution of preferences continues until the requisite number of seats is filled by candidates meeting the quota.

Case study   The Northern Ireland Assembly elections, 2011

Table 2.6 shows that the 2011 elections to the Northern Ireland Assembly produced a broadly proportional outcome. The UUP won more seats than the SDLP despite polling fewer first preferences, benefiting from the transfer of second and lower preferences.

Table 2.6 Elections to the Northern Ireland Assembly, 2011

Party	First preference votes	First preference votes (%)	Seats won	Seats won (%)
Democratic Unionist (DUP)	198,436	29.3	38	35.2
Sinn Fein	178,224	26.3	29	26.9
Social Democratic and Labour Party (SDLP)	94,286	13.9	14	13.0
Ulster Unionist (UUP)	87,531	12.9	16	14.8
Alliance	50,875	7.7	8	7.4
Traditional Unionist	16,480	2.4	1	0.9
Green	6,031	0.9	1	0.9
Others	29,873	6.6	1	0.9

Advantages of STV

The advantages of STV are:

➤ It has a good record of delivering proportional outcomes, and ensures that votes are largely of equal value.

➤ Only a party or group of parties that wins more than 50% of the popular vote can form a government.
➤ Voters can choose between a large range of candidates, including different candidates from the same party.

Disadvantages of STV

The disadvantages of STV are:

➤ The system is less accurate in translating votes into seats than list systems or some versions of AMS.
➤ It uses large multi-member constituencies that weaken the link between individual MPs and their constituency.
➤ It is likely to produce a **coalition government** that may be unstable and can give disproportional influence to minor parties that hold the balance of power.

Key term
➤ **Coalition government**
A government made up of more than one political party.

Additional member system

The additional member system (AMS) is a mixed electoral system. It has been used to elect the Scottish Parliament and Welsh Assembly since 1999, and the London Assembly since 2000. It is also used for general elections in Germany. The main features of AMS are:

➤ A proportion of seats in the legislative assembly are elected using FPTP in single-member constituencies; 73 out of 129 members of the Scottish Parliament (57%) are elected in single-member constituencies, as are 40 of the 60 members of the Welsh Assembly (67%).
➤ A smaller number of representatives — additional members — are elected in multi-member constituencies; 56 members of the Scottish Parliament (43%) and 20 members of the Welsh Assembly (33%) are elected in this way.
➤ Electors cast two votes: one for their favoured candidate in a single-member constituency, and one for their favoured party from a party list in a multi-member constituency
➤ List seats (additional members) are allocated on a corrective basis to ensure that the total number of seats for parties in the assembly is proportional to the number of votes they won. These seats are allocated using the d'Hondt rule (see case study).
➤ To win seats in the London Assembly, a party must pass a threshold of 5% of the vote. There is no threshold for Scottish Parliament and Welsh Assembly elections.

Advantages of AMS

The advantages of AMS are:

➤ It balances the desirability of constituency representation with that of fairness in election outcomes.
➤ Results are broadly proportional and votes are less likely to be wasted.
➤ Voters have greater choice. **Split-ticket voting** is allowed. Here, a voter uses their constituency vote to support a candidate from one party, and their list vote to support a different party.

Key term

➤ **Split-ticket voting** The practice of voting for candidates from different parties in an election where an elector is permitted to cast more than one vote.

Disadvantages of AMS

The weaknesses of AMS are:

➤ It creates two categories of representative, one with constituency duties and one without.
➤ Parties can have significant control over the party lists used to elect additional members.
➤ Smaller parties are often under-represented because multi-member seats elect relatively few representatives.

Case study The d'Hondt formula

The d'Hondt formula is a mathematical formula for allocating seats proportionally. It was invented by the nineteenth-century Belgian academic Victor d'Hondt. It is a highest average system that uses a divisor method rather than a quota. The formula does not deliver strict proportionality because it slightly favours large parties over smaller ones.

Under d'Hondt, the total votes of each party are divided by the number of seats it already has, plus the next seat to be allocated. Thus, the party totals are divided first by 1 (0 seats plus 1), then by 2 (1 seat plus 1) and so on. The first seat goes to the party with the largest number, the next seat to the next highest number and so on.

Table 2.7 shows the regional list election in Mid and West Wales in the 1999 Welsh Assembly election. The number of constituency seats won by each party in the region was taken into account in allocating the first list seat. The calculations for subsequent seats then took the list and constituency seats into account. The Conservatives won two of the four list seats, having failed to secure a constituency seat in the region.

Table 2.7 The regional list election in Mid and West Wales, 1999

	Con	Lab	Lib Dem	Plaid Cymru	Winner
Constituency seats won	0	2	2	4	
List votes	36,622	53,842	31,683	84,544	
First divisor	1	3	3	5	
First seat	36,622	17,947	10,561	16,910	Con
Second divisor	2	3	3	5	
Second seat	18,311	17,947	10,561	16,910	Con
Third divisor	3	3	3	5	
Third seat	12,207	17,947	10,561	16,910	Lab
Fourth divisor	3	4	3	5	
Fourth seat	12,207	13,460	10,561	16,910	Plaid Cymru

Source: Bradbury, J. (1999) 'Labour's bloody nose', *Politics Review*, Vol. 9, No. 2, p. 7.

Case study The Scottish Parliament elections, 2011

Table 2.8 shows the result of the 2011 elections to the Scottish Parliament. For the first time, the AMS system delivered a majority government as the SNP won 73% of constituency seats. Labour won more regional list seats than the SNP despite polling fewer votes because these were allocated in a corrective way. The Conservatives also benefited from the distribution of list seats. Smaller parties and independents performed better in the regional list contests than constituency contests, securing three seats.

Table 2.8 Elections to the Scottish Parliament, 2011

Party	Share of constituency vote (%)	Constituency seats won	Share of regional list vote (%)	List seats won	Total seats
Conservative	13.9	3	12.4	12	15
Labour	31.7	15	26.3	22	37
Lib Dem	7.9	2	5.2	3	5
SNP	45.4	53	44.0	16	69
Green	0	0	4.4	2	2
Others	1.1	0	7.7	1	1

Links to follow up

www.electoral-reform.org.uk — follow the links under 'Research and information' for the Electoral Reform Society's guide to electoral systems.

Impact of the new electoral systems

The most significant effects of the new electoral systems are:

➢ **Greater proportionality.** The results of elections conducted under the new electoral systems have been more proportional than Westminster elections. The number of seats won by parties more closely matches their share of the vote. Smaller parties have had a greater chance of representation. However, no electoral system can translate votes into seats perfectly, and some systems perform this task better than others (see case study on deviation from proportionality).

➢ **Multi-party systems.** The elections confirm that the UK has several party systems rather than a standard, nationwide two-party system. Many of these are multi-party systems. Labour has long won a majority of Scottish seats at Westminster, but has failed to do so in the devolved elections. Smaller parties that have been unable to make a breakthrough at Westminster have won seats in the devolved assemblies and the European Parliament. UKIP came second in the 2009 European Parliament elections with 16% of the vote.

➢ **Minority and coalition governments.** Only one of the elections to the devolved assemblies — the 2011 Scottish Parliament elections in which the SNP won a parliamentary majority — has produced a clear winner. No party has won a majority of the popular vote. Scotland has also seen two terms of Labour–Liberal Democrat coalition, and one

SNP **minority government**. In Wales, Labour has ruled as a minority government and in coalition with the Liberal Democrats and then Plaid Cymru. The Good Friday Agreement requires that the Northern Ireland executive includes the major unionist and nationalist parties.

Key term

➤ **Minority government**
A government formed by a political party that does not have an overall majority in the legislature.

➤ **Split-ticket voting.** Voting behaviour has become more complex. Minor parties and independent candidates have performed better in elections using the new systems because electors recognise that a vote for a minor party is less likely to be wasted. One in five voters engaged in split-ticket voting in the 1999 Scottish Parliament elections (and more did so subsequently), by supporting a major party in the constituency vote but giving their list vote to another party.

Case study Deviation from proportionality

'Deviation from proportionality' is a measure of the proportionality of electoral systems. Table 2.9 shows that FPTP is the least proportional of the systems used in the UK and STV is the most proportional.

Table 2.9 Deviation from proportionality under UK electoral systems

Institution	Electoral system	Year of election	Deviation from proportionality (%)
House of Commons	FPTP	2010	23
European Parliament (GB only)	Regional list PR	2009	18
Welsh Assembly	AMS (66:33)	2011	11
Scottish Parliament	AMS (57:43)	2011	10
Northern Ireland Assembly	STV	2011	8

Note: Deviation from proportionality is calculated by: calculating the difference between each party's percentage vote-share and seat-share, summing all deviations (ignoring minus signs) and halving the total.

Advocates of **electoral reform** see these outcomes as positive. However, the new systems have also brought problems:

➤ **Complexity.** Some voters have found the systems complex. The design of ballot papers was changed after the 2007 Scottish Parliament elections, when 146,000 ballots were rejected because they had not been completed correctly. In the 2012 London mayoral elections, only 589,000 of the 1,763,000 second preference

Key term

➤ **Electoral reform** Changes made to an electoral system or a change from one electoral system to an alternative (in Britain, the term commonly refers to the campaign to replace FPTP with PR).

votes were for the top two candidates. The other second preference votes did not influence the outcome and a further 435,000 electors did not cast a second preference.

➤ **Constituency links.** Tensions between constituency and regional list members have arisen in the Scottish Parliament and Welsh Assembly. Whereas the former have a significant constituency workload, the latter do not have a clear link with their constituents and undertake less of this work. Candidates were barred from standing for both constituency and regional list seats in the 2007 Welsh Assembly elections, but can do so in Scotland.

➤ **Low turnout.** Turnout in elections conducted under the new systems has often been low. Evidence from other countries shows that turnout in general elections conducted under PR elections is higher than that where FPTP is used. Turnout in second-order elections — contests that do not determine the government — is normally lower than for general elections. But turnout of 15% in the 2012 police and crime commissioner elections was disappointing.

Links to follow up

http://blogs.lse.ac.uk — follow the links under 'British politics and policy' for short articles by political scientists examining electoral reform (posted on the blog section of the LSE website).

Viewpoint Have the new electoral systems worked?

- Election results have been more proportional, translating votes cast into seats won more effectively.
- The rise of multi-party politics is reflected in election outcomes, with smaller parties winning seats and taking office.
- Voters have a greater choice as votes for small parties are less likely to be wasted.
- Majority, minority and coalition governments in the devolved assemblies have generally been stable.
- The new electoral systems have helped to produce more consensual and representative political systems.
- Voters have become more sophisticated, often engaging in split-ticket voting in elections to the devolved assemblies and voting differently in these elections from in Westminster elections.

- The new systems have not always delivered highly proportional outcomes (see Table 2.9).
- Extremist parties have gained seats, with the BNP winning 2 seats in the 2009 European Parliament elections.
- The closed list system used for European elections and the regional list element of elections for the devolved assemblies restricts voter choice.
- The new electoral systems weaken the relationship between representatives and constituents by using large multi-member constituencies or (in AMS) creating two classes of representative.
- Turnout has been low in elections conducted under the new electoral systems.
- Some voters appear confused by the new systems, evidenced in the relatively high number of spoiled ballot papers and wasted second preference votes.

Electoral reform

Campaigns for electoral reform have a long history. The Proportional Representation Society, forerunner of the Electoral Reform Society, was formed in 1884. In 1918, a Speaker's Conference recommended that a mixed electoral system should replace FPTP. A bill introducing AV was passed by the House of Commons but rejected by the House of Lords in 1931.

Labour's interest in electoral reform revived in opposition in the 1980s and 1990s. John Smith proposed a referendum on electoral reform for Westminster. In 1997 the Blair government established an Independent Commission on the Voting System to examine the case for reform. It was chaired by Lord (Roy) Jenkins, a Liberal Democrat peer and former Labour cabinet minister. Jenkins recommended 'AV Plus', a hybrid of the AMS and alternative vote systems. Most MPs would have been elected in single-member constituencies using AV, with the remaining 20% elected from open lists in multi-member regions and allocated on a corrective basis.

But Labour did not hold a referendum on electoral reform. Blair's doubts had hardened after Labour's experience of coalitions in Scotland and Wales. Many Labour MPs were also unwilling to replace a system that had given them parliamentary majorities on a minority of the popular vote. In 2010, however, Gordon Brown pledged that, if re-elected, Labour would hold a referendum on AV.

David Cameron agreed to hold a referendum on AV under the coalition agreement with the Liberal Democrats. The Liberal Democrats' preferred system is STV, but they accepted the Conservative offer on AV. The Electoral Reform Society suggested that the Liberal Democrats would have won an additional 22 seats if AV had been used for the 2010 general election, but 105 more under STV (see Table 2.10). The 2011 referendum produced a 68% vote against AV. This decisive vote against change, albeit to another majoritarian system, ended the prospect of electoral reform for Westminster in the medium term. Coalition plans for a reformed House of Lords elected by proportional representation were also shelved.

Links to follow up

www.electoral-reform.org.uk — the website of the Electoral Reform Society, a group advocating electoral reform, provides news and commentary.

Table 2.10 The 2010 general election under different voting systems

Party	First-past-the-post	Alternative vote	Single transferable vote
Conservative	307	281	246
Labour	258	262	207
Liberal Democrat	57	79	162
Others	28	28	35

Source: Electoral Reform Society, www.electoral-reform.org.uk.

Which electoral system for Westminster?

1   If asked to recommend an electoral system for Westminster, how would you decide? You might start by deciding what an electoral system should do. Rank the following in order of importance:

- allows voters to unseat the government
- clear link between MPs and constituents
- enhances the representation of women and ethnic minorities
- maximises voter choice between candidates
- produces stable government
- proportionality of outcome
- simple to understand

2   Now consider how three electoral systems used in the UK — FPTP, AMS and STV — perform these tasks. You could give each electoral system a score (e.g. 5 = very well; 1 = very poorly). On this basis, which of these electoral systems would you recommend?

Voting behaviour

Two main approaches have been prevalent in studies of voting behaviour:

➤ sociological approaches that focus on the social characteristics of voters, particularly **social class**, and their party loyalties

➤ rational choice approaches that focus on decisions made by individual voters on political issues, the economy, party leaders and governing competence

Key concept

➤ **Social class** A social group defined by social and economic status. The working class consists of people in manual occupations and the middle class is made up of those with non-manual jobs. The traditional way that opinion pollsters categorise social class is: AB – professional and managerial; C1 – white collar (non-manual) workers; C2 – blue collar (manual) workers; and DE – semi-skilled, unskilled and those reliant on state benefits. Government statisticians use more complex typologies.

Class voting and partisanship

Sociological approaches made two main claims about the social characteristics of voters in the period 1945–70:

➤ **Class voting.** A strong link existed between social class and voting. Most people voted for their 'natural' class party: that is, the party that best represented the interests of their social group. A majority of the working class (i.e. manual workers) voted for the Labour Party, while most of the middle class (i.e. non-manual workers) backed the Conservatives. There were, however, exceptions. At a time when the working class was the largest social

group, the Conservatives would not have won power without the support of a sizeable minority of working-class voters.

➤ **Partisanship.** Most voters had stable, long-term feelings of positive attachment to one of the main parties. This party identification developed through **socialisation** or social learning in the home (most people voted for the same party as their parents), school, workplace and neighbourhood.

Both class voting and partisanship have declined since 1970. Two trends have been apparent:

➤ **Class dealignment.** The relationship between social class and voting has weakened, with fewer people voting for their class party. This is because the distinctions between social classes have been eroded by greater affluence, improved access to higher education and changes in the labour market (e.g. the increase in women and part-time workers). The 'old working class' of manual workers who were employed in heavy industry and belonged to trade unions has shrunk. A 'new working class' of people working in the private sector, with better qualifications and owning their own home, emerged in the 1980s. New sectoral divisions have emerged, notably between those employed in the public and private sectors.

➤ **Partisan dealignment.** The number of voters who strongly identify with either Labour or the Conservatives has declined. In 1964, 43% of voters were 'very strong' supporters of one of the main parties, but by 2005 only 13% were. The **core vote** for the two main parties is therefore smaller — parties have to work harder to win over **floating voters** who do not have strong allegiances and may switch their vote from election to election. Partisan dealignment is also seen in the decline in party membership and the two-party system. Whereas more than 90% of voters in the 1950s voted for either Labour or the Conservatives, only 65% did so in 2010.

Key terms

➤ **Socialisation**. The process by which individuals acquire their values and beliefs.
➤ **Class dealignment** The decline in the relationship between social class and voting.
➤ **Partisan dealignment**. The decline in strong voter identification with political parties.
➤ **Core vote** Voters who feel a strong attachment to a political party and vote for it in election after election.
➤ **Floating voters** Voters without a strong attachment to a particular party, who may switch their vote from election to election.

Class voting has been less pronounced in recent general elections. The Conservatives gained support from the working class in the 1980s, while Labour made significant gains among middle-class voters in 1997. New Labour was a 'catch-all' party with a cross-class appeal. It made further gains among middle-class voters in 2001 and 2005, but its working-class support fell (see Table 2.11). Middle-class support for the Conservatives was no higher in 2010 than in their 1997 defeat.

Table 2.11 Class voting since 1974

Party	Middle class (ABC1)	Skilled working class (C2)	Unskilled working class (DE)
Conservative			
1974 (Oct.)	56	26	22
1979	59	41	34
1983	55	40	33
1987	54	40	30
1992	54	39	31
1997	39	27	21
2001	38	29	24
2005	37	33	25
2010	39	37	31
Labour			
1974 (Oct.)	19	49	57
1979	24	41	49
1983	16	32	41
1987	18	36	48
1992	22	40	49
1997	34	50	59
2001	34	49	55
2005	31	40	48
2010	27	29	40

Source: Ipsos MORI, www.ipsos-mori.com.

Despite the decline of class voting, it is important to recognise that Labour remains the most popular party among working-class voters and the Conservatives still perform best among middle-class voters.

Links to follow up

www.politicsresources.net — click on 'Elections in UK and US' and then 'Elections in the UK'.

Other social factors

A number of other social characteristics have an impact on voting behaviour:

➤ **Gender.** For much of the postwar period, there was a 'gender gap' in voting behaviour with women more likely to vote Conservative than men. This perhaps reflected social attitudes of the time and the fact that relatively few women went out to work. Since the 1990s, when Labour made significant gains among women voters, there has been little difference in the way men and women vote. However, younger women are more likely to vote Labour than older women. They may be attracted by Labour's welfare

policies — women are more likely to rely on state benefits than men — and efforts to increase the number of women MPs.

➤ **Age.** The Conservatives have long performed better among older voters than Labour. Voters acquire more responsibilities (e.g. a mortgage, children) as they grow older and may lose their youthful idealism. The political climate of the period in which a person grew up may also shape his or her longer-term outlook.

➤ **Ethnicity.** A majority of ethnic minority electors vote Labour. Ethnic minority voters are not, though, a homogeneous group —for example, those with Indian origins are more likely to vote Conservative (22% in 2010) than Black Africans (6%). Social class is a factor as ethnic minority voters are more likely to be manual workers or unemployed. The Iraq war contributed to a sharp fall in support for Labour in 2005 in constituencies with large Muslim populations, but Labour regained some of this support in 2010. As the number of ethnic minority voters grows, their negative perceptions of the Conservatives become more problematic for the party.

Links to follow up

www.ethnicpolitics.org — data and analysis of ethnic minorities' engagement in British politics.

British Asian voters entering a polling station in Dewsbury, West Yorkshire

➤ **Region.** There are important regional variations in voting. A 'north–south divide' is evident, with Conservative support highest in southern England, the suburbs and rural areas, while Labour does best in the north of England, Scotland and Wales, in large urban areas and on council estates. Regional patterns of support are explained partly by the distribution of social classes (e.g. manual workers are concentrated in urban areas), but also by local political factors. The 2010 general election saw Labour–Conservative contests in London, the Midlands, the northwest and Yorkshire. The main electoral battles in the southwest were between the Conservatives and Liberal Democrats, while some northern cities saw Labour–Liberal Democrat rivalry. Nationalist parties came second in Scotland and Wales. Northern Ireland has a distinctive party system and pattern of voting.

Rational choice approaches

The **rational choice model** of voting behaviour examines the choices made by individual voters. Variants of the model focus on short-term factors such as issues, the performance of parties and their leaders, and the state of the economy.

Key term

➤ **Rational choice model** An approach to the study of politics that focuses on the actions of rational individuals who pursue their own interests.

Issue voting

The issue voting perspective claims that people compare party policies and vote for the party whose position is closest to their own. For it to be significant, a sizeable number of voters must feel an issue is important, identify the same party as having the best policy, and vote for it. The spatial model of issue voting focuses on issues on which the main parties offer different policies. However, many voters see little difference between the main parties on key issues.

Valence issues

Issues on which there is broad agreement between the parties (e.g. the economy, health) are **valence issues**. The valence model claims that voter judgements on trust and competence on these issues are crucial. In 1997, 2001 and 2005, Labour enjoyed strong leads over the Conservatives on health and education. Voters believed that Labour was more likely to deliver a sound economy and good-quality public services than the Conservatives.

Key concept

➤ **Valence issue** A valence issue is a policy issue on which the main parties are in broad agreement. When parties adopt a similar position, voters make judgements about their relative competence and ability to deliver the desired outcomes. A party will campaign on those valence issues on which voters believe it is the most competent.

The broader valence politics perspective suggests that voters make a judgement about the overall performance of parties and their leaders. If the governing party is widely perceived to have performed well in office, it will be rewarded. Attributes of governing competence might include policy success (particularly a sound economy), strong leadership, a clear agenda and party unity. In 1997, voters reached a negative verdict on the Conservatives' performance in government and believed Labour would prove more effective. Voter satisfaction with Labour declined by 2005, but perceptions of the Conservatives were even more negative. Although these improved by 2010, many voters were not convinced that the Conservatives were ready for government.

Party leaders have become more important in shaping electoral outcomes because of partisan dealignment and the personalisation of politics. Leaders are the public face of their party and carry much of the responsibility for communicating party policy. This was especially true in the 2010 election campaign when the Conservative, Labour and Liberal Democrat leaders took part in three televised debates. Voters use their judgements about the character and competence of leaders as short-cuts to reach verdicts about political parties as a whole.

Economic voting

The economic voting model claims that voters are more likely to support the governing party if it has delivered a healthy economy. By looking at economic data (e.g. interest rates) and voters' personal economic expectations (i.e. whether they will be better or worse off), the model predicted the results of recent elections with a good degree of accuracy. A decline in economic pessimism as the UK emerged from recession saw support for Labour increase early in 2010, helping to deny the Conservatives a parliamentary majority.

Links to follow up

www.ipsos-mori.com — a leading opinion pollster whose website includes detailed information on political trends.

Campaigns and the media

Political parties spend a great deal of time and money (£31 million in 2010) on their nationwide general election campaigns. They aim to set the agenda by promoting the issues on which they are favoured by voters. Parties also engage in negative campaigning by rubbishing the policies and leaders of their rivals in the hope of persuading voters to switch, or at least making supporters of other parties consider whether to vote at all.

Evidence on the significance of these national campaigns is patchy. Most voters have already made their mind up before the campaign gets under way. There is likely to be some movement in the opinion polls during a campaign, but much of it is 'churning' in which voters switch between parties rather than moving uniformly towards one party. The 2010 campaign saw an unusually high number of voters make up their minds late (one in four decided in the final week) or change their minds (particularly those considering voting Liberal Democrat).

Local campaigning can be significant. Parties focus much of their effort on marginal seats, in which small swings in support can change the outcome of the contest. Local campaigns are coordinated from the centre to a much greater extent than previously, but an active local party can play an important role in canvassing voters.

The 2010 leaders' debates were the first to be broadcast live in the run-up to a UK election

Voters get much of their information on politics from the media. Television is a crucial medium, particularly with the advent of leaders' debates in 2010. One in four voters said that they changed their mind on how to vote after the first debate. Studies of the impact of newspapers on voting behaviour have not produced a definitive verdict. Rather, there are three broad perspectives:

➤ **Influence.** This perspective suggests that newspapers have a direct influence over the voting behaviour of their readers. Evidence suggests that, allowing for class and existing attitudes, readers of Labour-supporting newspapers are more likely to vote for Labour than are readers of pro-Conservative newspapers. The *Sun* claimed to have influenced the outcome of the 1992 election and that of 1997, when it switched support to Labour. It backed the Conservatives in 2010.

➤ **Reinforcement.** This view suggests that newspapers reinforce views already held by their readers. Most people read a newspaper that reflects their political views. But they often rely on television rather than newspapers for non-partisan coverage of politics.

> **Agenda shaping.** This perspective claims that the press is unlikely to have a direct influence on voting, but that newspaper coverage does help shape the political agenda. Newspaper coverage of, say, immigration or crime helps to frame the way in which these issues are perceived by voters.

Turnout

Turnout of around 60% in the 2001 and 2005 general elections was significantly lower than the postwar average of 78%. It increased in 2010, but only to 65%. Studies of low turnout focus on three areas:

> **Rational choice.** Rational choice theory suggests that voters will not vote if the costs outweigh the potential benefits. Many non-voters cite practical reasons (e.g. inconvenience) for their abstention. People are more likely to vote in a close contest because their vote is more likely to make a difference to the outcome. Most people believe that voting is a civic duty, but the number is declining and is particularly low among young people.

> **Disillusion and apathy.** Dissatisfaction with Westminster politics and the main political parties has contributed to low turnout. The proportion of people who trust politicians or feel a strong attachment to a political party has declined. Some of the anger felt by voters about the MPs' expenses scandal had dissipated by the 2010 election, but it still depressed turnout. Recent general election campaigns have failed to motivate potential voters.

> **Social groups.** Turnout varies across social groups. It is highest among elderly, middle-class and university-educated people, and higher in rural than urban areas.

The 2010 general election

The 2010 general election was the first to produce a hung parliament since February 1974. The Conservatives won 307 seats, falling short of the 326 needed for an overall majority in the House of Commons. The result was disappointing for the Conservatives given their healthy lead in the opinion polls in 2009 and Labour's unpopularity. But the Conservatives made a net gain of 97 seats and the Labour to Conservative swing of 5% was their largest since 1979.

Labour suffered a net loss of 91 seats and its 29% share of the UK vote was only marginally better than its 1983 postwar low. But Labour did enough to prevent a Conservative majority and saw off a brief surge in support for the Liberal Democrats.

The Conservatives and Labour together polled fewer than two-thirds of the vote for the first time in postwar politics. The Liberal Democrats' opinion poll ratings surged after Nick Clegg's performance in the first televised leadership debate, but the election delivered only a small rise in their share of the vote and a net loss of five seats. Nonetheless, they entered government as junior coalition partner.

Caroline Lucas became the first Green MP, but the party's nationwide vote share fell. UKIP polled over 900,000 votes and the BNP more than 500,000, their highest general election totals, but they managed only six third-placed finishes between them. The two independents elected in 2005 were defeated, although Respect MP George Galloway returned to parliament at the 2012 Bradford West by-election.

Social characteristics of voting

Table 2.12 shows the social characteristics of voting at the 2010 general election. The most significant developments were:

➤ **Social class.** The Conservatives remained the favoured party of middle-class voters and Labour of working-class voters, but support for Labour fell among C2 (manual) and DE (semi-skilled and unskilled) voters. People employed in the public sector were less likely to vote Conservative than those working in the private sector.

➤ **Gender and age.** Labour again had more support from women than men, although the Conservatives overtook Labour in terms of overall support from women voters. All parties had identified young mothers as a critical sub-set of the electorate. The Conservatives and Liberal Democrats made gains among women under 35, but Labour lost ground. The Liberal Democrats gained support from young voters, while the Conservatives retained their lead among older voters.

➤ **Region.** There was no uniform nationwide swing. A north–south divide in party support resurfaced. The Conservatives again did best in southern England and overtook Labour in the Midlands. Labour came top in northern England. Labour's best performance was in Scotland where it increased its share of the vote while the Conservatives remained fourth, winning only one seat. The Conservatives gained five seats in Wales but in Northern Ireland an alliance with the Ulster Unionist Party flopped.

The swing to the Conservatives was slightly higher in Labour–Conservative marginals than elsewhere. The swing to the Conservatives in Liberal Democrat–Conservative marginals was only 1%, allowing the Liberal Democrats to retain seats in southwest England. Labour topped the poll in London and the Conservatives failed to win seats in other large cities. They also underperformed in seats with a high proportion of ethnic minority voters. Finally, incumbent Labour MPs tended to suffer smaller swings to the Conservatives than new candidates.

Rational choice voting

To understand fully why the Conservatives made gains but did not win a majority, we must examine rational choice accounts of the 2010 general election. Key factors include:

➤ **The economy and other issues.** Management of the economy was the issue ranked most important by voters. 29% of voters felt that the Conservatives had the best policy, a 3% lead over Labour, but 36% believed that no party had the best economic policy. The

Table 2.12 The 2010 general election

	Conservative		Labour		Liberal Democrat	
Share of the vote (%)	36.1	(+3.8)	29.0	(−6.2)	23.0	(+1.0)
Seats	307	(+97)	258	(−91)	57	(−5)
Social class						
AB	39	(+2)	26	(−2)	29	(0)
C1	39	(+2)	28	(−4)	24	(+1)
C2	37	(+6)	29	(−11)	22	(+3)
DE	31	(+6)	40	(−8)	17	(−1)
Gender						
Men	38	(+4)	28	(−6)	22	(0)
Women	36	(+4)	31	(−7)	26	(+3)
Age						
18–24	30	(+2)	31	(−7)	30	(+4)
25–34	35	(+10)	30	(−8)	29	(+2)
35–44	34	(+7)	31	(−10)	26	(+3)
45–54	34	(+3)	28	(−7)	26	(+1)
55–64	38	(−1)	28	(−3)	23	(+1)
65+	44	(+3)	31	(−4)	16	(−2)
Region						
North East	24	(+4)	44	(−9)	24	(+0)
Yorkshire and the Humber	33	(+4)	35	(−9)	23	(+2)
North West	32	(+3)	40	(−6)	22	(+0)
West Midlands	40	(+5)	31	(−8)	21	(+2)
East Midlands	41	(+4)	30	(−9)	21	(+2)
Eastern	47	(+4)	20	(−10)	24	(+2)
London	35	(+3)	37	(−2)	22	(+0)
South East	50	(+5)	16	(−8)	26	(+1)
South West	43	(+4)	15	(−7)	35	(+2)
Scotland	18	(+1)	42	(+3)	19	(−4)
Wales	26	(+5)	36	(−7)	20	(+2)

Note: Figures in brackets refer to change since 2005.

Sources: BBC election website, www.bbc.co.uk/election/results/; Ipsos MORI, www.ipsos-mori.com/researchspecialisms/socialresearch/specareas/politics/trends.aspx

Conservatives had failed to convince voters despite the economic problems of the Brown government. They enjoyed large leads over Labour on immigration, crime and defence, but Labour led on health and unemployment. However, many voters had little faith in the policies of the established parties.

➤ **Party leaders.** Voters' opinions of the party leaders were as important as party policies in determining how people voted. David Cameron was preferred to Gordon Brown as the 'most capable prime minister', but only by a narrow margin. Voters who thought that a leader had done well in the televised leadership debates became more likely to vote for his party, and less likely to vote for a party whose leader performed poorly.

➤ **Competence.** A majority of voters agreed that it was time for change, but four in ten voters did not believe that the Conservatives were ready for government. Cameron had neutralised the negative image that his party had in earlier elections, but had not built convincing opinion poll leads on key issues, governing competence or his capability as a potential prime minister.

Links to follow up

www.bbc.co.uk/election — election results and analysis from the BBC.

What you should know

❯ Elections are central to politics in a liberal democracy. Their main functions include determining and legitimising the government, holding politicians to account, and ensuring the democratic participation and representation of the people.

❯ A representative should act in the interests of their constituents but is also free to exercise their own judgement. If a representative body should resemble society, then more women, ethnic minority and young MPs ought to sit in the House of Commons than do at present.

❯ The first-past-the-post system is used for general elections. The winning candidate in a single-member constituency needs only a plurality (i.e. one more vote than their nearest rival). Supporters of FPTP claim that it produces strong, stable and responsible government. Critics argue that it is disproportional, produces wasted votes and denies voters real choice.

❯ Four other electoral systems are used for elections beyond Westminster: the majoritarian supplementary vote, two proportional representation systems (the regional list system and the single transferable vote) and the mixed additional member system.

❯ The new electoral systems have produced more proportional outcomes than FPTP, although smaller parties may still be under-represented. They have also led to minority and coalition governments, reflecting the development of multi-party systems in the UK.

❯ The impetus for electoral reform for Westminster stalled when the 2011 referendum delivered a decisive 'no' vote on introducing the alternative vote.

❯ Class and party identity played a crucial role in voting behaviour in the period 1945–70, but their importance has declined. However, the Conservatives still perform best among middle-class voters and Labour among working-class voters. Voter perceptions of the relative competence of the main parties and their leaders have been significant in recent general elections.

UK/US comparison

Electoral systems

➤ There are separate elections for the president and for Congress in the USA. Elections take place at fixed terms. Presidential elections take place every 4 years. Members of the House of Representatives are elected every 2 years. Senators serve a 6-year term, but there are rolling elections with one-third of the Senate elected every 2 years. Hundreds of thousands of other positions (from judges to local officials) are subject to election. In the UK, the prime minister is not directly elected.

➤ Members of the House of Representatives are elected in single-member constituencies known as districts. Each of the 50 US states sends two representatives to the Senate. In the UK, the House of Lords is unelected.

➤ The simple plurality system is used for elections to Congress. In presidential elections, the candidate who secures a plurality of votes in a state receives all the electoral college votes for that state. As in the UK, simple plurality can deliver a 'winner's bonus' and may produce the wrong result — Republican George W. Bush won the 2000 presidential election yet Democrat Al Gore polled more votes nationwide.

➤ The USA retains a classic two-party system, whereas that in the UK is in decline. The Republicans and Democrats win most votes and seats in Congress, and have shared the presidency in modern times. Third-party candidates rarely have an impact.

➤ Social factors are less important in voting behaviour in the USA than in the UK, although the Democrats do better among poorer voters and the Republicans perform better among the well-off. Black and women voters are more likely to support the Democrats. Election campaigns have a greater impact than in the UK, and the character of the presidential candidates is often crucial.

Further reading

Curtice, J. (2010) 'So what went wrong with the electoral system? The 2010 election result and the debate about electoral reform', *Parliamentary Affairs*, Vol. 63, No. 4, pp. 623–38.

Denver, D., Carman, C. and Johns, R. (2012) *Elections and Voters in Britain*, 3rd edition, Palgrave.

Green, J. (2012) 'Voting behaviour: how important is issue voting?', *Politics Review*, Vol. 22, No. 2, pp. 26–29.

Hix, S., Johnston, R. and McLean, I. (2010) 'Electoral reform: a vote for change?', *Political Insight*, Vol. 1, No. 2, pp. 61–63.

Johnston, R. (2011) 'Which electoral systems are best for Westminster?', *Politics Review*, Vol. 21, No. 2, pp. 2–5.

Kavanagh, D. and Cowley, P. (2010) *The British General Election of 2010*, Palgrave.

Smith, N. (2011) *UK Elections and Electoral Reform*, 2nd edition, Philip Allan Updates.

Exam focus

Short response questions (around 5–6 minutes each)

1 What is an election?
2 Define wasted votes.
3 What is dealignment?
4 Define proportional representation.
5 Define tactical voting.

Mid-length response questions (around 10–12 minutes each)

1 Distinguish between majoritarian and proportional electoral systems.
2 Explain the ways that elections promote democracy.
3 Outline and explain *three* advantages of the first-past-the-post (FPTP) electoral system used in the UK.
4 Using examples, explain the workings of *three* electoral systems, other than FPTP, used in the UK.
5 Outline and explain the role played by the media in influencing elections in the UK.

Mini-essay questions (around 25–30 minutes each)

1 To what extent do elections play a vital role in the UK's democratic system?
2 'The UK should replace the first-past-the-post electoral system with a more proportional alternative.' Discuss.
3 How has the use of more proportional electoral systems affected party representation in the UK?
4 'The rational choice voting model is the most convincing explanation of voting behaviour in the UK.' Discuss.

 Extra resources to help you revise and consolidate your knowledge for this chapter are provided online at **www.hodderplus.co.uk/philipallan**. These include a revision PowerPoint, extension tasks and up-to-date weblinks.

Chapter 3

Political parties: structure

Key questions answered in this chapter

➤ What is a political party?

➤ What role do parties perform in the UK system?

➤ How are the main UK parties organised?

➤ How internally democratic are the main UK parties?

➤ How are the main UK parties funded and why is party funding so controversial?

What is a political party?

Political parties are groups of like-minded individuals who seek to realise their shared goals by fielding candidates at elections and thereby securing election to public office.

Most conventional UK parties would ultimately aim to emerge victorious at a general election, and thereby earn the right to form a government at Westminster. In this respect, parties differ significantly from **pressure groups**, for while some pressure groups employ electoral candidacy as a means of raising public awareness of their chosen cause, they generally have little interest in, or prospect of, being returned to office.

The origins of modern UK parties

Before the Great Reform Act of 1832, UK parties existed not as mass-membership organisations with formal structures outside of parliament, but as groups of like-minded individuals within the legislature; these groups were bound together by shared ideals, friendship or family ties. With electoral reform came the need to organise in order to mobilise the growing electorate. It was at this point that UK political parties as we know them today began to emerge.

Political parties and pressure groups

Political parties

- Political parties tend to offer a broad portfolio of policies, informed by a guiding ideology.
- The main UK political parties have open membership structures and are therefore inclusive.
- Political parties contest elections with a view to securing control of governmental power.
- The main UK parties are highly organised and offer their members an input into key decisions through formalised rules and procedures.

Pressure groups

- Pressure groups generally pursue a narrower cause or sectional interest.
- Many pressure groups — particularly sectional groups — are more exclusive in their membership.
- Those pressure groups that field candidates in elections generally do so simply as a means of raising their own profile — or encouraging candidates representing mainstream parties to adjust their policies for fear of losing votes.
- Even the larger, more established pressure groups are often dominated by a small leading clique; few pressure groups display high levels of internal democracy.

Different types of political party

Mainstream parties

UK politics is dominated by three main political parties: the Conservative Party, which emerged from the Tory group within parliament in the mid-nineteenth century; the Labour Party, formed by trade unions and socialist organisations at the start of the twentieth century; and the Liberal Democrats (Lib Dems), which came into being as a result of the merger between the Liberal Party and the Social Democratic Party (SDP) in 1988.

Minority or 'niche' parties

- **Nationalist parties.** Nationalist parties look to nurture the shared cultural identity and language of those indigenous to a given geographical area — whether a 'nation', as in the case of the Scottish National Party (SNP), or a region, as in the case of Mebyon Kernow ('Sons of Cornwall'). While some nationalist parties campaign for full independence for their region or nation (e.g. the SNP), others do not (e.g. Plaid Cymru in Wales). The British National Party is different from most other nationalist parties in that it campaigns in support of the way of life and values that it claims are common to all indigenous UK peoples.
- **Single-issue parties.** Recent years have seen a rise in the number of single-issue parties contesting elections in the UK. In some cases these parties offer a wide-ranging programme of policies rooted in a particular ideological perspective (e.g. the Green Party). In other cases, these smaller parties campaign on a particular issue (e.g. UKIP on the European Union), or even a specific policy (e.g. the Pro-Life Alliance on abortion). Recent elections have also seen the rise of local single-issue parties such as the Independent Kidderminster Hospital and Health Concern Party, whose candidate Dr Richard Taylor

won the Wyre Forest constituency at the 2001 and 2005 general elections. In many cases, such single-issue or ideological parties blur the boundary between political parties and pressure groups, as their primary goal is to raise awareness of a particular issue as opposed to winning an election and/or securing power.

Caroline Lucas became the Green Party's first MP at the May 2010 general election

⟷ Stretch and challenge

The Green Party: political party or attitude cause group?

It is possible for one or more pressure groups to evolve into a political party. A good case in point is the Green Party. Known prior to 1985 as the Ecology Party, the Green Party's origins can be found in a pressure group called 'People' that was formed in 1973. Although the Green Party itself initially appeared to be little more than a glorified single-issue group, it has developed a broader range of policies in recent years in an effort to improve its electoral prospects.

Questions

1 Does it make more sense to see the Green Party as a political party or an attitude cause group?

2 Which other UK political parties could be said to straddle the same divide?

The growing appeal of niche parties

It is significant that the membership of many niche parties has risen at the same time that mainstream parties have continued to haemorrhage members (see Table 3.1). Some argue that this is a function of the way in which the main UK parties have moved towards the centre of the political spectrum in recent years, thereby leaving some voters feeling unrepresented. Support for such niche parties at the ballot box may also reflect the fact that they provide an obvious vehicle for those looking to send a message to government or the main opposition parties by casting a protest vote.

Table 3.1 Individual party membership for the BNP, Green Party, SNP and UKIP (000s)

Year	BNP	Green	SNP	UKIP
2002	3.1	5.9	16.1	10.0
2003	5.5	5.3	9.5	16.0
2004	7.9	6.3	10.9	26.0
2005	6.5	7.1	11.0	19.0
2006	6.3	7.0	12.6	16.0
2007	9.8	7.4	13.9	15.9
2008	11.8	8.0	15.1	14.6
2009	12.6	9.6	15.6	16.3
2010	10.3	12.8	16.2	15.5
2011	7.7	12.8	20.1	17.2

Source: McGuinness, F. (2012)
Membership of UK political parties,
House of Commons Library SN/SG/5125.

Links to follow up

'Membership of UK political parties' (SN/SG/5125) 3 December 2012, **www.parliament.uk** — the relevant Standard Note from the House of Commons Library.

The UK party system

Despite the rise of the Liberal Democrats and some niche parties in recent years, most commentators still characterise Britain as a **two-party system**.

However, not all nations operate under a two-party system.

 Key term

> **Two-party system** Where two fairly equally matched parties compete for power at elections and others have little realistic chance of breaking their duopoly.

Single-party systems

In a single-party system, one party dominates, bans other parties and exercises total control over candidacy at elections — where elections occur at all e.g. in Nazi Germany or the Democratic People's Republic of Korea (North Korea).

Dominant-party systems

In a dominant-party system, a number of parties exist but only one holds government power (e.g. Japan under the Liberal Democratic Party between 1955 and 1993). Some argue that the UK party system has, at times, resembled a dominant party system — with the Conservatives in office 1979–97 and Labour in power 1997–2010.

Multi-party systems

In a multi-party system, many parties compete for power and the government consists of a series of coalitions formed by different combinations of parties e.g. Italy between 1945 and 1993.

Viewpoint Is Britain a two-party system?

YES

- The Labour and Conservative parties are the only parties that have a realistic chance of forming a government or being the senior partner in a coalition.
- Even in 2010, the Labour and Conservative parties secured 65.1% of the popular vote (down just 2.6% on 2005), winning 86.8% of the 650 seats contested (up 1.2% on 2005).
- The Liberal Democrats (in third) are still a long way behind the second-placed party (6% of the vote and 201 seats behind Labour in 2010).

NO

- 34.9% of voters backed parties other than the 'big two' in 2010.
- Although the Liberal Democrats are the 'third party', they are often second to Labour in the north and west and to the Conservatives in the south and east.
- The UK has the potential to evolve into a 'two-and-a-half party system' — where the the LibDems would be involved in a series of coalitions with one or other of the big two.
- In reality, different parts of the UK operate under different party systems. For example, in some parts of Scotland there is genuine four-way competition.
- Any party that could mobilise non-voters — 34.9% of registered voters at the 2010 general election — would stand a chance of winning the election.

The roles performed by UK political parties

Political parties perform five main roles: providing representation; facilitating political participation; engaging in political recruitment; formulating policy; and providing stable government.

Representation

Traditionally, parties were said to represent the views of their members. This was certainly true in an age of mass-membership parties, when parties and voters were clearly divided along class lines. Partisan and class dealignment, accompanied by the rise of centrist 'catch-all parties', could be said to have undermined this primary role.

Participation

Parties encourage political participation by encouraging citizens to engage with the democratic process and giving them the opportunity to exercise power within their chosen party. The quality of participation afforded to members is shaped largely by the extent to which political parties are themselves internally democratic.

Political recruitment

Parties assess the qualities of those seeking election to public office, casting aside those who are, for whatever reason, considered unsuitable. Parties also give those who will ultimately become the nation's leaders an opportunity to serve a political apprenticeship at a local level before 'graduating' to high office.

Policy formulation

Parties discuss and develop policy proposals, before presenting them to voters in a single coherent programme (i.e. their manifesto). It is argued that this process is likely to result in a more considered, 'joined-up' style of government than that which might emerge in the absence of political parties.

Providing stable government

Without parties, it is argued, the Commons would simply be a gathering of individuals, driven by their personal goals and political ambitions. Parties present the voters with a clear choice, while also providing order following the general election — by allowing a single party to form a government and secure the safe passage of its legislative proposals through the Commons.

The organisation of the main UK parties

Local and national level

Labour Party

Those who join the Labour Party are assigned to a local branch — the lowest level of the party organisation. Branches select candidates for local elections and send delegates to the General Committee of the Constituency Labour Party (CLP). The CLP organises the party at constituency level. It takes the lead in local and national election campaigns and plays a part in selecting candidates for parliamentary elections, although the extension of one-member-one-vote (OMOV) has diminished the role of constituency party leaders in relation to regular members.

The National Executive Committee (NEC) is the main national organ of the Labour Party. It enforces party discipline, ensures the smooth running of the party, has the final say on the selection of parliamentary candidates, and oversees the preparation of policy proposals. Although the annual conference was once the party's sovereign policy-making body, its role diminished somewhat in the 1990s.

Conservative Party

The Conservative Party has a similar structure to the Labour Party at the local level. Branches corresponding to local council wards operate below the constituency-level Conservative Associations (CA). The CA play a key role in organising the party at grassroots level, planning election campaigns, and selecting parliamentary candidates. As with the Labour Party, however, the CA no longer have a free rein in selecting parliamentary candidates.

The national party is organised around the Conservative Campaign Headquarters (CCHQ) at Millbank, Westminster. The party's headquarters were previously referred to as Conservative Central Office.

UK parties sitting in the European Parliament

UK members of the European Parliament (MEPs) sit in a number of transnational groups as opposed to a single UK block within the chamber. Following the UK elections to the European Parliament in 2009, the 25 Conservative MEPs elected sat with the newly formed European Conservatives and Reformists (ECR) group, the 13 Labour MEPs sat with the Progressive Alliance of Socialists and Democrats (PASD), and the 11 Lib Dem MEPs sat with the Alliance of Liberals and Democrats for Europe (ALDE).

Internal party democracy

As political parties seek to exercise control over our democratic institutions, it is only proper for commentators to question the extent to which parties are themselves internally democratic.

Choosing and removing party leaders

One significant indicator of **internal party democracy** is the extent to which regular members are given an input into the process by which the party leader is chosen.

> **Key concept**
> ➤ **Internal party democracy** A measure of the extent to which rank-and-file members
>   have genuine power within a given political party. Three processes are commonly
>   considered when assessing how internally democratic a political party is: the way in
>   which leaders are chosen; the way in which candidates for parliamentary elections are
>   selected; and the way in which party policy is formulated.

Conservative Party

The current system for electing Conservative leaders was introduced by William Hague in 1998 — with Hague's successor, Iain Duncan Smith, becoming the first Conservative Party leader to be elected under the new system in 2001. Only sitting Conservative MPs, who take the party whip, and have been nominated and seconded by fellow Conservative MPs may stand. Once nominations close, a series of ballots is held among Conservative MPs with the lowest-placed candidate being eliminated at the end of each round. Individual party members are then invited to choose between the two surviving candidates in a run-off election conducted by postal ballot.

A criticism of the current system is that those in the parliamentary party can manipulate the final choice presented to rank-and-file members by voting tactically in the ballots of MPs. In 2001, for example, those on the right of the party deliberately switched their support in the final ballot of MPs, with the effect of eliminating the early favourite Michael Portillo and presenting the rank-and-file members with a choice between their chosen candidate — the Eurosceptic Iain Duncan Smith — and the moderate Kenneth Clarke, a candidate whom Duncan Smith's supporters knew would not be able to defeat 'their man' in a ballot of individual party members.

Although it might appear sensible to offer individual party members the final say in such contests, doing so can prove problematic when the membership of all three main parties as a percentage of the electorate has contracted significantly in recent years (see Figure 3.1) and the members are themselves increasingly unrepresentative of the broader population. While Iain Duncan Smith was the clear favourite among Conservative Party members back in 2001, he proved singularly unable to capture the imagination of the broader electorate and was ultimately forced to resign by his own parliamentary party after just 2 years as leader.

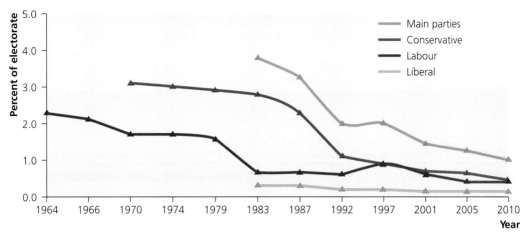

Figure 3.1 Membership of the main UK parties as a percentage of the UK electorate, 1964–2010

Source: McGuinness, F. (2012), *Membership of UK Political Parties*,
House of Commons Library SN/SG/5125.

Case study **The 2005 Conservative Party leadership contest**

Table 3.2 Results of the 2005 Conservative leadership contest

Candidate		Date declared
Kenneth Clarke		30 August
Liam Fox		8 September
David Davis		29 September
David Cameron		29 September
First ballot of MPs (18 October)		**Votes**
1	David Davis	62
2	David Cameron	56
3	Liam Fox	42
4	Kenneth Clarke	38
Second ballot of MPs (20 October)		**Votes**
1	David Cameron	90
2	David Davis	57
3	Liam Fox	51
Postal ballot of party members (closed 5 December)		**Votes**
1	David Cameron	134,446 (68%)
2	David Davis	64,398 (32%)
Eligible voters		253,689
Turnout		78%

Source: Kelly, R. and Lester, P. (2005) *Leadership Elections: Conservative Party*,
House of Commons Standard Note SN/PC/1366.

It was telling that individual members were excluded from the process of electing Duncan-Smith's successor in 2003 as a result of Michael Howard's unopposed 'coronation' as leader. There was, however, a full ballot to elect Howard's successor in 2005 (see case study above).

Labour Party

The Labour leader was once chosen by the Parliamentary Labour Party (PLP) alone. Since the 1980s, however, leadership elections have operated under an electoral college employing alternative vote (AV). In its present incarnation this electoral college is divided into three distinct sections, with one-third of the votes held by the Parliamentary Labour Party and the party's MEPs, one-third in the hands of **affiliated organisations**, and the final third being cast by **ordinary party members**. Since 1993 such contests have operated on an OMOV basis.

> **Key concept**
> ➤ **Affiliated organisations** Groups that are formally linked to the Labour Party without their members holding regular membership of the party. Most trade unions are affiliated to the Labour Party, as are many socialist societies such as the Fabian Society and the Cooperative Society.

Those seeking election as Labour leader must be nominated by at least 12.5% of the party's MPs where there is a vacancy — or 20% of MPs where they seek to challenge the incumbent. If no candidate secures more than half of the votes cast on the first ballot, further ballots must be held on an elimination basis, using preferences, until a clear winner emerges.

Although the system is obviously far more democratic than the one it replaced, rank-and-file members still have a fairly limited influence relative to individual MPs and the affiliated organisations. Indeed, individual members only have a say in the event that more than one candidate is able to secure the support necessary to validate their nomination: when Tony Blair stood down as party leader in 2007, Gordon Brown was elected unopposed. It is also far harder than it once was to remove a Labour Party leader while the party is in government — such a challenge can now only proceed following a majority vote at the annual party conference.

Viewpoint | **Is the system by which the Labour Party selects its leaders fair?**

YES
- The electoral college system puts individual party members on an equal footing with MPs/MEPs and members of affiliated organisations.
- The voting for all three sections operates on an OMOV basis.
- The weighting of the union vote was reduced from 40% to 33.33% in 1993.
- It is right that unions and other affiliated organisations retain a say in electing the party leader as they played a key role in founding the Labour Party.

- There are far more individual party members than MPs/MEPs — yet the electoral college gives these two sections an equal voice.
- The unions still have a massive input, even though most of their members are not regular members of the party.
- The nomination rules prevent hopefuls from outside of the PLP from qualifying for the ballot.
- There may be no election where only one candidate is nominated (as with Gordon Brown in 2007).
- A candidate can win without majority support among either the PLP or individual party members (see case study below).

Case study | The 2010 Labour Party leadership contest

Ed Miliband's victory in the 2010 Labour leadership contest resulted from his ability to campaign as a left-leaning 'party outsider' — thereby attracting the endorsement of many powerful trade unions. David Miliband lost the contest, despite commanding majority support both within the PLP and among individual members in all four ballots.

Table 3.3 Results of the 2010 Labour leadership contest (% share of the vote)

First ballot		MPs/MEPs	Members	Affiliates	Total
1	David Miliband	13.91	14.69	9.18	37.78
2	Ed Miliband	10.53	9.98	13.82	34.33
3	Ed Balls	5.01	3.37	3.41	11.79
4	Andy Burnham	3.01	2.85	2.83	8.68
5	Diane Abbot	0.88	2.45	4.09	7.42 (eliminated)
Second ballot		**MPs/MEPs**	**Members**	**Affiliates**	**Total**
1	David Miliband	14.02	15.08	9.80	38.89
2	Ed Miliband	11.11	11.13	15.23	37.47
3	Ed Balls	5.18	3.83	4.22	13.23
4	Andy Burnham	3.03	3.30	4.08	10.41 (eliminated)
Third ballot		**MPs/MEPs**	**Members**	**Affiliates**	**Total**
1	David Miliband	15.78	16.08	10.86	42.72
2	Ed Miliband	12.12	12.43	16.71	41.26
3	Ed Balls	5.43	4.82	5.77	16.02 (eliminated)
Fourth ballot		**MPs/MEPs**	**Members**	**Affiliates**	**Total**
1	Ed Miliband	15.52	15.20	19.93	50.65 (elected)
2	David Miliband	17.81	18.14	13.40	49.35

Source: data adapted from Labour Party website (www2.labour.org.uk/votes-by-round).

Liberal Democrats

Those wishing to stand must have the support of at least 10% of the parliamentary party and be nominated by no fewer than 200 members from at least 20 different local parties. The election itself then operates on an OMOV basis under a preferential, single transferable

Distinguish between

Ordinary party members and ordinary Members of Parliament

Ordinary party members

➤ The term 'ordinary party members' refers to individual members of a party or the 'rank-and-file', 'grassroots' membership — those paid-up party members who do not hold senior positions within their chosen party.

Ordinary Members of Parliament

➤ These are Members of Parliament (also known as backbenchers) who do not hold front-bench responsibilities as a government minister, shadow minister or party spokesperson.
➤ Although every MP will be a paid-up member of his or her chosen party, a question on ordinary party members will expect you to focus on the issue of internal party democracy — rather than the influence of backbenchers.

vote (STV) system — with losing candidates being eliminated and their votes transferred until one candidate commands the support of more than 50% of those members casting a ballot. In 2007, Nick Clegg defeated his chief rival for the leadership, Chris Huhne, by just 511 votes. Some commentators claimed that Huhne would have won, were it not for the fact that significant numbers of ballot papers had been held up in the Christmas post.

Candidate selection

As we have noted, political parties play a key role in political recruitment because they select and train up the political leaders of tomorrow. Potential candidates thus serve a kind of political apprenticeship within the party.

Separating 'the wheat from the chaff'

The number of individuals wanting to be elected to parliament exceeds the number of seats available. Parties play a key role in separating the genuine contenders from the 'no-hopers'.

All three major parties have traditionally employed a similar three-stage process in selecting parliamentary candidates: first, hopefuls must get their names on to a centrally vetted, 'approved list' of prospective candidates; second, the local party draws up a shortlist from those approved candidates who have expressed an interest; and third, constituency members vote for their preferred candidate, whether in person at a meeting or by postal ballot.

Conservative Party

Traditionally, those seeking to represent the Conservative Party in parliamentary elections were subject to a tortuous and largely 'closed' process:

➤ Prospective candidates had to get their names on to an 'approved' list of candidates by attending a formal panel interview.
➤ Approved candidates would apply to a constituency Conservative Association and succeed in getting their name onto a shortlist.

➤ Short-listed candidates would need to garner the support of those party activists attending a constituency general meeting.

Even those candidates who were successful in securing the nomination of their constituency association by such means could still find their nominations vetoed by the national party's Ethics and Integrity Committee, established in the 1990s by the party leader William Hague.

Under the leadership of David Cameron the party looked to broaden the range of candidates selected significantly, first by introducing the so-called A-lists and later by trialling hustings and primaries.

➤ **A-lists.** A-lists required Conservative Associations to include women and those from ethnic minorities on their shortlists. This move was seen as echoing Labour's use of women-only shortlists. However, the A-list scheme did not require local associations to select candidates from certain backgrounds; it merely forced them to draw up more socially diverse shortlists. Many of those candidates ultimately selected still fitted the Conservative stereotype of white, middle-aged men.

➤ **Hustings.** Open hustings events allow local voters as well as paid-up, card-carrying local party activists to attend a meeting at which the audience listens to and can pass judgement on the prospective parliamentary candidates assembled before them. Such hustings, sometimes referred to as primaries, were used in around 100 contests ahead of the 2010 general election.

➤ **Open primaries.** August 2009 saw the Conservative Party select its candidate in the parliamentary constituency of Totnes by means of an open primary — a popular ballot in which all registered voters (i.e. not just party members) have a hand in selecting the candidate who will run in the election proper. This was the first time that a major UK party had employed such a device in selecting a parliamentary candidate. Where the Totnes primary differed from the hustings used elsewhere was that participation was widened not simply by inviting non-members to attend a one-off meeting, but by sending out postal ballots to all 68,000 registered voters in the constituency — at an estimated cost to the party of £38,000.

Labour Party

Those wishing to become prospective parliamentary candidates for the Labour Party must first get their names on to the National Executive Committee's approved list (the parliamentary panel). This list is forwarded to Constituency Labour Parties, which draw up shortlists from those approved candidates who have applied, before selecting their preferred candidate under OMOV. Crucially, even where the CLP has already made a selection, the NEC is free to set aside the entire process and impose its own choice of candidate. The choice of members has also been limited by the introduction of **women-only shortlists** in many of Labour's safer seats.

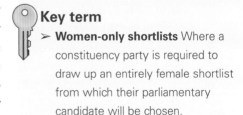

Key term

➤ **Women-only shortlists** Where a constituency party is required to draw up an entirely female shortlist from which their parliamentary candidate will be chosen.

Stretch and challenge

Women-only shortlists

The Labour Party's practice of employing women-only shortlists existed in its original form between 1993 and 1996. Although it was briefly outlawed in 1996 — under the Sex Discrimination Act — the government subsequently amended the legislation to allow such lists. This exemption to anti-discrimination legislation was subsequently enshrined in the Equality Act (2010).

The use of all-women shortlists in many safe Labour seats contributed to the significant increase in the number of women MPs returned to parliament at the 1997 general election (see Table 3.4). However, such shortlists have proven controversial — not least because they serve to discriminate against suitably able and qualified male candidates. At the 2005 general election, the independent candidate Peter Law was elected to represent the constituency of Blaenau Gwent, having been prevented from seeking selection as the official Labour Party candidate by the party's imposition of an all-women shortlist.

Table 3.4 Number of women MPs

General election	Female MPs	Percentage
1992	60	10
1997	120	18
2001	118	18
2005	128	20
2010	143	22

Questions

1 Outline the case in favour of using all-women shortlists.

2 Why is the use of such all-women shortlists so controversial?

Liberal Democrats

Those wishing to become prospective parliamentary candidates for the party must be vetted by their national party (England, Scotland or Wales). Those selected as approved candidates can then apply to individual constituencies for selection. Candidates short-listed by the constituency party go forward to a ballot of all constituency party members.

The deselection and imposition of candidates

Although the constituency-level party in all three major parties is normally allowed the final say in selecting parliamentary candidates from the approved lists, this is not always the case. In 1986, for example, the Labour Party under Neil Kinnock deselected MPs Dave Nellist and Terry Fields for being part of the banned Militant Tendency. The Labour Party has also imposed candidates on constituencies (for example, parachuting the former Conservative MP Shaun Woodward in as the Labour candidate for the safe seat of St Helens South ahead of the 2001 general election). More recently, the scandal over MPs' expenses saw both the Conservative Party and the Labour Party seeking to bar certain MPs from defending their seats at the 2010 general election.

Policy making

Conservative Party

Until the late 1990s, Conservative Party policy was largely determined by the leader of the day. Although the party leader was expected to canvass the views of senior colleagues on the front benches, the 1922 Committee, party elders and the grassroots membership, it was an unashamedly top-down process. As John Major famously said of the party's 1992 general election manifesto, 'it was all me'.

In 1998 the system appeared to have been democratised somewhat as part of the then party leader William Hague's 'Fresh Future' initiative. This programme saw the creation of a national party Policy Forum, alongside a number of other initiatives ostensibly aimed at enhancing participation within the party. Critics argued that these changes were more of style than substance. While the party's 2001 manifesto appeared to have been the product of greater consultation, the Policy Forum was downgraded under Iain Duncan-Smith and the 2005 manifesto was largely decided by party leader Michael Howard and advisers such as the party's Australian campaign consultant Lynton Crosby. In a similar vein, the party's 2010 general election manifesto was said to have been framed by David Cameron, Oliver Letwin and Steve Hilton — Cameron's director of strategy.

Labour Party

The Labour Party conferences of the past were genuine policy-making events. From 1997, however, the party adopted a 2-year policy-making cycle (see Figure 3.2). The National Policy Forum appointed policy commissions to make proposals which were then

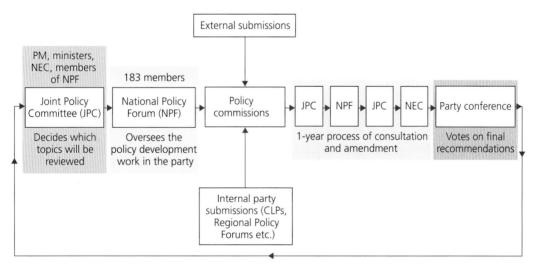

Source: Webb, P. (2000) 'Political parties: adapting to the electoral market' in P. Dunleavy et al., *Developments in British Politics 6*, Macmillan Press.

Figure 3.2 Labour's 2-year rolling policy-making cycle

formalised in the National Executive Committee, before passing to the party conference for approval. This process afforded the party leader more control and helped the party to avoid the kinds of nasty surprises and public shows of disunity that characterised earlier party conferences. Critics have argued that these reforms have seen the conference transformed from being a sovereign policy-making body, to little more than a rubber stamp for policies agreed elsewhere: Ed Miliband — the man who later succeeded Gordon Brown as Labour leader — was widely credited with having drafted the party's 2010 general election manifesto.

Liberal Democrats

The party is federal in structure, comprising English, Scottish and Welsh state parties with a number of organisational tiers below each national party. What this means in practice is that policy that will only affect Scotland, for example, will be developed by the Scottish party and confirmed at the conference of that party. Policies affecting England and the whole of the UK are dealt with at the main national conference — the Federal Conference — which meets twice-yearly. This conference is the supreme policy-making body of the party, but it spends most of its time considering proposals from the Federal Policy Committee, state parties, regional parties and local parties. The party leadership's influence over the Federal Policy Committee allows them to steer policy, at least to a degree.

Striking the right balance on policy

In an age of mass-membership parties, the views of members might have been a fair indication of how the broader public would react to a given policy. In the modern era, however, party membership is falling and those who do join are increasingly unrepresentative of the broader population. In this context, allowing regular members to determine policy in isolation could constitute electoral suicide.

While the Liberal Democrats are seen as having the most democratic method for determining party policy, some argue that some of the policies adopted in the past — for example, on cannabis possession and asylum seekers — were rather too easily picked-off by Labour and Conservative activists during general election campaigns.

Party funding

The changing basis of party funding

Most political parties receive income in the form of membership subscriptions. Until the 1990s, however, the lion's share of Labour Party funding came from fees paid by trade unions and other affiliated organisations, while the Conservative Party was said to be bank-rolled by wealthy business interests.

The decline of UK political parties as mass-member organisations has adversely impacted on party finances. The efforts to reduce the influence of trade unions within the Labour Party, under Neil Kinnock, John Smith and Tony Blair, also resulted in falling revenues. Such developments led parties to court donations from wealthy individuals such as Bernie Ecclestone and Lord Sainsbury for Labour, and Sir Paul Getty and Stuart Wheeler for the Conservatives (though the latter later defected to UKIP, becoming the party's treasurer).

Why has party funding provoked controversy?

The rise of large individual donations to political parties since the 1990s led to the perception that one might be able to buy access or political influence. For example, some felt that Bernie Ecclestone's £1 million donation to the Labour Party in 1997 may have prompted the subsequent delay in the introduction of the ban on tobacco advertising in Formula 1 motor racing. Such controversy inevitably led to calls for regulation.

Bernie Ecclestone

Political Parties, Elections and Referendum Act (PPERA)

The PPERA (2000) imposed an overall limit on party spending in general election campaigns (£30,000 per constituency), established additional spending limits for elections to devolved bodies and the European Parliament, and required parties to declare all donations over £5,000 to the Electoral Commission. In so doing, the Act sought to make parties less reliant on wealthy individual backers.

Political Parties and Elections Act (PPEA)

The PPEA (2009) built upon the regulations established under the PPERA:
- ➢ It allowed for the appointment of commissioners with more recent experience.
- ➢ It imposed tighter regulations on spending by candidates in the run-up to an election.
- ➢ It allowed the Electoral Commission to investigate cases and impose fines.
- ➢ It raised the threshold at which donations must be declared from £5,000 to £7,500.
- ➢ It restricted donations over £7,500 to those who could prove that they were UK residents for tax purposes.

Links to follow up

www.electoralcommission.org.uk — the Electoral Commission outlines the current legislation on party funding under 'Party finance'.

The Phillips report (2007)

The 'Phillips Report' (*Strengthening Democracy: Fair and Sustainable Funding of Political Parties*) concluded that one way forward might be greater state funding for UK political parties, perhaps through some form of 'pence-per-voter' or 'pence-per-member' funding formula.

Creeping towards the state-funding of political parties?

Although the case in favour of the comprehensive funding of UK political parties is still widely contested, it is worth remembering that 'public funds' have long been in place in the form of the Policy Development Grants (PDGs) established under Section 12 of the PPERA (2000) — **Short money** and **Cranborne money**. The PDGs are particularly significant as they are available not only to the main opposition parties — but as a share of a £2 million annual pot to any party that has two or more sitting MPs taking the oath of allegiance (see Table 3.5): there were seven such parties in 2012. Parties also receive subsidies in respect of their television broadcasts and help with their postage costs during election campaigns. Scottish parties receive assistance from the Scottish Parliament under the Assistance to Registered Parties scheme.

Key concepts

> **Short money** Short money comprises those funds paid to opposition parties in order to help them cover their administrative costs and thereby provide for proper scrutiny of the government. It is available to all opposition parties that win at least two seats — or win a single seat while also securing over 150,000 votes nationally — at a general election. The Labour Party received £5,917,159 under this scheme in 2011.

> **Cranborne money** In the House of Lords, such payments to opposition parties are known as Cranborne money. The Labour Party received £548,752 under this scheme in 2011.

Table 3.5 Policy Development Grant allocations in 2012 (rounded)

Party	Grant available	Expenditure submitted and approved	Total grant paid
Conservative and Unionist Party	£458,695	£256,517	£256,517
Democratic Unionist Party (DUP)	£155,577	£156,288	£155,577
Labour Party	£458,695	£458,695	£458,695
Liberal Democrats	£458,695	£473,503	£458,695
Plaid Cymru — The Party of Wales	£152,075	£165,617	£152,075
Scottish National Party (SNP)	£160,686	£217,063	£160,686
Social Democratic and Labour Party (SDLP)	£155,577	£155,647	£155,577

Source: Electoral Commission.

Links to follow up

www.electoralcommission.org.uk — the official website of the Electoral Commission providing background on various pieces of legislation together with data on donations, both recent and historic.

Viewpoint   Should political parties be state-funded?

- If parties are not funded by taxpayers, they will be funded by interest groups.
- State funding would allow politicians to focus on representing their constituents.
- Parties such as the Liberal Democrats could compete on an equal financial footing.

- Why should taxpayers bankroll parties that they oppose?
- Politicians could become isolated if they are denied contact with interest groups.
- Parties will always have unequal resources, even if state funding is introduced.

Has the reformed system worked?

Although the new system has made party funding more transparent, there have been significant teething problems — not least the Labour Party's efforts to circumvent the PPERA's regulation of 'donations' by encouraging supporters to offer the party long-term, low-interest 'loans'. It was this tactic, and the inducements supposedly offered to secure such lines of credit (specifically, the alleged offer of ennoblement), that gave rise to the 'Loans for Peerages' scandal. Although the police investigation into the scandal ultimately ended without any prosecutions being brought, it is clear that the issue of party funding is still controversial. This can be seen, for example, in the efforts to address the status of donors not registered as taxpayers in the UK under the PPEA — a measure that many saw as being aimed squarely at individuals such as the long-term Conservative Party backer and party deputy chairman Lord Ashcroft, whose tax status provoked debate and controversy until March 2010, when he finally revealed that he did not pay UK tax on his overseas earnings.

Statutory regulation and public funds aside, it is clear that the main UK political parties still receive considerable sums in donations: the three main parties were all reporting significant 'gifts' in the run-up to the 2010 general election (see Table 3.6). It is clear also that the wealthy individual backers that the PPERA (2000) sought to identify have not been put off by the prospect of losing their anonymity. For example, the Labour Party received two £1 million + donations in the last quarter of 2009 alone: one from Lord Sainsbury; the other from Nigel Doughty. Although the scale of donations to the main parties is obviously greatly reduced when there is no general election in prospect, the sums flowing into the parties' coffers in such years are significant nonetheless. In 2011, for example, the Conservative Party received donations totalling some £14 million, with the Labour Party collecting £12 million and the Liberal Democrats banking £4 million.

Table 3.6 Registered donations to British political parties in 2009

Party	Donations Value (£)	Donations No.	Public funds Value (£)	Public funds No.	Total Value (£)	Total No.
Conservative Party	27,085,928	1,604	5,428,014	13	32,513,942	1,617
Labour Party	15,213,494	1,183	1,007,201	6	16,220,695	1,189
Liberal Democrats	3,886,634	1,020	2,326,175	15	6,212,809	1,035
UK Independence Party	1,403,987	184	0	0	1,403,987	184
Co-operative Party	924,916	59	0	0	924,916	59
Scottish National Party	160,879	20	260,142	18	421,021	38
Plaid Cymru — The Party of Wales	142,656	27	271,187	23	413,843	50
Green Party	352,163	143	0	0	352,163	143
Christian Party 'Proclaiming Christ's Lordship'	273,937	12	0	0	273,937	12
No2EU: Yes to Democracy	97,995	26	0	0	97,995	26
The New Party	72,500	11	0	0	72,500	11
Scottish Voice	70,000	2	0	0	70,000	2
Pro Democracy: Libertas.eu	69,491	11	0	0	69,491	11
Jury Team	50,000	3	0	0	50,000	3
British National Party	45,332	14	0	0	45,332	14
mums4justice	35,890	4	0	0	35,890	4
Mums' Army	26,918	3	0	0	26,918	3
United Kingdom First	25,441	8	0	0	25,441	8
East Hert People	22,048	2	0	0	22,048	2
Scottish Green Party	11,547	2	8,952	1	20,499	3
Fair Play Fair Trade	16,040	2	0	0	16,040	2
Christian People Alliance	13,630	24	0	0	13,630	24
Yes 2 Europe	12,000	4	0	0	12,000	4
Communist Party of Britain	10,084	2	0	0	10,084	2
Mebyon Kernow — The Party of Cornwall	9,411	4	0	0	9,411	4
Pirate Party UK	210	1	0	0	210	1
Grand total	50,033,130	4,375	9,301,670	76	59,334,800	4,451

Source: Electoral Commission.

Party funding: where to from here?

The cross-party talks prompted by the Phillips Report were suspended without substantive agreement late in 2007. As a result, no significant progress on the issue of party funding was made ahead of the 2010 general election. The coalition agreement published in the wake of that election committed the Conservatives and Liberal Democrats to 'pursue a detailed agreement on limiting donations and reforming party funding in order to remove big money from politics'. Although the deputy prime minister Nick Clegg — within whose portfolio this area of policy fell — made mention of party funding in the debates that followed the Queen's Speech, the government appeared content to pause until the Committee on Standards in Public Life (CSPL) had reported the findings of the 'Inquiry into Party Political Finance' it had launched back in July 2010.

The publication of that report — *Political Party Finance: Ending the Big Donor Culture* — in November 2011, appeared to offer a way forward. Once again, however, the hopes of reformers were dashed; with the government offering little more than warm words and the prospect of yet more cross-party talks.

Not even the coverage in *The Times* in March 2012 of footage showing the then Conservative Party co-treasurer Peter Cruddas, apparently offering direct access to the prime minister in return for a donation of £250,000, was enough to re-energise the debate. While all parties appear to accept that 'big money' in the form of donations should be removed from politics, few at Westminster believe that voters enduring an extended period of austerity could easily be convinced of the need for greater state funding of political parties at tax payers' expense. Moreover, while the Labour Party would be happy to impose tougher restrictions on individual donations, the Conservatives would only accept such an overt attack on their own income-streams if similar restrictions were placed on Labour's union backers. Thus further reform of party funding, like Lords reform, appears to have arrived at a natural impasse.

What you should know

- ❥ A political party is a group of like-minded individuals who come together with the aim of realising their shared goals by fielding candidates at elections and thereby securing election to public office.

- ❥ Parties differ from pressure groups in that the latter would normally only contest elections as a mean of raising the profile of their chosen cause or sectional interest, as opposed to having a genuine desire to be returned to office.

- ❥ The main UK political parties are highly hierarchical organisations comprising a number of different organisational levels, from local and constituency parties to the national party level. The MEPs elected to represent the main UK parties in the European Parliament sit in transnational ideological groupings as opposed to a single national group.

- ❥ Although smaller niche parties of all types have made great strides in recent years, in terms of both votes won and candidates elected, the UK is still generally characterised as a two-party system, in which two fairly equally matched parties compete for power at elections and others have little realistic chance of breaking their duopoly.

- ❥ The study of party organisation often focuses on the issue of internal party democracy — the extent to which ordinary rank-and-file members are given a say in decision making within a given party. Analysis of internal party democracy commonly focuses on how parties select their leaders, how they choose candidates for parliamentary elections, and how they formulate party policy.

- ❥ Although the three main UK parties all allow ordinary members some say in choosing their party leader, the policy-making processes within the two main UK parties, the Conservative

Party and Labour Party, leave a good deal of power and control in the hands of their party leaders.

🔿 Party funding has proven a contentious issue in recent years, as the revenue generated from membership subscriptions has declined and the main parties have become increasingly reliant on donations from wealthy individuals.

🔿 Attempts to reform party finance under the PPERA (2000) and the PPEA (2009) have addressed some of the main areas of concern, although many commentators still argue in favour of the introduction of a more comprehensive system of state funding of parties than exists at present.

UK/US comparison

Party structure and organisation in the USA

➤ The USA, like the UK, is generally characterised as a two-party system. Vacant seats aside, all 435 members of the House of Representatives were either Democrats or Republicans in 2013, along with 98 of 100 US Senators. Every president since 1853 has been either a Democrat or a Republican.

➤ Whereas some UK niche parties are permanent, most minor parties (or 'third parties') in the USA are short-lived. Indeed, many might be seen as pressure groups employing electoral candidacy as a means of raising awareness of and support for their cause or sectional interest, as opposed to true political parties.

➤ US parties have traditionally been more decentralised in their organisation than their UK counterparts. The main US parties have no party leader as such, and the national parties have a far more limited role than their UK equivalents outside of elections.

➤ Whereas candidate selection in the UK remains largely controlled by political parties, the introduction of primaries in most US states has seen this power transferred to regular voters.

➤ The 1974 Federal Election Campaign Act (FECA) — as amended by subsequent legislation and moderated by rulings by the US Supreme Court — established a form of state funding of elections and regulated donations to candidates and parties. Despite this, campaign finance remains just as controversial an issue in the USA as it is in the UK.

Further reading

Clarke, A. (2012) *Political Parties in the UK*, Palgrave.

Kelly, R. (2007) *Leadership Elections: Liberal Democrats*, House of Commons Library Standard Note SN/PC/3872.

Kelly, R. (2012) *In Brief: Party funding*, House of Commons Library Standard Note SN/PC/6123.

Kelly, R. and Lester, P. (2005) *Leadership Elections: Conservative Party*, House of Commons Library Standard Note SN/PC/1366.

Kelly, R., Lester, P. and Durkin, M. (2010) *Leadership Elections: Labour Party*, House of Commons Library Standard Note SN/PC/3938.

McGuiness, F. (2012) *Membership of UK Political Parties*, House of Commons Library Standard Note SN/SG/5125.

McNaughton, N., Fairclough, P. and Magee, E. (2013) 'Political parties: is there a case for state funding?', *UK Government and Politics Annual Update 2013*, Philip Allan.

Wilks-Heeg, S. (2011) 'Funding UK Political Parties: A Democratic Dilemma', *Political Insight*, Vol. 2, No.1.

Exam focus

Short response questions (around 5–6 minutes each)

1 What is a political party?
2 What is a party conference?
3 Define the term multi-party system.
4 Give three examples of the roles performed by political parties in the UK.
5 Define internal party democracy.

Mid-length response questions (around 10–12 minutes each)

1 Identify and explain *three* functions of political parties.
2 Distinguish between political parties and pressure groups.
3 What are the advantages and disadvantages of women-only shortlists?
4 Explain how the Labour and Conservative parties elect their leaders.
5 Do the advantages of *primary elections* outweigh the disadvantages?

Mini-essay questions (around 25–30 minutes each)

1 'The UK is now a multi-party system.' Discuss.
2 How effectively do the UK's main political parties fulfil their core roles and functions?
3 To what extent should political parties in the UK be funded by the state?
4 Discuss the view that political parties in the UK offer little real power to individual party members.

 Extra resources to help you revise and consolidate your knowledge for this chapter are provided online at **www.hodderplus.co.uk/philipallan**. These include a revision PowerPoint, extension tasks and up-to-date weblinks.

Chapter 4

Political parties: policies and ideas

Key questions answered in this chapter

➤ What do we mean by 'party ideology'?

➤ What is the 'political spectrum'?

➤ What ideological positions have the main British parties traditionally adopted and how has party ideology evolved in recent years?

➤ Have we entered a post-ideological age of 'catch-all' parties?

Party ideology

As we saw in Chapter 3, political parties are groups of like-minded individuals who seek to realise collectively held goals by fielding candidates at elections and thereby securing election to public office. The first British parties were loosely bound together by shared ideals, friendships or family ties. However, electoral reform in the nineteenth century brought the need to organise and present a clearer message to the growing electorate. It was at this time that political parties as we know them today began to emerge.

For most of the twentieth century, it was common to characterise the British parties in ideological terms because the members of such organisations were committed not simply to a raft of discrete policies, but also to a coherent set of ideas and beliefs that underpinned such headline proposals. Thus the Conservative Party was said to favour conservatism; the Liberals, liberalism; and the Labour Party, socialism. However, by the late 1990s commentators on all sides were referring to the 'end of ideology' and the rise of so-called 'catch-all' parties, which were driven by a desire to win power at all costs, rather than campaigning on the basis of deeply held ideological convictions.

In this chapter we chart the changing character of the main British parties and assess the extent to which they remain distinctive, in terms both of their stated policies and of the ideas and values that underpin them.

Distinguish between

Ideology and policy

Ideology

➤ An ideology is a coherent set of beliefs or values that guide one's actions. Most mainstream British political parties traditionally subscribed to an ideology. The Labour Party, for example, was established along socialist lines.

Policy

➤ A policy is a proposed or actual strategy aimed at addressing a particular issue or area of government provision. Policies are often based upon a deeply held ideological position. For example, the Labour Party's desire to nationalise key industries after the Second World War was rooted in its commitment to socialism. However, policy may also serve purposes that are not essentially ideological in nature, such as the desire to appeal to wavering voters at an election or to bring a potential coalition partner on board in the wake of a 'hung' (or 'balanced') parliament.

The political spectrum

Party ideology in the UK has generally been discussed in terms of the simple left–right **political spectrum** (see Figure 4.1) that emerged in revolutionary France at the end of the eighteenth century. In modern usage, those on the extreme left of the political spectrum are said to favour some form of communal existence, with all property being held 'collectively' as opposed to 'individually', while moderate left-wingers accept capitalism but favour greater government intervention in the economy and a more comprehensive welfare state. In contrast, those on the right are said to favour private enterprise over state provision, resulting in a process that the former Conservative prime minister Margaret Thatcher described as 'rolling back the frontiers of the state'.

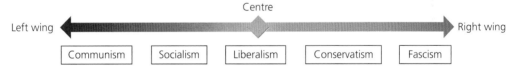

Figure 4.1 The left–right political spectrum

In the UK, where the extreme ideologies of communism (on the 'left') and fascism (on the 'right') have never really taken hold, the debate over the direction of government policy has generally centred on the battle between socialists and conservatives. However, all three of the main British parties are better seen as 'broad churches', each comprising members of various different political shades.

Key term

➤ **Political spectrum** A device by which different political standpoints can be mapped across one axis or more as a way of demonstrating their ideological position in relation to one another.

Critics of the left–right spectrum argue that it ignores significant differences between some of the groups that occupy each wing, as well as the significant overlaps between some of the groups that are said to occupy the polar opposites on the spectrum. For example, some forms of socialism and many of those regimes that would have described themselves as communist (e.g. Soviet Russia) appear similar in some respects to some of those on the extreme right (for example, Nazi Germany). While such problems can be partly explained by a certain confusion regarding precisely what communism entails, similar issues arise if one studies some of the major philosophical works of the nineteenth century.

The German philosopher Max Stirner is a case in point. In his 1845 work *The Ego and Its Own*, Stirner championed the importance of the individual and attacked **authoritarian** forms of government. Yet Stirner is said to have inspired both anarchists (on the 'left') and neo-liberals on the conservative right who rail against the state and champion the importance of individual liberty.

Some commentators have therefore argued that it is better to see the linear political spectrum as a circle or 'horseshoe' with the extremes of 'left' and 'right' coming together (see Figure 4.2).

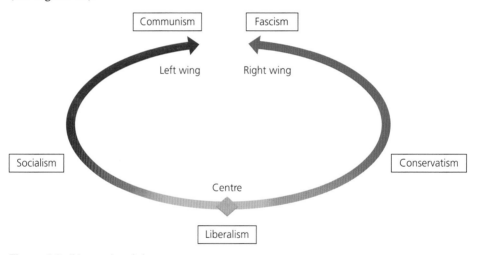

Figure 4.2 'Horseshoe' theory

Others argue that it makes more sense to move towards a four-pointed 'compass' because this allows us to make a distinction between those approaches to government which are more authoritarian and those which are more **libertarian** (see Figure 4.3).

Key terms

> **Authoritarian** In the political sense, describing any approach that favours strict obedience to the authority of the state.

> **Libertarian** Any approach that favours civil liberties and the rights of the individual over the authority of the state. Libertarians generally believe that society as a whole is best served by allowing citizens to operate relatively free from state intervention.

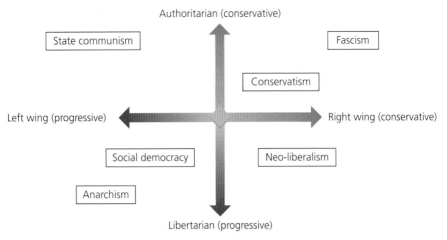

Figure 4.3 The ideological compass

Links to follow up

www.politicalcompass.org — a site that allows you to position yourself on the political spectrum by answering a series of question relating to how you feel about different aspects of policy.

Ideology and policy in the Conservative Party

Conservative ideology

The Conservative Party emerged from the Tory Party in the 1830s, with many dating its birth to Robert Peel's Tamworth Manifesto (1834). In the twentieth century, the party was in office (either alone or in coalition) for 67 years and enjoyed two extended periods in office:

➢ 1951–64 under Churchill, Eden, Macmillan and Home
➢ 1979–97 under Thatcher and then Major

One-nation conservatism

For most of the twentieth century, the Conservative Party was truly conservative in ideology: that is, rooted in pragmatism and the belief in gradual improvements founded on experience and existing institutions. This was a form of collectivist or **paternalist conservatism** which favoured pluralism and social inclusion, and held that while authority should be centralised, the state should be benevolent, caring for the neediest.

Key term

➢ **Paternalism** Where power and authority are held centrally but the state acts benevolently, caring for the neediest. Paternalism is said to be a key characteristic of traditional one-nation conservatism.

The proponents of this form of conservatism, now commonly referred to as one-nation Tories, were committed to: a mixed economy (Keynesianism); more significant state intervention, where necessary; slow, gradual change (evolution, not revolution); internationalism and increasing European integration; and support for a universal welfare state.

One-nation conservatism versus Thatcherism

The late 1970s and early 1980s saw the rise of a new form of liberal or libertarian conservatism on both sides of the Atlantic. Dubbed the 'New Right', this movement combined a belief in **monetarism**, free market economics and deregulation (an approach commonly referred to as **neo-liberalism**) with a more orthodox conservative approach in the sphere of social policy: for example, support for the traditional family unit and more traditional views on sexual orientation. The US president Ronald Reagan (1981–89) and UK prime minister Margaret Thatcher (1979–90) were key figures in this movement — the latter to such an extent that this broad approach has become known simply as **Thatcherism** in the UK. The advent of Thatcherism marked the death of the **postwar consensus** and the rise of a more **adversarial politics**.

Supporters of this approach, known as Thatcherites, favoured the importance of the individual over the needs of society as a whole, offering a radical agenda including policies such as:
➤ deregulation in the field of business
➤ privatisation of publicly owned industries

> **Key terms**
> ➤ **Monetarism** An economic theory advocating controlling the money supply as a means
> of keeping inflation in check.
> ➤ **Postwar consensus** The broad agreement between the Labour and Conservative
> parties over domestic and foreign policy that emerged after the Second World War.
> The consensus saw the parties cooperating over the creation of the welfare state and
> the adoption of a Keynesian economic policy. The postwar consensus began to break
> down in the 1970s and was said to have ended with the more ideological, adversarial
> approach that accompanied Thatcherism.
> ➤ **Adversarial politics** (or 'yah-boo' politics) The instinctive antagonism between the two
> main Westminster parties. The term was used by Professor S. E. Finer and commonly
> applied to UK politics from the 1970s.

Key concepts

> **Neo-liberalism** A political ideology closely related to classical liberalism. Neo-liberals stress the importance of the free market, individual rights and limited government. In the UK context, neo-liberalism is closely associated with Thatcherism.

> **Thatcherism** An ideological approach combining a free-market, neo-liberal economic policy with a more orthodox conservative social policy in areas such as the family and law and order. Thatcherism was the dominant Conservative Party ideology of the 1980s and 1990s, and was closely associated with the ideas of Sir Keith Joseph and right-wing think-tanks such as the Adam Smith Institute.

> statutory limits on the power of trade unions

> a smaller state ('rolling back the frontiers of the state') and more limited state intervention in the economy

> a greater emphasis on national sovereignty

> more limited state welfare provision (a lower 'safety net')

Thatcher referred to those who were not prepared to sign up to this agenda, in many cases the old one-nation Tories, as 'wets'. Committed Thatcherites, in contrast, were referred to as 'dries' — with the then prime minister's most loyal acolytes dubbed 'ultra dry'.

Ronald Reagan and Margaret Thatcher in 1988

Intra-party squabbles

The factional infighting that came to the fore as a result of this shift in direction under Margaret Thatcher led to formal challenges to her leadership of the party in 1989 (Anthony Meyer) and 1990 (Michael Heseltine). Though the latter led to Thatcher's resignation, in November 1990, the Conservative leaders who followed on from her — Major, Hague, Duncan Smith, Howard and Cameron — often struggled to command the full confidence of the entire parliamentary party due to internal party factions and personal rivalries.

In the 1990s Philip Norton identified seven broad and overlapping factions within the parliamentary Conservative Party. By 2013, Richard Kelly was able to identify three broad ideological strands (see Table 4.1).

Table 4.1 Conservative factions in 2013

Ideological strand	Group(s)	Key individuals
(1) Pre-Thatcherites or 'one-nation Tories'	Tory Reform Group	Kenneth Clarke, Nicholas Soames
(2) Thatchertites	Conservative Voice, Bruges Group	John Redwood, Liam Fox
(3) Post-Thatcherites:		
(a) Red Tories	ResPublica	Philip Blond, Iain Duncan-Smith, Jesse Norman
(b) Liberal Conservatives	Bright Blue, Free Enterprise Group	Boris Johnson, Nick Boles

One-nation conservatism and Thatcherism

Distinguish between

One-nation conservatism
- pragmatic
- incremental change
- paternalistic
- mixed economy

Thatcherism
- dogmatic
- radical change
- individualistic
- free-market economy

The Conservatives under Cameron

David Cameron's election as party leader in 2006, following three successive general election defeats for the Conservatives in 1997, 2001 and 2005, was widely seen as analogous to the kind of watershed or epiphany that the Labour Party had experienced a decade earlier under Tony Blair. Cameron's election was significant because it marked the point at which rank-and-file party members recognised the need to choose a leader who could appeal to those outside of the party — and thereby win an election.

Cameron sought to lead the Conservatives away from those areas of policy over which the party was deeply divided (e.g. Europe) and towards those where it could gain electoral advantage (e.g. the environment). He recognised the extent to which the party had come to be regarded as unelectable and set about 'detoxifying' the Conservative brand. This shift towards the centre saw the 'greening of conservatism'. The desire to challenge the perception that the Conservatives were the 'nasty party' was also reflected in former Conservative leader Iain Duncan Smith's association with the Centre for Social Justice, whose work was at the heart of the Conservatives' 2010 general election pledge to fix 'broken Britain'.

Many commentators drew parallels between the Cameron–Osborne double act and that of Blair–Brown in the early days of New Labour. Some dubbed Cameron's Conservatives the 'New Tories' or, as Cameron himself put it on at least one occasion, 'liberal Conservatives' (see Table 4.1). Cameron himself was widely referred to as 'the heir to Blair'.

Locating the 'Cameroons' on the political spectrum

Back in 2008, Richard Kelly offered three possible early judgements on Cameron's conservatism:

- first, that it represented a 'flagrant capitulation to New Labour'
- second, that it should be seen as a 'subtle continuation of Thatcherism'
- third, that it amounted to little more than 'shameless opportunism'

In reality, while there are elements of truth in all three judgements on the approach that Cameron has taken since becoming party leader, it was the last that presented the biggest obstacle as he looked to move the Conservatives from the mentality of a party in opposition to that of a party in power.

The substance of policy

Although David Cameron's Conservative Party issued a swathe of policy proposals in the run-up to the 2010 general election, the leader was frequently accused of 'playing to the galleries' with carefully crafted rhetoric as opposed to coming forward with substantive detail on specific policies. This is a failing forgivable in a party in opposition but less so in one on the verge of taking up the reins of power. Talk of replacing the Human Rights Act (1998) with a new UK Bill of Rights, mooted early on in Cameron's stewardship of the party, appeared without further elaboration in the party's 2010 manifesto. The same was true of many of Cameron's other proposals in the area of democratic renewal.

The party's position on tax appeared similarly opaque. Back in 2007 the emphasis had been on bringing back the married person's allowance (even extending it to same-sex couples in civil partnerships) and raising the threshold for inheritance tax. By the time of the 2010 general election, however, the focus had switched to pensions and public sector pay cuts, with the party even giving up its inheritance tax pledge as part of the coalition deal brokered with the Liberal Democrats in the wake of the election.

While the unravelling global credit crisis clearly played a part in reordering the party's priorities, some criticised what they saw as a tendency to issue policy statements for short-term effect without really taking the time to consider the mid- to long-term consequences of what was being proposed.

Reaching beyond the party's core support

As we have seen, Cameron sought to detoxify the Conservative brand as a means of making it more appealing to those who might not normally have considered supporting the party. He attempted to court the 'green vote' — not least through the adoption of the new green tree logo in preference to the long-established blue torch and the suggestion that voters should 'vote blue, go green'. Cameron's decision to side with the Liberal Democrats and the Gurkhas in their fight with the incumbent Labour government over residency rights also played well with many voters, as did the party's admission that Margaret Thatcher was 'wrong' when she asserted that there is 'no such thing as society', with Cameron asserting that there was such a thing as 'society' — but that 'society' was not the same as 'the state'.

A new 'Third Way'?

Even in the wake of the 2010 general election, it remained unclear as to just how Cameron intended to reconcile (or 'triangulate') his desire to adopt traditionally liberal positions on the environment and social welfare with his commitment to pursue the Thatcherite agenda of 'rolling back the frontiers of the state'. The kinds of change envisaged could surely not be brought about entirely by voluntary groups and charitable institutions, the 'little platoons' championed by many Cameroons. Yet there was little appetite for simply 'throwing money' at these problems while the economy continued to founder. Moreover, the need to keep their coalition partners engaged made it difficult for the Conservatives to deliver on those very few explicit promises that they had made in the run-up to the 2010 general election — an issue that we will revisit towards the end of this chapter.

Ideology and policy in the Labour Party

Labour Party ideology

The Labour Party was created at the start of the twentieth century. Although the Independent Labour Party, the Fabians and the Social Democratic Federation were involved in forming the Labour Representation Committee in 1900, it is important not to underestimate the role of the Trades Union Congress (TUC): 94% of the Labour Representation Committee's affiliated membership in 1900 was from the unions, and in the 1990s they still controlled around 80% of the votes at party conference and provided a similar proportion of the party's annual income.

The Labour Party was formed to represent the working classes at a time when the franchise had not yet been extended to such groups. The decision to give all men over 21 the right to vote in 1918 provided the Labour Party with the potential base of support necessary to launch a serious electoral challenge.

The party's origins in the unions and socialist societies of the late nineteenth and early twentieth centuries meant that it originally pursued an agenda centred on **socialism**.

Labour Party constitution (1918)

The extension of the franchise to all adult men in 1918 coincided with the adoption of the new Labour Party constitution. Clause Four of that constitution (see stretch and challenge activity) provided a clear commitment to public ownership of key industries and the redistribution of wealth.

Labour factions

Despite its left-wing origins, the party was the home to a number of ideological factions by the 1970s. For example, the Labour prime minister James Callaghan (1976–79) and those on the right of the party took the view that public sector pay demands had to be resisted, whereas those on the left (e.g. Michael Foot and Tony Benn) still favoured greater wealth redistribution.

Labour's defeat in the 1979 general election, which came in the wake of the period of industrial unrest known as the 'Winter of Discontent', saw those on the left gain control of the party under the leadership of Michael Foot. Foot led Labour into the 1983 general election with one of the most left-wing manifestos in the party's history. It included commitments to state control of all major industries, tighter regulation of business, enhanced workers' rights,

Key concepts
Socialism

A political ideology advocating greater equality and the redistribution of wealth. Socialists are suspicious of capitalism. They favour greater government intervention, both in economic policy and in social policy.

In the nineteenth century, socialism was often seen as similar to communism. In the UK, socialism was closely associated with the Labour Party, from the party's creation at the start of the twentieth century through to the emergence of New Labour under Tony Blair in the 1990s.

Broadly speaking, socialism can be subdivided into two distinct strands:
➢ revisionist (or 'reformist') socialism, which looks to improve capitalism (e.g. **social democracy**).
➢ revolutionary (or 'fundamentalist') socialism, which aims to abolish capitalism and bring all property into common ownership (e.g. Marxist communism)

Social democracy

A political ideology that accepts the basic premise of capitalism, whilst advocating a more equitable distribution of wealth along the lines favoured by all socialists.

support for unilateral nuclear disarmament and a withdrawal from NATO. Dubbed 'the longest suicide note in history' by the then Labour leading-light Gerald Kaufman, the manifesto was seen as a key factor in the Conservative Party's landslide victory. Indeed, so left-wing was the manifesto that the Conservatives ran an advertisement in the *Daily Mirror* carrying the tag-line 'Like your manifesto, Comrade'; drawing parallels between key clauses in Labour's programme and the provisions of the Communist Party manifesto.

A Conservative Party advertisement from the 1983 general election campaign

Old Labour versus New Labour

Although the Labour Party was formed to represent the working classes, changes in the class and occupational structure of the nation since the 1960s, together with the general election defeats of 1979, 1983 and 1987, saw the party looking to broaden its appeal beyond this core support.

Key term
➢ **'Old Labour'** Characterising the Labour Party prior to the modernisation programme begun by Neil Kinnock in 1983 and completed by Tony Blair. It refers to the party's historic commitment to socialism and its links with socialist societies, trade unions and the old working class.

This process of 'outreach', started by leaders such as Neil Kinnock (leader 1983–92) and John Smith (1992–94), is most closely associated with the leadership of Tony Blair (1994–2007). Under Blair, the party was rebranded as **New Labour** and the iconic Clause Four was controversially reworded (see stretch and challenge activity). Some critics accused Blair and other Labour modernisers of abandoning the socialist principles upon which the party was founded.

Key concepts

➤ **New Labour** Characterising the party that emerged to fight the 1997 general election following a process of party modernisation completed by Tony Blair. Blair first used the phrase 'New Labour' when addressing the Labour conference as party leader in 1994. Labour's modernisation programme began under Neil Kinnock, following the party's landslide defeat at the 1983 general election. It involved a less powerful role for the trade unions and a rebranding exercise designed to make the party more appealing to middle-class voters. In ideological terms, the New Labour project was characterised by the concept of **triangulation**.

➤ **Triangulation** The process of melding together core Labour Party principles and values, such as the party's commitment to greater social justice, with the lessons learnt from Thatcherism. It was closely associated with New Labour and the notion of a **Third Way**.

➤ **Third Way** An ideological position said to exist between conventional socialism and mainstream capitalism, closely associated with Tony Blair and New Labour, and also referred to as the 'middle way'.

 ## Stretch and challenge

'Clause Four' of the Labour Party Constitution

1918

...to secure for the workers by hand or by brain the full fruits of their industry and the most equitable distribution thereof that may be possible upon the basis of the common ownership of the means of production...

1995

[We] work for a dynamic economy, serving the public interest in which the enterprise of the market and the rigour of competition are joined with the forces of partnership and cooperation to produce the wealth the nation needs and the opportunity for all to work and prosper, with a thriving private sector and high quality public services.

Questions

1 Assess the extent to which the 'new' Clause 4 adopted in 1995 represented a significant departure from the one agreed in 1918.

2 Explain why the Labour Party under Tony Blair felt the need to make this change.

Old Labour and New Labour

Old Labour	New Labour
➤ dogmatic	➤ pragmatic
➤ working class	➤ catch-all
➤ interventionist	➤ market economy
➤ public sector provision	➤ public–private partnerships
➤ social justice	➤ social inclusion
➤ universal welfare	➤ targeted welfare

Labour Party policy after Blair

Gordon Brown's accession as Labour leader in June 2007 was greeted with optimism by those on the left who felt that his commitment to the concept of **social justice** was greater than that of his predecessor, Tony Blair.

Key term

➤ **Social justice** The goal of greater equality of outcome, as opposed to equality of opportunity alone. It is achieved through progressive taxation and other forms of wealth redistribution. The idea is closely associated with the Labour Party and with other parties of the left and centre-left, such as the Greens.

As chancellor, Brown had favoured deregulation and a 'light touch' approach to economic management. As prime minister, Brown was forced to nationalise a number of high-street banks, while overseeing an apparent return to 'tax and spend'; with a higher top rate of income tax and an explicit commitment to maintain public spending during the recession. New Labour's hard-fought reputation for economic competence — key to the party securing three consecutive general election victories (1997, 2001 and 2005) — was ultimately surrendered, along with much of the political capital that the former chancellor had accrued during his decade in charge at the Treasury.

Even in the field of constitutional reform, where Brown had widely been expected to take the lead in a process that might result in a more fully codified constitutional settlement, the *Governance of Britain* Green Paper (2007), the Constitutional Renewal Bill (2008) and the Constitutional Reform and Governance Act (2010) that followed largely failed to fulfil expectations.

Goodbye New Labour, hello 'Next Labour'?

In the wake of the Labour Party's defeat at the 2010 general election, even the most ardent former Blairites, such as the then leadership candidate David Miliband, were keen to distance themselves from the New Labour tag. 'New Labour is not the future', the former foreign secretary acknowledged in an article in the *Observer* on 16 May 2010, 'I'm interested now in

Next Labour.' However, the question of precisely what 'Next Labour' might mean in practice has dogged the party's efforts to re-group under the leadership of the younger Miliband, Ed, following his narrow victory in the 2010 race to replace Gordon Brown as Labour leader.

⟷ Stretch and challenge

In search of 'Next Labour'

Inside the Labour Party, there has been general agreement since 2010 that New Labour should give way to 'Next Labour'. But there has been less agreement about what this might involve. Indeed, no fewer than five different tendencies emerged within Labour after 2010, each seeking to influence the party's new leadership:

- **The Old Left:** centred on the Tribune and Socialist Campaign Groups, the Old Left aimed to return the party to its ideological roots, harking back to the spirit of the party's 1983 manifesto.
- **The New Left:** shared the socialist sensibilities of the 'Old Left' but sought to address issues of race, gender, sexual orientation and disability alongside social class.
- **Blue Labour:** embraced the traditional one-nation Conservative themes of community and immigration, but from a progressive perspective.
- **Purple Labour:** opposed the Old Left's desire to turn the clock back to 1983, preferring instead to tweak and adapt the New Labour approach, essentially a form of 'neo-Blairism'.
- **Black Labour:** sought to re-build the party's shattered reputation for economic competence by focusing on the task of getting the economy back in to credit (i.e. 'back to black').

Source: adapted from Kelly, R. (2013) 'From Blue Labour to Red Tories: party factions in Britain today', *Politics Review*, Vol. 22, No. 4.

Questions

1 Using the article cited (below), or the internet, research and add detail to each of the brief definitions offered above.

2 To what extent are the various factions identified here represented within the current shadow cabinet?

Ideology and policy of the Liberal Democrats

Liberal Democrat ideology

The Liberal Democrats were formed in 1988 with the merger of the Liberal Party and the Social Democratic Party (SDP). The Liberal Party had been the main party of government in the early twentieth century but was a distant third by the 1960s, rarely polling more than 10% of the vote. The SDP, in contrast, had been formed as a result of the decision of four leading Labour politicians to leave the party in 1981. Roy Jenkins, David Owen, Bill Rodgers and Shirley Williams felt that the Labour Party had come under the control of hard-line left-wingers following the defeat of James Callaghan's moderate Labour administration in 1979.

This **Gang of Four**, as they were known, launched the SDP with their 1981 Limehouse Declaration. With the Labour Party in disarray, the SDP formed an electoral alliance with the Liberals (the **SDP–Liberal Alliance**) in 1983, securing 26% of the popular vote, yet only

Key terms

➤ **Gang of Four** Refers in the UK context to the four former Labour cabinet ministers who left the party in 1981 to form the Social Democratic Party (SDP). The four were Bill Rodgers, Roy Jenkins, Shirley Williams and David Owen. The creation of the new party was announced in the Limehouse Declaration of 25 January 1981. The Gang of Four left Labour believing that the party had fallen under the control of left-wingers in the wake of Labour's defeat at the 1979 general election. They lacked confidence in the party's then leader, Michael Foot.

➤ **SDP–Liberal Alliance** The electoral alliance between the Liberal Party and the Social Democratic Party in place at the time of the 1983 (26.0% of the vote, 23 seats) and 1987 (23.1% of the vote, 22 seats) general elections. The two parties merged in 1988 to form the Liberal Democrats.

gaining 23 seats in parliament. Following a similarly disappointing return for the Alliance in 1987, the parties merged in 1988 to form the Social and Liberal Democrats, with Paddy Ashdown being elected as party leader. The following year the party was renamed the Liberal Democratic Party (Liberal Democrats, or Lib Dems for short).

Whereas Conservatives traditionally emphasise the role of society in shaping individuals, **liberalism** places a greater emphasis on the importance of the individual. Traditionally, liberals looked to a society formed of free, autonomous individuals of equal worth.

Key concepts

➤ **Liberalism** A political ideology associated with notions of personal liberty, toleration and limited government. It is often subdivided into two separate strands:

➤ **Classical liberalism** An early form of liberalism favouring minimal state intervention, which emerged in the nineteenth century. Classical liberals stressed the importance of freedom, toleration and equality. They believed that self-reliance and self-improvement had a bigger part to play than the state in improving the lives of those from less privileged backgrounds. Some of the classical liberal agenda was adopted by the Thatcherite New Right from the later 1970s, resulting in their being referred to as neo-liberals.

➤ **Progressive (or 'new') liberalism** A more compassionate form of liberalism that saw the need for some regulation of the market as well as the provision of basic welfare. It was originally advanced by writers such as T. H. Green and L. T. Hobhouse. Progressive liberalism later developed into the mixed economy supported by John Maynard Keynes and William Beveridge. This second, more progressive form of liberalism — with its emphasis on reform, individual rights and a mixed economy — provided the ideological foundation for all of the liberal centre parties of the second half of the twentieth century, and most recently the Liberal Democrats.

The launch of the SDP in 1981 by (left to right) Roy Jenkins, David Owen, Bill Rodgers and Shirley Williams: the 'Gang of Four'

Liberal Democrat policy under Clegg

Under Nick Clegg's leadership, from 2007, the Lib Dems developed a programme for government that included more orthodox Lib Dem policies on issues such as constitutional reform and the protection of civil liberties, alongside other pledges that appeared to challenge the very tenets upon which the party had been founded.

Taxation and government spending

The Lib Dems have long been associated with a commitment to increase public spending and have not been afraid, in the past, to make public their plans to fund such programmes by increasing the basic rate of income tax. Ahead of the 2010 general election, however, Chris Huhne announced that it was 'time to try something different'. The result was a pledge to deliver around £20 billion of cuts in existing public spending as a means of funding improvements in areas such as education and offering voters a cut in income tax worth somewhere in the region 4–6p in the pound. Although many were stunned by the sheer scale of the tax cut proposed, Clegg was quick to defend the move. 'Aspiring to hand back money to people from central government', he argued in the *Guardian*, 'is impeccably liberal'.

This repositioning on tax marked the triumph of the Orange Book liberals over the social liberals (see Table 4.2), while also serving to make the possibility of a coalition with the Conservatives more conceivable.

Table 4.2 Key Lib Dem factions after 2010

Ideological strand	Positions	Key individuals
Orange Book liberals	Draw on 'classical liberalism' Influenced by the neo-liberalism of Milton Friedman and others Endorse Thatcherite economics	Nick Clegg, Ed Davey, David Laws
Social liberals	Draw on the 'new' or 'progressive liberalism' of Keynes and Beveridge Reject Thatcherite economics	Tim Farron, Simon Hughes

Repositioning on Europe

Of the three main UK parties, the Lib Dems have traditionally been the most enthusiastic supporters of the European project. Clegg himself had served as a leading official at the European Commission in the 1990s and was also an MEP for a time, before he was elected to the Commons in 2005. From 2008, however, the party sought to neutralise Europe as an electoral issue, by abandoning its previous Europhile position and offering the prospect of a referendum on continued UK membership of the EU. Significantly, this shift in emphasis also served to remove one more of the potential barriers to a coalition with the Conservatives.

A more realistic foreign policy

The party's 2010 manifesto called for 'a full defence review' in order to ensure that the UK's armed forces 'are equipped for modern threats'. Although Clegg's commitment to the operation in Afghanistan remained, it was suggested that the conventional military resources needed in such theatres of war could be funded in large part by a 50% cut in the UK's nuclear arsenal and a commitment 'not to replace the Trident nuclear weapons system on a like-for-like basis'.

The end of ideology?

Daniel Bell, in his 1960 book *The End of Ideology: On the Exhaustion of Political Ideas in the Fifties*, argued that the traditional ideological movements that had taken root in the nineteenth century and flourished in the early twentieth century had lost their power to inspire and mobilise the masses by the 1950s. Bell suggested that the postwar period had witnessed the rise of a new consensus around the social democratic model, and that in future political parties would be offering piecemeal, incremental changes as opposed to a more fundamental reordering of society along ideological lines.

In recent years, the phrase 'end of ideology' has been applied more specifically to characterise the changes that have taken place in the field of British party politics since the 1990s. As we have seen, British parties were once said to be ideologically based. In recent years, however, they are said to have moderated their traditional ideological positions as part of an effort to appeal to as wide a range of voters as possible. Although it is probably fair to say that British parties were always broad churches (or 'big tents'), these modern 'catch-all parties' are criticised as being little more than election-winning machines.

Viewpoint Have recent years witnessed 'the end of ideology'?

YES

- The three main parties are all essentially social democratic in nature. They are concerned with making piecemeal changes to the current arrangements as opposed to imposing an ideological model.
- The ideological wings of each of the three main parties have been marginalised.
- There are significant overlaps in the stated policies of the three main parties.
- Parties that once appeared fundamentally opposed to one another were able to enter into coalition in 2010.
- There is an increased emphasis on presentation and personality over substance.

NO

- The three main UK parties still have distinct ideological traditions and a committed core support that strongly identifies with such traditions.
- The ideological dividing lines became more apparent in the wake of the global financial crisis.
- The rise of smaller ideological and single-issue parties and pressure groups suggests that ideology still matters to a significant proportion of the electorate.

Party policy at the 2010 general election

The prevailing economic climate meant that all three of the main UK political parties were forced to accept that there would need to be significant spending cuts and tax rises in the wake of the 2010 general election. While the Institute for Fiscal Studies criticised all three party leaders for failing to identify the full scale of cuts needed when drafting their election manifestos, few voters would have been under any illusion as to what was to come. The only significant cleavage between the parties appeared to be on the issue of not 'if' but 'when' the cuts would come, with the Conservatives promising an emergency budget and cuts of up to £6 billion in the first year, and Labour and the Lib Dems favouring maintaining spending in the first year as a means of avoiding a so-called 'double-dip' recession.

As can be seen from the summary provided in Table 4.3, there was also significant agreement among two parties (e.g. over the scrapping of ID cards) or all three parties (e.g. over giving voters the right to recall MPs) in many other areas of policy.

Table 4.3 2010 party manifestos, the 2010 coalition agreement and government policy (2010–13)
Coalition pledges common to both party's manifestos are shown in green — as are areas of compromise.

Economic policy

Conservative Party	Labour Party	Liberal Democrats
Emergency budget within 50 days.	No major cuts in first year.	No major cuts in first year.
Up to £6 billion in public spending cuts in first year.	Sale of nationalised banks.	No income tax on first £10,000.
Cuts in corporation tax and National Insurance.	No increase in income tax.	'Mansion tax' on properties over £2 million.
Freeze on council tax.	A referendum before any decision to join the euro.	Close tax loopholes.
'No' to the euro.		Break up banks.
		Favour joining the euro, but only after a referendum.

Coalition agreement	Delivery	
Full Spending Review.	✓	
Banking reform.	✓	Draft Banking Reform Bill published in October 2012.
Emergency budget within 50 days.	✓	
Up to £6 billion in public spending cuts in first year.	✓	
'No' to the euro.	✓	In this parliament.
Freeze on council tax.	✓	Support through to 2013 for councils that freeze council tax.
Work towards no income tax on first £10,000.	✓	Ongoing.
Close tax loopholes.	✓	Ongoing.

Home affairs

Conservative Party	Labour Party	Liberal Democrats
Scrap ID-cards scheme. 'Grounding orders' for anti-social behaviour. Annual cap on immigration. Prison sentences for those carrying knives.	Maintain police numbers. Successful police forces to take over failing ones. Points-based system to limit immigration. More prison places.	Scrap ID-cards scheme. 'Amnesty' for most long-term illegal immigrants. 30,000 more police officers. Stop building new prisons. Regional, points-based immigration system.

Coalition agreement	Delivery	
Scrap ID-cards scheme.	✓	
Greater oversight of police through directly elected officials.	✓	Police and Crime Commissioners.
Annual cap on immigration.	✓	Not possible in respect of EU citizens; cap imposed on non-EU migrants in 2010.

Education policy

Conservative Party	Labour Party	Liberal Democrats
Reduce state control over schools. Give headteachers more control over teachers' salaries and school discipline. Raise entry qualifications to the teaching profession.	Take over around 1,000 mediocre or failing schools. Free school meals for primary school children. Widen access to university.	Slim down curriculum. Phase out university tuition fees. Help poorest students going to university. Additional £2.5 billion to help struggling pupils.

Coalition agreement	Delivery	
Allow for new state school providers.	✓	'Free Schools' — under the Academies Act (2010).
Await Lord Browne's report into higher education funding.	✓	Top-up fees trebled.
Give headteachers more control over teachers' salaries and school discipline.	✓	Education Act (2011).
Pupil Premium to help disadvantaged students.	✓	But withdrew Education Maintenance Allowance (EMA) from students in England.

Health policy

Conservative Party	Labour Party	Liberal Democrats
Access to GPs at weekends.	Access to GPs in the evenings.	Prioritise preventative care.
Keep accident and emergency and maternity wards open.	Cancer tests within a week of referral.	Limit managers' pay and restructure the Department of Health.
Abandon waiting list targets.	Enhance patient choice.	Give patients the right to go private.
	High-achieving hospitals to take over weaker ones.	Compulsory language and competence tests for doctors.

Coalition agreement	Delivery	
Reduce admin costs and quangos.	?	Arguable.
Keep accident and emergency and maternity wards open.	✓	Ongoing.
Compulsory language and competence tests for doctors.	✓	Ongoing.

Other social policy

Conservative Party	Labour Party	Liberal Democrats
Tax breaks for married couples on low to middle incomes.	Protect Sure Start centre budgets.	Time-off for fathers to attend antenatal appointments.
Remove tax credits for households earning more than £50,000.	15 hours' free nursery provision for 3–5-year-olds.	Shared parental leave extended to 18 months.
Form of national service for 16-year-olds.	Enhanced paternity leave.	Access to 20 hours of free childcare from age of 18 months.
Neighbourhood groups to take over badly performing public services.	Restore link between state pension and average earnings from 2012.	Scrap compulsory retirement ages.
		Immediately restore link between state pension and average earnings.

Coalition agreement	Delivery	
Create a single welfare to work programme.	✓	Alongside universal benefit.
Remove tax credits for households earning more than £50,000.	✓	Also removed child benefit for higher earners.
Scrap compulsory retirement ages.	✓	
Immediately restore link between state pension and average earnings.	✓	Implemented with a 'triple-lock' to protect the value of pensions.

Environment

Conservative Party	Labour Party	Liberal Democrats
Move towards a 'low carbon economy'.	400,000 new 'green jobs'.	Replace road tax with national road-pricing scheme.
Incentives for recycling and loans to help energy-saving home improvements.	40% clean electricity.	100% clean energy by 2050.
	Ban on unnecessary landfill.	Help with energy-saving home improvements.
Move towards renewable power generation, nuclear power and cleaner coal-fired power stations.	Green investment bank.	Push for strict international agreements on carbon emissions.
	Help to insulate homes.	

Coalition agreement	Delivery	
Cancel Heathrow Third Runway.	✓	
'Green Deal' support for energy-saving home improvements.	✓	Ongoing.
Move towards a 'low carbon economy'.	✓	Ongoing.
Move towards renewable power generation, nuclear power and cleaner coal-fired power stations.	✓	Lib Dems free to maintain opposition to new nuclear power stations.

Foreign policy and security

Conservative Party	Labour Party	Liberal Democrats
Replace Trident missile system. Establish US-style National Security Council.	Maintain nuclear deterrent and build two new aircraft carriers. Give aid to failing states. Regulate arms trade.	No direct replacement for Trident. Regulate arms exports. Inquiry into UK involvement in torture.

Coalition agreement	Delivery	
Review plans for Trident replacement.	✓	Decision postponed until 2016.
No further transfer of sovereignty to EU.	✓	Referendum ahead of any further transfer.
Establish US-style National Security Council.	✓	Established in May 2010.

Constitutional reform

Conservative Party	Labour Party	Liberal Democrats
Cut the number of MPs. Equalise the size of constituency electorates. Allow recall of MPs in cases of serious wrongdoing. Parliamentary debate for any public petition gaining 100,000 signatures. Prevent former ministers taking up lobbying posts within 2 years. Replace the Human Rights Act with a British Bill of Rights.	Recall of MPs Referendum on moving to the AV system for elections to the Westminster Parliament. Referendum on Lords reform. Greater power for local government. Fixed-term parliaments. Register of lobbyists. Votes for 16-year-olds.	Cut the number of MPs. Recall of MPs. Freedom Bill to regulate CCTV and protect Human Rights Act. Proportional system for elections to the Westminster Parliament. Fully elected second chamber. Greater power for local government. Fixed-term parliaments. Votes for 16-year-olds.

Coalition agreement	Delivery	
Freedom Bill.	✓	Protection of Freedoms Act (2012).
Establish a Commission on a British Bill of Rights.	✓	Reported, inconclusively, in December 2012.
Referendum on AV for UK general elections.	✓	Referendum in April 2011 brought a decisive 'No' vote.
Recall of MPs.	✗	Little progress.
Create a statutory register of lobbyists.	✓	Register to be introduced 'by 2015'.
Cut the number of MPs.	✗	Rejected in the wake of Lords reform reversal (see below).

Coalition agreement		Delivery
Equalise the size of constituency electorates.	✗	Rejected in the wake of Lords reform reversal (see below).
A committee to bring forward proposals for a wholly or mainly elected upper chamber elected under PR.	✓	House of Lords Reform Bill introduced in June 2012, but abandoned in August.
Greater power for local government.	?	Arguable.
Five-year fixed-term parliaments.	✓	Fixed-Term Parliaments Act (2011).

Party policy in an age of coalition government

Critics of coalition government commonly argue that it lacks legitimacy as a result of the horse-trading and compromise that inevitably follows in the wake of a hung (or 'balanced') parliament: where party ideology and principles are sacrificed upon the altar of political expediency. So it was that the Liberal Democrats were cast in the role of 'king-makers' in 2010, having to choose between returning Labour to office for a fourth consecutive term or, in effect, handing the baton on to David Cameron's Conservatives.

Yet the very fact that the Conservatives were able to reach an accommodation with the Liberal Democrats, forming a coalition that few on the left would previously have considered either likely or tenable, suggests that we might need to start thinking about the whole concept of party policy in an entirely different way.

The terms of the Conservative–Lib Dem coalition were indeed remarkable — with the Conservatives giving up their pledge on inheritance tax and accepting the Lib Dem policy of moving towards a personal income tax allowance of £10,000, as well as guaranteeing a referendum on the introduction of the alternative vote (AV) system for elections to the Westminster Parliament. Equally remarkable was the extent to which the parties were able to reach agreement on Europe (see Box 4.1); in part a result of Cameron's desire to avoid

Box 4.1 The 2010 Conservative–Lib Dem coalition deal on the EU (extracts)

…We agree that there should be no further transfer of sovereignty or powers over the course of the next parliament. We will examine the balance of the EU's existing competences and will, in particular, work to limit the application of the working time directive in the UK…

…We agree that we will amend the 1972 European Communities Act so that any proposed future treaty that transferred areas of power…would be subject to a referendum…

…We will examine the case for a UK sovereignty bill to make it clear that ultimate authority remains with parliament…

…We agree that Britain will not join or prepare to join the euro in this parliament.

reopening splits within his own party, but also a consequence of the shift in the Lib Dem approach towards Europe signalled 2 years earlier and discussed earlier in this chapter.

From theory into practice (the coalition in action)

In economic policy, the coalition partners have pursued those objectives they hold in common (with a concerted attempt to tackle the deficit and a steady 'creep' towards a personal tax allowance of £10,000), while placing the manifesto policies that divided them (for example, the Conservatives' pledge on inheritance tax and the Lib Dems' plans for a 'mansion tax') to one side.

In the area of constitutional reform, however, progress has been more haphazard. Although the Conservatives fulfilled their promise to deliver a nationwide poll on AV, most leading Conservatives campaigned for a 'No' vote in an acrimonious campaign that saw the proposal comprehensively defeated in the referendum held in 2011. The failure of the Conservative Party whips to mobilise the Tory backbenches in support of Lords reform (a key element of the Coalition Agreement), resulted in the Lib Dems' tit-for-tat refusal to approve the proposed changes to parliamentary constituency boundaries (another element of that agreement). The coalition also failed to deliver to voters the power of recall over their MPs — despite the fact that all three of the main UK parties had supported such a move at the time of the 2010 general election.

In areas not covered by the Coalition Agreement — for example on the implementation of the Leveson Report in 2013 and the abolition of the Educational Maintenance Allowance (EMA) in England back in 2010 — the Lib Dems have been willing to side with (or at least threaten to side with) the Labour opposition as a means of extracting the necessary concessions from their Conservative coalition partners. Such politicking between the coalition partners is likely to become more frequent as the two parties seek to 'disengage' and establish clearly delineated positions ahead of the 2015 general election.

A sign of things to come?

Should coalition government become more of a 'norm' in the coming years, it may well be that party manifestos will come to be seen less as an agenda for action — as has been the case in the past — than as a starting point for negotiations. Such a shift in thinking will necessarily involve a reassessment of many of the fundamental principles that are common to any study of UK government and politics — not least the doctrine of the **mandate**.

Key concept

> **Mandate** The right of the governing party to pursue the policies it sets out in its general election manifesto. The doctrine of the mandate gives the governing party the authority to pursue its stated policies, but it does not require it to do so or prevent it from drafting proposals not included in its manifesto.

What you should know

- ❯ We use the political spectrum as a means of distinguishing between different ideological traditions and locating individual parties in relation to one another.

- ❯ UK political parties were once regarded as ideological in character: the Labour Party being socialist; the Conservatives, conservative; and the Liberal Party and its successors, liberal.

- ❯ In reality, all three of the main UK parties were broadly social democratic in the postwar period, with competition between them centring on the 'detail' as opposed to the 'fundamentals' of policy. This was the postwar consensus.

- ❯ The emergence of New Right thinking in the 1970s and the Thatcherite revolution of the 1980s marked the end of consensus, with the two main UK parties once again adopting more ideologically coherent positions.

- ❯ The Conservatives under Margaret Thatcher pursued a neo-liberal agenda whereas the Labour Party under Michael Foot went into the 1983 general election on the basis of an orthodox left-wing manifesto that was later described as 'the longest suicide note in history'.

- ❯ Under the leadership of Neil Kinnock, John Smith and Tony Blair, the Labour Party sought to reposition itself on the political spectrum and broaden its appeal beyond traditional Labour voters.

- ❯ This modernisation programme involved adopting a Third Way, arrived at by triangulating traditional Labour values and approaches with the lessons learnt from Thatcherism.

- ❯ This New Labour project saw the party elected to three consecutive terms in office on a platform which rejected the 'tax and spend' approach of previous Labour administrations in favour of establishing partnerships between the public and private sectors and creating internal markets within public services as a way of improving efficiency.

- ❯ While Labour accepted many of the lessons of Thatcherism, the Thatcherite emphasis on the individual and Thatcher's suspicion of 'big government' notions of 'society' saw the Conservatives characterised as the 'nasty party'.

- ❯ David Cameron sought to 'detoxify' the Conservative brand by campaigning on issues such as the environment and social inclusion, thereby reaching out beyond his party's core support.

- ❯ Some argue that the convergence of the three main parties on the centre ground has led to the 'end of ideology'. There were more similarities in than differences between the manifestos published by the three main parties at the time of the 2010 general election.

- ❯ The fact that the Conservatives and the Lib Dems were able to reach agreement and form a joint administration suggests that we might be experiencing a new age of consensus.

UK/US comparison

Party policies and ideas in the USA

➤ The traditional 'left–right' political spectrum is less useful when discussing US politics because the two main parties are both regarded as right of centre. Instead, commentators tend to describe policies and parties as being 'more liberal' or 'more conservative'.

➤ Whereas UK parties were once seen as broadly ideological in character, the two main US parties have always been regarded as broad churches or 'big tents'.

➤ While one would expect a Conservative Association in Surrey to stand by the same broad programme of policies as one in Yorkshire, many commentators speak of the USA as having '50 party systems' or 100 distinctive parties (i.e. two per state).

➤ This is because the differences between Democrats (or between Republicans) in different states can be more significant than the differences between the official party platforms of the Democrats and Republicans nationally: in other words, there may be more differences within the parties than between them.

➤ While the UK is said to have undergone a period of ideological convergence in recent years, with the rise of catch-all parties, US parties have become more ideologically coherent and distinctive.

Further reading

Bale, T. and Sanderson-Nash, E. (2012) 'Coalition policy: is the yellow tail wagging the blue dog', *Politics Review*, Vol. 22, No. 1, pp. 30–33.

Beech, M. and Hickson, K. (2012) 'Which path for Labour', *Political Insight*, Vol. 3, No. 3, pp. 20–23.

Gallop, N. (2012) 'Constitutional reform and the coalition government', *Political Insight*, Vol. 3, No. 1, pp. 34–37.

Heppell, T. (2012) 'Ed Miliband: a post-New Labour leader?', *Politics Review*, Vol. 22, No. 2, pp. 2–5.

Hickson, K. and Williams, B. (2011) 'Conservatives and Lib Dems: closer than we thought?', *Politics Review*, Vol. 21, No. 2, pp. 24–27.

Kelly, R. (2013) 'From Blue Labour to Red Tories: party factions in Britain today', *Politics Review*, Vol. 22, No. 4, pp. 24–27.

McNaughton, N., Fairclough, P. and Magee, E. (2012) 'Ed Miliband: a new direction for Labour?', in *UK Government and Politics Annual Update 2012*, pp. 22–26, Philip Allan Updates.

McNaughton, N., Fairclough, P. and Magee, E. (2013) 'Coalition economic policy: austerity or growth?', in *UK Government and Politics Annual Update 2013*, pp. 17–22, Philip Allan Updates.

Moxon, K. (2012) 'Party approaches to the UK economy', *Politics Review*, Vol. 21, No. 4, pp. 12–15.

Exam focus

Short response questions (around 5–6 minutes each)

1 What is ideology?
2 What is conservatism?
3 What is meant by the term British socialism?
4 Define the term catch-all party.
5 What is a manifesto?

Mid-length response questions (around 10–12 minutes each)

1 Distinguish between adversarial and consensus politics.
2 Identify and explain *three* policy differences between the Conservative and Labour parties.
3 How could it be argued that the three main parties are all social democratic in character?
4 Distinguish between one-nation conservatism and Thatcherism.
5 Explain *three* ways in which New Labour differs from Old Labour.

Mini-essay questions (around 25–30 minutes each)

1 To what extent has the current Conservative Party abandoned Thatcherism and returned to its conservative roots?
2 'The Labour Party is no longer a socialist party.' To what extent do you agree with this statement?
3 How and to what extent did the formation of a coalition government require the Conservative and Liberal Democrat parties to depart from their traditional ideological principles?
4 To what extent have the three main parties abandoned their traditional ideological positions and adopted a pragmatic approach to policy issues to win votes?

 Extra resources to help you revise and consolidate your knowledge for this chapter are provided online at **www.hodderplus.co.uk/philipallan**. These include a revision PowerPoint, extension tasks and up-to-date weblinks.

Chapter 5

Pressure groups

Key questions answered in this chapter
➤ What are pressure groups and what roles do they perform in the British system?
➤ How are British pressure groups classified?
➤ What methods do pressure groups employ?
➤ How does membership of the EU affect pressure group activity in the UK?
➤ Why are some pressure groups more successful than others?
➤ Does pressure group activity threaten or enhance democracy in the UK?

What are pressure groups?

Pressure groups are groups of like-minded individuals who come together on the basis of shared interests or a commonly held cause in order to put pressure on policy-makers at Westminster and beyond. Pressure groups are significantly more numerous than political parties because whereas the parties tend to aggregate and accommodate a wide range of views in an effort to see their candidates elected to public office, pressure groups have a tendency to fragment opinion. Recent years have seen the emergence of looser **social movements** and more focused **single-issue groups**, replacing the larger, more traditional

 Key terms
➤ **Pressure group** A group of like-minded individuals who come together on the basis of shared interests or a commonly held cause in order to put pressure on policy-makers at Westminster and beyond.
➤ **Single-issue group** A pressure group or protest movement that focuses on a single issue as opposed to a range of issues underpinned by a broader set of guiding principles or an ideology. Single-issue groups often disband once their central objective is achieved (e.g. the Snowdrop Campaign).

groups common in the 1950s and 1960s. Many commentators see the rise of such groups as a fundamental change in the nature of political participation in the UK — as the emergence of a so-called **new pressure group politics**. It is even suggested that such changes threaten the very principles upon which democracy has traditionally operated in the UK.

Key term

> **New pressure group politics** Characterising the rise of more loosely organised social movements, protest movements, direct action campaigns and grassroots activities. It is distinct from the more tightly organised and choreographed pressure group activity of earlier decades.

Pressure groups and social movements

Distinguish between

Pressure groups

> Pressure groups tend to benefit from some kind of formal organisation. Many have formal membership structures and identifiable leaders, and most have offices and an officially sanctioned internet presence.

Social movements

> Social movements are far looser in terms of organisational structure. They generally bring together individuals who are also members of more organised pressure groups, and they are generally seen as bringing together political parties and pressure groups that operate in a given area of policy. For example, the 'green movement' in the UK can be said to include numerous pressure groups, such as the Soil Association, Greenpeace and Plane Stupid, as well as the Green Party.

Links to follow up

'1996: Handguns to be banned in the UK', BBC On this day, 16 October, **http://news.bbc.co.uk** — background on the Dunblane Massacre and the Snowdrop Campaign.

Pressure group roles

Pressure groups are traditionally said to perform three main roles within the UK system.

Participation

Pressure groups provide citizens with an avenue for participation between elections. Although the representative model of democracy (or **trustee model**) suggests

Key term

> **Trustee model** The Burkean model of representation provided for in a representative democracy. Politicians are returned to office on the understanding that they are free to use their judgement in the interests of their constituents and the nation as a whole.

that MPs should be free to use their judgement once elected, democracy demands that the channels of communication remain open between elections, and pressure groups play a key role in allowing for this.

By engaging citizens in a form of structured participation, pressure groups also serve to moderate the views of those who might otherwise adopt more extreme strategies in pursuit of their goals. Pressure group participation can also serve as a route into a career in politics, thereby serving a secondary function in the area of political recruitment.

Representation

Pressure groups enhance representation by aggregating and articulating the common interests or concerns of a given group of individuals. Whereas contemporary political parties are often criticised for being little more than 'catch-all', election-winning machines (see Chapter 4), pressure groups are able to represent the specific interests or concerns of citizens. For example, groups such as the Society for the Protection of Unborn Children (SPUC) serve to represent the interests of those who oppose abortion, at a time when the three main UK parties are broadly sympathetic to the availability of such practices and choose not to impose a party line on moral issues when votes are taken in the Commons.

Links to follow up

www.spuc.org.uk — the SPUC website.

Education

Pressure groups have an educative function. They act as a source of specialist knowledge, helping the government to weigh up the merits and demerits of proposed policies. This benefits the broader public by helping the government to avoid costly mistakes and unnecessary conflict. Pressure groups also serve to educate the broader public, making it more likely that the government will be held to account.

Pressure group typologies

Pressure groups are commonly classified according to two broad typologies. The first, the sectional group–cause group typology, classifies pressure groups according to their core aims. The second, the insider–outsider typology, classifies pressure groups according to their status in relation to the government.

Classifying pressure groups by core aims

First developed by writers such as J. D. Stewart in the 1950s, the sectional group–cause group typology seeks to classify pressure groups according to their core aims.

Sectional groups

Sometimes referred to as 'protectionist groups', 'private interest groups' or simply 'interest groups', sectional groups are those that aim to advance the shared interests of their members, as opposed to campaigning for a broader cause. Sectional groups are normally 'exclusive'; individuals must meet certain requirements in order to qualify for group membership. For example, those seeking to join the British Medical Association (BMA) must be qualified medical practitioners or students training to enter the profession.

Links to follow up

www.bma.org.uk — the website of the British Medical Association.

Cause groups

Also referred to as 'promotional groups' or 'public interest groups', cause groups seek to promote approaches, issues or ideas that are not of direct benefit to group members. Cause groups tend to be 'inclusive', in that they generally look to establish a wide membership base and do not put in place as many barriers to entry. The Royal Society for the Protection of Birds (RSPB), for example, has become one of the largest and most visible UK cause groups in recent years with somewhere in excess of 1 million members in 2013. The cause group category is commonly subdivided into three further categories: **attitude cause groups**, **political cause groups** and **sectional cause groups**.

Key terms

➤ **Attitude cause group** A group that seeks to change people's attitude on a particular issue (e.g. Greenpeace, www.greenpeace.org.uk).

➤ **Political cause group** A group that campaigns in pursuit of a cause that is essentially political in nature (e.g. Charter 88, now part of Unlock Democracy, www.unlockdemocracy.org.uk).

➤ **Sectional cause group** A group that represents a specific section of society that is distinct from its own membership (i.e. not simply a sectional group). For example, the National Society for the Prevention of Cruelty to Children (NSPCC, www.nspcc.org.uk) is a sectional cause group because it seeks to represent the interests of children but is not organised or run by children.

Links to follow up

www.rspb.org.uk — the website of the Royal Society for the Protection of Birds.

Sectional and cause groups

Distinguish between

Sectional groups
➤ Serve the interests of their members.
➤ Tend to be more 'exclusive' in terms of their membership, e.g. requiring members to be serving in a particular profession.

Cause groups
➤ Campaign on policies that they believe will benefit others or the interests of society as a whole.
➤ Generally seek a wider membership, i.e. 'inclusive'.

Problems associated with classifying groups according to their aims

Critics of the sectional group–cause group typology argue that it is more helpful to look at group 'status' than the nature of a group's aims when assessing its chances of success. A further criticism of the typology is that some groups do not fit neatly into any of the 'boxes' identified. For example, while a teaching union such as the NASUWT clearly campaigns for the sectional interests of its members (a sectional group), it would also claim to raise awareness and promote reform in the field of primary and secondary education (an attitude cause group), with a view to bringing immediate benefits to school pupils (a sectional cause group).

Classification by group status

The problems associated with classifying pressure groups according to their core aims led writers such as Wyn Grant to subdivide groups according to their status in relation to the government. The resulting insider–outsider typology largely sees group success as a function of the extent to which any given group is able to develop secure, positive relationships with politicians and officials.

Distinguish between

Insider and outsider groups

Insider groups
- Have regular contact with decision-makers.
- Generally work behind the scenes rather than engaging in high-profile publicity stunts that could embarrass the government and threaten the group's privileged status.
- Tend to have mainstream goals.

Outsider groups
- Do not have regular contact with decision-makers.
- Are often forced to engage in publicity stunts as a means of moving their cause or interest up the political agenda.
- Often campaign on issues that provoke controversy.

Insider groups

Those groups that enjoy closer and more positive relationships with those in government are referred to as insider groups. Those that have particularly strong two-way relationships with policy-makers across a broad range of issues (e.g. the BMA) are described as **core insiders**. Those granted such status within a more narrow area of expertise (e.g. the Worldwide Fund for Nature, WWF) are known as **specialist insiders**. A third group, **peripheral insiders**,

Key terms
- **Core insiders** Groups that work closely with government and are consulted regularly across a broad range of policy areas.
- **Specialist insiders** Groups with which the government consults across only a narrow range of policies.
- **Peripheral insiders** Groups whose areas of expertise or interest are so narrow that government would only rarely consult them.

are those who have access to, but are only rarely needed by, the government due to the narrow nature of their interest or cause (e.g. the Dogs Trust).

Links to follow up

www.wwf.org.uk — the website of the Worldwide Fund for Nature.

www.dogstrust.org.uk — the website of the Dogs Trust.

Outsider groups

Groups that work outside of the 'political loop' are referred to as outsider groups. Those which might one day gain insider status, but have not yet established good working relationships with those in government, are referred to as **potential insiders**. **Outsiders by necessity** are those groups that are forced to operate as outsiders because they are unlikely ever to achieve insider status — perhaps due to the nature of their cause or as a consequence of their preferred methodology. The term **ideological outsiders** refers to those groups that prefer to distance themselves from the government for reasons of ideology.

Key terms

➤ **Potential insiders** Groups that might ultimately achieve insider status but are currently lacking in terms of support and/or experience. Governments may be reluctant to grant such groups insider status because they regard them as lacking legitimacy.

➤ **Outsiders by necessity** Groups that are forced to operate as outsider groups as a result of there being no realistic prospect of regular consultation with government — whether because of the group's core aims or its chosen methods (e.g. Fathers4Justice).

➤ **Ideological outsiders** Groups that look to avoid establishing close working relationships with government for ideological reasons. Amnesty International, for example, must avoid becoming too closely associated with any national government if it is to preserve its reputation for impartiality. Those campaigning against globalisation may see government as part of the problem, rather than part of the solution.

Links to follow up

www.amnesty.org.uk — the website of Amnesty International.

Problems with the insider–outsider typology

Classifying different groups by group status (insider–outsider) addresses some of the problems inherent in categorising pressure groups by aims. It may also be more useful in terms of assessing the likelihood of a group achieving its central aims. However, such labels tend to ignore the fact that many groups can operate both as 'insiders' and 'outsiders', to a degree, and that groups can also move surprisingly quickly from 'outside' to 'inside' and vice versa. For example, the political cause group Charter 88 was clearly outside of the political loop before the 1997 general election, but assumed more influence following Labour's victory in that year. In contrast, the National Farmers' Union's long-held core insider status came under threat as a result of growing EU control over agricultural policy and a period of 13 years when the Conservative Party was out of office.

Consequently, Wyn Grant has argued that it might be more appropriate to divide insider groups into 'high-profile' insider groups (which court the media as well as working with government behind the scenes), 'low-profile' insider groups (which focus largely on establishing relationships behind the scenes) and so-called **'captive' or 'prisoner' groups**.

Key term

➤ **'Captive' or 'prisoner' groups** Groups that are dependent on government, either because they benefit from state funding or because the government played a part in their creation. For example, the Equality and Human Rights Commission (EHRC) was established under the Equality Act (2006).

Links to follow up

www.equalityhumanrights.com — the website of the Equality and Human Rights Commission.

Pressure group methods

The nature of pressure group activity is greatly dependent upon the scope and extent of group aims and objectives. Pressure groups can make use of a range of access points (see stretch and challenge activity). Those groups whose aims are local and limited in scale may be able to achieve their goals without ever needing to lobby at Westminster. Broader-based environmental groups will, in contrast, need to work at local, national and supranational levels in order to achieve their core aims.

Traditional pressure group methods

Many groups still favour traditional methods, such as letter writing campaigns, petitions, public demonstrations and conventional lobbying (see Box 5.1).

The anti-abortion organisation Life compiled a petition of more than 2 million names in the mid-1980s and employed postcard campaigns in 1989 and 1990 in opposition to the bill which ultimately became the Human Fertilisation and Embryology Act (1990).

Marches and demonstrations organised by the Anti-Poll Tax Federation in 1990 were said to have contributed both to Margaret Thatcher's downfall (in November of that year) and to the subsequent replacement of the community charge with the council tax in 1993. A decade later, in February 2003, an estimated 1 million took to the streets as part of the Stop the War Coalition's efforts to persuade the government not to deploy UK forces in Iraq.

Links to follow up

www.stopwar.org.uk — the website of the Stop the War Coalition.

⟷ Stretch and challenge

Access points

Access points are the points within the political system at which pressure groups and other interested parties can exert pressure on those who hold political power. In a unitary system, where sovereign power is held at the centre, access points tend to be less numerous and less meaningful than in a federal system, where the ultimate power over different areas of policy is held at different levels of government. Systems that incorporate a clear separation of powers and an entrenched system of checks and balances (e.g. the USA) are also likely to offer pressure groups a greater range of meaningful access points than those where the three main elements of state power (executive, legislative and judicial) are fused and the checks on the executive are weak.

A number of factors have served to increase the range of access points available to British pressure groups in recent years, for example: the establishment of a Scottish Parliament with wide-ranging primary legislative powers; the creation of assemblies and executives in Wales, Northern Ireland and London; and the creation of a more independent UK Supreme Court.

Questions

1 Explain why the UK was traditionally seen as benefiting from relatively few access points, in comparison with the USA.

2 Briefly outline the changes that are said to have led to an increase in the number of meaningful access points available to pressure groups operating within the UK system.

3 Explain, using examples, why individual pressure groups may choose to target specific access points.

Demonstration against the Iraq War, Hyde Park, London in February 2003

Box 5.1 Lobbying

John Kingdom defined lobbying as the 'act of seeking the ear of a member of government'. At a simple level, individuals or members of pressure groups may write to a government minister or visit the Palace of Westminster to lobby those who have influence over the group's area of interest or expertise face-to-face. However, in the modern era it has become more common for groups to employ lobbying firms that will, for a fee, direct professional lobbyists to use their contacts on behalf of the pressure group in question. For example, the lobbying group Ian Greer Associates arranged the initial contact between Mohamed Al Fayed and the then Conservative MP and junior trade minister Neil Hamilton — an association that was at the heart of the 'cash for questions scandal'.

Influencing the legislative process directly

As we have seen, core insider groups have the ability to influence the formation of policy at an early stage through consultation with ministers, civil servants and government-appointed bodies working on legislative proposals. Many larger groups employ lobbyists to pursue their legislative goals; some maintain permanent Westminster offices.

Embarking on legal action

Litigation can be an effective, if expensive, pressure group tactic. Such action can work on four levels:

➢ where a court finds that the government has acted beyond its authority (ultra vires)
➢ where the rules in place appear to violate EU law
➢ where an Act of Parliament or action of a public official is deemed incompatible with the Human Rights Act (1998)
➢ where litigation raises public awareness of a particular issue irrespective of the outcome of the case — as in the case of the Pro-Life Alliance's challenges over the application of the Human Fertilisation and Embryology Act (1990).

Working through a political party

The easiest time for pressure groups to gain a foothold within parties is when they are in opposition. Examples are the way in which anti-fox hunting groups and those favouring wholesale constitutional reform established links with the Labour Party between 1979 and 1997. Such relationships are far harder to develop when a party is in government, as the government is likely to be subject to far greater demands on its time and the policy-making process is necessarily more 'top-down'.

Direct action

Direct action is an increasingly popular form of pressure group action. It starts from the premise that conventional methods of influencing policy are flawed and that more visible and direct protests, perhaps even involving **civil disobedience** or illegality (possibly even violence), may offer the best opportunity of success because they attract media attention, raise public awareness and force politicians to sit up and listen.

Key concepts

➤ **Direct action** Direct action includes those forms of political protest that move beyond traditional pressure group methods, often involving a degree of civil disobedience. Those engaged in direct action generally aim to raise the profile of their chosen cause by attracting local or national media coverage. Direct action is said to have gained in popularity as groups adopting more conventional methods have failed to achieve their goals.

➤ **Civil disobedience** Civil disobedience is the act of refusing certain orders given by the state, without resorting to physical violence. It is closely associated with the 'non-violence' of political leaders such as Mahatma Gandhi in India and Martin Luther King Jr in the USA. The campaign against the poll tax saw widespread civil disobedience. Many thousands refused to register for the tax; others refused to pay and then failed to attend court when issued with a summons. Many local Anti-Poll Tax Unions used non-violent protest as a way of preventing their local councils from setting the level at which the tax would be charged. The scale of civil disobedience made it impossible for the courts to process all the cases arising. Occupy London's 2011–12 protests in the capital are another example of non-violent civil disobedience.

Although many feel that direct action techniques provide the most immediate way of articulating a view and achieving tangible results, critics argue that the rise in single-issue, direct action politics undermines representative democracy. This is because such campaigns prevent governments from implementing their programmes and from pursuing policies that address the 'bigger picture'.

The scope and scale of direct action campaigns have increased significantly since the 1990s. Anti-roads protests, the campaign against live animal exports, the campaigns against fox hunting and vivisection, the fuel protests and the campaigns by groups such as Fathers4Justice and environmental groups such as Greenpeace and Plane Stupid (see case study) have all been said to have had some effect on policy or opinion.

In recent years, direct action groups have increasingly sought to target suppliers, investors and those working in the transport industry as a way of curtailing the operations of those businesses they oppose.

Key term

➤ **Umbrella group (or 'peak group')** A pressure group that brings together or speaks on behalf of a number of pressure groups that share a common interest or campaign in favour of associated causes. The Trades Union Congress (TUC), for example, is a peak group speaking on behalf of a large number of individual trade unions.

Case study   Plane Stupid (www.planestupid.com)

An environmental **umbrella group** founded by university graduates Richard George, Graham Thompson and Joss Garman in 2005. The group employs direct action tactics in an effort to limit further airport expansion.

Aims:
➤ to end short haul flights and airport expansion

➤ to stop aviation advertising

➤ to campaign for a just transition to sustainable jobs and transport

Organisation:
➤ a loosely organised, non-hierarchical and consensual network of regional groups

➤ invites people to carry out protests in the group's name (as long as such protests are 'accountable, non-violent and focusing on aviation expansion')

Activists from the umbrella group Plane Stupid on the roof of the Palace of Westminster in February 2008

'Pressure groups' or 'terrorist groups'?

In some cases, the methods adopted by those engaging in direct action causes groups to cross that imperceptible line between 'pressure group' and 'terrorist group'. Direct action groups such as the Animal Liberation Front have been banned on both sides of the Atlantic and other groups have also courted controversy. Supporters of the anti-vivisection group Save the Newchurch Guinea Pigs (SNGP), which campaigned between 1999 and 2005, exhumed the body of one of the relatives of the owners of a farm criticised for supplying animals for experimentation; the farm subsequently closed in the wake of a campaign of harassment and intimidation. A similarly intense campaign against Huntingdon Life Sciences by the group Stop Huntingdon Animal Cruelty (SHAC) also proved controversial. In both of these cases, group activists received lengthy prison sentences as a result of the methods they employed in pursuit of their chosen cause.

Managing the media

Groups increasingly employ sophisticated media techniques to advance their cause or sectional interests. They may use paid media, taking out whole-page adverts in the national

press, using direct mail or producing and airing TV adverts. Established caring charities have also made widespread use of such tactics. For example, the NSPCC made extensive use of television advertising in support of its Full-Stop campaign, which sought to address violence against children. Groups can also use unpaid media, eliciting news coverage by organising stunts, planning marches or employing other direct action techniques.

Pressure groups and the European Union

Pressure groups in the UK increasingly look to organise and lobby at EU level as opposed to focusing their attention solely on British institutions. Pressure groups are particularly likely to turn to the EU where:

> they are faced with a national government that is unsympathetic to their cause, and/or
> their sectional interest or cause is supranational (i.e. Europe-wide)

Case study **Environmental pressure groups and the EU**

Environmental pressure groups have two good reasons to lobby at the EU level:

> Many environmental issues, by definition, do not respect territorial borders. It therefore makes more sense to deal with environmental issues at a European or international level, rather than simply at a national level.

> The EU is already committed to environmental protection and is, therefore, more sympathetic towards the core aims of many environmental pressure groups than are the national governments of most of the 28 EU member states.

In the broad areas of economic and environmental policy, the proliferation of Europe-wide regulation provides an opportunity for real influence not often afforded to pressure groups at a national level.

On issues such as the improvement of water quality, for example, environmental groups in the UK have made great progress by working through the European Union.

> Many beaches in England, previously categorised as unfit for bathing due to sewage pollution, have been improved under pressure from the EU.

> The policy of awarding blue flags for clean beaches has also had the effect of raising the public profile of the EU.

> Groups such as Surfers Against Sewage (**www.sas.org.uk**) have played a part in bringing about such changes.

The growing power of the EU

Under the terms of the European Communities Act (1972), European law takes precedence over British law where the two are in conflict. Pressure groups can therefore lobby in an effort to force change on their national governments by, in effect, going 'over their heads' to the EU.

Since 1986, decisions in the Council of the European Union (formerly known as the Council of Ministers) have increasingly been taken under a system of qualified majority voting (QMV) rather than on the basis of unanimity. This means that groups must work

| **Case study** | **The National Farmers' Union and COPA–COGECA** |

The National Farmers' Union (NFU) has a permanent office in Brussels, but it is also a member of the Eurogroup COPA–COGECA (**www.copa-cogeca.be**).

COPA is the umbrella organisation representing the main agricultural organisations in the EU.

COGECA is the equivalent organisation for agricultural cooperatives.

In 2013, COPA–COGECA had a total of 95 member organisations from EU states and many other affiliated organisations from beyond the EU's borders. In total, the group represented in excess of 30 million farmers and 40,000 co-operatives.

to build up a broader European support, rather than simply lobbying their own national governments to block measures using their national veto. Though QMV makes life more complicated, it also presents opportunities for pressure groups (see case study above). A UK-based group can, for example, campaign in favour of a measure affecting the UK in the knowledge that the British government alone cannot prevent it from happening. As the process of EU integration sees the Union move beyond the economic sphere into many aspects of social, foreign and security policy, a wider range of British pressure groups is likely to turn to Europe.

The emergence of Eurogroups

If pressure groups in each member state conducted their activities independently of one another, their voices might easily be lost. In fact, like-minded pressure groups from different EU member states often aggregate their efforts, establishing Eurogroups which, simply by virtue of their size and coverage, possess the resources and legitimacy needed to have their views heard.

The scale and structural complexity of the EU provides numerous access points. The European Commission, for example, has a massive appetite for information and recognises Eurogroups as a legitimate source of information. Clearly, the most successful Eurogroups will be those which possess the material resources needed to take advantage of such opportunities. While an EU office is the ideal, not all groups can afford a permanent office in Brussels.

Factors affecting pressure group success

Precisely how effective individual pressure groups are is often hard to gauge — not least because many core insider groups prefer not to publicise the extent of their influence, for fear of alienating the government and losing their privileged status. Similarly, while high-profile protests and stunts might appear impressive, they rarely affect the course of government policy. Indeed, even at the time of the nationwide 'fuel protests' in 2000, the government chose to speak to the Road Hauliers' Association, rather than to those blockading refineries and bringing motorways to a standstill.

At a simple level, we can measure the extent to which a pressure group is deemed 'a success' in terms of the degree to which it is able to achieve its central aims and objectives. If we are prepared to accept this narrow definition of success, a pressure group's chances of success will depend upon four key variables: group aims, group resources, group status and group methods.

However, the dividing lines between these four factors are not hard-and-fast. For example, while it is true that groups adopting extreme methods are unlikely to achieve success, such groups may only be adopting such tactics because their aims have failed to garner sufficient support among the public at large, and they have been unsuccessful in establishing a relationship with government. Similarly, those groups with large memberships (resources) are also likely to be seen by the government as more legitimate (thus affecting status).

Group aims

Group aims are vital to understanding why some groups are more successful than others. Central to this theme are the twin concepts of practical achievability and public receptivity.

Practical achievability means the extent to which a group's main goals are achievable in practice. For example, while the Snowdrop Campaign's aim of banning handguns in the UK was clearly an achievable goal in practical terms, the core aim of most anti-globalisation protesters is probably not. We might also regard small, local pressure group campaigns with limited goals (see Box 5.2) as being more practically achievable than campaigns that require major changes in UK statute or EU law.

Box 5.2	Relatively high 'achievability'? The Gurkha Justice Campaign

Aims: to gain the right to live in the UK for all Gurkhas who had served in the British Army prior to 1997 (those retiring after 1997 had already been granted residency rights).

Numbers directly affected: predicted to result in applications from between 10,000 and 15,000 former Gurkhas. Around 8,000 arrived in the 2 years that followed the decision to admit such individuals.

Financial impact: Gurkhas' representatives estimated that each entrant cost an average of £600–£700 per month in benefits.

Public receptivity refers to the extent to which the general public are sympathetic to group aims. Those groups which have aims that are diametrically opposed to the prevailing popular mood are unlikely to achieve success in the short term. In contrast, those groups whose aims are broadly in tune with the prevailing public mood are likely to find that they are, in effect, 'pushing at an open door'. This can be seen in the differing fortunes of those campaigning for better conditions in prisons (e.g. the Howard League for Penal Reform) and those seeking to help the victims of crime (e.g. Victim Support).

Crucially, however, while the practical achievability of group aims may remain fairly constant, the public mood — and with it the extent to which that group will be well received — will change over time. For example, while the Snowdrop Campaign's central aim was always achievable in practical terms, it was the public reaction to the Dunblane High School Massacre in 1996 that eased the passage of the Firearms (Amendment) (No. 2) Act (1997), banning private ownership of handguns. Anthony Downs' five-stage 'issue attention cycle' (see Box 5.3) seeks to offer one explanation as to why the fortunes of a given group might wax and wane over time.

Box 5.3   Anthony Downs' 'issue attention cycle'

1   **The pre-problem stage**
    The problem exists. Experts and activists may be 'alive' to the threat posed, but wider public remains unaware or unperturbed.

2   **Alarmed discovery and euphoric enthusiasm**
    The problem enters the public consciousness. There is a widespread sense that 'something must be done'. Politicians compete to offer 'solutions'.

3   **Realising the cost of significant progress**
    The general public recognise the potential costs and knock-on effects of the proposed 'solutions'. They may also recognise that the problem is a result of practices that have other significant benefits that they would not want to sacrifice.

4   **Gradual decline of intense public interest**
    The realisation that the costs of solving the problem outright are unacceptable results in an erosion of interest. At the same time, other problems might be entering stage 2.

5   **The post-problem stage**
    The problem has been replaced in the public consciousness by other, more pressing problems. Low-level efforts to tackle the original problem may continue, but it is no longer viewed as a priority.

Group resources

The extent to which a given group is able to campaign as it wishes will inevitably be shaped to a large degree by its resources. In simple terms, we can divide group resources into human resources (size and quality of membership, availability of technical skills, etc.) and material resources (money, equipment, offices, etc.). While it is certainly true that some groups are able to raise their profile without access to great material resources, such groups inevitably rely heavily on the skills of group members (i.e. human resources). For example, while the material resources available to the group Fathers4Justice were clearly limited, it benefited both from the presence of members who were prepared to risk personal injury in pursuit of their cause, and from a leader, Matt O'Connor, who was articulate, presentable and familiar with the world of public relations. Celebrity endorsement can also be significant, as witnessed in the case of Joanna Lumley's support for the Gurkha Justice Campaign and Jamie Oliver's involvement with the 'Feed Me Better' campaign for more nutritious food in schools.

Group status

Although outsider groups have enjoyed greater media coverage in recent years and could even be said to have contributed to some changes in policy (e.g. the work of groups such as Greenpeace and Plane Stupid in opposing the proposed third runway at Heathrow), it is generally accepted that groups which have at least some contact with government behind the scenes are more likely to achieve some or all of their objectives than those which do not.

Group methods

The methods adopted by a particular group will inevitably have an effect on its chances of success. While an inability to achieve insider status might force some groups into adopting more high-risk strategies as a means of attracting attention, groups that employ extreme methods involving high levels of violence and/or illegality are rarely successful. In truth, successful groups are often characterised by the wide range of tactics they employ in pursuit of their cause, although the ability to plan and resource pressure group campaigns on many fronts using different strategies may just as easily be a product of groups' success as a cause of it.

Anna Jones from Greenpeace delivers a message of thanks to No. 10 Downing Street, 2010, after the new coalition government scrapped plans for a third runway at Heathrow airport

Pressure groups and democracy

Are pressure groups a threat to democracy?

In Chapter 1 we explored the meaning of the term 'democracy' and considered the concepts of **representative democracy**, **liberal democracy** and **pluralist democracy**.

Key concepts

➤ **Representative democracy** A system under which citizens elect representatives who enact laws on their behalf — but there is no obligation on the part of those elected to seek further approval from citizens before they introduce new policies.

➤ **Liberal democracy** A style of democracy incorporating free and fair elections, and a belief in the importance of certain key rights and responsibilities.

➤ **Pluralist democracy** A system of government that encourages participation and allows for free and fair competition between competing interests.

While the concept of representative democracy might lead one to believe that those returned to the Commons should be left largely to their own devices in the wake of a general election, it is clear that pressure groups have a central role in both the liberal and pluralist models of democracy. In the case of liberal democracies, the protection afforded to fundamental rights such as the freedom of speech, the right of assembly and the right to petition the government for redress of grievances would all appear to point towards the likelihood of widespread pressure group activity. The pluralist model, with its emphasis on the open interplay of competing — or 'countervailing' — interests would also appear to necessitate the existence of pressure groups.

However, while all three models of democracy clearly 'allow' for the existence of pressure groups, it is often argued that the way in which certain groups operate does more to undermine than to enhance the political process as a whole. Such criticisms of pressure groups can be crystallised into three main arguments.

Pressure groups reinforce inequalities

When commenting on pluralism at work in some aspects of the US system of government, Ernest S. Griffiths remarked that the unwritten belief underpinning such democratic arrangements is that 'truth customarily emerges from a battle of protagonists'. However, the battle between those groups 'for' and 'against' a particular issue or policy proposal is rarely an even one, bringing into question the idea of countervailing interests (where opposing groups in effect serve to cancel one another out).

Groups representing business interests clearly have an advantage in open competition. First, while they often have considerable material resources and a significant financial incentive to lobby, such groups are generally free from the problems associated with organising mass-membership cause groups. Second, as Wyn Grant has noted, the government has a vested interest in listening to such groups, as its re-election will be based in part on delivering economic success.

In more general terms, it is commonly observed that the most successful groups tend to be those that benefit from both a highly skilled and articulate membership, and a sound financial base. As a result, it could be said that pressure groups representing middle-class interests are in a better position to compete — and that pressure group competition thus serves to reinforce as opposed to break down social inequalities. All of this suggests that, far from contributing to pluralism, pressure groups may in fact be a feature of **elitism**.

Key concept

➤ **Elite theory** The belief that modern societies are dominated by an elite that uses its privileged position to benefit its own members while at the same time excluding others from the key decision-making processes. Elite theory is closely associated with the work of US sociologist Charles Wright Mills and his seminal book *The Power Elite* (1956).

Pressure groups 'strangle efficient government'

It was the former Conservative cabinet minister Douglas Hurd who famously described pressure groups as 'serpents that strangle efficient government'. Hurd's criticism can be interpreted in two broad ways.

First, the way in which many insider groups have been able to become an established element in the machinery of government adds a further 'level' to the policy-making process. Groups such as the RSPB work closely with government and are consulted across a range of policy areas at the drafting stage. While some might argue that this is helpful, as it serves to reduce the likelihood of unforeseen problems emerging further down the legislative road, it is clear that the existence of such insider groups must by definition result in other groups being excluded from the process, thus undermining pluralism. The existence of such privileged groups also acts as an internal check on the ability of government to pursue its legislative agenda.

Second, while governments must weigh up the merits and demerits of different policies and, ultimately, seek to 'balance the books', pressure groups are generally concerned only with a specific area or at best a limited range of policies. Thus governments seeking to deliver 'joined-up' government are all too often forced to take a reactive stance when facing single-issue outsider campaigns, as opposed to being proactive in seeking to deliver on their manifesto pledges. In forcing the government to 'fire-fight' in this way, pressure groups distort the decision-making process and make it far harder for those in office to make the difficult decisions. This is particularly true in the broad area of central government finance, where the activities of pressure groups, campaigning publicly and privately for increased government expenditure in their area of interest, apply a relentless upward pressure on public sector spending and — particularly in times of economic downturn — public sector borrowing.

Pressure groups can be internally undemocratic

Although pressure groups are said to play a vital role within a liberal democracy, by providing avenues for representation and participation, many membership groups are themselves not internally democratic, affording little real power to individual members or supporters.

The growth of passive, 'cheque-book' group membership in recent years clearly has implications for the quality of participation provided for by pressure groups. More important, however, is the extent to which the level of internal democracy present in a group may have a bearing on its legitimacy. As Wyn Grant notes, 'we need [to be able] to ask questions about whom [groups] represent and how their policies are arrived at'. While some groups are clearly engaged in intense internal debate (e.g. the RSPCA over fox hunting), others (e.g. Greenpeace — see case study) have tended to be more centralised, despite having large individual memberships.

How are pressure group officers chosen?

In many cases, pressure group officers are appointed, as opposed to being elected by the group's members on a one member, one vote (OMOV) basis. This means that those leading pressure groups are often not directly accountable to members.

How do pressure groups make decisions?

In many pressure groups, key decisions are taken not by members, but by a central committee or board which is itself unelected. Neil McNaughton suggests that groups such as the British Medical Association and the Automobile Association are particularly poor at consulting their members over questions of policy and direction: in short, that the organisation of many groups reflects elitism rather than pluralism.

Some sectional groups, such as trade unions, have been forced to become more internally democratic as a result of employment and union legislation passed in the 1980s (e.g. the requirement to hold ballots before national strike action). Other sectional groups (e.g. non-membership business groups) may display little or no internal democracy. Many cause groups start as a small group of committed individuals and control often remains with these individuals, or their chosen successors, even when the group's membership expands significantly.

Case study — Is Greenpeace internally democratic?

According to Wyn Grant, Greenpeace is a hierarchical organisation that allows little democratic control over the direction of campaigns.

➤ It has a strictly bureaucratic, if not authoritarian, internal structure.

➤ A small group of people has control over the organisation both at the international level and within national chapters.

➤ Local action groups, which exist in some countries, are totally dependent on the central body.

➤ The rank and file is excluded from all decisions.

Viewpoint — Are pressure groups good for democracy?

YES

● Pressure groups occur naturally under any system of government. People have a natural desire to unite in furtherance of their own interests or a particular cause.

● Pressure groups allow people to organise and articulate their views between elections.

● Groups provide an additional avenue for participation, at a time when some other more traditional forms (e.g. party membership and voting) are waning.

● Pressure groups allow a wider range of opinions to be represented than is possible through political parties, particularly in a post-ideological age of catch-all parties.

● Groups play an essential role in moderating the views of their more extreme members. Without such groups, individuals with extreme views might never have their views challenged and changed.

● Pressure groups allow the strength (i.e. intensity) of opinions to be expressed, as opposed to simply counting the number of people supporting a view — as happens at elections.

● Pressure groups play a role in educating the public and providing the government with specialist information and expertise.

NO

- Many pressure groups lack legitimacy because they exhibit low levels of internal democracy.
- The quality of participation offered by pressure groups is often very low, even where membership is high. Many members do little more than pay their annual membership fee. This is referred to as 'passive membership' or 'cheque-book membership'.
- Many non-membership groups are simply fronts for wealthy and influential business interests which may have little interest in the greater public good. This is true of many core insider groups.
- Pressure groups do not compete on an equal financial footing. Less wealthy groups find it far harder to access the policy-making process.
- Groups tend to be more successful where they have articulate, educated leading members. This tends to favour groups run by the middle classes, thus favouring elitism over pluralism.
- Groups often have an effect on government that is disproportionate to their size or to the merit of their cause, particularly when employing direct action tactics.
- Pressure group activity gets in the way of joined-up government.
- The information produced by some groups is unreliable. Far from 'educating', many groups are in fact misleading or indoctrinating.

What you should know

- ❯ Pressure groups are groups of like-minded individuals who come together on the basis of shared interests or a commonly held cause in order to put pressure on policy-makers at Westminster and beyond.
- ❯ Recent years have seen the rise of less formally structured social movements and direct action campaigns.
- ❯ Pressure groups perform three main functions: a participatory function, a representative function and an educative function.
- ❯ The right to engage in pressure group activity is an essential element of the style of liberal democracy practised in the UK. This is because freedom of speech, freedom of association and the right to petition the government for redress of grievances are protected.
- ❯ Pressure groups are an essential feature of pluralist democracy, where competing interests (so-called countervailing groups) compete in support of their interests or cause.
- ❯ Pressure groups are normally classified either according to their core aims (under the sectional group–cause group typology) or in terms of their status in relation to government (under the insider–outsider typology).
- ❯ The UK's unitary system and the absence of a formal separation of powers traditionally limited the range of meaningful access points available to groups. However, new avenues have been opened up as a result of devolution and European integration.
- ❯ Pressure groups seek to advance their interests or cause by a variety of means: traditional methods (such as letter writing, public demonstrations and lobbying); cultivating links with political parties; direct action; accessing the mass media; and the use of legal action.
- ❯ A pressure group's chances of success will be shaped largely by the nature and appeal of its core aims, its resources, its status and its methods.
- ❯ Some commentators argue that pressure groups threaten to undermine democracy in the UK because they give undue influence to wealthy, well-educated groups (favouring elitism over pluralism), because they hinder the government's efforts to deliver joined-up government, and because many groups lack legitimacy as a result of their not being internally democratic.

UK/US comparison

Pressure groups in the USA

➤ While both the USA and the UK are said to be liberal democracies, the USA is generally seen as being further along the road towards pluralism.

➤ This view reflects the sheer diversity present in US society as well as the numerous access points created as a result of power being fragmented both vertically and horizontally, through federalism, the separation of powers and checks and balances.

➤ US pressure groups play a greater role at election time than their UK counterparts, not least due to the continued activities and influence of so-called Political Action Committees (PACS).

➤ The financial cost of running an election campaign in the USA makes elected politicians far more receptive to those groups that back their election campaigns. Senator Barbara Mikulski went as far as to describe the US legislature as a 'coin-operated Congress'.

➤ Single-issue groups have a far greater role in US politics than has traditionally been the case in the UK. Many of these groups campaign on issues of great political or moral controversy, e.g. 'abortion rights'. Candidates who take positions that run contrary to group aims often become a target for group-funded negative campaigns, called 'attack-ads'.

➤ The presence of a codified constitution in the USA means that the use of legal action as a pressure group tactic is far more prevalent there than in the UK, with groups often sponsoring test cases in an effort to establish a legal precedent in their favour. As Alexis de Tocqueville once noted, 'scarcely any political question arises in the US that is not resolved sooner or later into a judicial question'.

Further reading

Fairclough, P. (2011) 'Pressure groups: a new age of protest?', *Politics Review*, Vol. 21, No. 1, pp. 2–4.

Fairclough, P. (2013) 'Pressure groups: what makes them successful?', *Politics Review*, Vol. 23, No. 1, pp. 2–5.

Heffernan, R. (2012) 'Pressure groups: do promotional groups strengthen democracy?', *Politics Review*, Vol. 22, No. 1, pp. 24–27.

McNaughton, N., Fairclough, P. and Magee, E. (2012) 'Pressure groups: how democratic are direct action and mass protest?', in *UK Government and Politics Annual Update 2012*, pp. 27–34, Philip Allan Updates.

Sloam, J. (2013) 'The outraged young: how young Europeans are reshaping the political landscape', *Political Insight*, Vol. 4, No. 1, pp. 4–7.

Exam focus

Short response questions (around 5–6 minutes each)

1 What is pluralism?
2 What is elitism?
3 What is direct action?
4 What is meant by the term 'new pressure group politics'?
5 Define the term 'access point'.

Mid-length response questions (around 10–12 minutes each)

1 Distinguish between pressure groups and political parties.
2 Why do some pressure groups seek to preserve their outsider status?
3 What are the advantages and disadvantages of direct action?
4 Identify and explain *three* ways in which pressure groups seek to influence the legislative process.
5 How do pressure groups encourage political participation?

Mini-essay questions (around 25–30 minutes each)

1 To what extent is wealth the most important factor in determining pressure group success?
2 'Pressure group activity is fundamentally undemocratic.' Discuss.
3 How and why have the methods of pressure groups changed in recent years?
4 'Pressure groups rarely have any effect on the course of government policy.' To what extent do you agree with this statement?

 Extra resources to help you revise and consolidate your knowledge for this chapter are provided online at **www.hodderplus.co.uk/philipallan**. These include a revision PowerPoint, extension tasks and up-to-date weblinks.

Chapter 6

The constitution

Key questions answered in this chapter
- ➢ What are the key sources and principles of the British constitution?
- ➢ What are the main strengths and weaknesses of the traditional constitution?
- ➢ Is parliament sovereign?
- ➢ How significant are the constitutional reforms introduced by the Labour governments (1997–2010), and the Conservative–Liberal Democrat coalition?
- ➢ Should the UK adopt a codified constitution?

What is a constitution?

A **constitution** comprises the laws, rules and practices by which a state is governed. It specifies the powers of the governing institutions, while also setting out the formal relationships between them, and the relationship between citizens and the state. It provides the framework for the political system, establishing the main institutions of government, determining where decision-making authority resides and protecting the basic rights of citizens (often in a **Bill of Rights**).

In liberal democracies, the constitution provides an important defence against the abuse of power by the state and its institutions. It upholds a system of **limited government** in which a system of checks and balances prevents over-mighty government, and the rights of the citizen are protected from arbitrary state power. Reference to the constitution can determine when state action is lawful and legitimate (i.e. is constitutional) and when it is not (i.e. is unconstitutional).

Key terms
- ➢ **Bill of Rights** An authoritative statement of the rights of citizens, often entrenched as part of a codified constitution.
- ➢ **Limited government**. A system in which the powers of government are subject to legal constraints, and checks and balances within the political system.

Constitutions should not be seen as existing outside normal political activity. Instead, they impact upon day-to-day politics and are inherently political. A constitution is not static: the rules and practices it sets out have to be interpreted and sometimes adapted to meet changing circumstances. Nor are constitutions neutral: the framework they provide (e.g. the electoral system) may favour some actors, while others may seek to change it.

Key concepts

➤ **Constitution** The House of Lords Select Committee on the Constitution (2001) defined a constitution as 'the set of laws, rules and practices that create the basic institutions of the state and its component and related parts, and stipulate the powers of those institutions and the relationship between the different institutions, and between those institutions and the individual'.

➤ **Constitutionalism** The theory and practice of government according to the rules and principles of a constitution. A constitutional democracy is one which operates within the framework of a constitution that sets limits on the powers of government institutions and provides protection for the rights of citizens. A government or public authority acts in an unconstitutional manner when its actions are not in accord with the principles and practices set out in the constitution.

Codified and uncodified constitutions

A key distinction is that between codified and uncodified constitutions. A **codified constitution** is one in which the major principles underpinning the political system are collected in a single authoritative document. This is a constitution with a capital 'C', such as the US Constitution. An **uncodified constitution** has no single source for these principles; rather, they are found in a number of places. The UK constitution is the prime

Key concepts

➤ **Codified constitution** A codified constitution is a single document that sets out the laws, rules and principles on how a state is to be governed, and the rights of citizens. The key provisions governing the political system are collected in one authoritative document, often called 'the Constitution'.

➤ **Uncodified constitution** An uncodified constitution is one in which the laws, rules and principles specifying how a state is to be governed are not gathered in a single document. Instead they are found in a variety of sources, some written (e.g. statute laws) and some unwritten (e.g. conventions).

The distinction between codified and uncodified constitutions is significant, but it should be remembered that no constitution is either entirely written or unwritten, and that codified constitutions often have some flexibility.

example. It is frequently described as 'unwritten', but this is misleading. While it is true that constitutional principles are not gathered in a single document, most are written down, notably in the form of statute law (Acts of Parliament) and decisions of the higher courts. But others take the form of unwritten conventions that lack the clarity of a codified constitution.

The distinction between codified and uncodified constitutions is not as sharp as it might appear. No constitution ever spells out each and every practice. All constitutions contain a mixture of written and unwritten rules. Students of American politics will, for example, learn little about the formal powers of the Supreme Court or the informal powers of the president from reading the US Constitution. The US Constitution has been periodically reinterpreted by the Supreme Court so that its eighteenth-century principles make sense in the modern world. A codified constitution is, then, not a detailed blueprint but a reference point for an evolving political system.

Features of codified constitutions

There are nevertheless significant differences between codified and uncodified constitutions. Codified constitutions are often produced at a critical juncture in a nation's history: for example, after independence (the US Constitution in 1787), authoritarian rule or war (West Germany's Basic Law in 1949). In this situation, institutions derive their authority from the constitution. By contrast, the UK constitution has evolved over time and is not based upon a definitive statement of abstract principles. Some of its features (e.g. prerogative powers) are centuries old, whereas others (e.g. the Scottish Parliament) are recent additions.

A codified constitution has the status of **fundamental law** or higher law, placing it above ordinary law made by the legislature. There is a two-tier legal system with the constitution having a higher status than all other law. A constitutional (or supreme) court determines whether its provisions have been violated. The provisions of a codified constitution are also **entrenched**: that is, there are special procedures for its amendment which make it more difficult to change than ordinary legislation. For the constitution to be amended, a super-majority (a higher fraction than a half) in the legislature or approval in a referendum may be required. Codified constitutions are characterised as rigid and uncodified constitutions as flexible. But degrees of flexibility are also evident in codified constitutions — only 17 amendments have been added to the US Constitution since the 1791 Bill of Rights (which consists of the first ten amendments), but the 1958 constitution of the French Fifth Republic was amended 17 times in 50 years.

 Key terms
➤ **Fundamental law** The law which forms the foundation of the government of a state.
➤ **Entrenched** Secured; difficult to change.

The UK's uncodified constitution

There are no special legal mechanisms for amending the British constitution — the uncodified constitution can be amended by a simple Act of Parliament. The British constitution is, in a sense then, reducible to what parliament enacts. Nor, in a single-tier legal system, is there fundamental law. There are no constitutional 'no go areas' into which parliament cannot step. As we will see below, the doctrine of parliamentary sovereignty endows parliament with legislative supremacy, enabling it to legislate on any matter of its choosing and to overturn any existing law. Parliament can change the constitution in the same way that it can amend any other legislation.

Parliamentary sovereignty and an uncodified constitution mean that **judicial review** is limited in the UK. Judicial review is the power of the courts to determine whether the government and public authorities have acted within the bounds of their authority when making decisions. Without a codified constitution, there is no definitive criterion for determining what is unconstitutional. However, as Chapter 9 examines, judicial review of legislation and ministerial decisions has increased significantly in recent decades.

Key term

➤ **Judicial review** The power of senior judges to review the actions of government and public authorities, declaring them unlawful if they have exceeded their authority.

Links to follow up

www.politicsresources.net/const.htm — includes the texts of many national constitutions.

Codified and uncodified constitution

Distinguish between

Codified constitution

➤ The rules and principles governing the state are collected in a single authoritative document — 'the Constitution'.
➤ It has the status of fundamental law, being above all other law.
➤ It is entrenched, with special procedures for its amendment that make it difficult to change.
➤ The courts, particularly a constitutional court, use it to determine if actions are constitutional.

Uncodified constitution

➤ There is no single authoritative document; rather the rules and principles governing the state are found in a number of sources, both written and unwritten.
➤ It has the status of ordinary law; there is no hierarchy of laws.
➤ It is not entrenched, but can be amended in the same way as ordinary law.
➤ Judicial review is limited; there is no single authoritative document that senior judges can use to determine if an action is unconstitutional.

Sources of the British constitution

In the absence of a codified document, we must look for the key rules and practices of the UK's political system in different places. There are five principal sources of the British constitution:

➢ statute law
➢ common law
➢ conventions
➢ authoritative works
➢ European Union law

Statute law

Statute law is law created by parliament. In the legislative process, Acts of Parliament have to be approved by the House of Commons, the House of Lords and the monarch before they are placed on the statute book (i.e. gain the force of law). They are then implemented by the executive and enforced by the courts. Statute law is the most important source of the principles and rules making up the British constitution because parliament is the sovereign body.

Not all Acts are of constitutional significance: legislation on funding for schools will have an important effect on policy but not on the constitution. Examples of statute law that have been of historical constitutional importance include:

➢ the Great Reform Act (1832), which extended the franchise
➢ the Parliament Act (1911), which established the House of Commons as the dominant chamber of parliament
➢ the European Communities Act (1972), by which the UK joined the European Economic Community (EEC)

More recent examples are:

➢ the Scotland Act (1998), which created a Scottish Parliament
➢ the Human Rights Act (1998), which enshrined key rights in UK law
➢ the Fixed-term Parliaments Act (2011), which established fixed-term elections for Westminster

Common law

The **common law** includes legal principles that have been developed and applied by UK courts. The courts interpret and clarify the law where there is no clear statute law. Common law is thus legal precedent made by judges concerning, for example, the rights of homeowners to tackle intruders who enter their property. Judicial decisions have clarified the rights of citizens *vis-à-vis* the state. Such case law (or 'judge-made-law') becomes part of the body of the common law and serves as a guide to future lawmakers. In recent years, however, judges

Key terms

➢ **Statute law** Law derived from Acts of Parliament and subordinate legislation.
➢ **Common law** Law derived from decisions in court cases and from general customs.

have been more likely to look to the Human Rights Act (1998) than to precedents in common law. Government ministers may clarify or amend common law through Acts of Parliament.

The common law also includes customs and precedents that have become accepted practice. They relate to the role of the monarchy, parliament and the executive. Particularly important is the **royal prerogative** — the powers exercised in the name of the Crown. The Crown retains a number of formal powers that date back to the period before the UK became a constitutional monarchy in the late seventeenth century. The Crown's prerogative powers traditionally included the right to:

➢ give royal assent to legislation
➢ declare war and negotiate treaties
➢ appoint ministers

Many of these powers were exercised by government ministers in the name of the Crown. The Brown government and the Conservative–Liberal Democrat government introduced measures limiting the royal prerogative and enhancing the role of parliament. The prerogative power to dissolve parliament was, for example, ended by the Fixed-term Parliaments Act (2011). The Constitutional Reform and Governance Act (2010) put parliamentary scrutiny of treaties on a statutory basis. However, papers released in 2013 revealed that the monarch has been specifically asked to approve bills relating to prerogative powers and was advised by the government to withhold consent to a 1999 Private Member's Bill which sought to transfer the power to declare war from the monarch to parliament.

Conventions

Conventions are rules or norms that are considered to be binding. They are neither codified nor enforced by courts of law; it is long usage that gives conventions their authority. The British constitution is regarded as flexible because some of its key elements are based on convention. By convention, the monarch must assent to Acts of Parliament: if the queen were to refuse, a constitutional crisis would ensue.

Recent governments have created what may become seen as new conventions. Gordon Brown announced that the UK would not declare war without a parliamentary vote. Holding referendums on devolution and electoral reform has raised expectations that major constitutional reforms should be put to a popular vote.

The Cabinet Office has also clarified the status of conventions in its *Cabinet Manual* (2011). It has 11 chapters covering, for example, the role of the monarch, elections and government formation and collective cabinet decision-making. The *Cabinet Manual* is intended as a guide

Key terms

➢ **Royal prerogative** Discretionary powers of the Crown that are exercised in the monarch's name by government ministers.
➢ **Conventions** Established norms of political behaviour rooted in past experience rather than the law.

to the current position rather than a legally binding source of rules, but will establish greater clarity in the interpretation of conventions.

Conventions have been an imprecise guide to what should be considered constitutional. Three examples illustrate this ambiguity.

Links to follow up

www.cabinetoffice.gov.uk — click on 'Publications' for the *Cabinet Manual* and related documents.

Appointing the prime minister

It is the monarch who appoints the prime minister. Convention dictates that the leader of the largest party in the House of Commons after a general election will be invited to form a government. The last member of the House of Lords to become prime minister was Alec Douglas-Home in 1963. It had become a convention that the prime minister should be a member of the Commons, so he resigned from the Lords and successfully fought a by-election to take a seat as an MP.

The first-past-the-post (FPTP) electoral system usually produces a clear outcome, rendering the monarch's decision on which party will form the next government a formality. However, should a general election produce a hung parliament — one in which no single party has an overall majority — the monarch could face a difficult decision. The 2010 general election produced a hung parliament with the Conservatives the largest party. Following Cabinet Office guidance, Gordon Brown remained in office for 5 days while coalition negotiations took place. Brown resigned when it became apparent that there was no prospect of a deal between Labour and the Liberal Democrats. David Cameron was then appointed prime minister even though coalition negotiations between the Conservatives and Liberal Democrats had not formally concluded.

Ministerial responsibility

The circumstances under which government ministers ought to resign are also governed by convention. The convention of collective ministerial responsibility suggests that ministers who cannot accept a policy position agreed by the cabinet should leave the government. That of individual ministerial responsibility holds that ministers should resign if they, or their department, are guilty of serious political mistakes. As we will see in Chapter 8, neither convention is clear cut or holds fast for all cases.

Salisbury Convention

The Salisbury Convention (also known as the Salisbury–Addison Convention) states that the House of Lords should not vote down or wreck bills that seek to enact a manifesto commitment of the governing party. It marked an acceptance in the 1940s that an unelected upper house with an inbuilt Conservative majority should not frustrate the will of the Commons and the electorate. This convention has been challenged in recent years. Liberal Democrat and Conservative peers voted against legislation on identity cards even though

it had featured in Labour's 2005 election manifesto. They argued that Labour did not have a sufficient mandate (it won just 35% of the vote on a low turnout) and that no party now had a majority in a reformed House of Lords stripped of most hereditary peers. The coalition government has also been defeated in the Lords as peers claim that the coalition does not have a clear mandate, particularly for legislation (e.g. on NHS reforms) not explicitly signalled in the Conservative or Liberal Democrat manifestos.

Authoritative works

A number of established legal and political texts have become accepted as works of authority on the British constitution. These texts have no formal legal authority but they do have 'persuasive authority' as guides to the workings of institutions and the political system in general. They thus prove helpful in interpreting the core values that underpin the constitution, and shed light on the more obscure areas of constitutional practice.

There are only a handful of examples:

➤ Erskine May's *Treatise on the Law, Privileges, Proceedings and Usage of Parliament* (1844) is regarded as the 'Bible' of parliamentary practice, providing a detailed guide to its rules and practices.

➤ Walter Bagehot's *The English Constitution* (1867) set out the role of the cabinet and the prime minister, describing the latter as 'first among equals'.

➤ V. Dicey's *An Introduction to the Study of the Law of the Constitution* (1884) examined the relationship between the law and the nineteenth-century constitution, focusing on parliamentary sovereignty and the rule of law. It described a system of responsible cabinet government in a parliamentary democracy with a constitutional monarchy, where parliament was legally sovereign and the people politically sovereign.

European Union law

On 1 January 1973, the UK became a member of the European Economic Community. This was subsequently renamed the European Community (EC) and, after the Maastricht Treaty came into force in 1993, the European Union (EU). The treaties establishing the European Union, legislation emanating from the EU and judgments of the European Court of Justice have all become a part of the British constitution.

Basic principles of the British constitution

Four core principles formed the building blocks of the traditional British constitution:
➤ parliamentary sovereignty
➤ the rule of law
➤ the unitary state
➤ parliamentary government in a constitutional monarchy

Membership of the European Union has added a fifth main characteristic. Here it is discussed in the context of parliamentary sovereignty, with the nature of the EU and the UK's membership examined in greater depth in Chapter 11.

Parliamentary sovereignty

Parliamentary sovereignty is the cornerstone of the UK constitution. It states that the Westminster Parliament is the supreme law-making body. **Sovereignty** means legal supremacy: parliament has ultimate law-making authority. This legislative supremacy is constructed around three propositions:

> **Key term**
> ➢ **Sovereignty** Legal supremacy; absolute law-making authority that is not subject to a higher authority.

➢ Parliament can legislate on any subject of its choosing.
➢ Legislation cannot be overturned by any higher authority.
➢ No parliament can bind its successors.

The nature of parliamentary sovereignty and the constraints upon it are examined in detail in the next section of this chapter.

 Key concept
> ➢ **Parliamentary sovereignty** The doctrine that parliament has absolute legal authority within the state. It enjoys legislative supremacy: parliament may make law on any matter it chooses, its decisions may not be overturned by any higher authority and it may not bind its successors. Parliamentary sovereignty is a legal theory concerning the location of law-making authority. EU membership, devolution, the judicial review of legislation and the use of referendums raise questions about how meaningful it is. There is also a gap between legal theory and political reality, for no institution has absolute power to do as it wishes.

Parliamentary sovereignty states that the Westminster parliament is the supreme law-making body

The rule of law

The **rule of law** concerns the relationship between the state and its citizens, ensuring that state action is limited and responsible. All UK citizens must obey the law and are equal under it. The courts can hold government ministers, police officers and public officials accountable for their actions if they have acted outside the law or been negligent in their duties.

Laws passed by parliament must be interpreted and applied by an independent judiciary, free from political interference. The rights of citizens are thus protected from arbitrary executive action. Aggrieved citizens can take the government or a local authority to court if they feel they have been treated improperly. Individuals charged under the law are also entitled to a fair trial and should not be imprisoned without due regard for the legal process.

The rule of law is an essential feature of a liberal democracy. Parliamentary sovereignty theoretically enables parliament to abolish these rights. However, a sustained effort to overturn the key elements of the rule of law would be widely regarded as illegitimate and anti-democratic, making it untenable. As we will see below, the Human Rights Act (1998) gives greater protection to basic **civil liberties**.

Key terms

> **Rule of law** A system of rule where the relationship between the state and the individual is governed by law, protecting the individual from arbitrary state action.
> **Civil liberties** Fundamental individual rights and freedoms that ought to be protected from interference by the state.

Links to follow up

www.liberty-human-rights.org.uk — the website of Liberty, a civil liberties pressure group.

A unitary state

Constitutions may be classified according to whether they concentrate political power at the centre, or divide it between central and regional tiers of government. An important distinction is that between **unitary constitutions** and **federal constitutions**. The traditional British

Key concepts

> **Unitary constitution** A unitary constitution is one in which sovereignty is located at the centre. Central government has supremacy over other tiers of government, which it can reform or abolish. A unitary state is a centralised and homogeneous state: political power is concentrated in central government and all parts of the state are governed in the same way.
> **Federal constitution** A federal constitution divides sovereignty between (normally) two tiers of government. Power is shared between national government (the federal government) and regional government (the states). Regional government is protected by the constitution: it cannot be abolished or reformed significantly against its will.

constitution is a unitary constitution. Although the United Kingdom consists of four component nations — England, Scotland, Wales and Northern Ireland — it has been a highly centralised state in which sovereignty is located at Westminster. In a unitary constitution, subnational institutions do not have autonomous powers that are constitutionally safeguarded. Local government has had little power and regional government has historically been weak or non-existent.

In a federal constitution, such as in Germany or the USA, power is shared between national (i.e. federal) and regional (i.e. state) governments. Each tier of government is given specific powers and granted significant autonomy; one tier of government cannot abolish the other.

The UK has traditionally been described as a unitary state, but the label does not reflect fully its multinational character. An alternative is to see the UK as a union state. A **unitary state** exhibits a high degree of both centralisation and standardisation: all parts of the state are governed in the same way and share a common political culture. In a **union state**, by contrast, important political and cultural differences remain. These asymmetries reflect the different ways in which parts of the state were united.

Key terms

➤ **Unitary state** A homogeneous state in which power is concentrated at the political centre and all parts of the state are governed in the same way.

➤ **Union state** A state in which there are cultural differences and where, despite a strong centre, different parts of the state are governed in slightly different ways.

The component nations of the UK came together in different ways: Wales was invaded by England, Scotland joined the union through an international treaty, while Northern Ireland remained part of the UK after the establishment of the Irish Free State. Political and cultural differences survived. Scotland retained its own legal system, Wales its own language and Northern Ireland separate institutions and political parties. By the second half of the twentieth century, the interests of each nation were represented in London by a government department headed by a cabinet minister. But these departments were relatively weak and political power was concentrated at the centre.

As we will see below, the devolution of some policy responsibilities from central government to new institutions in Scotland, Wales and Northern Ireland has raised further questions about the classification of the UK state and its constitution. Vernon Bogdanor claims that the constitution is now 'quasi-federal'. In practice, but not in legal theory, Westminster no longer has the power to make domestic policy in many areas for Scotland. The Supreme Court can rule on which body has constitutional authority where disputes about competence arise, and other institutions have been created to manage relations between the UK government and the devolved bodies.

Parliamentary government in a constitutional monarchy

Under the UK constitution, government takes place through parliament under a **constitutional monarchy**. Government ministers are politically accountable to parliament and legally accountable to the Crown, and must face the verdict of the electorate every 5 years. Between general elections, a government relies upon its majority in the House of Commons to survive and enact its legislative programme.

The balance of power between the different institutions of the state has, of course, altered over time. The Glorious Revolution of 1689 established the supremacy of parliament over the monarchy. The key conventions of the constitutional monarchy gradually fell into place: the monarch retained formal powers (e.g. to assent to legislation) but their usage was constrained. The extension of the franchise enhanced the position of the House of Commons; it had overtaken the House of Lords as the predominant legislative chamber by the early twentieth century. Political parties emerged as key actors in the conduct of government. The FPTP electoral system and two-party system tended to produce single-party government. The majority party thus controlled the cabinet and exercised considerable discipline over its members in the House of Commons.

By the mid-nineteenth century, the UK political system was one of **cabinet government**. Cabinet was then the key policy-making body, but a century later considerable power was vested in the office of prime minister. This led some commentators to argue that **prime ministerial government** had replaced cabinet government (see Chapter 8).

Key terms

> **Constitutional monarchy** A political system in which the monarch is the formal head of state but the monarch's legal powers are exercised by government ministers.
> **Cabinet government** A system of government in which executive power is vested in a cabinet, whose members exercise collective responsibility, rather than a single office.
> **Parliamentary government** A political system in which government takes place through parliament, and in which the executive and legislative branches are fused.
> **Prime ministerial government** A system of government in which the prime minister is the dominant actor and is able to bypass the cabinet.

Sovereignty and the constitution

Characteristics of parliamentary sovereignty

The doctrine of parliamentary sovereignty establishes the Westminster Parliament as the supreme law-making body in the UK. According to legal theory:

> Parliament can legislate on any subject of its choosing.
> Legislation cannot be overturned by any higher authority.
> No parliament can bind its successors.

Law on any matter

There are no constitutional restrictions on the scope of parliament's legislative authority. Parliament's right to make retrospective laws and to reform itself provide useful examples. Concerning the former, the War Crimes Act (1991) gave the British courts the right to try people who became British citizens after 1990 for crimes they had committed in Nazi-occupied Europe in the Second World War (1939–45). Critics of the Act cautioned that evidence relating to events from over half a century ago could not be robust. Only one person has been convicted under the Act.

The Parliament Act (1911) is a prime example of parliament's right to reform itself. It stipulated that the House of Lords could no longer block bills approved by the House of Commons, but only delay them from entering into force for 2 years. This was reduced to 1 year in 1949. Parliamentary sovereignty effectively meant the sovereignty of the Commons. Opponents of the ban on fox hunting claimed that the Hunting Act (2004) was invalid as it was passed under the Parliament Act. But the Law Lords upheld the ban in the *Jackson* case (2005). Nick Clegg indicated in July 2012 that the government would invoke the Parliament Act if the upper House rejected the House of Lords Reform Bill (2012), but the bill was dropped after a rebellion in the Commons.

Legislative supremacy

The second element of parliamentary sovereignty is legislative supremacy. In many liberal democracies, a constitutional court (e.g. the Supreme Court in the United States) has the power to declare legislation unconstitutional and to annul it. But this is not the case in the UK. As parliament enjoys legislative supremacy, the courts cannot strike down statute law on the grounds that it is unconstitutional or that it conflicts with the common law.

Equality of legislation

Constitutional law has a higher status than other forms of law in many liberal democracies: it cannot be amended or repealed by simple majority votes in the legislature. This is not the case in the UK. Major changes to the constitution (e.g. devolution, reform of the House of Lords) have been enacted by simple majority votes in parliament. As no parliament may bind its successors, all legislation is of equal status. Legislation that brings about major constitutional change has the same status as, say, animal welfare law. It is not entrenched: one piece of legislation can be amended in the same way as any other.

Some constitutional experts, such as Vernon Bogdanor, argue that legislation of such constitutional significance should be considered *de facto* fundamental law. Although parliament retains the legal right to repeal the Scotland Act (1998), it is politically unthinkable that it would do so against the wishes of the Scottish Parliament and people. A similar view followed from *Thoburn* v *Sunderland City Council* (2002). The case concerned a campaign by market traders to use imperial rather than metric measures, but its main significance was the Law Lords' view that there was a hierarchy of Acts of Parliament: 'ordinary' statutes and 'constitutional' statutes, which had special status. Constitutional statutes — for example, the European Communities Act (1972), Human Rights Act (1998) and Scotland Act (1998) — should only be repealed when parliament does so by express provisions, rather than as an unintended consequence of a new law.

Fusion rather than separation of powers

Parliamentary sovereignty has contributed to the centralisation of power in the UK. In the USA, the three branches of government — the **legislature**, **executive** and **judiciary** — have different powers and different personnel. This is known as the **separation of powers**. But in the British legislature and executive there is a **fusion of powers**: members of the government are also Members of Parliament, and the executive dominates the legislature. It controls the parliamentary timetable and can normally use its parliamentary majority to push through its legislative programme.

Lord Hailsham, a Conservative who served three terms as Lord Chancellor, coined the term **elective dictatorship** in 1976 to describe the concentration of power in the executive branch. It implies that government can do whatever it wants because of parliamentary sovereignty, the FPTP electoral system that invariably gives one party a majority in the Commons, and executive dominance of the House of Commons. A government without a majority of the popular vote could change the constitution and introduce major policy change.

Key terms

> **Legislature** The branch of government responsible for making law.
> **Executive** The branch of government responsible for the implementation of policy.
> **Judiciary** The branch of government responsible for interpreting the law and deciding upon legal disputes.
> **Fusion of powers** The intermingling of personnel in the executive and legislative branches found in parliamentary systems.

Links to follow up

www.parliament.uk/business/publications — scroll down to 'Research publications' for guides to parliament and the constitution.

Lord Hailsham, who coined the term 'elective dictatorship'

Key concepts

> **Separation of powers** The separation of powers is the principle that the legislative, executive and judicial branches of government should be independent of each other. They should have different functions and distinctive memberships which should not overlap. The idea emerged in liberal thought as a means of preventing tyranny and the concentration of absolute power in one body (e.g. the Crown). The French philosopher Montesquieu (1689–1755) developed a theory of the separation of powers which influenced the American Founding Fathers. The US Constitution provides a rigid separation of powers. It also includes other checks and balances, such as a Bill of Rights, a bicameral legislature (i.e. one with two houses) and federalism.

> **Elective dictatorship** The excessive concentration of power in the executive branch. It implies that the only check on the power of government is the need to hold (and win) general elections at regular intervals. Beyond this, the government is regarded as free to do as it wishes because the constitution concentrates power in the executive branch and does not provide effective checks and balances.

Constraints on parliamentary sovereignty

The doctrine of parliamentary sovereignty means that, in legal theory, parliament can make or unmake any law of its choosing. In his *Commentaries on the Laws of England* (1765–69), Sir William Blackstone claimed that parliament 'can, in short, do every thing that is not naturally impossible'. In practice, a series of constraints limit parliament's ability to legislate successfully. The most significant political constraints on parliamentary sovereignty are:

> executive power
> membership of the European Union
> the Human Rights Act (1998)
> devolution
> referendums

**Key term**
> **Political sovereignty**
  Absolute political power.

Executive power

For students of politics, a major criticism of the doctrine of parliamentary sovereignty is that political reality is very different from legal theory. There are numerous informal and formal constraints on what parliament can do. Parliament is legally sovereign, but its authority derives from the electorate: were parliament systematically to ignore the wishes of the people, its legitimacy would be undermined. The doctrine of the mandate allows governments to claim that they have popular support for measures that featured in their election manifestos, but it also suggests that the right of governments to make law is less clear if their proposals have not received popular endorsement.

Parliamentary sovereignty concerns formal legal authority, whereas **political sovereignty** suggests absolute political power. The fusion of the legislative and executive branches means that parliamentary sovereignty gives the executive great power. As we have seen, this creates the potential for elective dictatorship. But government power is far from absolute. Government defeats in parliament are more numerous today than 40 years ago, although parliament still finds it difficult to impose its own will. The House of Lords has also become more assertive in the last decade. Defeat or the threat of defeat in the Lords forced the Blair government to amend bills on civil liberties issues such as the treatment of terrorist suspects, trial by jury and the introduction of the offence of incitement of racial hatred. Conventions and traditional modes of behaviour may also shape opinion on what is practicable and desirable. It is expected, for example, that proposals for significant constitutional reform should be put before the electorate before they are enacted.

European Union

The UK's membership of the EU provides the most significant challenge to the traditional view of parliamentary sovereignty. The legal basis for British membership of the then EEC was provided for by the European Communities Act (1972). Its provisions on Community (now EU) law in the UK have important constitutional implications:

➤ The Act gave legal force to existing and all future EU law. EU regulations do not need to receive the explicit assent of parliament before they become binding.

➤ The British courts apply EU law directly. Where questions of interpretation of EU law arise, they are referred to the European Court of Justice for a ruling.

➤ EU law has precedence over domestic British law. In the event of a conflict between the two, EU law must be applied. This may mean that British law has to be amended. The key example was provided in the 1990 *Factortame* case, which resulted in the Merchant Shipping Act (1988) being disapplied as its provisions restricting non-British citizens from registering fishing boats as British were contrary to Community law.

Recognition by British courts of the primacy of EU law fits uneasily with the legislative supremacy of parliament. But parliament retains sovereignty as it has the right to repeal the European Communities Act (1972), although the terms of British withdrawal from the EU would have to be negotiated. Section 18 of the European Union Act (2011) restated the sovereignty of parliament.

Membership of the European Union also impacts upon sovereignty in other ways:

➤ The range of policy areas in which the EU has competence (i.e. responsibility) has increased significantly since the Single European Act (1986). The EU has exclusive competence in trade, agriculture and fisheries policy. Policy responsibility for issues such as regional policy, working conditions and environmental policy is shared between the EU and its member states. The EU has gained competences in areas such as defence, immigration and monetary policy (although the UK has not adopted the euro) that have traditionally been the preserve of nation states.

➤ The Council of the European Union, in which ministers from national governments negotiate EU policy, increasingly takes decisions by qualified majority voting. This means that a member state opposing a policy decision cannot veto it. But unanimity remains the norm for particularly sensitive issues such as taxation and treaty change.

> The EU's supranational institutions have gained powers: the European Parliament acts as the EU's co-legislature with the Council of Ministers, and decisions of the European Court of Justice have furthered European integration.

Eurosceptics often speak of sovereignty in absolute terms: legislative supremacy cannot be diluted, for parliament either has ultimate authority or it does not. But they also focus on the democratic deficit within the EU — parliament and the electorate have little opportunity to hold EU decision-makers accountable. Eurosceptics would like to see policy competences restored to Westminster. For some Eurosceptics, withdrawal from the EU is the optimal means of restoring sovereignty.

Pro-Europeans argue that EU membership has had positive consequences. Instead of viewing sovereignty as a legal concept concerned with ultimate law-making authority, they define sovereignty in terms of effective influence and a practical capacity to act. The UK has **pooled sovereignty** rather than lost it. EU member states each delegate some of their sovereign authority to the EU and gain a greater capacity to achieve their policy objectives. By pooling sovereignty, the UK has achieved policy objectives such as the single European market which it could not have done alone, and more influence on the world stage.

Globalisation also means that no state can act fully independently on issues such as the environment, economic policy and terrorism. States exercise, and cede some of, their sovereignty by signing international treaties and joining international organisations.

 Key term

> **Globalisation** The widening and deepening interconnectedness between peoples and societies across the world in economic, political, social and cultural activities.

 Key concept

> **Pooled sovereignty** The decision-making authority of the member states of an international organisation is combined. This is said to enhance the collective power and achieve the joint interests of the member states, producing outcomes that could not be reached by individual state action or in a system in which member states could veto outcomes. The whole is greater than the sum of its parts.

Human Rights Act

The Human Rights Act (1998) incorporated the rights set out in the European Convention on Human Rights (ECHR) into UK statute law. All new legislation must be compatible with these rights and the British courts decide cases brought under the ECHR. Strictly speaking, parliamentary sovereignty is preserved by the Act because the courts cannot automatically strike down laws. If legislation is found to be incompatible with the ECHR, it is for parliament (in effect, ministers) to decide whether to either amend the law or launch an appeal. In practice, a law deemed contrary to human rights will lack moral authority and will be subject to further legal challenge. There had been 27 declarations of incompatibility by 2011, eight of which were overturned on appeal.

Devolution

Devolution means that, in many policy areas, Westminster no longer makes laws that apply across the entire territory of the UK. The Scottish Parliament, Northern Ireland Assembly and, since 2011, Welsh Assembly have primary legislative authority on devolved matters such as education and health.

Key concept

➤ **Devolution** Devolution is the transfer of political power from central government to regional or subnational government(s) with limited territorial jurisdiction. Sovereign authority is not divided but remains at the centre. The regional tier of government is subordinate to central government and can be changed or removed by it. This contrasts with federalism, where the autonomy of regional government is protected in a codified constitution. Legislative devolution is the most significant form of devolution because it involves the creation of separate parliaments with law-making powers.

Westminster no longer makes law on devolved matters, but it retains legislative supremacy. It has sole authority over 'reserved matters' such as the UK economy, social security and the constitution. The UK Parliament can also decide to legislate on Scottish, Welsh and Northern Irish matters, and abolish the devolved assemblies, but it would be politically difficult to do so in the face of elite and public opposition.

Many Scottish political commentators view parliamentary sovereignty as an English doctrine and regard **popular sovereignty** as an important element of Scottish political culture. The Scottish Parliament does not have the authority to change the UK's constitution, but the UK government and Scottish government agreed that a referendum on independence will be held in 2014.

Links to follow up

http://devolutionmatters.wordpress.com — blog examining devolution developments by the academic Alan Trench.

Referendums

Referendums have been proposed by UK governments on a number of constitutional issues. Only two UK-wide referendums have been held: the 1975 vote in favour of continued membership of the European Economic Community and the 2011 vote against introducing

Key terms

➤ **Popular sovereignty** Supreme authority resides with the people.
➤ **Referendum** A vote in which the electorate is asked to express its view on a specific issue of public policy.

The Scottish Parliament in session in Edinburgh

the alternative vote for Westminster elections. But devolution for Scotland, Wales and Northern Ireland was approved in referendums in these nations. The Blair governments proposed referendums on the European single currency and the EU Constitution but abandoned them when, first, they decided against joining the euro and, second, voters in France and the Netherlands rejected the EU Constitution. The European Union Act (2011) requires a referendum to be held if powers are transferred to the European Union.

Adherents to the traditional view of parliamentary sovereignty oppose referendums because they place decision making in the hands of the electorate rather than MPs and peers. The increased use of referendums suggests a shift towards popular sovereignty, but parliament retains ultimate authority: although parliament risks damaging its legitimacy if it ignores the outcome, referendums are still advisory rather than binding.

The main parties appear to have accepted that, because devolution was supported in referendums in the late 1990s, further major changes to the powers of the devolved bodies should also be put to a popular vote. However, the refusal of the Labour government to hold a referendum on the Lisbon Treaty, having earlier promised one on the EU Constitution, confirmed that it is up to the government to decide if an issue warrants a referendum — and governments are loath to hold referendums that they might lose.

Strengths and weaknesses of the traditional constitution

Strengths

The UK's traditional constitution is known as the **Westminster model**. This not only provides a description of the workings of the British political system but also claims (or assumes) that this is how a political system ought to operate. Supporters of the traditional constitutional settlement argue that it has a number of enduring strengths. While they recognise that improvements are required, they believe that reform should be limited and pragmatic. Changes should work with the grain of the existing constitution rather than overhaul it.

Key term

➤ **Westminster model** A form of government exemplified by the British political system, in which parliament is sovereign, the executive and legislature are fused and political power is centralised.

Adaptability

One perceived strength of the traditional constitution is its proven worth. The constitution has proved its value by operating effectively over many years. Pragmatic reforms, introduced where there is a clear case for change, have enabled the constitution to adapt to changed circumstances. This flexibility is another positive feature, as the mechanics of the constitution can be adapted smoothly and speedily.

Evolution

Conservatives view the constitution as an organic body of rules rather than an artificial creation. It has evolved over time and reflects the history and enduring values of the British people. The rules and practices that make up the constitution form a coherent and intelligible whole.

Strong government

The traditional constitution provides for strong and effective government. The doctrine of parliamentary sovereignty establishes supreme authority within the political system. But it is the government, particularly the core executive, rather than Parliament that is at the heart of the policy-making process. The process of government is conducted by political parties: the cabinet is party-based and the governing party exercises significant control over the legislative process in the House of Commons. Power is thus concentrated at the centre, enabling the government of the day to implement most of its political objectives. Ministers, not judges or bureaucrats (or the people), make crucial political decisions.

Accountability

Strong government is also responsible government. The government is accountable to parliament, which scrutinises its activities, and responsive to the electorate. In a general election in a two-party system, voters effectively choose between alternative governments. The FPTP electoral system usually gives the winning party a parliamentary majority, allowing it to fulfil its mandate. An unpopular government will pay the price at the polls. Government is also responsible, as the rule of law protects citizens against arbitrary power.

Viewpoint Was the traditional British constitution effective?

YES
- It was tried and tested, evolving in response to genuine needs.
- Its rules and principles added up to a coherent whole: the Westminster model.
- It provided a clear centre of authority, ensuring strong government.
- It provided for responsible government that is accountable to the electorate.
- The rule of law protected the rights of citizens against the state.
- It was sufficiently flexible to accommodate political and social change.

NO
- It was outdated, with pre-democratic elements unsuitable for a modern liberal democracy.
- It produced an excessive centralisation of power, with few checks and balances.
- It provided few opportunities for citizens to get involved in decision making.
- The rights afforded to individuals were weak and not adequately protected.
- It was prone to manipulation by single-party governments.

Weaknesses

Critics of the traditional constitution argue that it had a number of serious weaknesses that could only be rectified by a significant reform programme.

Lack of clarity

The uncodified nature of the constitution creates problems of clarity and interpretation. It is not always clear when a government has acted unconstitutionally: conventions on ministerial responsibility, for example, are unclear. Parliament, which is controlled by the government of the day, is the final arbiter of the constitution. There is no constitutional court to check the power of the state and defend civil liberties.

Concentration of power

Power is concentrated dangerously at the centre. There are few safeguards against the arbitrary exercise of state power. Parliamentary sovereignty and the absence of a codified constitution mean that even the key tenets of the rule of law are not fully protected. A government with a strong majority can force through legislation undermining civil liberties and weakening other institutions. It can overturn traditional principles and practices in response to populist sentiment. There are insufficient checks and balances, and there is no formal separation of powers. The executive exercises considerable control over the legislative process. Neither local nor subnational government has constitutionally protected status.

Outdated and undemocratic

Critics of the traditional constitution depict it as outdated, inefficient and undemocratic. Conventions are unclear and key elements of the common law, notably the royal prerogative, date back to a pre-modern era. The House of Lords is also a throwback to a pre-democratic era: the hereditary principle cannot be justified in a liberal democratic state.

The constitution under pressure

For much of the twentieth century, there was a broad political consensus supportive of the constitution and the key institutions of the UK state. The Westminster model was held up as a paragon of constitutional theory and practice. The constitution evolved in a largely peaceful and pragmatic fashion. Governments of different political persuasions were happy to work within the existing constitutional framework. Political elites and the electorate regarded the constitution as legitimate and effective.

Early twentieth century

At times, however, the constitution was the focus of serious political dispute. The 'Irish Question' came close to provoking civil war before a solution of sorts was reached in 1921–22 with the creation of the Irish Free State (which became the Republic of Ireland in 1949) and a six-county Northern Ireland that remained part of the UK. A constitutional crisis also arose when the House of Lords refused to support the Liberal government's budget of 1909. It was resolved when the Parliament Act (1911) reduced the powers of the House of Lords.

The 1970s

The 1970s brought further challenges to the traditional constitution, including the decline of the two-party system, the 'Troubles' in Northern Ireland and EEC membership. Conservative politician Lord Hailsham warned that executive dominance of the legislature created an elective dictatorship and proposed a codified constitution. Political scientist S. E. Finer believed that the FPTP electoral system produced adversarial politics in which parties entering government systematically overturned the policies of their predecessors, creating instability. He advocated proportional representation (PR) as a remedy.

Thatcher and Major

The Conservative governments of Margaret Thatcher (1979–90) and John Major (1990–97) had important constitutional consequences. There was a further centralisation of political power, evident in the abolition of the Greater London Council. In areas where the Conservatives maintained the constitutional status quo — by refusing demands for Scottish devolution, for example — they were criticised for undermining the legitimacy and efficiency of the traditional constitution. The FPTP electoral system came under further pressure, for it enabled the Conservatives to carry out radical reforms having won four successive elections without securing a majority of the popular vote.

In the 1990s, traditional methods of government gave way to new forms of **governance**. Formal institutions such as government departments and local authorities had been responsible for allocating public funds and implementing policy decisions, but many of these functions were now transferred to quangos. Nationalised industries were privatised

Key term

➤ **Governance** A form of decision making in which a wide range of institutions, networks and relationships are involved.

and new regulatory agencies established. Public trust in parliament and politicians waned as **sleaze** cases hit the headlines. Not even the monarchy was immune from this loss of faith in the traditional constitution.

The case for reform

In response, a coherent case for constitutional reform was developed by bodies such as the pressure group Charter 88 (now Unlock Democracy). It was taken up by the Liberal Democrats and, most significantly, the Labour Party. For much of its history, Labour had viewed constitutional reform as an unwelcome distraction from its main goal of improving conditions for the working class. Now it embraced a liberal perspective on reform which focused on a number of key themes:

➢ **Modernisation.** Institutions such as parliament, the executive and the civil service were using outdated and inefficient procedures that were in need of reform.

➢ **Democratisation.** Participation in the political process would be encouraged through electoral reform and greater use of referendums.

➢ **Decentralisation.** Decision-making powers would be devolved to new institutions in Scotland and Wales, and the role of local government enhanced.

➢ **Rights.** The rights of citizens would be strengthened and safeguarded.

Labour advocated policies such as devolution, a Bill of Rights and reform of the House of Lords, but it did not support electoral reform for Westminster or a written constitution. Labour and the Liberal Democrats worked together to develop proposals for Scottish devolution, and after Labour's 1997 general election victory, senior Liberal Democrats sat on a cabinet subcommittee examining constitutional reform.

Reforming the constitution: the Labour governments, 1997–2010

The constitutional reforms introduced by the Labour governments (1997–2010) are discussed in detail in other chapters. Here, the main reforms are outlined and their significance assessed (see Table 6.1). Most of the reforms were introduced by Blair's first government (1997–2001). The pace and extent of reform then fell away, although major changes to the judiciary were announced in Blair's second term. Constitutional reform was an early priority for the Brown government, but attention shifted to the financial crisis from 2008.

Human rights

The Human Rights Act (HRA, 1998) enshrined most of the provisions of the European Convention on Human Rights (ECHR) in UK law. The rights protected by the convention include:

➢ the right to life

➢ the right to liberty and security of person

Table 6.1 Labour governments' constitutional reforms, 1997–2010

Area	Reforms	Frustrated or incomplete reforms
Rights	Human Rights Act (1998) incorporates European Convention on Human Rights into UK law. Freedom of Information Act (2000) gives greater access to information held by public bodies.	Derogation from Article 5 of Human Rights Act (2001–05) overturned. New Bill of Rights and Duties was proposed but no legislation was introduced.
Devolution	Scottish Parliament with primary legislative and tax-raising powers. Welsh Assembly with secondary legislative powers. Northern Ireland Assembly with primary legislative powers.	Proposal for regional assemblies in England dropped after 2004 'no' vote in referendum in northeast England.
Decentralisation	Elected mayor of London and London Assembly. Elected mayors in some English authorities.	Only 12 local authorities adopted the elected mayor model.
Electoral reform	New electoral systems for devolved assemblies, European Parliament and elected mayors.	No action on 1998 Jenkins Report on electoral reform for Westminster.
Parliament	All but 92 hereditary peers removed from the House of Lords. Limited reforms to business of House of Commons.	Unable to forge consensus on next stage of House of Lords reform. MPs' expenses scandal damaged trust in parliament. Some *Governance of Britain* proposals not enacted.
Judiciary	Supreme Court started work in 2009. New judicial appointments system. Changes to role of Lord Chancellor.	Reforms of office of Lord Chancellor were diluted.
Participation	Referendums on devolution in Scotland, Wales and Northern Ireland. Referendums on mayor of London and regional assembly for northeast England. Political Parties, Elections and Referendums Act (2000) regulates conduct of parties and elections.	Proposed referendums on electoral reform, European single currency and EU Constitution were shelved. Trials of alternative voting methods produced mixed results.

> the right to a fair trial
> respect for private and family life
> freedom of thought and expression
> freedom of peaceful assembly and association
> the right to marry and found a family
> freedom from torture and degrading treatment
> freedom from discrimination

The HRA requires the British government to ensure that legislation is compatible with the convention. All bills introduced at Westminster (and in the devolved assemblies) must receive a declaration of compatibility with the ECHR from lawyers. UK courts and tribunals decide cases brought under the convention — before the HRA, cases were heard by the European Court of Human Rights in Strasbourg. The UK courts can declare legislation incompatible with the ECHR and overturn executive decisions. But the courts cannot automatically overturn legislation that is declared incompatible: it is up to ministers to decide whether to amend it through a fast-track process in parliament or appeal against the court's decision.

The government introduced a derogation (i.e. a temporary exemption) from Article 5 of the ECHR, the right to liberty and security, in 2001 to allow the indefinite detention without charge of those foreign nationals suspected of terrorist activity who could not be deported to a safe country. This ended in 2005 after the House of Lords ruled that it was unlawful because it discriminated against foreign nationals.

Links to follow up

www.justice.gov.uk — website of the Ministry of Justice, responsible for human rights, democracy and the legal system.

Devolution

Devolution involves the transfer of powers — legislative, executive and tax-raising — from central government to subnational institutions. In 1999 power was devolved to new institutions in Scotland, Wales and Northern Ireland, following 'yes' votes in referendums in each nation. The new system was one of asymmetric devolution — rather than following a standardised blueprint, the devolved bodies have different powers and distinctive features. Devolution has been a process rather than an event, with further powers devolved since 1999.

The Scottish Parliament has primary legislative and tax-varying powers. It and the Scottish government have sole responsibility for policy on issues such as education, health and local government. The Calman Commission (2007–09) recommended the devolution of further powers. The Conservative–Liberal Democrat coalition enacted these changes. The National Assembly for Wales, commonly referred to as the Welsh Assembly, was initially weaker. It had secondary legislative and executive powers, but not primary legislative authority. This meant that it could only fill in the details of, and implement, legislation passed by Westminster in policy areas such as education and health. In 2006, Labour paved the way for the Assembly to gain primary legislative powers — which duly occurred after a referendum in 2011. The Northern Ireland Assembly has legislative powers over a similar range of policy areas to the Scottish Parliament, but does not have tax-raising powers. Special procedures exist in the Assembly to ensure cross-community support.

Constitutional implications of devolution

Devolution has had a significant impact on the traditional constitutional settlement. The UK no longer fits the classic definition of a unitary state — although even the pre-devolution UK was more like a union state. Nor does the UK fit the standard definition of a federal state: that is, a state in which power is shared between different tiers of government, with autonomous subnational institutions enjoying significant authority.

The new constitutional settlement has **quasi-federal** features: central government does not make some domestic policy for parts of the UK and disputes over competences

> ### Key concept
>
> ➤ **Quasi-federalism** Quasi-federalism occurs when the central government of a unitary state devolves some of its powers to subnational governments. It exhibits some of the features of a unitary state and some of a federal state. In legal theory there is one supreme legal authority located at the centre, as in a unitary state. But in practice the centre no longer makes domestic policy for some parts of the state and it would be difficult politically for the centre to abolish the subnational tier of government. Different policy frameworks operate within the state. Senior judges rule on questions concerning the division of competences.

are decided by senior judges. New bodies were created to handle relations between the UK government and the devolved bodies (i.e. intergovernmental relations). The legislation creating the devolved institutions, however, sought to safeguard parliamentary sovereignty and place limits on the powers of the new bodies. Westminster remains sovereign and retains the right to overrule or abolish the devolved institutions. The legislation also identified 'reserved powers' that remain exclusive to Westminster. These include crucial areas such as economic policy, foreign and defence policy, and constitutional affairs.

Devolution has also raised questions about how England should be governed. There is, for example, no simple answer to the 'West Lothian Question', which asks why Scottish MPs at Westminster should be able to vote on purely English matters when English MPs can no longer vote on matters devolved to the Scottish Parliament. The Blair governments' policy of creating (weak) assemblies in the English regions was abandoned after a 'no' vote in a referendum in northeast England in 2004.

Decentralisation

The Blair governments also made changes to local government in England, notably in London. Here an executive mayor has powers in areas such as the environment and transport, the latter leading to the creation of a congestion charge for motorists entering central London. The directly elected London Assembly scrutinises the mayor's actions. All local authorities

In London, the mayor has powers in areas such as transport, which in 2003 led to the introduction of the congestion charge

were obliged to reform their political management, but by 2010 only 12 had adopted the government's preferred option of a directly elected mayor. (Five more authorities established an elected mayor under the Conservative–Liberal Democrat coalition.)

Electoral reform

The Blair governments' record on electoral reform was a mixed one. Proportional representation was introduced for elections to the Scottish Parliament, Welsh Assembly, Northern Ireland Assembly and European Parliament, and for directly elected mayors in a number of towns and cities. However, no action was taken to change the FPTP system used in general elections. The government set up an Independent Commission on the Voting System chaired by Roy Jenkins to examine the case for using proportional representation in general elections. The Jenkins Report (1998) recommended a mixed electoral system called 'AV plus' in which most MPs would be elected by FPTP and a minority by the alternative vote system. The government did not endorse the report and a promised referendum on electoral reform was never held.

The new electoral systems introduced in the UK are not uniform (see Chapter 2). The additional member system is used in elections for the Scottish Parliament and Welsh Assembly. This is a mixed electoral system in which a majority of representatives are elected by FPTP in single-member constituencies, with the remainder elected by a regional list system of proportional representation in multi-member constituencies. The latter are 'top-up seats' allocated to political parties on a corrective basis. A closed list system of proportional representation is used in Great Britain for elections to the European Parliament. Electors cast one vote for their favoured party in multi-member regions, but they cannot choose between candidates on the party's list.

Directly elected mayors, such as in London, are elected by the supplementary vote in which electors indicate their first and second preferences. All but the top two candidates are eliminated and second preferences cast for them are added to their total. The single transferable vote system is used to elect the Northern Ireland Assembly and, following a decision by the Scottish Parliament, Scottish local authorities. Electors rank their preferred candidates in multi-member constituencies. To win, a candidate must achieve a fixed quota of votes; votes are redistributed until all seats are filled.

Links to follow up

www.electoral-reform.org.uk — the website of the Electoral Reform Society, a pressure group that promotes electoral reform.

Parliamentary reform

The House of Lords Act (1999) abolished the right of all but 92 hereditary peers (i.e. those who inherited their titles) to sit and vote in the upper house. This was intended as the first stage of the reform process. The Lords now comprised mainly life peers, and no political party had an overall majority. But the Labour governments made little progress with stage two of the reforms, when the final composition and powers of the reformed House of Lords would be settled. MPs and peers rejected a series of options for reform, including an all-appointed Lords and a hybrid house containing both elected and appointed peers. In 2007 MPs voted for a 100% elected or 80% elected House of Lords, but no legislation followed in the short term. Lords reform is examined in more detail in Chapter 7.

Blair's initiatives on reform of the House of Commons were less spectacular. Changes to Prime Minister's Question Time and the working hours of the Commons, plus additional sittings in Westminster Hall modernised proceedings. Parliament was given greater opportunity to scrutinise the government's legislative proposals. Devolution also changed procedures: matters devolved to the Scottish Parliament cannot, for example, be dealt with at Westminster.

The Brown government gave greater priority to reform of the Commons. The 2010 'Governance of Britain' Green Paper aimed to limit the powers of the executive and make it more accountable to Parliament. Reforms such as House of Commons hearings for some public appointments followed. But progress stalled as attention turned to the financial crisis. However, the 2009 MPs' expenses scandal prompted further action to restore the reputation of parliament. An independent Parliamentary Standards Authority was created to manage MPs' expenses.

The Reform of the House of Commons Committee (2009), chaired by Tony Wright, recommended that:

➢ chairs of select committees should be elected by backbenchers
➢ a backbench business committee should determine the business of the House of Commons for 1 day a week
➢ a procedure petitions committee should select issues for debate that had been suggested by the public via e-petitions

These proposals were accepted by MPs but did not come into force until after the 2010 general election.

The judiciary

The Constitutional Reform Act (2005) focused on judicial reform. A Supreme Court, which started work in 2009, became the UK's highest court and removed the judicial role of the House of Lords. This enhanced the separation of powers, but the Supreme Court does not have the authority to strike down legislation. The government had intended to abolish the office of Lord Chancellor and so bring about the separation of the legislative, executive and judicial functions of the office. The Lord Chancellor was a member of the cabinet (with responsibility for the law and rights), the legislature (as speaker of the House of Lords) and head of the judiciary. But it proved difficult to disentangle these roles and the office was retained, shorn of some of its some judicial responsibilities, such as the appointment of judges. A Judicial Appointments Commission is now responsible for the latter (see Chapter 9).

Links to follow up

www.judiciary.gov.uk — official site of the judiciary of England and Wales.

Freedom of information

The Freedom of Information Act (2000) gave individuals a general right of access to personal information held on them by public bodies. But there are a number of crucial exemptions. Information can be withheld on the grounds of national security or public safety, while citizens do not have an automatic right to see the policy advice provided to ministers. In 2009 the government exercised its right to veto a decision by the Information Tribunal that the minutes of cabinet meetings concerning the legality of the 2003 invasion of Iraq should be released. Politicians, journalists and citizens have used the Act to gain access to information on matters such as government policy, the activities of local authorities and police forces, school inspections and the performance of hospital surgeons.

Links to follow up

www.ico.gov.uk — website of the Information Commissioner's Office.

Elections, referendums and parties

The Political Parties, Elections and Referendums Act (2000) established an independent Electoral Commission to administer elections and referendums, set an upper limit on national campaign expenditure by political parties, required parties to disclose donors and donations, and banned foreign donations. But discussions on a new system of state funding for political parties failed to produce agreement. The Blair governments also encouraged alternative methods of voting (e.g. all-postal ballots) to increase turnout, although these led to concerns about electoral fraud.

The Blair governments used referendums more frequently than any of their predecessors. Devolution referendums were held in Scotland, Wales and Northern Ireland, while a number of English towns and cities held local referendums on creating a directly elected mayor. But proposed referendums on electoral reform for Westminster, membership of the European single currency and the EU Constitution did not take place. Some local authorities used legislation allowing them to hold referendums on local issues. A referendum in Manchester in 2008, for example, voted against a congestion charge.

Links to follow up

www.ucl.ac.uk/constitution-unit — website of the Constitution Unit, an academic research centre that provides authoritative analysis of constitutional issues. The 'Monitor' newsletter provides regular updates.

A new constitutional settlement

The Labour governments (1997–2010) introduced the most important package of constitutional reform in modern British history. Commentators talked of a 'new constitutional settlement' replacing the traditional constitution. Many of the rules, procedures and principles of the traditional constitution were affected. Few key institutions remained untouched. Devolution, new electoral systems, the Human Rights Act and reform of the House of Lords changed the constitutional landscape. Overall, the reforms brought about a rebalancing of the relationship between state institutions and between the citizen and the state. More checks and balances were introduced: the Human Rights Act increased judicial review of legislation, the reformed House of Lords proved more willing to amend or block government legislation, electoral reform produced coalition government in the devolved assemblies and they departed from central government policy frameworks.

Impact of the reforms

Labour's reforms enhanced British democracy, although falling turnout in general elections and low levels of public trust in the political system were causes for concern. However, the reforms were evolutionary rather than revolutionary. Change was introduced in a piecemeal rather than 'big bang' fashion. The Labour governments did not produce a written constitution or a tailor-made UK Bill of Rights. Significantly, the underlying principles of the British constitution were adapted rather than overturned. Labour was careful to avoid too many direct challenges to the core principles of the constitution. The impact of the reforms on four principal features of the constitution was as follows:

> **Uncodified constitution.** The reforms did not introduce a codified constitution, but they did establish key principles and procedures (e.g. human rights, devolution) in statute law.
> **Parliamentary sovereignty.** The legislative supremacy of parliament has been preserved, but parliament has ceded significant powers. The Scotland Act (1998) states that the Westminster Parliament remains sovereign and retains the power to make laws for Scotland. It can also repeal the Act itself. However, Westminster will not legislate on matters devolved to the Scottish Parliament, so parliamentary sovereignty no longer means a real power to make law across the UK. The Human Rights Act (1998) also preserved the sovereignty of parliament. If the courts find legislation incompatible with the ECHR, that legislation is not automatically struck down. It is up to parliament to decide on amendments. Similarly, the Constitutional Reform Act (2005) states that the Supreme Court cannot overturn legislation. These important statutes have, in practice if not in theory, the status of fundamental law because they are unlikely to be overturned without the express approval of parliament and the electorate.
> **The rule of law.** The power of the state was restricted and the rights of citizens were strengthened by the Human Rights Act (1998) and the Freedom of Information Act (2000), although these did not go as far as some reformers had hoped for.
> **The unitary state.** Asymmetric devolution means that the component parts of the UK are governed in different ways. Policy differences have also emerged, so elements of the welfare state are no longer uniform across the UK.

Appraisal of the reforms

When judged in relation to the themes of modernisation, democratisation, decentralisation and rights, the verdict on Labour's reforms is mixed:

> **Modernisation.** Most hereditary peers were removed from the House of Lords, but 92 remained and reform was incomplete. Some of the proposals for reform of prerogative powers were not put into action. The constitution remained uncodified.

> **Democratisation.** New electoral systems were introduced for the devolved assemblies, European elections and mayoral elections. But FPTP remained in place for Westminster elections and continues to produce disproportional outcomes. Elections and political parties were better regulated, but turnout fell and public faith in politicians was low.

> **Decentralisation.** Power was devolved to new institutions in Scotland, Wales and Northern Ireland, bringing government closer to the people. But local government remained weak and questions about how England should be governed were not addressed effectively. In other respects, political power became still more concentrated in Downing Street and the executive continued to dominate the legislature.

> **Rights.** The Human Rights Act (1998) put the rights of citizens on a stronger statutory footing and has been used by the courts to put limits on state power. But other measures restricted civil liberties (e.g. the right to trial by jury).

⟷ Stretch and challenge

Majoritarian and consensual democracy

Dutch political scientist Arend Lijphart located liberal democracies on a spectrum with majoritarian democracy at one extreme and consensual democracy at the other. In a majoritarian democracy, political power is concentrated at the centre and there are few limits to its exercise. Common features include a flexible constitution, a FPTP electoral system, a two-party system, a dominant executive and a unitary state. In a consensual democracy, political power is diffused. Typical features are a rigid constitution, proportional representation, multiparty politics, the separation of powers and a federal system. There are also important differences in political culture. Politics is adversarial in a majoritarian democracy, whereas power sharing is the norm in a consensual democracy (see 'Distinguish between: majoritarian and consensual democracy' box).

The British Westminster model is the archetypal majoritarian democracy, while Switzerland is a leading example of consensual democracy. The constitutional reforms of the Labour governments introduced elements of consensual democracy, notably devolution and the Human Rights Act. But the UK is still close to the majoritarian extreme. Parliamentary sovereignty remains the guiding constitutional principle, the fusion of the legislature and executive has not been disturbed greatly, and the FPTP system is still used for Westminster elections.

Question

To what extent has the UK moved from a majoritarian to a consensual democracy?

Links to follow up

http://democraticaudituk.wordpress.com — the Democratic Audit, an independent research unit, analyses the state of British democracy.

Majoritarian and consensual democracy

Distinguish between

Majoritarian democracy

➤ Uncodified constitution which can be amended by a simple legislative majority.
➤ Dominant executive controls the legislative branch.
➤ Legislature determines the constitutionality of its laws.
➤ Unitary state with power concentrated at the centre.
➤ FPTP.
➤ Adversarial two-party system.

Consensual democracy

➤ Codified constitution which can be amended only by a weighted majority.
➤ Balance of power between the executive and legislative branches.
➤ Laws can be struck down by a constitutional court.
➤ Federal system with power divided between tiers of government.
➤ Proportional representation.
➤ Cooperative multiparty system.

Viewpoint

Did Labour's reforms (1997–2010) produce a new constitutional settlement?

YES

● They were the most extensive package of reforms in modern times, with few institutions untouched.
● Reform is an ongoing process whose effects will continue to be felt for years to come.
● The balance of power between institutions changed, with further checks and balances introduced.
● The rights of citizens were strengthened and given greater protection.
● Key legislation has *de facto* status as fundamental law and is likely to endure.

NO

● They were evolutionary rather than revolutionary, developing rather than dismantling the key principles of the constitution.
● They did not add up to a coherent whole and lacked an overarching vision.
● They were unfinished and raised new problems (e.g. the government of England).
● More radical changes were rejected or not attempted, notably electoral reform for Westminster and a codified constitution.
● Parliament remains sovereign and power is still concentrated in the executive.

Criticisms of Labour's reforms

Labour's reforms were subject to criticism from two broad perspectives: a liberal perspective which argued that the reforms did not go far enough, and a conservative perspective which held that Labour had damaged the traditional British constitution. Both accused the Blair and Brown governments of incoherence: changes were introduced without an overarching philosophy or sufficient thought on their impact. So, little consideration was given to how devolution might impact upon the role of the House of Lords. In addition, some reforms were incomplete. Labour did not deliver on its early promises on an elected House of Lords, devolution in England and a referendum on electoral reform for Westminster. The Blair governments' reform programme largely ran out of steam after 2001. Brown tried to pick up the pace on some issues that had not been addressed fully (e.g. prerogative powers) but delivered little as the economic situation worsened. In its 2010 manifesto, Labour proposed referendums on electoral reform and reform of the House of Lords.

Liberal critique

Labour's reforms grew out of a liberal agenda for constitutional change. But proponents of the liberal model of constitutional reform were critical of both the details and vision of Labour's reforms. They questioned the coherence and comprehensiveness of the new constitutional settlement. Although much changed, liberal reformers argued that Blair and Brown had adopted a minimalist rather than a maximalist reform agenda. They were also concerned by perceived infringements of civil liberties, particularly after the 11 September 2001 terrorist attacks on New York and Washington and those in London on 7 July 2005.

An alternative maximalist reform package might include:

➢ a written constitution
➢ a Bill of Rights
➢ a federal state with regional assemblies in the English regions and a federal parliament at Westminster
➢ a wholly-elected upper chamber of parliament
➢ proportional representation for general elections
➢ state funding of political parties
➢ a transfer of power from quangos to elected local authorities
➢ reform of the monarchy (or its abolition)

This liberal perspective is associated with the Liberal Democrats, who support many of the demands listed above. Having worked with Labour on constitutional reform in the 1990s, they became more critical after the 2001 election.

Links to follow up

www.unlockdemocracy.org.uk — website of Unlock Democracy, an influential advocate of liberal constitutional reform.

Conservative critique

The conservative perspective supports the traditional constitution, believing that it required only limited reform. Its critique argues that Labour's reforms damaged the fabric of the constitution so that its component parts no longer form a coherent and effective whole. The reforms also brought new problems in their wake. Devolution raised questions about the government of England; the Human Rights Act increased the political role of the judiciary and opened up a can of worms on the nature of rights such as privacy. The academic and Conservative peer Lord (Philip) Norton is a leading advocate of this conservative critique.

Before the 1997 general election, the conservative critique was most associated with the Conservative Party. It opposed Labour's proposals for reform of the House of Lords, electoral reform and the incorporation of the European Convention of Human Rights into domestic law. The Conservatives claimed that legislative devolution would bring about the break-up of the Union. But the Conservatives adopted a more pragmatic position on many areas of constitutional reform following their election defeat in 1997. After the 'yes' results in the Scottish and Welsh referendums, the Conservatives accepted devolution and pledged to work constructively with the new institutions.

The conservative perspective on the constitution has often been a defensive one. But with much of the traditional constitution changed by the Labour governments, some conservatives (e.g. the journalist Simon Heffer) argue that radical reforms are needed to restore parliamentary sovereignty. These include the return from the EU to Westminster of substantial policy responsibilities, or withdrawal from the EU. Some conservatives also support an English Parliament, or even English independence.

Links to follow up

www.nortonview.wordpress.com — a blog by Conservative peer and constitutional expert Lord Norton.

The Conservative–Lib Dem coalition

The Conservatives and Liberal Democrats formed a coalition government after the 2010 general election. There was some common ground on constitutional reforms in their election manifestos. Both parties proposed reform of the House of Lords, supported proposals made by independent commissions for the devolution of further powers to Scotland and Wales, and reform of the House of Commons, although the Liberal Democrats attached greater importance to constitutional reform than the Conservatives. There were, however, important differences on electoral reform and the Human Rights Act (see Table 6.2).

These differences necessitated compromises in the coalition agreement. The Conservatives opposed electoral reform for Westminster while the Liberal Democrats supported the single transferable vote system. They agreed to hold a referendum on introducing the alternative vote system, but the two parties would be free to campaign on opposing sides. In other areas of dispute, the coalition agreement proposed commissions to examine the West Lothian Question and a UK Bill of Rights. The commission on a Bill of Rights failed to reach consensus, although a majority of its members favoured a new UK Bill of Rights that incorporated and built on the ECHR.

The constitutional reforms proposed by the coalition government are outlined here and the progress made by early 2013 assessed (see Table 6.2).

Electoral reform

A referendum on replacing the first-past-the-post system with the alternative vote for general elections was held in May 2011. The Liberal Democrats supported AV and the Conservatives campaigned aggressively for a 'no' vote. The referendum produced a 68% vote against AV, a significant setback for the prospects of electoral reform.

Table 6.2 The Conservative–Liberal Democrat coalition and constitutional reform

Area	2010 Conservative and Lib Dem manifestos	Coalition agreement	Progress by early 2013
Electoral reform	Cons: retain FPTP; Lib Dems: introduce PR.	Bill on alternative vote for general elections if approved in a referendum.	68% 'no' vote in May 2011 referendum.
House of Lords	Cons: build consensus for mainly-elected Lords; Lib Dems: wholly-elected Lords.	Committee to propose a wholly or mainly elected House of Lords.	Joint Committee, White Paper and draft bill, but plans dropped in 2012.
House of Commons	Lib Dems: fixed-term parliaments; Cons: greater parliamentary control of royal prerogative.	Five-year fixed-term parliaments.	Fixed-term Parliaments Act 2011 established 5-year fixed-term parliaments.
	Both: smaller House of Commons.	Reduce number of MPs to 600.	Boundary commission reviews began, but Lib Dems withdrew support in 2012.
	Both: right of recall of MPs in event of serious wrongdoing.	Power of recall of MPs in event of serious wrongdoing.	2011 White Paper and Draft Bill.
Devolution	Both: support Calman Commission recommendations on new powers for Scottish Parliament.	Implement Calman Commission recommendations on new powers for Scottish Parliament.	Scotland Act (2012) implemented Calman recommendations. Referendum on Scottish independence to be held in 2014.
	Both: referendum on new powers for Welsh Assembly.	Referendum on primary legislative powers for Welsh Assembly.	64% 'yes' vote in March 2011 referendum; powers transferred to Welsh Assembly.
	Cons: English votes on English laws at Westminster; Lib Dems: federal UK.	Commission to consider the West Lothian Question.	McKay Commission proposes limited changes to Commons procedures.
Human Rights Act	Cons: replace HRA with UK Bill of Rights; Lib Dems: protect HRA, citizens' convention to draw up a codified constitution.	Commission to investigate the creation of a British Bill of Rights incorporating and building on the ECHR.	Commission on a Bill of Rights report (2012) — majority favoured a new UK Bill of Rights incorporating and building on the ECHR.
European Union	Cons: 'referendum lock' requiring referendums on future EU treaties, Sovereignty Bill restating parliamentary sovereignty; Lib Dems: 'In/Out' referendum when UK next agrees fundamental change in relationship with EU.	Amend the European Communities Act (1972) to ensure that any future treaty transferring powers would be subject to a referendum. Examine the case for a UK Sovereignty Bill making it clear that ultimate authority remains with parliament.	European Union Act (2011): referendums required for new treaties transferring powers from the UK to the EU; parliamentary sovereignty restated.

The result of the AV referendum was a setback for electoral reform

Parliamentary reform

The coalition proposed a number of reforms of parliament, but some ran into difficulties.

> **Fixed-term parliaments.** Under the Fixed-term Parliaments Act 2011, general elections will be held after a fixed 5-year parliamentary term, with the next election scheduled for 7 May 2015. Parliament can, however, be dissolved earlier if the government is defeated on a motion of no confidence or a motion calling for an early general election is supported by two-thirds of MPs.

> **Reduction in the number of MPs.** The coalition proposed reducing the number of MPs from 650 to 600 for the next general election, and equalising the size of parliamentary constituencies. Legislation establishing boundary reviews was passed, but the Liberal Democrats withdrew their support for the process after plans to reform the House of Lords were abandoned in 2012. The Liberal Democrats and Labour would have been net losers under the boundary review, but the Conservatives would have gained some 20 seats.

> **Recall of MPs.** A 2011 White Paper and draft bill proposed that MPs found guilty of serious wrongdoing by the courts or parliament could be subject to recall. A by-election would be triggered if 10% of constituents signed a recall petition. However, following criticism from the House of Commons Political and Constitutional Reform Committee, legislation was delayed.

> **The Wright reforms**. Reforms recommended by the Wright Committee before the general election came into effect under the coalition. The Backbench Business Committee recommends issues for debate in the Commons, selecting some proposed by the public via e-petitions. Chairs of select committees are now elected by a secret ballot of MPs and committee members elected within their party groups rather than nominated by the whips.
> **House of Lords reform.** A Joint Committee of both Houses could not reach consensus on Lords reform, although a majority of its members supported an upper chamber with 80% elected members serving 15 year terms. The Commons approved the House of Lords Reform Bill in principle in July 2012, but concerns about the role and composition of the upper House saw 91 Conservative MPs rebel. With the proposals facing an arduous passage, the government abandoned the bill.

Devolution

Further powers have been devolved to the Welsh Assembly and Scottish Parliament. Following a 64% vote in favour of additional legislative powers in the 2011 referendum, the Welsh Assembly was granted full primary legislative power in the 20 devolved areas. The Silk Commission, set up by the UK government to examine the transfer of fiscal and other powers, recommended that responsibility for income tax be shared by the UK and Welsh governments from 2020, subject to approval in a referendum.

The key recommendations of the 2009 Calman Commission report were implemented through the Scotland Act (2012). It gives the Scottish Parliament additional powers over taxation (e.g. a Scottish rate of income tax) and borrowing. However, the debate had moved on with the Scottish National Party government pressing for a referendum on Scottish independence. In October 2012, the UK and Scottish governments agreed that a single-question referendum on independence will be held on 18 September 2014.

European Union

The European Union Act (2011) provides a 'referendum lock' under which any future treaty transferring powers from the UK to the EU must be put to a binding referendum. A referendum must also be held if, for example, the government seeks to joins the euro or give up the national veto. Section 18 of the Act restates the sovereignty of parliament, but does not alter the relationship between the UK and EU.

Appraisal of the reforms

By the mid-point of its term in office, the coalition's constitutional reform programme had run into trouble. The search for consensus on Lords reform proved fruitless and enthusiasm for reform of the Commons waned. Divisions between the Conservatives and the Liberal Democrats were inevitable given their attachment, to greater or lesser degrees, to the competing conservative and liberal perspective visions of the constitution. The two parties had different priorities: Lords reform and electoral reform had long been core Liberal Democrat goals, while Conservative backbenchers wanted to replace the Human Rights Act and loosen relations with the EU. They also had competing interests: AV and House of Lords reform were detrimental to the Conservatives' prospects of holding power, while the Liberal Democrats would be net losers under the review of constituency boundaries. These differences produced dissent in the Commons with Liberal Democrats rebelling on constitutional issues and Conservatives on European integration. Divisions extended to the heart of government when Cameron announced that he was unable to deliver Conservative support for Lords reform and Clegg responded by withdrawing Liberal Democrat support for boundary changes.

Although the move to fixed-term parliaments is significant, the coalition is unlikely to deliver fundamental changes to the constitution. The result of the AV referendum rendered electoral reform unlikely for the foreseeable future, the prospects for consensus on Lords reform look slim and there is no majority in parliament for replacing the Human Rights Act with a UK Bill of Rights.

A codified constitution for the UK?

Labour's reforms brought about a greater codification of the British constitution. The Human Rights Act (1998) and the Scotland Act (1998), for example, wrote important constitutional principles into statute law. Some scholars and judges claim that such Acts have *de facto* status as fundamental law or 'constitutional statutes'. But the Labour governments did not take their constitutional reforms to what the liberal perspective viewed as their logical conclusion — a codified constitution. Labour and the Liberal Democrats proposed moves towards a codified constitution in their 2010 election manifestos, but the coalition agreement did not include a similar commitment.

Arguments for a codified constitution

Supporters of a codified constitution claim that it would provide greater clarity on what is, and what is not, constitutional. The rules governing the British political system would be set out in an authoritative document, reducing the ambiguities that exist in the current uncodified constitution and its myriad conventions. The rights of citizens would also be given further constitutional protection. A codified constitution would also tackle the centralisation of power (and the potential for elective dictatorship) by setting limits on the power of the executive and introducing more effective institutional checks and balances. Local and subnational governments would enjoy constitutional protection.

In drawing up a codified constitution, politicians and the public would have to give greater thought to the core principles of the British constitution than was evident during Labour's reform programme. The process of drawing up the new constitution would also educate citizens and, proponents hope, provide the people with a greater sense of shared values and citizenship, while bestowing additional legitimacy on the political system.

Arguments against a codified constitution

Opponents argue that codification would remove the flexibility and adaptability that is often seen as a key strength of the existing uncodified constitution. The British constitution has endured because it has developed organically and been adapted when the case for change has been proven. A codified constitution may reflect the mood of the time when it was produced — although this too may be doubtful, given the difficulty of forging consensus — but values change and constitutional legislation often requires amendment within a few years because of unintended consequences or the emergence of new issues. Codified constitutions are rigid and not easy to change. Codification, critics argue, will place too much power in the hands of judges because they will be called upon to determine whether laws and political processes are constitutional. A government acting on a popular mandate to introduce, say, stricter measures on law and order could find its legislation overturned by the courts. Judges would become more overtly political and this might reduce faith in the legal system.

A move to a codified constitution would bring about a fundamental change in the British political system and in the country's political culture. The traditional view is that a codified constitution would be incompatible with parliamentary sovereignty. Whereas codified constitutions set limits on the powers of the legislature and executive, the doctrine of parliamentary sovereignty gives Westminster supreme authority. A codified constitution could not be entrenched or have the status of fundamental law for so long as parliament retains the power to alter it at will.

An extensive national debate that produces elite and popular consensus on the guiding principles of the political system and authorising their codification might offer a way out of this conundrum. In such circumstances, parliament would be reluctant to counter the express will of the people. But disputes over the treatment of England in the post-devolution UK, reform of the House of Lords and the future of the Human Rights Act suggest that elite (and popular) consensus on the constitution is some way off.

Viewpoint Should the UK have a codified constitution?

YES
- It is the logical conclusion of recent constitutional reforms.
- It would provide greater clarity on what is constitutional.
- It would be an authoritative reference point for the courts.
- It would set limits on the powers of the state and its institutions.
- It would provide greater protection for the rights of citizens.
- It would better inform citizens about the values and workings of the political system.

NO
- Pragmatic adaptation has worked well and is preferable.
- There is no agreed process for establishing a codified constitution.
- There is no elite consensus on what a codified constitution should include.
- It would be rigid and difficult to amend.
- It would give judges, who are unaccountable, greater political power.
- There is no great popular demand and other issues are more important.

What you should know

❯ The British constitution is uncodified. The most important provisions are not gathered in one document, but are found in a variety of sources: Acts of Parliament, the common law, conventions, works of authority, and the treaties and law of the European Union. The uncodified nature of the British constitution means that it can be adapted to meet new political realities, but also that there is no definitive view of what is unconstitutional and that protection of individual rights is limited.

❯ Parliamentary sovereignty is the core principle of the British constitution. It establishes parliament as the supreme law-making body. But this legal theory has come under pressure given EU membership, the Human Rights Act, devolution and the use of referendums. Political practice also differs significantly from legal theory. No institution has absolute power; all are subject to significant internal and external constraints. The UK, however, has been a highly centralised state.

❯ The constitution was changed significantly by the Labour governments (1997–2010). Devolution, the Human Rights Act, new electoral systems and reform of the House of Lords changed the constitutional landscape. They provided greater protection for the rights of citizens and introduced more effective checks and balances and more democratic elements into the political system. The reforms have important implications for parliamentary sovereignty. Critics claim that the reform programme was incomplete and lacked a unifying vision.

❯ The new constitutional settlement continues to evolve. The Scottish Parliament and Welsh Assembly have gained more powers and the coalition government has introduced fixed-term parliaments, although the 2011 AV referendum ended the immediate prospect of electoral reform. Debates continue on reform of the House of Lords, the government of England, the Human Rights Act and codification of the constitution. The constitution is not above politics, but is an important political issue in its own right.

UK/US comparison

The US and UK constitutions

➤ The US Constitution is codified. It was produced by the Founding Fathers in 1787 following the Declaration of Independence. The constitution has just seven articles setting out the role and powers of the legislature, executive and judiciary. Some important features of the US political system (e.g. the Supreme Court's power of judicial review) are not described in the constitution but have emerged through case law or as conventions. The British constitution is not codified.

➤ The US Constitution is entrenched. The constitution establishes special procedures for its amendment. Amendments must be approved by two-thirds of members in both houses of Congress and ratified by three-quarters of state legislatures in the 50 states. Since the first ten amendments, which form the Bill of Rights, were approved in 1791, only 17 other amendments have come into force (two of which, the 18th and 21st, cancel each other out). The British constitution is not entrenched: there are no special procedures for its amendment.

➢ The US Constitution is subject to extensive judicial review. The Supreme Court can declare Acts of Congress and the actions of the executive, and those of state legislatures and executives, to be unconstitutional and strike them down. Some Supreme Court decisions (e.g. *Roe* v *Wade* 1973 on abortion) have provided crucial contemporary interpretations of the eighteenth-century constitution. Parliamentary sovereignty and the uncodified constitution mean that judicial review is limited in the UK.

➢ The US Constitution is a federal constitution. The 10th Amendment states that all powers not delegated to the federal government by the constitution, nor prohibited by it to the states, are reserved to the states or the people. Sovereignty is divided rather than located in a single authority. The UK has traditionally been a highly centralised state but has developed quasi-federal features since devolution.

➢ The US Constitution is inspired by liberal and republican principles. It establishes a strict separation of powers, reflecting the Founding Fathers' fear of despotism. The executive, legislature and judiciary have different powers and personnel. There is also an extensive system of checks and balances to prevent one branch of government becoming pre-eminent. In the UK, there is a fusion rather than separation of powers. The executive dominates the legislature.

➢ The Bill of Rights sets out the rights of individual American citizens and protects them from state encroachment. The Human Rights Act (1998) incorporated ECHR rights into UK statute law.

➢ The US Constitution establishes a presidential system of government in which the head of the executive branch is directly elected, the executive and legislative branches have distinct membership and functions, and neither branch can dismiss the other. The UK has a parliamentary system in which the prime minister is the leader of the largest party in the House of Commons, the executive and legislative branches are fused, and the House of Commons can dismiss the government.

Further reading

Bogdanor, V. (2009) *The New British Constitution*, Hart.

Bogdanor, V. (2011) *The Coalition and the Constitution*, Hart.

Cabinet Office (2011) *The Cabinet Manual*.

Gallop, N. (2011) *The Constitution and Constitutional Reform*, Philip Allan Updates.

Norton, P. (2011) 'Coalition government: a new era of constitutional reform?', *Politics Review*, Vol. 21, No. 2, pp. 8–11.

Norton, P. (2013) 'The UK constitution: why has it been criticised?', *Politics Review*, Vol. 22, No. 3, pp. 12–14.

Russell, M. (2011) 'Constitutional politics', in R. Heffernan, P. Cowley and C. Hay (eds.), *Developments in British Politics 9*, Palgrave Macmillan, pp. 7–28.

Exam focus

Short response questions (around 5–6 minutes each)

1 What is an uncodified constitution?
2 Define parliamentary sovereignty.
3 What are constitutional conventions?
4 What is the rule of law?
5 Define the term entrenchment.

Mid-length response questions (around 10–12 minutes each)

1 Outline and explain *three* functions of constitutions.
2 Distinguish between unitary and federal constitutions.
3 What are the advantages and disadvantages of a fusion of powers?
4 Explain the view that parliament is no longer sovereign.
5 Distinguish between parliamentary and presidential government.

Mini-essay questions (around 25–30 minutes each)

1 'The UK should replace its constitution with a codified alternative.' Discuss.
2 To what extent have the UK's central constitutional principles of parliamentary sovereignty, the rule of law and the unitary state been eroded in recent years?
3 Does the UK's constitution provide a sufficient check on executive power?
4 Critically assess the benefits of the constitutional reforms brought in since 1997.

 Extra resources to help you revise and consolidate your knowledge for this chapter are provided online at **www.hodderplus.co.uk/philipallan**. These include a revision PowerPoint, extension tasks and up-to-date weblinks.

Chapter 7

Parliament

Key questions answered in this chapter

➤ What are the main features of parliamentary government?

➤ What are the powers and composition of the House of Commons and House of Lords?

➤ What are the functions of parliament, and how well does it perform them?

➤ How has the House of Commons been reformed?

➤ How has the House of Lords been reformed? Are these reforms sufficient?

The Houses of Parliament, located in the Palace of Westminster on the banks of the River Thames, are a familiar symbol of British democracy. The importance of **parliament** is reflected in the description of the British political system as the 'Westminster model'.

Parliamentary government

The UK has a parliamentary system of government. The key features of a parliamentary system are as follows:

➤ **The executive and legislative branches are fused.** There is overlap between membership of the two branches, with the government consisting of members of the **legislature**.

➤ **The legislature can dismiss the executive.** The government is accountable to parliament, which can remove the government through a vote of no confidence. The government may be able to dissolve parliament by calling a general election.

➤ **Parliamentary elections decide the government.** Governments are formed according to their strength in parliament. The person who commands a majority in parliament, usually the leader of the largest party, becomes prime minister.

Key terms

➤ **Parliament** An assembly that has the power to debate and make laws.

➤ **Legislature** The branch of government responsible for passing laws.

> **Collective government.** The executive branch is led by a prime minister who, in theory at least, is 'first among equals' in a cabinet of senior ministers (see Chapter 8).
> **Separate head of state.** The head of the executive branch (the prime minister) is not the **head of state**. The latter is often a ceremonial role with little political power, as in the case of the UK monarchy.

Presidential government is the main alternative system. In a presidential system, there is a clear separation of powers between the executive and legislative branches, and the executive is dominated by a single individual (the president) who is directly elected.

> **Key term**
> **Head of state** The chief public representative of a country, such as a monarch or president.

Parliamentary and presidential government

Distinguish between

Parliamentary government
> The executive and legislative branches are fused — government ministers must be members of the legislature, and are responsible to it.
> Parliament can dismiss the government through a vote of confidence; the government can dissolve parliament by calling a general election.
> Power is exercised collectively within the executive branch — the prime minister is the head of a cabinet.
> The prime minister is the person who can command a majority in the parliament following a general election.
> The head of the executive is not the head of state.

Presidential government
> There is a clear separation of powers between the executive and legislative branches — members of the executive cannot be members of the legislature.
> The legislature cannot dismiss the president, except in special circumstances, and the executive cannot dissolve the legislature.
> Power in the executive is concentrated in the office of president.
> The president is directly elected by the people.
> The president is also head of state.

The Westminster model

The **Westminster model** is the traditional way of understanding British politics. As the name suggests, it puts parliament at the heart of the British political system — the guiding principle of the constitution is that parliament has supreme law-making authority.

> **Key concept**
> **The Westminster model** The traditional way of understanding the British political system, focusing on the constitution and major institutions. It both describes the British system and claims that it is the ideal. The key features of the Westminster model are parliamentary sovereignty, an uncodified constitution, cabinet government, the first-past-the-post electoral system, a two-party system and a unitary state (see Chapter 5). These face significant challenges which raise important questions about the future of the Westminster model.

The Westminster model not only describes the British political system, but also claims or assumes that it is the model of how a political system should operate. Two of its main virtues are said to be:

➢ **Representative government.** Government takes place through parliament, where decisions are taken by elected representatives of the people. The people do not make decisions on public policy directly, electing MPs to do so on their behalf.

➢ **Responsible government.** The government is accountable to parliament for its actions, and accountable to the people through elections. Collective responsibility means that the government can be forced to resign by parliament. Individual ministerial responsibility means that ministers must account for their actions in parliament (see Chapter 8). Voters can remove the government at a general election.

The usefulness of the Westminster model as a description of how the British political system works is disputed. There is a significant disparity between the ideal presented by the model and the reality. In particular, there is a clear imbalance in the relationship between the executive and legislature. A parliamentary majority, party discipline in the House of Commons and government control of the parliamentary timetable enable the executive to dominate parliament.

Structure of Parliament

The UK has a **bicameral** legislature — that is, parliament has two chambers. Formally, the UK Parliament actually has three component institutions:

➢ the House of Commons
➢ the House of Lords
➢ the monarchy (the 'Crown in Parliament')

Key concept

➢ **Bicameralism** A political system in which there are two chambers in the legislature. The lower house is usually elected in a general election and tends to be the dominant chamber. The composition of upper houses varies: they may be directly elected or indirectly elected (e.g. appointed by ministers), or be a hybrid of both. Bicameralism has a number of benefits: the upper house provides checks and balances, provides for greater scrutiny and revision of legislation, and may represent different interests (e.g. states in a federal system). Problems associated with bicameralism include:

(i) institutional conflict between the two houses can produce legislative gridlock;

(ii) an indirectly elected upper house may frustrate the will of the democratically elected lower house.

Links to follow up

www.parliament.uk — home page of the UK Parliament, with information on its composition and functions.

House of Commons

The House of Commons is the lower house of the UK Parliament. It has been the dominant chamber for over a century. The role and functions of the House of Commons will be examined in detail later in this chapter, but it is important to note at this stage two key powers of parliament that are, in effect, exercised by the Commons:

➤ **Parliamentary sovereignty.** A central principle of the British constitution, this gives parliament legislative supremacy. Parliament has ultimate law-making authority within the UK. In theory, this means that parliament can legislate on any matter of its choosing and these laws cannot be overturned by any higher authority (see Chapter 5).

Key concept

➤ **Parliamentary sovereignty** The doctrine that parliament has absolute legal authority within the state. Parliament can make law on any matter it chooses, its decisions may not be overturned by any higher authority and it may not bind its successors. Parliamentary sovereignty is a legal theory concerning the location of law-making authority. But EU membership and devolution raise questions about how meaningful it is in practice (see Chapter 5).

MPs gather in the House of Commons

➤ **Motion of no confidence.** The House of Commons can remove the government by defeating it in a motion of no confidence (also known as a vote of confidence). The Fixed-term Parliaments Act (2011) states that parliament will be dissolved if the government is defeated on a motion of no confidence and no alternative government is approved by the

Commons within 14 days. The only government defeat on a motion of no confidence since 1924 occurred when James Callaghan's Labour government lost by one vote in March 1979.

Key term
> **Motion of no confidence** A parliamentary motion which, if passed, requires the resignation of the government.

Composition

The House of Commons is a democratically elected chamber consisting of 650 Members of Parliament (MPs). Each MP is elected in a single-member constituency by the first-past-the-post electoral system (see Chapter 2). The number of MPs is not fixed, but can change following reviews of parliamentary constituencies. Conservative proposals to reduce the number of MPs to 600 were defeated in the Commons in 2013.

In the chamber, the governing party (or parties) sit on the benches to the right of the Speaker's chair, and members of opposition parties on the benches to its left. More than 100 MPs hold ministerial positions in the government. The main opposition party appoints 'shadow ministers' to confront their rivals. Ministers and shadow ministers are known as **frontbenchers** because they occupy the benches closest to the floor of the chamber. The majority of MPs have no ministerial or shadow ministerial posts and are known as **backbenchers**.

Almost all MPs are elected as a representative of a political party. Two independent MPs were elected in 2005, but a further 13 resigned from, or were expelled by, their party during the 2005–10 parliament. Only one independent, Lady Sylvia Hermon in Down North, was elected in 2010. The party system in the House of Commons has traditionally been strong. Each party appoints a number of MPs to act as **whips**. They have three main roles:
> Ensuring that MPs attend parliamentary **divisions** (votes), or approving the absence of MPs when their vote will not be required.
> Issuing instructions on how MPs should vote. Each week, MPs receive instructions on their attendance — also known as a **whip**. Debates where there will be a vote are underlined on this letter. A 'three-line whip' is a strict instruction to attend and vote according to the party line, or face disciplinary action. It is usually issued on only the most important divisions.

Key terms
> **Frontbencher** An MP who holds a ministerial or shadow ministerial position.
> **Backbencher** An MP who does not hold a ministerial or shadow ministerial position.
> **Division** A vote in parliament.
> **Whip** (a) A party official responsible for ensuring that MPs turn up to parliamentary votes and follow party instructions on how to vote. (b) An instruction to vote that is issued to MPs by political parties.

> Enforcing discipline within the parliamentary party. The whips seek to persuade wavering MPs to vote with their party by providing assurances, making offers and issuing threats. Rebel MPs may be expelled from the parliamentary party by having the whip withdrawn.

Links to follow up

www.parliament.uk/business/commons — detailed information on the work of the House of Commons.

Case study   The speaker

The speaker of the House of Commons presides over debates in the chamber, selecting speakers and maintaining order. He or she may temporarily suspend MPs who break parliamentary rules. The speaker is elected by MPs in a secret ballot. He or she must stand down at a general election but is normally re-elected at the start of the next parliament. Once chosen, the speaker gives up his or her party affiliation and is non-partisan. The speaker does not vote unless there is a tie, in which case he or she has the casting vote — but uses it to provide further debate rather than a final decision.

Former Labour MP Michael Martin became the first speaker to be forced from office in 174 years when he resigned in 2009. Martin had been criticised for his handling of the MPs' expenses scandal and viewed as an obstacle to reform. He stepped down before a formal motion of no confidence could be heard. Conservative MP John Bercow was then chosen as speaker, winning an absolute majority on a third ballot of MPs.

The Lord Speaker chairs proceedings in the House of Lords. He or she is elected by **peers** and is politically neutral. The Lord Chancellor, a cabinet minister, had overseen debates in the Lords until stripped of this role by the Constitutional Reform Act (2005). Baroness D'Souza became Lord Speaker in 2011.

House of Lords

The House of Lords is the upper house of the UK Parliament. It is an unelected chamber and is subordinate to the House of Commons. The House of Lords can delay most bills passed by the House of Commons for up to 1 year. Prior to 1911, it could block bills passed by the Commons indefinitely. The Parliament Act (1911) restricted this veto power to two parliamentary sessions (i.e. 2 years), which was subsequently reduced to 1 year by the Parliament Act (1949). The 1911 Act also prevented the Lords from delaying 'money bills': that is, bills that include significant provisions on taxation or expenditure.

Key term

> **Peer** A member of the House of Lords.

These measures transformed the House of Lords into a revising chamber. The Lords can propose amendments to bills passed by the Commons (except money bills). The Commons can then accept these amendments, reject them or introduce new amendments of its own. The Lords cannot force the Commons to accept its amendments. If the Commons refuses to accept the wishes of the Lords, the upper house is faced with the choice of backing down or blocking the bill from becoming law for 1 year. If it chooses the latter, the bill can be passed unchanged in the following session of parliament without the consent of the Lords using the Parliament Act (1949). This has been invoked on only four occasions:

➢ the War Crimes Act (1991)
➢ the European Parliamentary Elections Act (1999)
➢ the Sexual Offences (Amendment) Act (2000)
➢ the Hunting Act (2004)

The Salisbury–Addison convention states that the House of Lords should not reject or wreck bills that seek to enact a manifesto commitment of the governing party. As a convention, it does not have the force of law. It arose in the 1940s as an acceptance that the unelected Lords should not frustrate the will of the elected Commons. The convention has come under strain. In 2006, peers voted against an identity cards bill despite it featuring in Labour's 2005 manifesto. Liberal Democrats argued that Labour had not won sufficient support at the election to have a valid mandate, and that the convention applied to a time when the upper house had an inbuilt Conservative majority. Application of the convention to the Conservative–Liberal Democrat coalition is still more questionable because the coalition agreement was not put before voters.

Until 2009, the House of Lords also had a judicial role. The Law Lords — senior judges who sat in the Lords — acted as the UK's highest court of appeal. The Supreme Court took over this role in 2009.

The House of Lords consists of:

➢ hereditary peers
➢ life peers
➢ Lords Spiritual — two archbishops and 24 senior bishops of the Church of England

The first two categories will now be examined in more detail.

Hereditary peers

The House of Lords Act (1999) ended the right of all but 92 hereditary peers to sit and vote in the Lords. Before the Act came into force, the House of Lords contained more than 750 hereditary peers who had inherited their title and a place in the upper house. Some hereditary peerages dated back centuries, but most were created in the nineteenth and early twentieth centuries when the power of the aristocracy was in decline.

The Peerages Act (1963) allowed hereditary peers to renounce their titles and membership of the Lords. It enabled Alec Douglas-Home, the 14th Earl of Home, to leave the Lords and win a by-election to the House of Commons when he became Conservative Party leader and prime minister in 1963. Labour MP Tony Benn also renounced his peerage. The Act also allowed women hereditary peers to sit in the Lords. The right of primogeniture, under which aristocratic titles are transferred to a male heir, means that almost all hereditary peers are men.

The House of Lords Act (1999) transformed the hereditary element of the Lords into a new category of 'elected hereditary peers'. The 15 hereditary peers who became deputy speakers were chosen in a ballot of the whole House. Two others hold royal appointments.

The remaining 75 were elected by ballots of hereditary peers from their party and crossbench groups. When an elected hereditary peer dies, a by-election is held in which peers from the same group as the deceased member choose a replacement from the register of hereditary peers — 17 such by-elections had been held by March 2013.

Life peers

The Life Peerages Act (1958) gave the prime minister the right to appoint members of the upper house for life. Their title and right to sit in the Lords cannot be inherited. With the removal of most hereditary peers, life peers now form the largest category of members of the upper house, numbering 647 in March 2013 (see Table 7.1). An independent House of Lords Appointments Commission recommends individuals for appointment as non-party peers, and vets those nominated by political parties.

The Life Peerages Act (1958) and the House of Lords Act (1999) brought about significant changes to the composition and day-to-day working of the upper house. The creation of life peers increased the diversity and professionalism of the House of Lords. The body of life peers includes former ministers and MPs, as well as leading figures from business, education and the arts. Life peers have also proved more likely to play an active role in the house. Many hereditary peers, known as 'backwoodsmen', did not attend regularly.

The House of Lords Act (1999) also ended the historical predominance of the Conservative Party in the upper house. Many hereditary peers had taken the Conservative whip. Following the removal of all but 92 hereditary peers, no party had a majority (see Table 7.1). Crossbench members of the upper house have no formal party allegiance. The removal of hereditary peers also increased the proportion of women in the Lords. In March 2013, there were 172 women peers — 23% of the house compared to 9% before 1999.

Table 7.1 The House of Lords by party, October 1999 and March 2013

Party	October 1999			March 2013		
	Life peers	Hereditary	Total	Life peers	Hereditary	Total
Conservative	172	299	471	165	49	214
Labour	160	19	179	218	4	222
Lib Dem	49	23	72	86	4	90
Crossbench	128	225	353	147	31	178
Bishops	0	0	26	0	0	25
Other	32	80	112	31	1	32
Total	541	646	1,213	647	89	761

Note: Figures for October 1999 exclude 113 hereditary peers and 4 life peers on leave of absence.
Figures for March 2013 exclude 38 peers on leave of absence,
11 disqualified as senior members of the judiciary and 1 disqualified as an MEP.

Links to follow up

www.parliament.uk/business/lords — detailed information on the role, composition and business of the House of Lords.

The monarchy

The monarchy retains a formal and ceremonial role in parliament. Its role entails:

➤ **The royal assent.** Approval by the monarch is the final stage in the legislative process. Only when a bill has been signed by the monarch can it become law. Constitutional convention dictates that the monarch always grants royal assent.

➤ **Appointing the prime minister.** The monarch appoints the prime minister. This is often a formality, with the leader of the largest party in the House of Commons invited to form a government. If no party has a majority, the monarch awaits the outcome of discussions between the parties, avoiding personal involvement in the process of forming a government.

The State Opening of Parliament

➤ **Proroguing parliament.** The monarch's prerogative power to dissolve parliament was ended by the Fixed-term Parliaments Act (2011). The monarch retains a formal role in proroguing parliament, i.e. bringing a parliamentary session to an end.

➤ **The Queen's Speech.** At the State Opening of Parliament, the monarch opens the new parliamentary session and delivers the Queen's Speech. It sets out the main bills that the government intends to introduce that year. The speech is drawn up by the government not the monarch.

Links to follow up

www.royal.gov.uk — official site of the British monarchy.

Functions of parliament

Parliament performs a number of functions in the British political system. The most significant are:

➤ legislation
➤ scrutiny and accountability
➤ representation
➤ recruitment of ministers
➤ legitimacy

This section outlines the main parliamentary procedures for dealing with these functions, with a particular focus on the House of Commons given its status as the dominant chamber. It also assesses how effective parliament is in performing these roles.

Legislation

Parliament is the legislative branch (the 'legislature') of a political system. The term reflects parliament's primary function — making law.

The legislative process

A **bill** is a draft legislative proposal that is debated in parliament. When a bill has completed the legislative process and enters into law, it is known as an **Act** of Parliament. The most significant bills are **public bills**. These are promoted by a government minister and concern general issues of public policy. Public bills are also the most common because the executive exercises significant control over the parliamentary timetable.

The government sets out its legislative programme in the Queen's Speech at the beginning of a parliamentary session. For a minority government, the votes at the end of this debate may determine its chances of survival. The government may produce a consultative **Green Paper** setting out options for legislation, and/or a **White Paper** explaining the objectives of government policy.

Legislation follows an established process of debate, scrutiny and amendment (see Figure 7.1). Most legislation originates in the House of Commons, but some bills on non-controversial or complex matters of law are introduced in the House of Lords. The

Key terms

➤ **Bill** A legislative proposal that has yet to complete the parliamentary legislative process.
➤ **Act** A legislative proposal that has completed the legislative process and entered into law.
➤ **Public bill** A bill concerning a general issue of public policy, introduced by a government minister.
➤ **Green Paper.** A government document setting out various options for legislation and inviting comment.
➤ **White Paper** A government document setting out a detailed proposal for legislation.

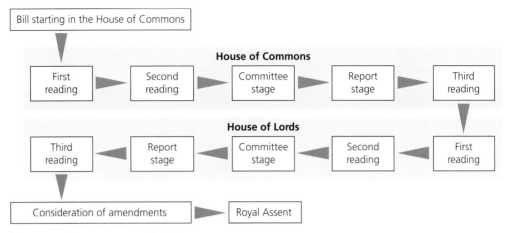

Figure 7.1 The passage of a bill

main stages in the legislative process for a bill introduced in the House of Commons (except a money bill) are as follows:

➤ **First reading.** The formal presentation of the title of the bill on the floor of the house by a minister from the responsible department. There is no debate or vote at this stage.

➤ **Second reading.** The main debate on the principle of the bill. The government minister explains and justifies the objectives of the bill, the shadow minister responds and backbenchers contribute to the debate. If the bill is contested, a vote is taken. Government defeats at second reading stage are extremely rare, occurring only twice since 1945. The last was in 1986 when the Sunday Trading Bill, which would allow more shops to open on Sundays, was defeated by 14 votes despite a government majority of 140.

➤ **Committee stage.** Bills are sent to a public bill committee — known as a standing committee until 2006 — where detailed scrutiny of each clause occurs and amendments can be made. A new public bill committee is established for each bill, and is named after it. Once the bill has completed this stage, that committee is dissolved. In the 2010–12 session, there were 36 public bill committees.

The membership of the committee, which ranges from 16 to 50, reflects party strength in the Commons and whips instruct MPs how to vote. Public bill committees may take evidence from outside experts. Finance bills and bills of particular constitutional significance are scrutinised on the floor of the house, in a **Committee of the Whole House**.

Key term

➤ **Committee of the Whole House** A meeting held in the chamber in which the full House of Commons considers the committee stage of a public bill.

➤ **Report stage.** Amendments made in committee are considered by the full house. It may accept, reject or alter them. The Major government lost a report stage vote on the Maastricht Treaty in 1993, but then made the issue a matter of confidence and won by 40 votes.

> **Third reading.** This is a debate on the amended bill on the floor of the house. No further amendments are permitted.
> **House of Lords stages.** The bill is sent to the House of Lords, where it follows the same procedure. If amendments to the bill are made in the Lords, the Commons may agree to them, reject them or amend them further. A bill may go back and forth between the two houses in a process known as 'parliamentary ping pong'. In 2010–12, the Commons overturned a series of amendments made by the Lords to legislation on legal aid and welfare reform. If agreement cannot be reached, the government must decide whether to accept changes made by the Lords, drop the bill or invoke the Parliament Act.

Some government bills are subject to pre-legislative and/or post-legislative scrutiny; 56 draft bills were scrutinised by committee between 1997 and 2010, and 9 in the 2010–12 session. Committee recommendations may influence debate on the bill, but the government can ignore objections and pursue its favoured course. The coalition government has piloted a 'public reading stage' in which members of the public may post comments online about proposed legislation. In post-legislative scrutiny, government departments submit memorandums on legislation to select committees 3 to 5 years after it came into force. The committee may conduct an inquiry into the act.

Other bills

Two other types of legislative proposal are also noteworthy: private members' bills and secondary legislation.

Legislative proposals initiated by backbench MPs rather than by the government are known as **private members' bills**. Early in each parliamentary session, 20 names of MPs who wish to introduce a bill are drawn in a ballot. Some will already have a cause they wish to pursue; others will take soundings from lobbyists or their party. MPs can also introduce Ten Minute Rule bills, which offer a brief slot to introduce a legislative proposal, but few get beyond this first hurdle.

A handful of private members' bills become law in each parliamentary session. These tend to enjoy the support, or benevolent neutrality, of the government. Time constraints and the difficulty of persuading other MPs to back a proposal mean that most fall at an early stage. Two landmark laws to originate as private members' bills were the Murder (Abolition of Death Penalty) Act (1965) and the Abortion Act (1967). Both had government support. More recent examples include the Autism Act (2009) and the Sustainable Communities Act (2006), which were promoted by lobbying organisations and supported by government.

The authority to issue **secondary legislation** in specific policy areas is delegated by parliament to government ministers. Some 2,500 pieces of secondary legislation, known as

Key terms

> **Private member's bill** A bill sponsored by a backbench MP.
> **Secondary legislation** Law made by ministers, who have been granted this authority by an Act of parliament, rather than by parliament.

statutory instruments, are issued each year on matters such as immigration, taxation and education. Parliamentary scrutiny is limited to examination by the statutory instruments committee.

Effectiveness of legislatures

In theory, the UK parliament can make, amend or repeal any laws it chooses. In practice, the situation is very different. The government is responsible for most of the laws passed by parliament. Philip Norton, an academic expert on parliament and member of the House of Lords, developed a threefold classification of legislatures:

- **Policy-making legislatures.** These amend or reject legislative proposals made by the executive, and can put forward alternative bills.
- **Policy-influencing legislatures.** These can modify or reject legislative proposals from the executive but are unable to develop extensive legislative proposals of their own.
- **Legislatures with little or no policy influence.** These are unable to modify or veto legislative proposals from the executive, and cannot formulate meaningful alternative policy proposals of their own.

The UK parliament is a policy-influencing legislature. Law making occurs through, not by, parliament. It has only modest influence over policy and reacts to government proposals rather than taking the lead in formulating policy. Parliament can vote against government bills and pass amendments. But parliament's effectiveness in making and scrutinising law is limited by the dominance of the executive. This is evidenced by:

- **Government bills.** Most bills that come before parliament originate from the government. Private members' bills have little chance of success unless they have government backing.
- **Parliamentary timetable.** The executive controls much of the legislative timetable and can use 'guillotine motions' to curtail debate.
- **Party discipline.** The whip system ensures that government proposals are rarely defeated and that most amendments are acceptable to it.
- **House of Lords.** The upper house scrutinises and revises legislation, but does not alter the key features of most bills.

Links to follow up

www.parliament.uk/business/bills-and-legislation — information on bills before parliament and the legislative process.

Scrutiny and accountability

In addition to scrutinising a government's legislative proposals, parliament also exercises a general scrutiny and oversight role. It scrutinises the actions of the executive and ensures government **accountability** by requiring ministers to explain and justify their actions. The convention of individual ministerial responsibility states that ministers are accountable to parliament; they must explain and justify their policies and actions — and those of their department — in parliament (see Chapter 8).

There are a number of routes for scrutinising the executive.

> **Key concept**
>
> ➤ **Accountability** The principle that an office holder or institution must account for their actions. In a system of parliamentary government, ministers are accountable to parliament and to the electorate. They have a duty to explain their policies and actions to parliament. Ministers may also be held responsible for policy failures (see Chapter 8). MPs face the electorate at a general election, where their constituents may take their record in office into account when deciding whether to vote for them.

Question Time

Government ministers face questions from MPs on the floor of the house. The parliamentary timetable includes question sessions for ministers from each government department. The most high-profile event is Prime Minister's Questions, which takes place each Wednesday at noon for half an hour. This provides an opportunity for the leader of the opposition, the leader of the third largest party and backbenchers to question the prime minister. A backbencher might raise a constituency matter, but many ask questions drafted by the whips. The leader of the opposition may try to embarrass the prime minister by highlighting a policy failure. Overall, Prime Minister's Questions provides parliamentary theatre rather than effective scrutiny.

MPs also send written questions to ministers requesting information on issues of public policy.

The opposition

The largest party not included in the government forms the official opposition. The very architecture of the House of Commons is confrontational, with the government and opposition facing each other across the chamber. The party in opposition is expected to perform two major tasks that do not always sit easily together. First, it will oppose many of the government's legislative proposals, and harry the government throughout the legislative process by tabling amendments and forcing votes. But the opposition will also try to appear as an alternative government-in-waiting. It will need to develop its own policies and might consider supporting government measures that it agrees with. When the government has a comfortable majority, a period in opposition can prove frustrating. But when it has a small majority or none at all, the opposition may be able to force government u-turns or inflict defeats.

The government enjoys significant institutional advantages in parliament. It can draw upon the expertise of the civil service, while the opposition relies on limited state funding ('Short money') to fund researchers. Government control over the parliamentary timetable also means that the opposition has few opportunities to set the agenda. The opposition parties are permitted to choose the topic for debate on 20 days in the parliamentary year ('opposition days'). A 2009 Liberal Democrat motion on British citizenship for Gurkha veterans produced a rare government defeat on an opposition motion.

Debates

MPs can also express their views and try to influence policy in debates on current events and government actions. Half-hour adjournment debates at the end of each day give MPs a chance to raise a particular issue. Ministers also make statements to parliament on major issues, and these are followed by debate. Speaker John Bercow has required ministers to answer 'urgent questions' more frequently.

Many debates are poorly attended, but those at times of crisis can provide moments of high drama. In 1940, prime minister Neville Chamberlain resigned after losing the support of his party following a debate on the German invasion of Norway. The debate that preceded the 2003 invasion of Iraq saw high-quality contributions from both sides of the argument, and reflected the difference of opinion within the nation as a whole.

The Backbench Business Committee, which was created in 2010, gives MPs greater opportunity to shape the parliamentary agenda. It decides the topic for debate on the floor of the Commons and in Westminster Hall for roughly 1 day per week. The committee takes account of backbench opinion, select committee reports and e-petitions when determining subjects for debate. Topics selected in 2010–12 included a referendum on the European Union and the release of documents on the 1989 Hillsborough disaster.

Links to follow up

www.parliament.uk/business/publications — scroll down to 'Commons Hansard' for official verbatim reports of proceedings in the House of Commons.

Select committees

Select committees have proved more effective at scrutinising the actions of the executive and holding it to account. Departmental select committees were created in 1979 to scrutinise the policy, administration and expenditure of government departments. There were 19 departmental select committees in 2013 (see Table 7.2).

Membership of select committees is fixed at 11 backbench MPs and reflects the party balance in the Commons. Chairs of committees are allocated to parties according to their relative strength. Since the implementation of the Wright Committee recommendations in 2010, select committee chairs are elected by all MPs in a secret ballot using the alternative vote system. Successful candidates often have a reputation for independence. Members of select committees are elected by secret ballot within party groups. Prior to 2010, members were appointed by party whips.

Since a unanimous select committee report is likely to carry maximum weight, members aim to strike compromises across party lines. Over time, committee members can become more expert in their chosen field than the relevant ministers, who usually have short tenures in a specific office.

Select committees decide which issues they are going to examine. They have wide powers to summon witnesses and to examine restricted documents. Committees spend much of their time questioning ministers, officials and outside experts. Some witnesses are, however, reluctant to provide full and frank evidence.

Table 7.2 Departmental select committees, 2013

Select committee	Chair (party)
Business, Innovation and Skills	Adrian Bailey (Labour)
Communities and Local Government	Clive Betts (Labour)
Culture, Media and Sport	John Whittingdale (Conservative)
Defence	James Arbuthnot (Conservative)
Education	Graham Stuart (Conservative)
Energy and Climate Change	Tim Yeo (Conservative)
Environment, Food and Rural Affairs	Anne McIntosh (Conservative)
Foreign Affairs	Richard Ottaway (Conservative)
Health	Stephen Dorrell (Conservative)
Home Affairs	Keith Vaz (Labour)
International Development	Sir Malcolm Bruce (Liberal Democrat)
Justice	Sir Alan Beith (Liberal Democrat)
Northern Ireland Affairs	Laurence Robertson (Conservative)
Science and Technology	Andrew Miller (Labour)
Scottish Affairs	Ian Davidson (Labour)
Transport	Louise Ellman (Labour)
Treasury	Andrew Tyrie (Conservative)
Welsh Affairs	David Davies (Conservative)
Work and Pensions	Dame Anne Begg (Labour)

Rupert Murdoch giving evidence in July 2011 to the Culture, Media and Sport Select Committee into phone-hacking at News International

⟨⟩ Stretch and challenge

Select committees in action

High profile select committee inquiries of recent years include:

- **Culture, Media and Sport Select Committee** inquiry (2009–10) into press standards, privacy and libel was critical of the conduct of the press. It heard evidence of illegal phone-hacking by journalists at the *News of the World*, prompting police investigations and the Leveson Inquiry on press conduct.
- **Culture, Media and Sports Select Committee** inquiry (2011–12) into phone-hacking at News International heard evidence from Rupert Murdoch and James Murdoch (twice).
- **Home Affairs Select Committee** inquiry (2011) into policing large-scale disorder examined the causes and police response to the riots in English cities.
- **Health Select Committee** inquiry (2011) into public health identified concerns about the coalition government's proposals for NHS reform. It helped persuade the government to make significant changes to the Health and Social Care Bill.

Questions

1 Choose a recent House of Commons select committee inquiry using the Parliament website: **www.parliament.uk/business/committees**.

2 Examine the role and influence of your chosen committee by exploring the following:
- What were the aims of the inquiry?
- Who were the witnesses questioned by the committee?
- What were the key recommendations of the select committee report?
- Were they broadly supportive or critical of government policy?
- Did the government accept the committee's recommendations in its response?

The government must respond to select committee reports but is not required to accept their recommendations. A study by the Constitution Unit (2011) found that governments accept around 40% of select committee recommendations. Many of these recommend limited policy change.

Other important (non-departmental) select committees in the House of Commons include:

➤ **Public Accounts Committee.** The oldest committee in parliament, this examines government expenditure to check that value for money is being achieved. It does not consider the merits of government policy. It is chaired by a senior opposition MP.

➤ **Standards and Privileges Committee.** This examines the conduct of MPs, overseeing the Register of Interests and dealing with disciplinary cases against MPs.

➤ **Modernisation Committee.** Established in 2005, this examines how the practices and procedures of the House of Commons might be reformed. Unusually, it is chaired by a government minister, the leader of the House of Commons.

➤ **Liaison Committee.** This includes the chairs of all select committees. Its most significant meetings are the twice-yearly sessions in which the prime minister is questioned on public policy.

➤ **European Scrutiny Committee.** This assesses the significance of European Union documents, reporting in detail on about 475 of the 1,000 or more it receives each year.

> **Political and Constitutional Affairs Committee.** Established in 2010, this examines the work of the deputy prime minister on political and constitutional reform.

In the House of Lords, a smaller number of committees conduct in-depth inquiries on topical issues. The European Union Committee, which has six subcommittees, and the Constitution Committee have developed impressive bodies of work.

Effectiveness of scrutiny and accountability

The select committee system has improved and extended parliament's scrutiny of the executive. Committees highlight important issues, bring expert contributions to topical debates, hold the government accountable for policy problems and issue evidence-based recommendations. The remit of select committees has been widened in recent years. They now scrutinise legislation that has come into force and hold hearings on some public appointments. Election of select committee chairs and members has enhanced their independence.

Viewpoint Are select committees effective in scrutinising the executive?

YES
- Select committees scrutinise the policies and actions of government, conducting detailed examinations of controversial issues.
- They question ministers, civil servants and outside experts, and can request access to government papers.
- Many select committee recommendations are accepted by the government.
- The election of chairs and members by MPs has enhanced the independence of select committees.

NO
- A government with a majority in the Commons will also have a majority in committees.
- Ministers and civil servants may not provide much information when questioned, and access to documents may be denied.
- They have no power to propose policy — governments can ignore recommendations made by select committees.
- Some members do not attend regularly; some may be overly abrasive when questioning witnesses.

Links to follow up

www.parliament.uk/business/committees — information on, and documents from, parliamentary committees.

Representation

The House of Commons consists of 650 MPs, elected from single-member constituencies on the basis of universal suffrage among adults over 18. The geographical nature of representation is supposed to ensure that individual MPs can be identified as the exclusive representatives of their constituents, as opposed to the multi-member constituencies used in proportional representation systems (see Chapter 2).

Constituency work takes up a greater proportion of an MP's time than in the recent past — almost half of it, according to a 2005 Hansard Society study. MPs hold regular surgeries in which constituents can discuss problems. They may then take up grievances that individual constituents have against a public authority: for example, by contacting the relevant body, writing to a minister or raising the issue in the Commons. MPs also defend the interests of the constituency as a whole by, for example, campaigning to improve local services.

Some MPs win favourable local reputations for their constituency work and reap a sizeable personal vote in a general election. The Electoral Commission's 2007 *Audit of Political Engagement* showed that 41% of people were satisfied with the way their local MP was doing his or her job, and 12% dissatisfied. When asked how MPs in general were doing their job, 30% were satisfied and 37% dissatisfied.

Links to follow up

www.theyworkforyou.com — find your MP, read their speeches in parliament and discover how they have voted.

Descriptive representation

Descriptive representation occurs when a legislature mirrors the society it represents. In this perspective, parliament should be a microcosm of society with all major social groups included in numbers proportional to their size in the electorate. In the UK, attention has focused on the under-representation of women in the House of Commons. The number of women MPs has risen in recent decades, reaching 143 at the 2010 general election. But women make up only 22% of the Commons compared to 51% of the UK population (see Table 7.3).

Table 7.3 Women candidates and MPs, 1983–2010

	Conservative		Labour		Liberal Democrat		Total women MPs
	Candidates	MPs	Candidates	MPs	Candidates	MPs	
1983	40	13	78	10	75	0	23
1987	46	17	92	21	106	2	41
1992	63	20	138	37	143	2	60
1997	69	13	157	101	140	3	120
2001	92	14	146	95	135	5	118
2005	118	17	166	98	142	10	128
2010	151	49	189	81	137	7	143

Note: 'Total women MPs' includes MPs from other parties.

The main methods that parties have used to increase the number of women candidates are:

➤ **All-women shortlists.** These were used by Labour for the 1997, 2005 and 2010 general elections. Some constituency Labour parties were required to select their parliamentary candidate from a list consisting only of women. This boosted significantly the number of female Labour MPs elected in 1997. The Sex Discrimination (Election Candidates) Act (2002) permits political parties to use positive measures to reduce inequality in the

Most of the Labour Party's female MPs gather outside the Members' Entrance to the House of Commons for the first sitting of the House following the 2010 general election

number of women elected to parliament. All-women shortlists are 'equality guarantees': they ensure that a woman candidate will be selected in a constituency.

> **Priority lists.** David Cameron introduced a priority list (the 'A list') in 2005 for the top 100 Conservative target seats. This was an 'equality promotion' initiative that set a general target of more women MPs, but did not guarantee that women would be selected in winnable seats. Constituency associations chose from a priority list of aspirant candidates, half of whom were women. From 2006 constituency associations were required to draw up shortlists, on which at least half the aspirant candidates were women. In 2010, 49 women Conservative MPs were elected, although only 19 of them had been on the 'A list'.

These 'demand-side' initiatives have helped to increase the number of women MPs, but 'supply-side' obstacles remain. Career choices, family issues, money and a lack of political connections may prevent women from putting themselves forward as candidates. The 2010 speaker's conference on parliamentary representation recommended that if the number of women MPs did not increase significantly at that year's election (the proportion rose from 20% to 22%), then equality guarantees should be considered.

Other areas of under-representation in the House of Commons include:

> **Ethnic diversity.** In 2010, 26 black and minority ethnic (BME) MPs were elected, an increase of 11. This is only 4% of the house, compared to 14% of the population. The speaker's conference on parliamentary representation recommended all-BME shortlists.

➤ **Age.** The average age of MPs fell to 50 in 2010 because of the high number of MPs who stood down or were defeated in the election. Young and older people are under-represented in the Commons, with most MPs being in the 35 to 55 age range.

➤ **Sexual orientation.** There are 20 openly gay MPs in the 2010 parliament.

➤ **Education.** More than a third of MPs elected in 2010 attended a fee-paying school, but fewer than 10% of voters did. Nine out of ten MPs have been to university, with over a quarter going to either Oxford or Cambridge.

➤ **Social class.** The number of MPs who used to be manual workers has declined. Only 10% of Labour's MPs in 2005 had been manual workers. Occupations such as the law, financial services and public relations are well represented in the Commons. MPs who worked in business are more likely to be found on the Conservative benches, and those who worked in the public sector (e.g. teachers) on the Labour benches.

Recruitment of ministers

Government ministers must be members of either the House of Commons or the House of Lords. Parliament is, therefore, a recruiting ground for government. The number of government posts — the 'payroll vote' — has increased over the last 20 years with 95 MPs holding paid posts in 2012 and a further 43 unpaid positions as parliamentary private secretaries.

Traditionally, future ministers have learned about the political process and carved out their reputations in the House of Commons. However, parliament's effectiveness in this area is questionable:

➤ **Communications skills.** Being an effective communicator is important for the career prospects of an MP. But television rather than parliament is now the key arena in which MPs display their communications skills.

➤ **Experience.** A total of 227 new MPs entered the Commons in 2010. Government needs people with managerial, leadership and organisational skills, rather than just communications skills. The proportion of MPs who worked in politics (e.g. as researchers or advisers) before entering parliament reached 20% in 2010. The proliferation of career politicians with little experience of life beyond politics widens the gap between the 'political class' and ordinary voters.

➤ **Conformity.** Loyal MPs have a better chance of ministerial office than troublemakers. However, the strengthening of select committees offers an alternative career route for backbenchers.

Legitimacy

Parliament helps to maintain the legitimacy of the political system. Government policies are scrutinised and discussed by MPs who represent the people. MPs also hold the executive accountable and represent the interests of their constituents. Parliamentary debates provide some assurance that major issues are being considered.

However, there are limits to the legitimacy of parliament. The House of Lords plays an important role in revising legislation and constraining the executive. But its legitimacy is limited because it is unelected.

In the House of Commons, the partisan point-scoring of Prime Minister's Question Time fosters negative perceptions of parliament. Parliament's reputation has also been damaged by sleaze. Public trust in parliament declined after the 'cash for questions' scandal of the 1990s when some MPs accepted money to table parliamentary questions. The Committee on Standards in Public Life and a code of standards were established.

The 2009 MPs' expenses scandal further damaged the reputation of politicians and parliament. MPs had claimed expenses for items ranging from adult movies (Jacqui Smith) to the clearing of a moat (Douglas Hogg). More serious were tax avoidance and the 'flipping' of second homes — changing the property designated as a second home so that expenses could be claimed on different properties. Six Labour MPs faced criminal charges; four were jailed. An independent audit by Sir Thomas Legg required 373 MPs to pay back excessive claims.

Many of the claims fell within the rules of the Additional Costs Allowance (ACA). It covered costs up to £24,222 that MPs from constituencies outside London incurred attending parliament, including mortgage interest payments, fixtures and fittings, and utility bills. MPs had been reluctant to vote themselves higher salaries for fear of negative publicity. So the ACA was treated as a salary top-up to which MPs felt entitled.

Reforms to the expenses and allowances system followed:

➢ The Parliamentary Standards Act (2009) created an Independent Parliamentary Standards Authority to run the expenses system.
➢ The Kelly Report (2009), by the chair of the Committee on Standards in Public Life, recommended that MPs should not be able to claim towards buying a second home. They can now claim rent up to the value of a one-bedroom flat.

Links to follow up

www.hansardsociety.org.uk — an independent research body promoting parliamentary democracy.

Parliament and government

The relationship between parliament and government is an unequal one, with the executive the dominant actor. The government has significant control over the legislative process. If it did not, it might not be able to fulfil its manifesto commitments or govern effectively. However, executive dominance does not mean that parliament is impotent. The power to dismiss the government is an important weapon in the parliamentary armoury, albeit one of last resort. Select committees have enhanced parliament's ability to scrutinise the government and hold it to account.

The relationship between parliament and government is not determined simply by the institutional resources that each possesses, but is also shaped by the political context. Three contextual factors are of particular significance:

➢ the government's parliamentary majority
➢ the level of party unity
➢ the assertiveness of the House of Lords

Government majority

The size, or absence, of a majority for the governing party in the House of Commons is an important factor in the relationship between the legislature and executive. The first-past-the-post electoral system often, but not always, delivers a working majority for the party that wins most votes in a general election. A government with a large majority is in a commanding position, able to push its legislation through parliament by utilising the whip system and controlling the parliamentary timetable.

The larger a government's majority, the less likely it is that the other parties in the Commons will be able to defeat or amend government bills. The ability of backbenchers to influence policy is also limited because a government with a substantial majority can absorb dissent within its own ranks. With a majority of 167 at the 2001 election, the Blair government survived large rebellions from Labour backbenchers on Iraq, tuition fees and foundation hospitals. Within months of its majority being cut to 65 at the 2005 election, the government suffered its first Commons defeat.

A governing party that has a slender majority, or none at all, can find itself in a precarious position. A hung parliament occurs when no single party commands an absolute majority of seats in the House of Commons. Then, a minority government or coalition government is likely.

In a minority government, the party with the largest number of seats governs alone. It may be able to persuade a smaller party not to vote against it on key measures such as the budget or Queen's Speech. This is known as a 'confidence and supply' deal. But it must find parliamentary majorities on a bill-by-bill basis. A minority government may be relatively stable in the short term, particularly if other parties do not want another general election. But it is difficult to sustain a minority government for long.

There have been three postwar minority governments:

➤ **Wilson government, 1974.** Harold Wilson's Labour government had no majority after the February 1974 election. Wilson called another election that October and secured a majority of 3 seats.

➤ **Callaghan government, 1976–79.** James Callaghan succeeded Wilson as Labour prime minister in 1976, but his majority disappeared after by-election defeats. Under the 1977–78 'Lib–Lab pact', the Liberals supported the government on key votes in the Commons.

➤ **Conservative government, 1996–97.** John Major's government lost its majority in 1996 following by-election defeats and defections. It was supported by Ulster Unionist MPs on some divisions, but there was no formal deal.

Coalition government

In a coalition government, two or more parties form the government having reached a formal agreement on a legislative programme and the distribution of cabinet posts. When the 2010 election failed to deliver an outright majority for the Conservatives, they formed a coalition with the Liberal Democrats. The two parties agreed a programme covering the major areas of public policy, and five Liberal Democrats took seats in David Cameron's cabinet. This was the first coalition in Britain since that led by Winston Churchill (1940–45) during the Second World War, and the first in peacetime since the National Government of the 1930s.

The Conservative–Liberal Democrat coalition had a healthy working majority of 79 in March 2013. Although party unity may be strained in a coalition of parties with different ideological positions, this majority should be sufficient for the government to get its legislation through the Commons. The coalition agreement explicitly permitted the Liberal Democrats to abstain on parliamentary votes on tuition fees and nuclear power. David Cameron and Nick Clegg made separate parliamentary statements following the publication of the Leveson Report.

Coalition governments may break up because of disputes between the parties or within them. Relations between the Conservatives and Liberal Democrats worsened when rebel Conservative MPs voted against House of Lords reform. The bill was withdrawn and the Liberal Democrats retaliated by voting against the introduction of new constituency boundaries for the 2015 general election.

The Fixed-term Parliaments Act (2011) states that an early general election can only be called if (i) the government loses a motion of no confidence and no alternative government is formed, or (ii) a motion calling for an early general election is supported by two-thirds of MPs. Under the latter, neither the Conservatives acting alone nor the coalition parties acting together have the numbers to force an early election. Under the former, the collapse of the coalition would not necessarily bring about an immediate general election — the Conservatives might form a minority government, supported by the Liberal Democrats on a confidence and supply basis.

Party unity

It is a common perception that MPs slavishly follow the party whip. It is true that MPs vote with their party on the overwhelming majority of divisions in the Commons. When a **parliamentary rebellion**

Key term

➤ **Parliamentary rebellion**
A division in which MPs vote against their party whip.

⟷ Stretch and challenge

The Conservative–Liberal Democrat coalition

The coalition agreement envisages the Conservative–Liberal Democrat coalition serving a full 5-year term. But research on coalitions in other countries shows that many break up because of differences between and within the coalition parties.

Question

How likely are the following scenarios for the Conservative–Liberal Democrat coalition, and what would be their implications?

- The coalition government serves its full term, but tensions between the Conservatives and Liberal Democrats escalate as the election approaches.
- The coalition serves its full term and the Conservatives and Liberal Democrats agree an electoral pact.
- The Liberal Democrats leave the coalition and either reassert their independence or explore cooperation with Labour.
- The Conservatives break up the coalition following either a series of backbench rebellions or a strategic decision by the party leadership to go it alone.

occurs, it is usually small and can be easily absorbed by a government with a working majority. But rebellions have become more frequent in recent decades, and some have been dramatic.

In the 1950s and 1960s, the Conservative governments of Eden, Macmillan and Douglas-Home suffered no defeats in the Commons. Things changed in the 1970s when ideological divisions within the Labour and Conservative parties became more pronounced.

> **Heath government, 1970–74.** A rebellion by 39 Conservatives meant that European Communities Act (1972) was passed only because 69 Labour MPs defied a three-line whip.
> **Wilson (1974–76) and Callaghan (1976–79) governments.** Labour operated with either a slender parliamentary majority or none at all. Forty-five per cent of Labour MPs rebelled and the government suffered 59 defeats in the Commons, the final one on a motion of no confidence.
> **Major government (1992–97).** Conservative rebellions on the Maastricht Treaty (1992–93) saw Major call a confidence motion to force the treaty through the Commons. Further rebellions followed on gun control and VAT on domestic fuel.
> **Blair (1997–2007) and Brown (2007–10) governments.** The rebellion by 139 Labour MPs on the 2003 vote on the invasion of Iraq was the largest in a governing party in modern British politics. There were also significant rebellions on foundation hospitals (65 rebels) in 2003 and university tuition fees (72 rebels) in 2005. Research by Philip Cowley and Mark Stuart shows that the 2005–10 parliament was the most rebellious of the postwar era. Rebellions by Labour MPs occurred on 28% of divisions and 174 Labour MPs voted against the party line at least once. The government was defeated on 90-day detention of terrorist suspects (2005), the Racial and Religious Hatred Bill (2006) and the right of Gurkhas to live in the UK (2009). Labour needed support from other parties to win votes on the Education Bill (2006), renewal of the Trident nuclear weapons system, and the Counter Terrorism Bill (2008).
> **Conservative–Liberal Democrat coalition government (2010–).** In the long 2010–12 parliamentary session, Cowley and Stuart calculate that 153 MPs from the coalition parties voted against the whip and rebellions occurred on 44% of divisions. But Conservative and Liberal Democrat MPs tended to rebel on different issues. Conservative MPs rebelled on constitutional and European Union votes. In July 2012, 91 Conservatives opposed the House of Lords Bill and 81 Conservatives voted for a referendum on EU membership in October 2011. The government's first significant defeat came on a 2012 motion calling for a cut in the EU budget when 53 Conservatives voted with Labour. Liberal Democrat MPs rebelled most frequently on welfare and social policy. Their largest rebellion (27 MPs) was on university tuition fees in December 2010. Differences between the two parties were also evident when, on a free vote, 137 Conservatives but only 4 Liberal Democrats opposed the Marriage (Same Sex Couples) Bill in February 2013.

Ideological differences between the Conservatives and Liberal Democrats provide a partial explanation for the high level of dissent since 2010. Significantly, coalition MPs do not feel as obliged to support the coalition agreement as they would their party's manifesto. The incentives for Conservative MPs to toe the party line are also reduced if they believe that their

promotion prospects are reduced because government positions must be given to Liberal Democrats. MPs may also exert influence through more subtle methods than rebellion. If the whips expect significant opposition to a measure, the government may withdraw or revise it rather than risk defeat or cause ill-will by exerting pressure on MPs. In 2008, Labour ministers made important concessions to opponents of the budget proposals to abolish the 10% income tax band.

Links to follow up

www.revolts.co.uk — data on, and analysis of, parliamentary rebellions by Philip Cowley.

An assertive House of Lords

The 1999 reform of the House of Lords strengthened the upper house and helped it become more assertive in the legislative process. The Lords blocked the Sexual Offences (Amendment) Act (2000) and the Hunting Act (2004), forcing the government to employ the Parliament Act (1949) so that the legislation could come into force without the Lords' consent after a 1-year delay.

In the first decade since the removal of all but 92 hereditary peers, the House of Lords inflicted more than 400 defeats on the Labour government — compared to seven defeats in the Commons. Many of these defeats occurred on judicial and constitutional matters, which are of particular interest to the Lords. The coalition government suffered 48 defeats in the Lords in 2010–12.

Notable examples of government defeats in the House of Lords include:

➤ **Counter-terrorism.** In 2005, the Lords amended proposals on control orders for terrorist suspects and insisted that the legislation had a limited lifespan.

➤ **Religious hatred.** Proposals to introduce a new offence of incitement to religious hatred were amended or blocked by the Lords in 2001 and 2005.

➤ **Trial by jury.** The Lords blocked Labour's proposals to restrict the right to trial by jury in 2000 and 2007.

The increased effectiveness of the House of Lords in checking the powers of the executive and forcing changes to legislative proposals is a result of a number of factors:

➤ **Party balance.** No party has a majority in the House of Lords, so governments must win cross-party support for their legislation. The votes of crossbench and Liberal Democrat peers are crucial.

➤ **Enhanced legitimacy.** The reformed Lords is more confident of its legitimacy and more willing to flex its muscles on legal and constitutional issues.

➤ **Government mandate.** Liberal Democrat and crossbench peers argued that the Labour government elected in 2005 did not have a mandate to introduce legislation restricting the rights of citizens because it won the support of less than a third of the electorate. Peers have also questioned the mandate of the Conservative–Liberal Democrat coalition because the coalition agreement was not put before voters.

➢ **Support from MPs.** The Lords has been most effective in forcing the government to amend its proposals when MPs have accepted amendments made in the upper house. Backbench support for Lords' amendments limits the prospects of the government overturning the changes. It is then more likely to compromise during the 'parliamentary pingpong' in which bills are passed between the two houses, rather than risk defeat in the Commons or resort to the Parliament Act. Four out of every ten defeats in the Lords were substantially accepted by the Blair and Brown governments.

Links to follow up

http://lordsoftheblog.net — a blog on the work of the House of Lords, to which Lord Norton contributes.

Viewpoint — Is parliament an effective check on the power of the executive?

- The executive's control over the parliamentary timetable has been weakened by the creation of the Backbench Business Committee, which determines the business of the House of Commons for 1 day a week, and the greater use of 'urgent questions'.
- Backbench MPs provide greater checks on government policy than in the past; increased incidents of rebellion are a constraint on government action.
- The reformed House of Lords, in which no party has a majority, is a more effective revising chamber — amendments made in the Lords often force the government to rethink legislation.
- Select committees have become more influential in recent years, with governments accepting around 40% of their recommendations. The election of select committee chairs and members has enhanced their independence.

- The executive exercises significant control over the legislative timetable and MPs hoping to steer legislation through parliament face significant obstacles.
- Government defeats are rare — most backbench MPs from the governing party obey the whip on a majority of votes.
- The government is usually able to overturn hostile amendments made in the House of Lords, and can resort to the Parliament Act 1948 to bypass opposition in the Lords.
- Select committees have little power. The government is not required to accept their recommendations and often ignores proposals that run counter to its preferred policy.

Reform of the House of Commons

Extensive reform of the House of Commons was not part of Labour's constitutional reform agenda in 1997. The changes it introduced aimed to modernise the Commons' archaic procedures rather than shift power from the executive to the legislature. Opposition politicians complain about executive dominance of the Commons, but in office this becomes more attractive. The MPs' expenses scandal gave additional impetus to reform of the Commons. A Select Committee on Reform of the House of Commons (the Wright Committee) was established but its recommendations were not implemented until after the 2010 election.

Changes made to the Commons under Labour included:

➤ **Pre-legislative scrutiny.** Greater scrutiny of draft bills prior to the formal legislative process.
➤ **Carry-over of legislation.** Bills that fail to get through the legislative process in one parliamentary session can complete the process in the next, provided they pass in one calendar year.
➤ **Modernisation Committee.** This was set up to consider reforms of the Commons' procedures. Its recommendations included changes to working hours.
➤ **Liaison Committee.** Since 2002, the prime minister has faced questions from this committee twice a year. This allows for greater scrutiny than occurs in the more partisan atmosphere of the chamber.
➤ **Westminster Hall sittings.** These sittings deal with non-controversial issues, select committee reports and motions chosen by the Backbench Business Committee.
➤ **Hearings on public appointments.** Since 2008, select committees have held pre-appointment hearings for public appointments to some 60 positions (e.g. chair of Ofcom, Governor of the Bank of England). They do not have veto power. The government's candidate for Children's Commissioner for England was not endorsed by the select committee but was still appointed.

The devolution of primary legislative powers to the Scottish Parliament, Northern Ireland Assembly and, since 2011, the Welsh Assembly has changed procedures in the House of Commons. For example:

➤ Westminster no longer makes law on policies that have been devolved.
➤ Questions on devolved matters can no longer be addressed to UK government ministers at Westminster.
➤ Westminster can make law for Scotland on devolved areas when the Scottish Parliament requests that it does so through the 'Sewell motion' procedure.

Conservative–Liberal Democrat coalition

The coalition government has introduced a number of reforms of the House of Commons:

➤ **Fixed-term parliaments**. Under the Fixed-term Parliaments Act (2011), general elections will be held after a fixed 5-year parliamentary term. Parliament can still be dissolved earlier if (i) the government is defeated on a motion of no confidence and no alternative government is formed, or (ii) a motion calling for an early general election is supported by two-thirds of MPs.
➤ **Implementation of the Wright proposals**. Reforms initially suggested by the Wright Committee were introduced:
  – Chairs of select committees are elected by a secret ballot of MPs and committee members are elected within their party groups rather than nominated by the whips.
  – The Backbench Business Committee determines the business of the Commons for 1 day a week.

– Public e-petitions that attract more than 100,000 signatures may be considered for debate in parliament. In the first year of the scheme, 17 petitions led to parliamentary debates including on a referendum on the EU and a reduction in fuel duty.

– A 'public reading stage' in which members of the public can comment on proposed legislation was piloted for the Protection of Freedoms Bill (2011) and the Small Charitable Donations Bill (2012).

A number of reforms signalled in the coalition agreement were dropped or had not come into force by early 2013. These include:

➢ **Alternative vote.** In a referendum in 2011, voters rejected a proposal to replace the first-past-the-post system with the alternative vote system for elections to the House of Commons.

➢ **Reduction in the size of the Commons.** Proposals to reduce the number of MPs from 650 to 600 for the next general election and equalise the size of parliamentary constituencies were defeated in the House of Commons in 2013 after the Liberal Democrats withdrew support.

➢ **Recall of MPs.** A 2011 draft bill proposed that MPs found guilty of serious wrongdoing by the courts or parliament could be subject to recall. A by-election would be triggered if 10% of constituents signed a recall petition.

➢ **West Lothian Question.** In 2012, the McKay Commission recommended changes to parliamentary procedures to address the West Lothian Question — why Scottish MPs should be able to vote on purely English matters when English MPs can no longer vote on matters devolved to the Scottish Parliament.

Links to follow up

www.parliament.uk/business/publications — scroll down to 'Research publications' and click on 'Parliament and constitution research' for research briefings and papers on parliamentary reform.

Reform of the House of Lords

Labour's 1997 manifesto proposed that all hereditary peers be removed as a first stage in the reform process. But the government accepted an amendment from the House of Lords that 92 hereditary peers, elected by their fellow peers, would remain until the second stage of the reform process. When the House of Lords Act (1999) entered into force, 655 hereditary peers lost their right to attend and vote. There were no significant changes to the powers of the upper house.

The intention was that this 'transitional house' would not remain in place for long. However, a search for consensus on the composition of the Lords has proved fruitless and the second stage of the reform process has not come to fruition.

Viewpoint   Should the House of Lords be wholly elected?

YES

- A fully elected House of Lords would have the legitimacy that can only be derived from democratic elections.
- It would be more confident in its work scrutinising and amending government bills, improving the quality of legislation.
- If no party has a majority, as would be likely under proportional representation, it would challenge the dominance of the executive.
- If elected by proportional representation, it would be more representative of the electorate.

NO

- It would come into conflict with the House of Commons, as both would claim democratic legitimacy.
- Institutional conflict between two elected chambers with similar powers would produce legislative gridlock.
- An appointed house would retain the expertise and independence of crossbench peers.
- The problems associated with party control in the House of Commons would be duplicated in an elected upper house.

Failed proposals for reform

A series of proposals for Lords reform have been made since 1999, but none has garnered sufficient support. The main proposals have been:

➤ **The Wakeham Report, 2000.** This report of the Royal Commission on Reform of the House of Lords proposed that the majority of peers be appointed, with 20% recommended by an independent appointments body. Between 12% and 35% would be elected by proportional representation. The remaining hereditary peers would be removed.

➤ **White Paper, 2001.** This proposed that 20% of peers be elected, but this figure was criticised for being too low and was dropped. MPs were given a free vote in February 2003 on seven options proposed by a parliamentary joint committee. None attracted majority support. In the Lords, peers voted for a wholly appointed house.

➤ **White Paper, 2003.** This proposed a wholly appointed house, but was widely criticised.

➤ **White Paper, 2007.** This proposed a hybrid house: 50% appointed and 50% elected. A series of votes on reform options were held in parliament. A wholly elected house was approved, as was the 80% elected option. But some MPs who backed the former were trying to wreck the process. The Lords again voted for a wholly appointed house.

➤ **White Paper, 2008.** This set out how a wholly elected or 80% elected house might function.

➤ **Joint Committee of Both Houses of Parliament, 2012.** This was established by the Conservative–Liberal Democrat coalition to issue proposals on a wholly or mainly elected

Lords. A majority of the committee supported an 80% elected upper house, but 12 of its 26 members issued an alternative report.

➤ **House of Lords Bill, 2012.** This proposed that, after a transitional period, a reformed second chamber would consist of 360 elected members, 90 appointed members, 12 bishops and 8 'ministerial members'. Elected members would serve non-renewable 15-year terms. One-third of seats would be elected by proportional representation on the same date as elections for the House of Commons. Appointed members would be nominated by the House of Lords Appointments Commission. The Commons approved the second reading of the bill by 462 votes to 124 in July 2012. However, 91 Conservative MPs rebelled and Labour indicated that it would vote against a 'programme motion' that would ensure speedy passage of the bill. With a majority unlikely, the government abandoned the bill.

Supporters of a wholly or mainly elected upper house claim that only elections bring legitimacy and that an elected house would be better able to challenge executive power. If proportional representation were used, no single party would dominate and long non-renewable terms in office would encourage members to be independent. Those favouring an appointed house note that the Lords has a different role to the Commons. The Commons has 'input legitimacy' because of its composition (it is directly elected), whereas the Lords has 'output legitimacy' because of what it delivers (its scrutiny produces better quality legislation). An elected upper house would produce competing claims of legitimacy and legislative gridlock. Elections would strengthen the role of parties in the upper house and the expertise of crossbenchers would be lost.

There is broad agreement on removing the remaining hereditary peers, strengthening the Appointments Commission and reducing the size of the house. Votes in the Commons under Labour and the coalition suggest that a majority of MPs support in principle a wholly or mainly elected upper house. But the debates revealed that many fear that an elected upper house would rival the Commons. Differences over the details of reform — for example, how members of a reformed upper house should be elected, their term of office, the presence of bishops, and whether there should be a referendum — also limit the prospects of consensus.

In the absence of further reform, the coalition government appointed additional Conservative and Liberal Democrat peers so that the chamber better reflected the share of the vote won by parties in 2010.

Links to follow up

> **www.guardian.co.uk/politics/lordreform** — coverage of Lords reform from the *Guardian* newspaper.

Stretch and challenge

Designing a reformed second chamber

When considering reform of the House of Lords, we should think about both the composition of a reformed second chamber and its functions.

Questions

1 Consider whether the following functions of the upper house should be reduced, maintained or developed:
- scrutiny of government legislation
- initiating legislation
- holding the executive to account
- specialist investigation
- debating major issues
- representation

2 How should the House of Lords be composed? Consider the following:
- direct election of all members (how should they be elected?)
- direct election of a majority of members (what proportion?)
- members without party allegiance appointed by an independent body
- nominees of political parties who are represented in the House of Commons
- members appointed by virtue of the positions they hold (e.g. government ministers, representatives of the Church of England and other faiths)

What you should know

❯ The UK has a system of parliamentary government in which government takes place through parliament. There is a fusion rather than separation of powers. The executive is the dominant actor, but its ability to control proceedings in parliament is affected by the size of its majority, the extent of party unity and the assertiveness of the House of Lords.

❯ Parliament comprises the monarchy, the House of Lords and the House of Commons. The House of Commons is the dominant chamber. It consists of 650 MPs who are directly elected. Almost all are members of a political party. The House of Lords is a revising chamber and can delay legislation for a year. It is unelected. Since the 1999 reform that removed all but 92 hereditary peers, life peers make up the largest category of members. The judicial role of the House of Lords ended in 2009.

❯ Parliament is the supreme legislative body in the UK. But parliament is a policy-influencing rather than policy-making institution. Most successful bills originate from the government. Party discipline and government control of the parliamentary timetable ensure that most government proposals are accepted by the House of Commons.

❯ Parliament debates important issues, scrutinises government actions and holds it to account. Select committees carry out detailed examinations of the activities of government departments, but the government is not required to accept their recommendations.

❯ Reforms introduced by the Conservative–Liberal Democrat coalition have enhanced the status of select committees and given backbench MPs greater say over the parliamentary timetable. But the MPs' expenses scandal weakened public trust in parliament. The under-representation of women and rise of career politicians also damages the image of parliament.

● Reform of the House of Lords stalled after the completion of the first stage in 1999. Support has grown for a wholly elected or mainly elected upper house. This would enhance the legitimacy of the second chamber, but might create tensions between the Lords and Commons.

UK/US comparison

US Congress and UK Parliament

➤ The US Congress is a bicameral legislature. The lower chamber is the House of Representatives, which consists of 435 elected members. The Senate, which consists of 100 elected members, is the upper chamber. The two chambers have broadly equal powers. In the UK, only the House of Commons is elected. The unelected House of Lords is politically and legally subordinate.

➤ Congress is a policy-making legislature. It can reject or amend proposals from the president, and puts forward legislative proposals of its own. Most proposals come from the president, who has the power of veto — although this can be overridden by Congress. The UK parliament is a policy-influencing legislature that modifies government proposals, but does not propose extensive bills of its own.

➤ There is a strict separation of powers in the USA. Members of the executive branch cannot be members of the legislature. The president cannot dismiss Congress, but Congress can impeach the president. The US Constitution also gives Congress the power to declare war, and Senate the power to veto appointments made by the president.

➤ Party discipline has grown stronger in the USA, but it is still weaker than in the UK. A president cannot rely on the support of members of his own party in Congress. Members of Congress are more likely than MPs to place the interests of their constituents above those of party.

➤ Standing committees in Congress have significant influence over US government departments. Committee chairs are powerful figures in Congress. Departmental select committees in the UK are much less powerful.

Further reading

Kelso, A. (2010) 'The House of Commons: an effective legislature?', *Politics Review*, Vol. 20, No. 2, pp.18–21.

Kelso, A. (2012) 'Parliament: an effective check on coalition government?', *Politics Review*, Vol. 22, No. 2, pp. 18–21.

Norton, P. (2013) *Parliament in British Politics*, 2nd edition, Palgrave.

Renwick, A. (2012) 'Reforming the House of Lords: difficult but not impossible', *Political Insight*, Vol. 3, No. 3, pp.12–15.

Russell, M. and Benton, M. (2011) *Selective Influence: The Policy Impact of House of Commons Select Committees*, The Constitution Unit.

Exam focus

Short response questions (around 5–6 minutes each)

1 What is bicameralism?
2 Define the term 'Westminster model'.
3 What is meant by the term executive accountability?
4 What is a whipped vote?
5 Define the term parliamentary government.

Mid-length response questions (around 10–12 minutes each)

1 Distinguish between departmental select committees and Public Bill committees.
2 Outline and explain parliament's legislative process.
3 What are the advantages and disadvantages of unelected peers?
4 Identify and explain *three* ways that parliament scrutinises the executive.
5 How do the functions of the Commons differ from those of the Lords?

Mini-essay questions (around 25–30 minutes each)

1 'Parliament's executive scrutiny role is ineffective.' Discuss.
2 To what extent has the advent of a coalition government altered the relationship between the executive and the legislature?
3 How effectively does parliament perform its representative function?
4 Do the arguments in favour of an elected second chamber outweigh the arguments against?

Extra resources to help you revise and consolidate your knowledge for this chapter are provided online at **www.hodderplus.co.uk/philipallan**. These include a revision PowerPoint, extension tasks and up-to-date weblinks.

Chapter 8

The prime minister and the core executive

Key questions answered in this chapter

➢ What powers does the prime minister have?

➢ What are the constraints on the prime minister's power?

➢ What role does the cabinet play?

➢ In what circumstances do government ministers resign?

➢ Where does power lie within the executive?

The **executive** is the branch of government concerned with the formulation and implementation of policy. In the UK system of parliamentary government, all ministers are drawn from parliament and are accountable to it. The **prime minister** and **cabinet** are the main institutions within the executive.

Key terms

➢ **Executive** The branch of government responsible for policy making and policy implementation.

➢ **Prime minister** The head of government and of the executive branch. The prime minister chairs the cabinet.

➢ **Cabinet** The committee of senior cabinet ministers that is the main collective decision-making body of the government.

The prime minister

The prime minister is the head of the government. He or she provides political leadership within the cabinet system and the country at large, chairs the cabinet, appoints ministers and is leader of the largest party in the House of Commons. The office of prime minister emerged in the early eighteenth century and became the accepted title for the First Lord of the Treasury. Robert Walpole (1721–42) is recognised as the first prime minister because he commanded majority support in the Commons and cabinet. From the start of the twentieth century, prime ministers have used 10 Downing Street as their official residence. Postwar prime ministers are listed in Table 8.1.

Table 8.1 Postwar British prime ministers

Prime minister	Period in office	Governing party	Reason for leaving office
Clement Attlee	1945–51	Labour	Election defeat
Winston Churchill	1951–55	Conservative	Resigned — ill health, some pressure from party
Anthony Eden	1955–57	Conservative	Resigned — ill health, reputation damaged by Suez crisis
Harold Macmillan	1957–63	Conservative	Resigned — ill health
Alec Douglas-Home	1963–64	Conservative	Election defeat
Harold Wilson	1964–70	Labour	Election defeat
Edward Heath	1970–74	Conservative	Election defeat
Harold Wilson	1974–76	Labour	Resigned — exhausted by office, feared ill health
James Callaghan	1976–79	Labour	Election defeat
Margaret Thatcher	1979–90	Conservative	Resigned — failed to survive Conservative leadership challenge
John Major	1990–97	Conservative	Election defeat
Tony Blair	1997–2007	Labour	Resigned — decided date of departure after pressure from party
Gordon Brown	2007–10	Labour	Election defeat
David Cameron	2010–	Conservative–Liberal Democrat	

Requirements of a prime minister

Three requirements must be fulfilled for a person to become prime minister. First, he or she must be a member of the Westminster Parliament. Until the late nineteenth century, the prime minister was usually a member of the House of Lords. As the House of Commons emerged as the dominant chamber, it became a constitutional convention that the prime minister should be an MP in the Commons. When Harold Macmillan resigned as prime minister in 1963, the Earl of Home replaced him. He renounced his hereditary peerage to be known as Alec Douglas-Home, and stood successfully in a by-election for the Commons.

Second, he or she must be leader of a political party. The prime minister must command the support of their party. If forced to step down as leader of their party, they also relinquish the office of prime minister, as happened when Margaret Thatcher failed to achieve victory in the 1990 Conservative Party leadership election. Five postwar prime ministers took office having become party leader when the incumbent resigned, including John Major and Gordon Brown (see Table 8.1). The new prime minister is not required to call an immediate general election in these circumstances.

Third, the political party that he or she leads will normally have a majority in the House of Commons. Winning a general election is the most common route to becoming prime minister. The monarch invites the leader of the party that has won a majority of seats to form a government. Thatcher and Blair became prime minister as a result of election victories (each won three). Prime ministers defeated in a general election (e.g. Major in 1997) must resign. **Majority governments** are the norm at Westminster. A 'hung parliament' occurs when no party has an absolute majority of seats. In such circumstances, the incumbent prime minister is not required to resign immediately but is given the chance to negotiate with other parties to form a **minority government** or a **coalition government**. The 2010 general election produced a hung parliament and a Conservative–Liberal Democrat coalition government was formed (see case study).

The 2010 general election resulted in a coalition government

Distinguish **between**

Majority, minority and coalition government

Majority government
- One political party has an absolute majority of seats in the House of Commons and forms the government.
- Government ministers are members of this one party.

Minority government
- No political party has an absolute majority of seats in the House of Commons.
- A party without a majority (often, but not necessarily, the largest party) forms a government but must try to secure support from other parties for key measures.
- Government ministers are members of this one party.

Coalition government
- No political party has an absolute majority of seats in the House of Commons.
- Two or more parties agree a deal to form a government, following negotiations and a formal agreement on policy.
- Ministerial positions in the government are shared between two or more parties.

Links to follow up

www.number10.gov.uk — includes details of the office of prime minister and its holders.

Case study · Hung parliaments

If a general election produces a hung parliament in which no party has an absolute majority of seats, a minority government or coalition government may emerge. A second general election may also be called.

The February 1974 and 2010 general elections produced hung parliaments. In the former, Labour won 301 seats and the Conservatives 297, although the Conservatives polled more votes. Defeated Conservative prime minister Edward Heath exercised his right as incumbent to try to form a government, but negotiations with the Liberals and Ulster Unionists failed. Heath resigned and the Queen invited Labour leader Harold Wilson to form a minority government. Wilson called another general election in October 1974 and won a three-seat majority.

In 2010 the Conservatives won 307 seats, 19 short of an absolute majority. Prime minister Gordon Brown stayed in office but Liberal Democrat leader Nick Clegg negotiated with the Conservatives first because they had won more seats and votes. They initially discussed a 'confidence and supply' deal in which the Liberal Democrats would support a Conservative minority government on key votes in the House of Commons (e.g. the Queen's Speech and budget).

When talks with the Conservatives entered a fourth day, Clegg also opened negotiations with Labour. Brown had announced that he would stand down as Labour leader by the autumn. Many Liberal Democrat MPs were ideologically closer to Labour than to the Conservatives, but a Labour–Liberal Democrat coalition would not have had a parliamentary majority. The vocal opposition of some Labour MPs raised further doubts about a deal. Five days after the election, the Conservatives and Liberal Democrats agreed to form a coalition government with a detailed policy programme. (The average duration of coalition negotiations in the EU is 40 days.) Brown resigned and David Cameron became prime minister. Five Liberal Democrats joined the cabinet, with Clegg as deputy prime minister.

Role of the prime minister

The role of the prime minister is not set out in statute law. Tony Blair claimed that 'it is not possible to precisely define' the role. The key functions are accepted as being:

> **Political leadership.** The prime minister decides the political direction taken by the government, setting its priorities and broad strategy. He or she will determine (or at least shape) policy, particularly on high-profile issues.

> **National leadership.** The prime minister is the predominant political figure in the UK and provides national leadership at times of crisis such as war or terrorist attack. The heightened media focus on the prime minister has furthered their role as communicator-in-chief for the government.

> **Appointing the government.** The prime minister determines the membership of his or her cabinet and government, appointing and dismissing ministers.

- **Chairing the cabinet.** The prime minister chairs meetings of the cabinet, sets its agenda and steers its decisions. He or she also creates and makes appointments to cabinet committees, and holds bilateral meetings with ministers.
- **Managing the executive.** The prime minister is responsible for the overall organisation of the government and is head of the civil service. He or she can create or merge government departments, and reform the civil service.
- **Managing relations with parliament.** The prime minister makes statements to, and answers questions in, the House of Commons. He or she also shapes the government's legislative programme.
- **Representing the UK in international affairs.** As head of government, the prime minister represents the UK in the European Union, international organisations and meetings with other leaders.

Powers of the prime minister

These give the prime minister greater resources than other cabinet ministers. However, they do not automatically produce prime ministerial power. The resources available to the prime minister are subject to important constraints and vary according to circumstances.

The main resources available to the prime minister are:

- patronage
- authority within the cabinet system
- party leadership
- public standing
- policy-making role
- the Prime Minister's Office

Patronage

The prime minister has important powers of **patronage** that are not available to other cabinet ministers. The most significant is the power to appoint government ministers. Other patronage powers have been curtailed in recent years:

Key term
- **Patronage** The power of an individual to appoint someone to an important position.

- **Judicial and ecclesiastical appointments.** The prime minister's role in appointing judges and senior members of the Church of England was reduced by the Brown government. He or she now plays no role in judicial appointments, and is given only one name to approve for ecclesiastical appointments.
- **The honours system.** The prime minister's role in the honours system has also been reduced. A police inquiry into allegations of 'cash for honours' — that donors to the Labour Party were rewarded with peerages — ended in 2007 without criminal charges being brought. But Blair announced that the prime minister would accept the final list presented by independent honours committees. Cameron is more inclined to award honours for political service, creating a Parliamentary and Political Service

Honours Committee. He was criticised for awarding honours to ministers dismissed in the 2012 reshuffle.

> **Life peers.** The prime minister can appoint people to the House of Lords. He or she may do so in order to give them ministerial positions. Gordon Brown gave government portfolios and life peerages to five prominent public figures who were not politicians, including former CBI head Sir Digby Jones. But they made little impact in office. Peter Mandelson was given a seat in the Lords on his return to government. The power to nominate life peers enables prime ministers to alter the party balance within the Lords. Blair appointed a large number of Labour peers before embarking on Lords reform. An independent Appointments Commission makes recommendations on non-party appointments to the Lords, but the prime minister still makes political nominations.

Appointing cabinet ministers

The prime minister's power to appoint and dismiss government ministers, particularly at cabinet level, provides a crucial advantage over colleagues. The Conservative Party gives its leader a free hand in appointing cabinet ministers. Since 1981, a Labour prime minister forming his or her first cabinet after a spell in opposition must select it from MPs elected to the shadow cabinet. This tied Blair's hands in 1997 but not thereafter.

In theory, prime ministers can create a cabinet in their own image, rewarding supporters and penalising disloyal MPs. In practice, however, the prime minister does not have a free hand. The 2010 coalition agreement required David Cameron to appoint five Liberal Democrats to his cabinet, including Nick Clegg as deputy prime minister.

A prime minister is unlikely to overlook senior party figures, some of whom may be rivals for their job. John Major's opponents in the 1990 Conservative leadership election, Michael Heseltine and Douglas Hurd, were given cabinet posts. John Prescott and Margaret Beckett lost out to Blair in the 1994 Labour leadership contest but were included in his cabinet. Senior politicians may have claims to office because of their high profile or standing within the party. Some might demand a post of their own choosing. Gordon Brown agreed not to stand in the 1994 Labour leadership election in order to improve Blair's chances of victory. In return, Brown gained assurances that he would become chancellor of the exchequer in a future Labour government and would exercise significant influence over government policy.

Ideological considerations are also important. A cabinet that contains politicians from only one wing of a party may not have the full support of that party. Margaret Thatcher included both economic 'dries' (Thatcherites) and 'wets' (one-nation Conservatives) in her first cabinet, but gave her allies key positions. Major ensured that the pro-European and Eurosceptic wings of his party were represented in cabinet, but sought to prevent either from garnering enough strength to challenge his authority. Blair's cabinets contained mainly 'New' Labour politicians, although 'Old' Labour was appeased by the appointment of John Prescott as deputy prime minister. When Brown faced unrest within the Labour Party in

2008, he brought prominent Blairite Lord (Peter) Mandelson back into the cabinet. Cameron's cabinet includes five Liberal Democrats and Conservatives from the left and right of the party, although some Conservative MPs bemoaned the underrepresentation of the Eurosceptic right.

The prime minister's choice of ministers is also constrained by the talent available. Rising stars should be promoted to give them experience of government. A party that has had a long spell in power, such as the Conservatives in the 1990s, may become stale.

Cabinet reshuffles

Prime ministers can also reshuffle cabinet portfolios. Some ministers might be moved to another post and others dismissed entirely. This allows the prime minister to promote successful ministers, demote those who have underachieved and freshen up the team. Ministers whose continued presence might damage the standing of the government can be axed. The prime minister decides the timing of a **cabinet reshuffle**, but a sudden resignation may force an unwanted reshuffle.

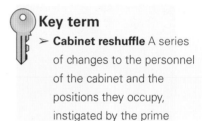

Key term

➤ **Cabinet reshuffle** A series of changes to the personnel of the cabinet and the positions they occupy, instigated by the prime minister.

The Coalition Agreement for Stability and Reform limits Cameron's patronage powers. The initial allocation of cabinet positions was agreed between Cameron and Clegg. Any changes in the allocation of portfolios must also be agreed by both. In reshuffles, Cameron nominates Conservative ministers and Clegg Liberal Democrats. When David Laws and Chris Huhne resigned, they were replaced by Liberal Democrats. Cameron cannot dismiss a Liberal Democrat minister without 'full consultation' with Clegg.

The power to dismiss cabinet ministers is a blunt weapon that may backfire. A botched reshuffle may raise questions about the prime minister's judgement, reveal cabinet divisions and highlight policy failings. This was true of Harold Macmillan's 1962 reshuffle, dubbed the 'night of the long knives', in which he sacked seven cabinet ministers. Thatcher's demotion of foreign secretary Sir Geoffrey Howe in 1989 also had damaging consequences. A year later, Howe resigned and his criticism of Thatcher triggered her downfall. Major was accused of not being ruthless enough. He seemed reluctant to dismiss ministers associated with policy failure (e.g. chancellor Norman Lamont after sterling's 1992 exit from the exchange rate mechanism [ERM]) or personal scandal (e.g. David Mellor). Blair speedily dismissed ministers whose behaviour was questioned, notably Peter Mandelson who was twice forced to resign.

After the 2005 election, Blair negotiated the distribution of some cabinet positions with Brown, his heir apparent. The refusal of ministers to change posts may also thwart a prime minister's plans. Brown intended to make Ed Balls chancellor of the exchequer in 2009, but the incumbent, Alastair Darling, let it be known that he would refuse to accept another post. Fearing the damage that the resignation of his chancellor would cause, Brown relented.

After Sir Geoffrey Howe's resignation in 1990 he launched a withering attack on the prime minister that helped bring about her downfall

Authority in the cabinet system

With the post of prime minister comes specific authority within the core executive. The prime minister:

➤ chairs cabinet meetings
➤ manages the agenda of cabinet meetings, and determines their frequency and length
➤ directs and sums up cabinet discussions
➤ creates cabinet committees and appoints their members
➤ holds bilateral meetings with ministers
➤ appoints senior civil servants
➤ organises the structure of government

This gives the prime minister a significant advantage over other cabinet ministers. As chair of the cabinet, the prime minister steers discussions and sums up. Skilful prime ministers can ensure that their favoured position prevails. However, if a group of senior ministers promote an alternative viewpoint, the prime minister may not get his or her way so easily. Poor management of the cabinet by a prime minister who is either too domineering or too indecisive will weaken his or her authority. An effective prime minister will act as coordinator or broker on disputed issues. It is the prime minister's role to direct the government's general strategy, giving a sense of purpose, cohesion and direction.

Agenda setting

The prime minister can determine the agenda of cabinet meetings by:

- controlling the information presented to ministers by determining which issues and papers should be brought before cabinet
- keeping potentially difficult issues off the cabinet agenda, dealing with them in a cabinet committee or in **bilateral** discussions with the relevant minister instead
- deciding the chair, membership and remit of cabinet committees, where much detailed policy work occurs

Key term

- **Bilateral** A meeting between the prime minister and a departmental minister in which policy is agreed.

The prime minister can establish committees to examine issues that he or she wants to promote. But he or she is unlikely to take a direct role in proceedings and cannot control all aspects of decision making at this level.

The prime minister can also reshape the structure and top personnel of central government. Harold Wilson created a short-lived Ministry of Economic Affairs to rival the Treasury in the late 1960s. Blair merged responsibility for the environment and agriculture in a new Department for the Environment, Food and Rural Affairs in 2001. Cameron transferred responsibility for media and broadcasting from the Department of Business, Innovation and Skills to the Department of Culture, Media and Sport after business secretary Vince Cable's hostile comments about Rupert Murdoch were made public in 2010. The prime minister also makes appointments to the top posts in the civil service and can reform the role and organisation of the civil service.

Party leadership

The prime minister is leader of the largest party in the House of Commons. A working majority in parliament strengthens the position of the prime minister, as it means that he or she is more likely to enjoy the confidence of the Commons and be able to enact the government's programme. However, the increased incidence of rebellion by backbench MPs suggests that a prime minister cannot always rely on their support. Blair suffered sizeable rebellions on the war in Iraq, university tuition fees and foundation hospitals in his second term. Brown made concessions to see off a rebellion on the abolition of the 10p income tax band. Coalition government proposals on reform of the House of Lords were dropped after a rebellion by Conservative MPs, after which the Liberal Democrats withdrew support for changes to constituency boundaries.

Party leadership strengthens the authority of the prime minister. Labour and Conservative leaders are elected by their MPs and party members. This legitimises their position. The length and cost of the leadership election process makes the sudden removal of a prime minister by his or her party less likely.

A party's support for its leader is not unconditional. Thatcher was forced out of Downing Street when she failed to muster sufficient support from Conservative MPs to win the 1990 leadership contest. The party leadership rules at that time dictated that the leader could face an annual leadership challenge even if they were also prime minister. Major resigned as leader of the Conservative Party — but not as prime minister — in 1995, calling a leadership contest to reassert his authority. Major secured a 218 to 89 vote victory over Eurosceptic John Redwood, who resigned from the cabinet to stand against him, but one-third of the party failed to support him.

Blair enjoyed great authority within his party in his first years in office, having secured two landslide election victories and reformed Labour's organisation so as to enhance the position of the leader. But support for Blair within the Labour Party waned after the war in Iraq in 2003. Ahead of the 2005 general election, Blair announced that he would not serve another full term as prime minister. But this did not satisfy some supporters of Gordon Brown, who launched failed attempts to oust Blair during his third term. A junior minister and six ministerial aides resigned in an attempt to force a change of leadership in 2006, but the rebellion petered out. Blair stepped down in 2007, before he had originally intended, because support for him in the Labour Party was ebbing away.

Brown became prime minister having being elected as Labour leader unopposed. But he had to survive efforts by Labour MPs to force him out. In 2009, James Purnell resigned from the cabinet and called for Brown to step down. An attempt by former cabinet ministers Geoff Hoon and Patricia Hewitt to force a secret ballot on Brown's leadership failed in 2010.

Unease among right-wing Conservatives about policy compromises made in coalition with the Liberal Democrats has increased since 2010. For a vote of confidence in Cameron's leadership to be called, 15% of Conservative MPs (46 MPs) must write to the chair of the backbench 1922 committee proposing a vote.

Public standing

The prime minister enjoys a high public profile. He or she provides political leadership at home and represents the UK in international affairs. The prime minister has regular discussions with other world leaders and attends formal meetings of heads of government, such as European Union summits. Thatcher and Blair made a significant impact on the world stage, in part because they forged a strong relationship with the president of the United States.

The media spotlight has focused more on the prime minister in recent years. The prime minister has taken on the role of communicator-in-chief for the government, articulating its policy programme and objectives. The prime minister's monthly press conferences and twice-yearly appearances before the House of Commons Liaison Committee are a formal expression of this. High opinion poll ratings strengthen the prime minister's position: a prime minister regarded as a strong and effective leader has much greater authority than one perceived as weak or out of touch.

Thatcher polarised public opinion but was widely regarded as a determined leader with a clear agenda. This image was a profitable one for much of her premiership, but towards the end she became associated with unpopular policies (e.g. the poll tax) and was viewed as autocratic. Major enjoyed record poll ratings in the 1991 Gulf War, but his popularity fell sharply when his government ran into a series of problems. Blair enjoyed high poll ratings during his first term, but the war in Iraq damaged his standing, after which he was trusted by fewer voters. Brown was seen as competent and experienced on becoming prime minister, but his standing plummeted to a record low in 2009. Cameron's opinion poll ratings fell after he entered office as economic recovery proved elusive and austerity measures were implemented.

Policy-making input

The prime minister's policy-making role is not confined to a specific field. Instead, he or she has licence to get involved in issues across the political spectrum. A prime minister with a strong interest in an issue can give it a central place in the government's programme.

The prime minister is the most important actor when political crises occur. Prime ministers will also take an active interest in economic and foreign policy. The chancellor of the exchequer and foreign secretary are powerful actors in their own right, but the prime minister is likely to play an active role in setting objectives, and directing and coordinating policy in these crucial areas. The prime minister needs the backing of senior figures on controversial matters. Chancellor Nigel Lawson and foreign secretary Geoffrey Howe forced Thatcher to shift government policy on the ERM in 1989 by threatening to resign if she continued to rule out British entry.

Thatcher was a hands-on politician who played an active role in many policy fields. Instances of policy success (e.g. the 1982 Falklands War) strengthened her position. But in the case of the poll tax, policy failure undermined her authority. Both Major and Blair played an active role in the Northern Ireland peace process. Blair sidelined secretary of state for Northern Ireland Mo Mowlam in the final stages of talks on the 1998 Good Friday Agreement, taking charge of the negotiations himself. Despite the rapid removal of Saddam Hussein, the 2003 invasion of Iraq undermined Blair's position. Doubts about the government's case for war raised questions about his judgement and trustworthiness.

Neither Major nor Blair enjoyed the success they hoped for in some domestic policy areas on which they focused their energies. Major's Citizen's Charter changed the nature of governance, but did not bring great political reward. Blair was frustrated that increased public spending in health and education delivered only a gradual improvement in services. Brown forged a reputation for competence as chancellor, but the credit crunch and recession undermined his economic credibility when he was prime minister. The coalition agreement on the government's core objectives limits Cameron's room for policy manoeuvre. But he has been able to set the overall agenda (e.g. maintaining the deficit reduction strategy) and determine responses to emerging issues (e.g. military intervention in Libya in 2011).

The Prime Minister's Office

The prime minister does not head a government department, nor is there a formal prime minister's department. Within **10 Downing Street**, however, lies the **Prime Minister's**

Office and this has grown in importance. Its staff of some 190 people contains a mix of career civil servants and special advisers.

> ### Key terms
> ➤ **10 Downing Street** The residence and office of the prime minister. 'Number 10' and 'Downing Street' are sometimes used to refer to the Prime Minister's Office.
> ➤ **Prime Minister's Office** The group of senior civil servants and special advisers, based at 10 Downing Street, who provide advice and support for the prime minister, particularly on policy and communications with government, parliament and the media.

The Prime Minister's Office has a number of different roles carried out by individual directorates and units. Two important aspects of its work are:

➤ **Policy advice.** The Prime Minister's Office provides the prime minister with policy advice, and may offer alternative views to those he or she receives from cabinet ministers. Prime ministers appoint their own senior advisers on Europe and foreign affairs. The Prime Minister's Office also engages in strategic thinking, helping to forge the future direction of government policy. Since Blair's premiership, it has also had an important role coordinating policy making and policy implementation across government. Cameron initially scaled back this strategic and policy role but subsequently strengthened Number 10's oversight of Whitehall by establishing a Policy and Implementation Unit in 2011.

➤ **Communications.** The Prime Minister's Office is responsible for the presentation of government policy. This has grown in importance given the intensification of the media focus on the prime minister. Thatcher's press officer, Bernard Ingham, was one of her most important advisers. Alastair Campbell, as press officer and then communications director, was an influential member of Blair's inner circle until his resignation in 2003. Following criticism of the politicisation of communications, responsibility for government communications was then transferred to a senior civil servant. Cameron appointed former News of the World editor Andy Coulson as his Director of Communications in 2010. Coulson resigned in 2011 following allegations about his role in the phone-hacking scandal and subsequently faced criminal charges.

Blair's desire for a strong centre meant that something akin to a prime minister's department was created in practice if not in name. This template was accepted by Brown and Cameron. But strategic and policy implementation shortcomings were evident in the Prime Minister's Office during their premierships and turnover among senior staff was high.

Prime ministerial leadership style

The structural advantages that the office of prime minister brings its incumbent are important but not sufficient for understanding the location of power within the executive. Power is not static, but dynamic. The context in which a prime minister operates is significant. Policy success and a large parliamentary majority can strengthen a prime minister's position considerably. But policy failure, divisions within their political party and unforeseen crises

Viewpoint

Do the resources the prime minister has bring him or her significant power?

	YES	NO
Patronage	Appoints ministers.	Senior colleagues have claims to posts.
	Can place allies in key roles.	Desirability of ideological balance.
	Dismisses ministers.	Botched reshuffles create rivals.
	Can appoint outsiders to government.	Availability of talent.
Authority in the cabinet system	Chairs and manages cabinet meetings.	Problems arise if senior ministers feel ignored.
	Steers, and sums up cabinet discussions.	Senior ministers may challenge prime minister's policy preference.
	Creates cabinet committees and appoints their members.	Not involved in detailed policy making in cabinet committees.
	Uses bilateral meetings with ministers to steer policy.	Ministers represent departmental interests.
Party leadership	Authority as party leader.	Support of party is not unconditional.
	Elected as leader by MPs and party members.	Party rules allow for a leadership challenge.
	Party normally has majority in the House of Commons.	Backbench rebellions have become more frequent.
Public standing	Has higher public profile than other ministers.	Unpopularity with voters undermines authority.
	Communicator-in-chief for the government.	Blamed for government's failings.
	National leader in times of crisis.	Expected to represent the public mood.
Policy-making role	Directs government policy and sets agenda.	Expected to be able to articulate a vision.
	Can direct policy in areas of their choosing.	Lacks time and expertise.
	Represents UK in international affairs.	Globalisation has reduced scope for action.
Prime Minister's Office	Provides advice and support.	Has limited resources.

can weaken them. For Harold Macmillan, it was 'events, dear boy, events' that a prime minister feared.

A prime minister's style of **leadership** is critical. Vision and political will are important, as are the prime minister's relationship with senior ministers.

Thatcher as prime minister

Margaret Thatcher made less use of cabinet than her predecessors. Detailed policy work was done in cabinet committees or bilateral meetings with ministers. Thatcher often began cabinet discussions by announcing the government's policy and kept some issues away from

> ### Key concept
> #### Leadership
>
> Political leadership is the exercise of power over public policy making by an individual or institution. The study of political leadership has focused on institutional structures (e.g. the offices of president and prime minister), relations between leaders and followers, the personality traits of leaders (e.g. their charisma) and styles of leadership. On the latter, James Macgregor Burns' book *Leadership* (1978) identified three styles of leader:
> - ➤ laissez-faire leaders, who adopt a hands-off approach to issues and delegate decision-making responsibility
> - ➤ transactional leaders, who favour collective decision making and broker compromise deals
> - ➤ transformational leaders, who are conviction politicians and seek to impose their own strong views
>
> John Major is an example of a transactional leader, while Margaret Thatcher and Tony Blair were transformational leaders.

cabinet. Senior ministers like Nigel Lawson accused her of paying greater attention to her advisers than to ministers.

Early in her premiership, Thatcher's skilful management of the cabinet enabled her to cement her authority at a time when many ministers doubted her policies. Her refusal to bow to pressure to tone down the monetarist budget of 1981 — and her colleagues' unwillingness to flex their muscles — proved decisive. Thatcher was then able to construct a cabinet of ideological allies.

By 1990, Thatcher had few loyal allies left in the cabinet. Chancellor John Major exploited her relative weakness to persuade Thatcher to agree entry into the ERM — a policy she had opposed. Within weeks, Thatcher failed to win on the first ballot of the Conservative leadership election. She then met her cabinet ministers one by one, but few offered their full support and Thatcher resigned. Economic problems, unpopular policies, cabinet divisions and low opinion poll ratings were factors in her downfall. However, Thatcher was in part the author of her own misfortune. By ignoring the concerns of ministers and bypassing cabinet, she had not strengthened her position but weakened it, alienating colleagues whose support she needed. When Thatcher was vulnerable, ministers struck back.

Links to follow up

www.margaretthatcher.org — website of the Margaret Thatcher Foundation. It includes key documents from her premiership.

Major as prime minister

John Major adopted a more collegiate style. Cabinet discussed government policy and exercised greater influence over policy direction. Major has been portrayed as a weak prime minister. He failed to put across a clear vision, was unable to set the agenda and appeared overwhelmed by events. But Major recognised the limitations of his authority, managing his cabinet in a way that ensured he stayed in office for over 6 years despite never appearing totally secure. He used cabinet meetings to bind pro-European and Eurosceptic ministers to government policy. By working closely with senior figures such as Michael Heseltine and Ken Clarke, he lessened the chances of a serious rival emerging.

Blair as prime minister

In Tony Blair's first years in office, seasoned observers such as Peter Hennessy, Dennis Kavanagh and Michael Foley depicted him as a more dominant prime minister than Major and even Thatcher. For Hennessy, Blair's was a 'command premiership', while Kavanagh described Blair's leadership style as 'Napoleonic'. Foley argued that the Blair era offered confirmation of the 'presidentialisation' of the office of prime minister. Blair took key decisions and acted as communicator-in-chief for the government.

Blair had little time for cabinet government, preferring to conduct government business through bilateral meetings in which he agreed policy objectives with individual ministers. Key decisions were reached in informal meetings of an inner circle of advisers. This style of government was dubbed 'sofa government'. It was criticised by former head of the home civil service, Lord Butler, in his 2004 report on the use of intelligence on Iraq's weapons of mass destruction. Butler was 'concerned that the informality and circumscribed character of the government's procedures which we saw in the context of policy-making towards Iraq risks reducing the scope for informed collective political judgement'.

Blair strengthened the Prime Minister's Office and brought parts of the Cabinet Office within the prime minister's remit. He sought to command swathes of government policy from Downing Street and improve policy coordination and delivery.

In his first two terms, Blair enjoyed big parliamentary majorities, a strong position within his party and a largely loyal cabinet. But he faced rebellions by Labour MPs on Iraq, foundation hospitals and tuition fees in his second term, and his opinion poll ratings fell. Labour won a third election in 2005, but its reduced majority limited Blair's room for manoeuvre. Blair's announcement that he would step down during this third term weakened his authority and he had to fend off attempts from within his own party to hasten his departure. By stepping down in June 2007, Blair may have jumped before he was pushed.

The Blair government was unusual for the extent of chancellor Gordon Brown's influence. Commentators talked of a 'dual monarchy' in which Blair and Brown had their own spheres of influence and 'courts'. They met regularly to bargain over policy. Blair allowed Brown unparalleled influence in areas such as pensions, enterprise and welfare-to-work that stretched beyond a chancellor's usual domain. Comprehensive spending reviews allowed Brown to shape government priorities.

The relationship was often fraught. In Labour's second term, it came under severe strain over foundation hospitals, tuition fees and the European single currency. Brown's supporters were prominent in failed attempts to force Blair out of office in his third term. Although often bitter and damaging to the operation of the government, the relationship between Blair and Brown was also one of mutual dependence: one could not maintain his position without the support of the other.

Links to follow up

'The Blair years 1997-2007', **http://news.bbc.co.uk** — BBC News analysis of Blair's period as prime minister.

Brown as prime minister

Gordon Brown enjoyed a strong start to his period as prime minister. He secured the Labour leadership without a challenge, responded steadfastly to terrorist attacks, and gave the impression that his was a government with new ideas (e.g. on democratic renewal) but without the 'spin' of the Blair period. The tide turned when Brown allowed speculation about an early election to intensify in autumn 2007, only to then rule it out. He was thereafter perceived as indecisive and his reputation was dented by the economic crisis.

Brown promised a more collegiate style, but soon reverted to reliance on an inner circle. He struggled to articulate a vision and intervened in minor policy decisions. Brown survived demands from senior Labour MPs for him to step down in 2009 and 2010 as cabinet ministers proved unwilling to force him out. But his authority was damaged and he was unable to impose his will. Brown enjoyed few obvious policy successes as the economic crisis forced other issues off the agenda, but by propping up the banking system he staved off an even greater crisis.

Cameron as prime minister

David Cameron has adopted a collegial style, in part because coalition requires regular negotiation between Conservative and Liberal Democrat ministers. Key decisions are taken in bilateral meetings between Cameron and Clegg, and in meetings of the 'Quad' (Cameron, Clegg, George Osborne and Danny Alexander). Cabinet committees are also important.

Cameron appears temperamentally suited to coalition, taking a pragmatic view of politics and enjoying good personal relationships with Clegg and Osborne. Relations between the key figures in the cabinet appear smoother than under Blair and Brown. Cameron has allowed ministers greater freedom to get on with their jobs. However, he has been criticised for failing to articulate a positive vision and for making a number of policy U-turns.

Coalition has constrained Cameron's powers of patronage and his ability to dictate policy. Party management has also proved problematic, with Conservative MPs rebelling on European integration and constitutional reform. Cameron's 2013 announcement that a future Conservative government would renegotiate Britain's relationship with the European Union then hold an 'in-out' referendum illustrated both the constraints of coalition (the Liberal Democrats would not support renegotiation and a referendum) and problems of party management (the pledge was an attempt to quell Conservative dissent). Yet had Cameron formed a minority government, party management may have been trickier still as Conservative backbenchers would have been better placed to defeat the government.

Viewpoint

Is coalition government a significant constraint on the power of the prime minister?

YES

- The Coalition Agreement for Stability and Reform sets the number of Liberal Democrat cabinet ministers. Cameron cannot dismiss or reshuffle Liberal Democrat ministers without Clegg's approval.
- The government's principal policies are set out in the coalition Programme for Government.
- Coalition requires a more collective style of government, with key issues discussed in the cabinet system to ensure the agreement of both parties.
- The prime minister must manage tensions between Conservatives and Liberal Democrats, and dissent within the Conservative Party.

NO

- The prime minister retains significant patronage powers, for example, creating and making appointments to cabinet committees.
- The prime minister determines the overall direction of government policy and shapes its response to new issues.
- Key decisions are taken by the prime minister in consultation with Clegg or in the 'Quad', where relations appear smoother than those between Blair and Brown.
- Coalition with the Liberal Democrats ensures Cameron has a healthy parliamentary majority.

Links to follow up

www.ucl.ac.uk/constitution-unit — Constitution Unit research on coalition government and the core executive.

Stretch and challenge

Rating prime ministers

In a 2010 survey, 106 political scientists and historians rated the success in office of postwar prime ministers on a scale of 0 to 10 (see K. Theakston and M. Gill, 'The postwar premiership league', *Political Quarterly*, Vol. 82, No.1, 2011, pp.67–80). The top three were: Clement Attlee (mean score of 8.1), Margaret Thatcher (6.9) and Tony Blair (6.40). Gordon Brown (3.9), Alec Douglas-Home (3.7) and Anthony Eden (2.3) made up the bottom three.

A similar survey by Ipsos-Mori and the University of Leeds in 2004 asked about the characteristics most important for prime ministerial success. The top ones were: leadership skills (chosen by 64%), sound judgement (42%), good in a crisis (24%), decisiveness (22%) and luck (22%).

Questions

1 What do you think are the most important personal attributes for a successful prime minister?

2 Use your list of core attributes to evaluate the strengths and weaknesses of recent prime ministers.

3 How important are external factors and luck in determining whether a prime minister is successful?

Theories of executive power

Cabinet government versus prime ministerial government

For much of the twentieth century, the main debate about executive power was whether the UK still had a system of **cabinet government** or had developed one of **prime ministerial government**. In his classic text *The English Constitution* (1867), Walter Bagehot described a system of cabinet government in which the prime minister was 'first among equals' (or *primus inter pares*) but decision making was a collective endeavour. By the second half of the twentieth century, however, the cabinet had been weakened and the powers of the prime minister had expanded. Proponents of the prime ministerial government thesis argued that the prime minister was now the dominant actor and bypassed the cabinet when taking key decisions.

Key concepts

> **Cabinet government** A system of government in which executive power is vested in a cabinet whose members exercise collective responsibility, rather than in a single office. Within the cabinet, the prime minister is 'first among equals'. Although the prime minister has institutional resources that other ministers do not have, he or she cannot act unilaterally.

> **Prime ministerial government** A system of government in which the prime minister is the dominant actor in the executive. The prime minister sets the direction of government, makes the major decisions and intervenes decisively in policy areas of his or her choosing. The cabinet is able to advise and warn the prime minister, but does not decide policy.

The core executive model

The term **core executive** covers those organisations and actors that coordinate central government activity, including the prime minister and his or her advisers, the cabinet and its committees, and coordinating bodies such as the Prime Minister's Office and Cabinet Office (see Figure 8.1).

Key concept

> **Core executive** The core executive is the heart of government, consisting of those organisations and actors who coordinate central government activity, including the prime minister, cabinet, cabinet committees, bilateral meetings between the prime minister and ministers, the Prime Minister's Office, coordinating departments (e.g. the Cabinet Office and Treasury) and top civil servants. The core executive model claims that power is based on dependence rather than command.

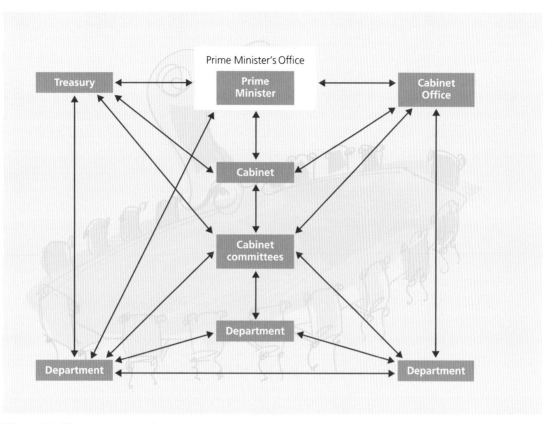

Figure 8.1 The core executive

The core executive model argues that the debate on whether the UK has either prime ministerial government or cabinet government is flawed. Power is not located inevitably in one or the other; instead it is shared between actors who are mutually dependent. The decline in the power of the cabinet does not inevitably mean that the prime minister is dominant. The key actors in the core executive all have resources, but to achieve their goals they need to cooperate and exchange resources with each other. Power is based on dependence, not command. A prime minister needs the support of cabinet ministers and officials to achieve his or her objectives. If this cooperation is not forthcoming, success will be difficult.

The prime minister has considerable resources at his or her disposal. However, the powers of the prime minister are not fixed but depend on a number of variables. These include external factors (e.g. policy success, parliamentary majority, government popularity) and the strategies of resource exchange (e.g. the leadership style) adopted by the prime minister. Cabinet ministers also have resources. Most head a government department, giving them authority and policy knowledge. They may also enjoy policy success and support within their party. Departmental civil servants are also significant, having detailed knowledge and experience as well as links with colleagues across Whitehall.

Martin Smith argues that Margaret Thatcher's downfall was inevitable, given her failure to recognise her dependence on the support of cabinet ministers at a time of wider political difficulties. By contrast, John Major recognised that in difficult times a prime minister needs the support of other actors within the core executive.

The core executive model recognises that the resources available to the prime minister have increased in recent years. The Prime Minister's Office has been strengthened and the prime minister's media profile has increased. However, other developments have made it more difficult for the prime minister to command policy. These include:

➤ the devolution of power to Scotland, Wales and Northern Ireland
➤ the continued transfer of policy competences to the European Union
➤ giving the Bank of England's Monetary Policy Committee the power to set interest rates
➤ privatisation and the transfer of functions to executive agencies, which make policy coordination more difficult

Prime ministerial predominance

Richard Heffernan describes a system of prime ministerial predominance. The prime minister is the predominant figure within the core executive. They have the potential to exercise leadership by utilising their institutional resources (e.g. leadership of the government allows them to set the policy agenda) and making judicious use of their own personal skills (e.g. being a good media performer). The more institutional and personal power resources the prime minister has, the more likely they are to be predominant. The prime minister cannot have a monopoly of power, however. They have to work with ministers because government is a collective endeavour, and they must also respond to parliamentary and public opinion.

The prime minister, then, leads but does not command the executive, and directs rather than controls its policy agenda. The political context is also important: policy success, public popularity and high standing in the party strengthen the prime minister's position, but policy failure and bad luck will damage it.

A British presidency?

Michael Foley has argued that the office of prime minister has become more 'presidential': that a 'de facto British presidency' has emerged. Three trends are central to **presidentialisation**:

➤ **Personalised leadership.** The prime minister is expected to be a dominant political personality who stamps his or her imprint on the government, and imposes a personal vision. Thatcher was a conviction politician whose ideology set the political agenda, while Blair and Cameron modernised their parties. Thatcher and Blair, rather than their governments as a whole, were personally associated with major policy initiatives. The personalisation of leadership is also evident in election campaigns and party organisation. Election victory is proclaimed as a personal mandate by the prime minister. The televised leadership debates held during the 2010 general election campaign reinforced this focus on party leaders.

Key concept

> **Presidentialisation** The idea that UK prime ministers have taken on some of the characteristics of presidents because of the emergence of a personalised form of leadership. It is characterised by spatial leadership (the distancing of the prime minister from his or her government) and public outreach (the tendency of the prime minister to reach out to the public directly). The concept of presidentialisation does not claim necessarily that the office of UK prime minister is becoming the same as that of US president.

> **Public outreach.** Political leaders have become public commodities. The political and media spotlight falls on the prime minister to a far greater extent than any other minister. He or she becomes communicator-in-chief for the government. The prime minister is also expected to connect with the popular mood and act as spokesperson for the nation. He or she claims to represent the public interest, and takes his or her message directly to the public through the popular media (e.g. on 'soft format' chat shows rather than heavyweight political programmes).

> **Spatial leadership.** A sense of distance has been created between the prime minister and his or her government and party. The prime minister relies more on his or her own inner circle of advisers than on the cabinet system, as in Blair's 'sofa government' and the 'Quad' in the coalition government. Blair and Cameron presented themselves as outsiders in their own parties.

The leadership stretch that characterises presidentialisation has strengthened the position of the prime minister. But it can also create problems. Just as the prime minister gains credit for policy success, so he or she is blamed personally for policy failure. Blair eroded the institutional foundations of prime ministerial power and developed instead an individual power base. But his position became exposed after the invasion of Iraq, when trust in his leadership declined and his leadership style was questioned. Brown was also blamed personally for the declining fortunes of his government, and faced criticism over his inability to connect with the public and communicate a clear vision.

Viewpoint
Has there been a presidentialisation of the office of prime minister?

 YES

- Leadership in the executive has been personalised, with the prime minister expected to impose his or her personality and agenda.
- Prime ministers rely on a close circle of senior ministers and advisers.
- Prime ministers have created a 'strategic space' between themselves and their governments, distancing themselves from other actors in the executive.
- Prime ministers appeal to the public directly, through the media, and claim a personal mandate from the electorate.
- Prime ministers have additional authority as party leaders, where they are elected by MPs and members, and exercise personalised leadership.

NO

- The prime minister leads but cannot command the executive, particularly in coalition, and directs rather than controls the agenda.
- Senior ministers enjoy support from government departments and have their own special advisers.
- The prime minister needs the support of ministers and officials to achieve his or her objectives.
- The prime minister's position is strong only if he or she enjoys policy success and popular approval, and makes effective use of his or her own personal abilities
- Support from the party is not unconditional, and unpopular leaders face concerted attempts to remove them.

Criticisms of the presidentialisation thesis

Critics argue that the notion of a British presidency misrepresents the nature of power within the core executive, overstating the room for manoeuvre that a prime minister has and underestimating their dependence on cabinet ministers and their party. The prime minister's power is constrained further in coalition government. Crude versions can also be criticised for ignoring the significant differences between the British and US political systems (see US/UK comparison, page 258).

Foley's presidentialisation thesis does not claim, however, that the office of British prime minister is becoming the same as, or even a pale imitation of, that of the US president. Nor has the UK become a presidential system of government. Important institutional differences between the British prime minister and the US president remain. The prime minister is indirectly elected, is accountable to the legislature and is head of a collegial executive. But a British prime minister also has greater resources than a US president, given that the former is leader of a disciplined political party and the British system allows for executive dominance whereas the separation of powers is a guiding principle of the US Constitution.

The cabinet

The traditional constitutional view is that executive power in the UK is vested in a **cabinet** whose members exercise collective responsibility. But the importance of the cabinet waned in the modern era. It now plays only a limited role in decision making, as many key policy decisions are made elsewhere in the executive. Suggestions

Key term
➤ **Cabinet** The meeting of senior ministers and heads of government departments. It is formally the key decision-making body in British government.

that the cabinet has joined the ranks of Walter Bagehot's 'dignified institutions' — those that retain a symbolic role but have no real influence — may be premature. As Thatcher's resignation illustrated, a prime minister who fails to recognise his or her dependence on senior cabinet colleagues risks losing office. Coalition government has also enhanced the status of the cabinet.

Cabinet ministers

The cabinet consists of the senior ministers in the government. Membership averaged just over 20 in the twentieth century. The number who can receive a cabinet minister's salary is limited to 22. After the 2012 reshuffle, Cameron's cabinet included a further 10 ministers who attend despite not being cabinet ministers (see Table 8.2). Only four cabinet ministers were women, compared with eight in 2006.

Table 8.2 The cabinet, 2013

Minister	Post	Party
David Cameron	Prime minister	Conservative
Nick Clegg	Deputy prime minister	Liberal Democrat
William Hague	Foreign secretary, first secretary of state	Conservative
George Osborne	Chancellor of the exchequer	Conservative
Danny Alexander	Chief secretary to the treasury	Liberal Democrat
Theresa May	Home secretary	Conservative
Philip Hammond	Secretary of state for defence	Conservative
Vincent Cable	Secretary of state for business, innovation and skills	Liberal Democrat
Iain Duncan Smith	Secretary of state for work and pensions	Conservative
Chris Grayling	Lord chancellor, secretary of state for justice	Conservative
Michael Gove	Secretary of state for education	Conservative
Eric Pickles	Secretary of state for communities and local government	Conservative
Jeremy Hunt	Secretary of state for health	Conservative
Owen Paterson	Secretary of state for environment, food and rural affairs	Conservative
Justine Greening	Secretary of state for international development	Conservative
Michael Moore	Secretary of state for Scotland	Liberal Democrat
Edward Davey	Secretary of state for energy and climate change	Liberal Democrat
Patrick McLoughlin	Secretary of state for transport	Conservative
Maria Miller	Secretary of state for culture, media and sport; minister for women and equalities	Conservative
Theresa Villiers	Secretary of state for Northern Ireland	Conservative
David Jones	Secretary of state for Wales	Conservative
Lord Hill of Oareford	Leader of the House of Lords, chancellor of the Duchy of Lancaster	Conservative

Note: 10 further ministers also attend cabinet: Kenneth Clarke (Minister without portfolio; Conservative); Andrew Lansley (Leader of the House of Commons; Conservative); Sir George Young (Chief whip; Conservative); Francis Maude (Minister for the cabinet office; Conservative); Oliver Letwin (Minister for government policy, cabinet office; Conservative); David Laws (Minister of state, cabinet office and education; Liberal Democrat); Grant Shapps (Minister without portfolio; Conservative); Baroness Warsi (Senior minister of faith; department of communities and local government and foreign office; Conservative); David Willetts (Minister of state, department of business, skills and innovation); Dominic Grieve (Attorney general; Conservative).

Most cabinet ministers are heads of government departments. Departments such as the Treasury, Foreign Office and Home Office have long been represented in cabinet. The lead ministers in spending departments such as health, education and social security have also been fixtures in the cabinet in the postwar period. Other cabinet posts are more recent creations (e.g. international development, created in 1997).

The first cabinet meeting following the 2012 ministerial reshuffle

Cabinet ministers must be Members of Parliament, to which they are politically accountable. Most are drawn from the House of Commons. It is rare for members of the Lords to hold senior cabinet posts. An exception was Lord Mandelson, secretary of state for business, innovation and skills, and first secretary in the Brown government.

Cabinet meetings

The frequency and length of cabinet meetings have fallen steadily since the 1950s. Then it tended to meet twice per week, whereas under Blair, Brown and Cameron the cabinet meets once a week when parliament is in session. Cabinet meetings under Blair tended to last about an hour, with some over in half that time. Recently, some cabinet meetings have been held outside London.

Cabinet meetings are rather formal affairs: there is a fixed seating arrangement; the agenda is settled in advance; and items are introduced by departmental ministers, with interventions from senior ministers and relevant departmental ministers given priority.

The role of the cabinet

The *Ministerial Code* and the *Cabinet Manual* set out the role and functions of the cabinet and its committees, acting as authoritative guides to the **cabinet system** for ministers and civil servants. The functions of the cabinet are as follows:

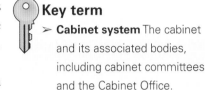

Key term

➤ **Cabinet system** The cabinet and its associated bodies, including cabinet committees and the Cabinet Office.

➤ registering and ratifying decisions taken elsewhere in the cabinet system
➤ discussing and deciding on major issues
➤ receiving reports on key developments and determining government business in parliament
➤ settling disputes between government departments

Links to follow up

www.cabinetoffice.gov.uk — click on 'Publications' for the *Cabinet Manual* and the *Ministerial Code.*

Registering decisions

The main business of the cabinet and cabinet committees concerns:

➤ questions that engage the collective responsibility of government because they raise major policy issues or are of critical public importance
➤ matters on which there is an unresolved dispute between government departments

Many issues are decided at lower level in cabinet committees, in bilateral meetings between the prime minister and a minister, or in correspondence between departments. Decisions are taken in committee and reported to the cabinet as 'done deals'. The cabinet thus acts as a clearing house for policy, registering or ratifying decisions taken elsewhere. If the prime minister and cabinet minister responsible for the policy in question are agreed, other ministers will have little chance of changing a decision. Ministers are discouraged from reopening issues where a decision has already been reached.

The ability of cabinet to decide policy is constrained by the infrequency of meetings, its size and the detailed nature of policy. It is impractical to engage in detailed discussions across a range of issues. Most cabinet ministers are primarily concerned with policy in their department. They have little time to study policy in other departments, lack expertise and may not see the relevant papers. This need not stop ministers offering their opinion on an issue outside their brief, but it curbs their influence. The frequent turnover of ministers also limits their impact.

The cabinet takes fewer decisions than it used to. Diaries of cabinet ministers from the 1960s and 1970s reveal that on issues such as UK membership of the European Economic Community and economic policy, the cabinet held lengthy discussions in which most ministers expressed their views. But Thatcher and Blair avoided lengthy cabinet discussions.

Discussions are more frequent in the coalition cabinet, where differences between Conservative and Liberal Democrat ministers have been evident on reform of the NHS. But the emphasis on settling issues before they reach cabinet remains.

Discussing or deciding major issues

Formally, the cabinet remains the supreme decision-making body in UK government. Yet for most areas of government activity, the cabinet is not a critical actor in the decision-making process. It may play a more active role when:

➤ issues are especially important or sensitive
➤ major or unexpected developments require a rapid decision
➤ government departments and ministerial committees have been unable to reach agreement

Even when the cabinet does consider major issues, however, its role is largely advisory. In June 2003, a special cabinet meeting was devoted to the Treasury's verdict on UK membership of the euro. Ministers aired their views, but in reality the cabinet was endorsing a decision — that the UK was not ready to adopt the euro — already taken by the prime minister and chancellor. The Butler report of 2004 noted that the cabinet was briefed on Iraq on 24 occasions in the year before the invasion. But ministers did not have access to key papers. Without these, Butler concluded, ministers would not have been able to 'bring their political judgement and experience to bear'.

Ministers can advise and warn, but it is the prime minister who must ultimately decide. The prime minister sums up the discussions and announces a verdict. Votes are very rarely taken as they would reveal divisions.

Government policy may, then, often be settled with little or no discussion in cabinet. The final decision on the poll tax was taken by a cabinet committee and discussed only briefly in cabinet. The prime minister may also want to keep a sensitive issue away from cabinet to minimise the possibility of his or her views being challenged. Thatcher did not want open discussion on membership of the ERM. Only a handful of senior ministers were consulted about Blair and Brown's decision to give operational independence to the Bank of England in 1997.

Reports and discussions

The cabinet hears reports on current developments, allowing ministers to keep abreast of events and policy change. It also allows ministers to discuss policy and the government's priorities.

Cabinet meetings have a formal agenda, with the following reports as standard:

➤ parliamentary business
➤ economic and home affairs
➤ foreign affairs

In the parliamentary report, the leaders of the House of Commons and House of Lords outline the following week's business. This reflects the cabinet's formal role in timetabling government bills and ministerial statements.

On domestic and foreign affairs, ministers may wish to clarify or question policy. They may offer their personal view, or that of a department or a section of their party. But the cabinet is not a debating society and time for discussion is limited. Only a small number of interventions, usually by senior ministers, will be taken. Blocking discussion of sensitive issues may prove counterproductive for a prime minister, as it allows discontent to fester. It will be better to gauge the views of colleagues, assure them that they are being considered and persuade them of the worth of the policy and of cabinet unity.

Settling disputes

It is a key working principle of the cabinet system that decisions should, where possible, be reached in cabinet committees or bilateral agreements. If an issue cannot be settled in committee, it will be referred up to the cabinet. Some appeals are relatively straightforward matters of arbitration between competing claims of departments. Examples include disputes between departments and the Treasury over spending allocations or where more than one department wants to be the lead actor. The cabinet judges the strength of the cases and reaches a binding decision.

Appeals to the cabinet are only permitted in special circumstances. Government could not work efficiently if ministers were continually required to wade through complex policy papers and force departments to give ground. This role as a court of appeal does not always work smoothly. In the 1985 Westland affair, secretary of state for defence Michael Heseltine resigned because he was unhappy with Thatcher's ruling that cabinet would not hear his appeal against a cabinet committee decision on the award of a defence contract. Secretary of state for trade and industry Leon Brittan then resigned after instructing a civil servant to leak information on the case.

Cabinet committees

A considerable proportion of decision making occurs within **cabinet committees**. These include:

➢ ministerial standing committees, which are permanent for the prime minister's term of office
➢ ministerial subcommittees, which report to a standing committee
➢ ad hoc committees — temporary committees set up to deal with a particular issue
➢ official committees of civil servants, which shadow ministerial committees

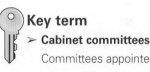

Key term

➢ **Cabinet committees**
Committees appointed by the prime minister to consider aspects of government business. They include standing committees and ad hoc committees.

Policy decisions are also reached in bilateral meetings between the prime minister and a departmental minister. Blair conducted much government business in this manner. Bilateral meetings between Cameron and Clegg are crucial to the operation of the coalition government.

Ministerial standing committees have considerable autonomy to determine the direction and detail of policy. Only where a final verdict has not been reached will the cabinet concern itself with the deliberations of a ministerial committee. The prime minister is responsible for the creation, membership, chairmanship and terms of reference of cabinet committees. In the coalition, government committees and their membership are agreed by Cameron and Clegg. Each cabinet committee and subcommittee has a chair from one party and deputy chair from the other. Liberal Democrat ministers chaired or co-chaired two committees and chaired five subcommittees in 2012 (see Table 8.3). Following criticism in the Hutton report of Blair's preference for informal meetings, cabinet committees were given greater priority. They have gained further importance under the coalition as forums for strategic discussions and resolution of policy differences.

The most important cabinet committees are those working on:

➤ domestic affairs
➤ economic affairs
➤ public expenditure
➤ national security
➤ the government's legislative programme

Table 8.3 Cabinet committees and subcommittees, 2013

Cabinet committee	Conservative members	Liberal Democrat members	Chair (party)
Coalition Committee	6	6	Prime minister (Con) and deputy prime minister (LD)
National Security Council (NSC)	8	3	Prime minister (Con)
NSC (Threats, Hazards, Resilience and Contingencies) Subcommittee	15	3	Prime minister (Con)
NSC (Nuclear Deterrence and Security) Subcommittee	5	2	Prime minister (Con)
NSC (Emerging Powers) Subcommittee	9	4	Foreign secretary (Con)
NSC (Afghanistan) Subcommittee	7	3	Prime minister (Con)
European Affairs Committee	10	5	Foreign secretary (Con)
European Affairs Subcommittee	9	4	Minister of state, Europe (Con)
Social Justice Committee	10	3	Secretary of state for work and pensions (Con)
Social Justice (Child Poverty) Subcommittee	6	2	Minister of state, education/cabinet office (LD)
Home Affairs Committee	19	6	Deputy prime minister (LD)
Home Affairs (Armed Forces Covenant) Subcommittee	12	3	Minister of state, cabinet office (Con)

Cabinet committee	Conservative members	Liberal Democrat members	Chair (party)
Home Affairs (Green Government Commitments) Subcommittee	11	4	Secretary of state for environment, food and rural affairs (Con)
Olympic and Paralympic Legacy	13	2	Prime minister (Con)
Economic Affairs Committee	14	4	Chancellor of the exchequer (Con)
Economic Affairs (Growth Implementation) Subcommittee	4+	3+	Chancellor of the exchequer (Con)
Economic Affairs (Infrastructure) Subcommittee	10	4	Chief secretary to the treasury (LD)
Economic Affairs (Reducing Regulation) Subcommittee	9	6	Secretary of state for business, innovation and skills (LD)
Economic Affairs (Trade and Investment) Subcommittee	13	3	Minister of state, foreign office/ business, innovation and skills (Con)
Banking Reform Committee	5	2	Chancellor of the exchequer (Con)
Scotland Committee	6	4	Chancellor of the exchequer (Con)
Parliamentary Business and Legislation Committee	9	9	Leader of the House of Commons (Con)
Public Expenditure Committee	5	2	Chancellor of the exchequer (Con)
Public Expenditure (Pay and Pensions) Subcommittee	11	3	Chancellor of the exchequer (Con)
Public Expenditure (Asset Sales) Subcommittee	8	2	Minister for the cabinet office (Con)
Public Expenditure (Impacts) Subcommittee	5	3	Chief secretary to the treasury (LD)
Public Expenditure (Efficiency and Reform) Subcommittee	14	5	Chief secretary to the treasury (LD)

Links to follow up

'The Cabinet Committees system and list of Cabinet Committees', **www.cabinetoffice.gov.uk** — details of cabinet committees and subcommittees.

Two committees were created to manage relations between the Conservatives and Liberal Democrats in the coalition government. The Coalition Committee, co-chaired by Cameron and Clegg, manages government business and resolves disputes. Research from the Constitution Unit reveals that it meets infrequently as differences tend to be resolved in informal meetings between Cameron and Clegg, or of the 'Quad'. The Coalition Operation and Strategic Planning Group is a small working group rather than a cabinet committee. It too has met rarely as issues are handled in meetings between Oliver Letwin and Danny Alexander.

The detailed content of material entering the cabinet system is largely determined in government departments. Legislative and policy proposals to be considered in cabinet committees must receive prior approval from the Treasury and government law officers. If a proposal impacts upon the work of another department, the lead minister should seek its views.

'Inner cabinet'

Prime ministers periodically hold meetings with small groups of ministers, advisers and officials. In times of crisis, a select group of ministers may meet regularly to discuss developments and formulate policy. When this occurs, the group is often dubbed an **inner cabinet** or kitchen cabinet. No such institution exists officially, although Harold Wilson created a short-lived inner cabinet to deal with the 1968–69 sterling crisis. 'War cabinets' of senior ministers and defence chiefs were in place during the Falklands War (1982), the war in Iraq (2003) and intervention in Libya (2011). The 'Quad' of Cameron, Clegg, Osborne and Alexander is a key forum for resolving issues in the coalition government.

The Cabinet Office

The **Cabinet Office** was created in 1916 to provide support for the cabinet system. Its key unit is the Cabinet Secretariat, which regulates and coordinates cabinet business. It calls meetings, circulates papers, prepares the agenda and writes the minutes of meetings. The secretariat also coordinates work on issues that bridge departments, and acts as a facilitator in case of disputes between departments. It is responsible to the prime minister and to committee chairs.

Key terms

➤ **Inner cabinet** An informal grouping of the prime minister's senior ministerial colleagues.

➤ **Cabinet Office** A government department responsible for supporting the cabinet system and the prime minister, and managing the civil service.

The role of cabinet secretary was redefined in 2012. Jeremy Heywood became cabinet secretary and principal policy adviser to the prime minister. Ian Watmore was appointed permanent secretary for the Cabinet Office and Sir Bob Kerslake head of the home civil service.

Under Blair, the Cabinet Office took a leading role in policy delivery and public service reform. The Strategy Unit (2002–10) coordinated policy on issues that cut across departments. The Cabinet Office was, in effect, brought within the remit of 10 Downing Street. In the coalition government, the Cabinet Office supports the deputy prime minister Nick Clegg, particularly on political and constitutional reform, and oversees policy on the 'big society'.

Links to follow up

www.cabinetoffice.gov.uk — details the role and organisation of the Cabinet Office.

Government ministers

There are more than 100 ministers in the UK government. Ministers are allocated positions in government departments. Senior ministers hold the rank of secretary of state, sit in the cabinet and head government departments. Below them in the hierarchy come the posts of minister of state and parliamentary under-secretary. These junior ministers are given specific policy roles in a department. In the coalition government, the Home Office has one secretary of state, three ministers of state (responsible for immigration, crime prevention, and policing and criminal justice) and two parliamentary under-secretaries. Finally, parliamentary private secretaries are unpaid assistants to ministers, but do not have ministerial status.

Ministerial roles

The main roles performed by ministers are as follows:

➤ **Policy leadership.** A minister does not have the time or knowledge to play a hands-on role in all detailed policy, but plays an important role in policy initiation and selection. Only a small number of ministers, such as home secretaries Michael Howard and David Blunkett, have changed their department's policy framework dramatically. Cameron granted ministers such as secretary of state for education Michael Gove greater policy autonomy than was the norm under Blair and Brown.

➤ **Representing departmental interests.** Ministers represent the interests of their department in the cabinet and negotiate for funding increases. They represent both the government and their department in meetings of the Council of the European Union.

➤ **Departmental management.** Ministers play a strategic role in managing the work of their department, setting objectives and shaping the internal distribution of resources.

➤ **Relations with parliament.** Ministers perform two main roles in parliament. First, they steer their department's bills through parliament. Second, they are accountable to parliament for decisions taken in their department, answering questions in the House and appearing before select committees.

Collective responsibility

The cabinet is theoretically a united body. Ministers are usually members of the same party who stood on an agreed manifesto at the general election. However, the sense of unity is undermined by departmental and personal rivalries. As well as being members of the government, ministers are also heads of government departments, whose interests they fight for in cabinet. Money and influence are scarce resources for which ministers must bargain. Departments provide ministers with authority, policy advice and technical information, so they may be tempted to act primarily as departmental chiefs rather than as members of a collegiate body.

Collective responsibility is a core principle of collective government. It has three main elements:

➤ **Secrecy.** Ministers must keep the details of discussions in the cabinet system secret. This ensures that sensitive information does not enter the public domain and prevents differences of opinion from being revealed.

> **Binding decisions.** Once a decision is reached in the cabinet system, it becomes binding on all cabinet and junior ministers regardless of whether they had opposed it or were not directly involved in the decision-making process. Those unable to accept this should resign or expect to be dismissed. Senior ministers who have resigned because of their disagreement with government policy include Nigel Lawson (1989), Sir Geoffrey Howe (1990) and Robin Cook (2003) (see Table 8.4). The Blair and Brown governments saw some ministers resigning in an attempt to force a change of leader. Junior minister Tom Watson resigned in 2006, having urged Blair to resign. Secretary of state for work and pensions James Purnell resigned in 2009, calling on Brown to stand aside.

> **Confidence vote.** The entire government must resign if it is defeated in a vote of confidence (i.e. one explicitly concerning the life of the government). This last happened in 1979 when James Callaghan's Labour government lost a vote of confidence after its bill on Scottish devolution was defeated in the House of Commons.

Key concept

Collective responsibility

The convention that all members of the government are responsible as a group. It has three main elements:

> Discussions in government should be kept secret.
> Decisions made in government are binding on all ministers.
> The government as a whole must resign if defeated on a vote of confidence in parliament.

Table 8.4 Ministerial resignations over collective responsibility: examples

Date	Minister	Post	Reason for resignation
1986	Michael Heseltine	Secretary of state for defence	Opposed defence procurement policy (Westland affair)
1989	Nigel Lawson	Chancellor of the exchequer	Opposed prime minister's conduct of economic policy
1990	Sir Geoffrey Howe	Leader of the House of Commons	Opposed policy on Europe
1995	John Redwood	Secretary of state for Wales	Launched leadership challenge
1998	Frank Field	Minister of state for social security and welfare reform	Opposed welfare policy
2003	Robin Cook (and two junior ministers)	President of the Council and leader of the House of Commons	Opposed invasion of Iraq
2003	Clare Short	Secretary of state for international development	Opposed policy on Iraq
2006	Tom Watson	Under-secretary of state for defence	Signed letter calling on Blair to resign
2009	James Purnell	Secretary of state for work and pensions	Called on Brown to stand down
2009	Caroline Flint	Minister of state (Europe), Foreign Office	Critical of Brown's leadership style

The convention under strain

The convention of collective responsibility has, however, been steadily eroded. Five main factors account for this:

➤ **Temporary suspension.** On rare occasions, prime ministers have suspended collective responsibility temporarily to prevent ministerial resignations. Harold Wilson allowed ministers to campaign for either a 'yes' or a 'no' vote during the 1975 referendum on the European Economic Community, despite the government supporting a 'yes' vote. This allowed a government that was divided on Europe to function in a more united fashion on other issues. Brown granted ministers a 'free vote' on three specific areas of the 2008 Human Fertilisation and Embryology Bill, but they were required to support it in its entirety at second and third reading. Three cabinet ministers — Des Browne, Ruth Kelly and Paul Murphy — backed an unsuccessful attempt to ban research on 'hybrid' embryos. Browne and Murphy supported the legislation at second and third reading, but Kelly missed the second reading vote and opposed the bill at third reading, by which time she had left the government.

➤ **Leaks.** Disgruntled ministers and their advisers may leak information on cabinet discussions to the media. They may want dissatisfaction about the policy or conduct of government to be aired, but do not want to go public with their criticism. In the 1990s, the press published details of divisions on Europe in Major's cabinet and purportedly verbatim accounts of discussions in the Blair cabinet. Cabinet discussions have also been made public in diaries written by cabinet ministers such as Tony Benn and Robin Cook. Alastair Campbell told the Chilcot inquiry into the Iraq war that secretary of state for international development Clare Short had been excluded from some discussions because of fears that she would leak sensitive material.

➤ **Dissent and non-resignation.** Cabinet ministers who oppose important aspects of government policy have survived in office even when their concerns have been made public. 'Wets' in Thatcher's first cabinet scarcely concealed their opposition to her economic policy. None resigned and Thatcher dismissed them only when her position was secure. Eurosceptic ministers like Michael Portillo remained in Major's cabinet despite their sympathy for backbench rebels. Clare Short stayed in the cabinet for 2 months after publicly expressing concerns about the 2003 invasion of Iraq, before finally resigning.

➤ **Prime ministerial dominance.** Some cabinet ministers who served under Thatcher and Blair believed that the prime minister had undermined collective responsibility by ignoring the cabinet. Heseltine, Lawson and Howe all cited Thatcher's contempt for collegiality as a reason for their resignation. Mo Mowlam and Clare Short complained that Blair did not consult cabinet sufficiently. Caroline Flint resigned from Brown's cabinet in 2009, accusing him of running a two-tier government with an inner circle that included few women.

➤ **Coalition**. The 2010 Conservative–Liberal Democrat coalition agreement set out four issues on which Liberal Democrat ministers would not be bound by collective responsibility. They were permitted to abstain on the construction of new nuclear power stations, tax allowances for married couples and higher education funding, and make the case against renewal of the Trident nuclear deterrent. Ministers were also free to campaign on different sides in the 2011 referendum on the alternative vote. Collective responsibility has also broken down where significant differences have emerged between the coalition partners. Cameron and Clegg initially took different positions on the Leveson Report before cross-party agreement was reached. Liberal Democrats responded to the abandonment of legislation on House of Lords reform by withdrawing support for constituency boundary changes, their ministers voting against them in 2013. Liberal Democrat business secretary Vince Cable has called for a 'mansion tax' and criticised the reduction in the 50p income tax band. Conservative junior energy minister John Hayes criticised Liberal Democrat energy secretary Ed Davey's support for wind farms in 2012. As the next election nears, the trade-off between government unity and party distinctiveness is likely to become more difficult to manage.

Individual ministerial responsibility

The convention of **individual ministerial responsibility** states that ministers are accountable to parliament for their own personal conduct, the general conduct of their department and the policies they pursue. The convention is not a rigid one, however, and confusion exists as to when a minister should be obliged to resign.

Key concept

Individual ministerial responsibility

The convention that ministers are accountable to parliament for their personal conduct, the general conduct of their department and the policies they pursue, the actions of officials within their department, and their own personal conduct. Governments have redefined the convention so that ministers should *not* be held personally responsible for:

➤ decisions made in their department that they had no knowledge of
➤ operational matters handled by officials in departments or executive agencies

Governments have long drawn a distinction between ministerial accountability (i.e. a minister's duty to give an account to parliament) and their individual responsibility. Home secretary Sir David Maxwell-Fyfe stated in 1954 that ministers cannot be held responsible for decisions taken by civil servants which they had no knowledge of, or which they disagreed with. Ministers are not obliged to resign if failings are traceable to the actions (or inaction) of civil servants. But they are constitutionally responsible for informing parliament of the actions of their department.

The 1996 Scott Report on the sale of arms to Iraq stated that ministers had a duty to be as open as possible, withholding information only when disclosure would not be in the public interest, but ministers were culpable only if they misled parliament 'knowingly'. It chronicled a number of occasions on which ministers misled parliament about changes in government policy, but none resigned because they denied culpability. The *Ministerial*

Code states that ministers must give 'accurate and truthful information to Parliament'; those who 'knowingly mislead Parliament will be expected to offer their resignation'. Immigration minister Beverley Hughes resigned in 2004 after admitting that she had unwittingly given parliament a 'misleading impression' on checks on migrants from eastern Europe.

A further distinction is that between policy and operations. Ministers are responsible for policy, but officials are responsible for day-to-day operational matters. Home Secretary Michael Howard sacked Derek Lewis, chief executive of the Prison Service, in 1995, blaming him for escapes from prison. But Lewis claimed that Howard had intervened in operational decisions. The head of the UK Border Force, Brodie Clark, was suspended in 2011 and then resigned after border controls were relaxed without ministerial agreement. He went beyond a pilot scheme requiring fewer mandatory checks on passengers by also suspending some passport checks, action which Home Secretary Theresa May had not authorised.

The transfer of policy implementation functions from government departments to executive agencies, which operate at arm's length from government, has added to the complexity surrounding ministerial responsibility.

Grounds for resignation

Four main categories of resignation on the grounds of individual ministerial responsibility can be identified, but in practice they overlap (see Table 8.5).

➤ **Mistakes made within departments.** Agriculture minister Sir Thomas Dugdale resigned in 1954 when mistakes made by civil servants in the Crichel Down case came to light — although he had come under pressure to resign. Such cases are rare. Reports into the sale of arms to Iraq (1996) and BSE (2000) uncovered mistakes in departments, but ministers survived. Ministers also remained in post when errors by civil servants forced the cancellation of competition for the West Coast Main Line franchise in 2012.

➤ **Policy failure.** Resignations following policy failure include that of chancellor of the exchequer James Callaghan after the 1967 devaluation of sterling, although he became home secretary in the ensuing cabinet reshuffle. However, Norman Lamont did not resign as chancellor when sterling left the ERM in 1992. Foreign secretary Lord Carrington and two junior ministers resigned after Argentina invaded the Falkland Islands in 1982. This is often cited as an example of ministers standing down because of policy failure. But Carrington stated that the situation had not been mishandled, and that he had resigned to ensure national unity in the build-up to war. Defence secretary John Nott remained in office.

➤ **Personal misconduct.** Ministers are expected to follow the 'seven principles of public life' set out by the 1995 Nolan Committee on Standards in Public Life and included in the *Ministerial Code*. They are selflessness, integrity, objectivity, accountability, openness, honesty and leadership. The Nolan Committee was set up after the 'cash for questions' case which led to the resignations of Neil Hamilton and Tim Smith. Ministers who break the *Ministerial Code* are expected to resign (e.g. Liam Fox in 2011). Peter Mandelson and David Blunkett both left the Blair cabinet twice after allegations about their private interests and/or conduct in office. Chris Huhne resigned in 2012 after being charged with perverting the course of justice in relation to a 2003 motoring offence for which his wife took the penalty points. Cecil Parkinson resigned in 1983 following revelations about his private life, but others (e.g. John Prescott) survived personal scandal.

Table 8.5 Ministerial resignations over individual responsibility: examples

Date	Minister	Post	Reason for resignation
1963	John Profumo	Minister of war	*Personal misconduct* — sex scandal and lying to House of Commons
1967	James Callaghan	Chancellor of the exchequer	*Policy failure* — devaluation of sterling
1972	Reginald Maudling	Home secretary	*Personal misconduct* — financial affairs
1982	Lord Carrington (and two junior ministers)	Foreign secretary	*Policy failure* — misjudgements before Argentina invaded the Falkland Islands
1983	Cecil Parkinson	Secretary of state for trade and industry	*Personal misconduct* — extramarital affair
1986	Leon Brittan	Secretary of state for trade and industry	*Political pressure* — leak of letter in Westland affair
1988	Edwina Currie	Minister of state, department of health	*Policy failure* — criticised for her warning about salmonella in eggs
1994	Neil Hamilton	Minister of corporate affairs, Board of Trade	*Personal misconduct* — 'cash for questions'
1998	Peter Mandelson	Secretary of state for trade and industry	*Personal misconduct* — financial affairs
2001	Peter Mandelson	Secretary of state for Northern Ireland	*Personal misconduct* — allegations of abuse of office
2002	Stephen Byers	Secretary of state for transport	*Political pressure* — disputes in Department of Local Government, Transport and the Regions, and policy problems
2004	David Blunkett	Home secretary	*Personal misconduct* — allegations of abuse of office
2005	David Blunkett	Secretary of state for work and pensions	*Personal misconduct* — broke the *Ministerial Code* on private sector job
2008	Peter Hain	Secretary of state for work and pensions; secretary of state for Wales	*Personal misconduct* — police investigation into political donations
2010	David Laws	Chief secretary to the treasury	*Personal misconduct* — past expense claims
2011	Liam Fox	Secretary of state for defence	*Personal misconduct* — working relationship with Adam Werrity broke the *Ministerial Code*
2012	Chris Huhne	Secretary of state for energy and climate change	*Personal misconduct* — charged with perverting the course of justice
2012	Andrew Mitchell	Chief whip	*Personal misconduct* — accused of insulting policemen in Downing Street

> **Political pressure.** This category is looser because it covers resignations that are not attributable to a single policy problem or scandal. Instead, they result from a period of sustained pressure from parliament, the party or the press about a minister's performance. In 2002, secretary of state for transport Stephen Byers resigned after an accumulation of problems including policy failure, disputes between civil servants and special advisers in his department, press criticism and Byers' admission that he had given inaccurate information to parliament.

Chris Huhne, who resigned in 2012

There are, then, no hard-and-fast rules on individual ministerial responsibility. Resignations often result from cumulative pressure rather than a single incidence of failure. The prime minister, House of Commons, political party and media can all apply pressure on underperforming ministers. Chief whip Andrew Mitchell resigned in 2012 weeks after he was alleged to have insulted police officers at the entrance to Downing Street, pressure on his position having escalated. Crucially, a minister is unlikely to remain in office if the prime minister considers ongoing media publicity too damaging or has lost faith in them.

Links to follow up

    www.cabinetoffice.gov.uk — click on 'Publications' for the *Ministerial Code*.

Ministers and civil servants

Government departments are staffed by **civil servants**: that is, officials appointed by the Crown. Some civil servants provide policy advice to ministers. In doing so, they may have advantages over ministers, such as experience, expertise and access to information. Civil servants are required to provide impartial advice, but can define which policy options are practicable and affordable. The Constitutional Reform and Governance Act (2010) put the civil service and *Civil Service Code* on a statutory footing. The latter sets out four core values: integrity, honesty, objectivity and impartiality.

 Key term

> **Civil servant** An official employed in a civil capacity by the Crown, responsible for policy advice or policy implementation.

Ministers, civil servants and special advisers

Distinguish between

Ministers

➢ MPs and peers.
➢ Make policy decisions.
➢ Required to support government policy.
➢ Accountable to parliament.
➢ Bound by *Ministerial Code*.
➢ Temporary.

Civil servants

➢ Officials appointed by the Crown.
➢ Advise on policy options.
➢ Politically neutral.
➢ Anonymity.
➢ Bound by *Civil Service Code*.
➢ Permanent.

Special advisers

➢ Political appointments made by ministers.
➢ Advise on policy options.
➢ Politically partisan.
➢ Accountable to ministers.
➢ *Code of Conduct* provides guidance on role.
➢ Temporary.

Claims that senior civil servants had too much influence over policy were common in the 1970s and 1980s. Tony Benn, for example, complained that civil servants had frustrated his policies when he was a minister. The 1980s BBC television comedy *Yes Minister* depicted a senior civil servant manipulating his often hapless ministerial boss (but often getting his comeuppance).

Special advisers and spin doctors

By the late 1990s, ministers had tilted the balance back in their favour. Rather than relying on advice from officials, they employed **special advisers** while many civil servants were engaged in operational activities. Special advisers are political appointments employed as temporary civil servants. They carry out policy advice or media liaison roles, the latter being known as **spin doctors**. The BBC comedy *The Thick of It* reflected the changed times by pitching spin doctors against ministers and civil servants. The coalition government initially pledged to reduce the number of special advisers. In 2012, there were 81 special advisers across government, a slight decline from the 2005 peak of 84 but more than double the number employed in the early 1990s. The number of special advisers at Number 10 reached a high of 36 in 2012.

The role of special advisers has proved controversial. Two of Blair's advisers, chief of staff Jonathan Powell and communications director Alastair Campbell (1997–2003), were given the power to issue instructions to civil servants. Brown ended this. In 2001–02, a dispute between advisers and civil servants spiralled out of control in the Department of Transport,

Key terms

➢ **Special adviser** A temporary political appointment made by a government minister.
➢ **Spin doctor** A special adviser employed to promote the image of the minister and his or her policy in the media.

Local Government and the Regions. Secretary of state Stephen Byers, his media adviser Jo Moore and Martin Sixsmith, the civil servant in charge of the department's communications, all lost their jobs. Brown's media adviser, Damian McBride, resigned in 2009 when e-mails making unfounded allegations about Conservative politicians became public. Adam Smith, adviser to culture secretary Jeremy Hunt, resigned in 2012 after evidence to the Leveson Inquiry showed that he had been in regular contact with News International when Hunt was considering the company's bid for control of BSkyB.

The Constitutional Reform and Governance Act (2010) sets out the role and responsibilities of special advisers. A code of conduct was revised to reflect the advent of coalition, with special advisers required to serve the government as a whole not just their minister.

Links to follow up

www.civilservice.gov.uk — civil service website, with information on its structure and values.

Civil service reform

Principles of the civil service

The civil service is a **bureaucracy** that operates according to a clear set of procedures and has a hierarchical structure. It has traditionally operated according to four principles:

➤ **Impartiality.** Civil servants serve the Crown rather than the government of the day. They are expected to be politically neutral and not become involved in overtly party political tasks.

➤ **Anonymity.** Individual civil servants should not be identified as the author of advice to ministers. Some may be called before parliamentary committees, but they give evidence under the direction of ministers. Civil servants sign the Official Secrets Act.

➤ **Permanence.** Civil servants stay in their posts when there is a change of government.

➤ **Meritocracy.** Civil servants are not political appointments. Instead, the civil service is staffed by generalists, recruited through competitive exams and interviews.

 Key concept

➤ **Bureaucracy** A large organisation that enacts policy and operates according to a clear set of rules and procedures. The role of each official within a bureaucracy is defined by these rules, and appointments are based on merit. There is a hierarchy of positions, with junior officials responsible to senior officials. A bureaucracy is impersonal: officials act on behalf of the organisation rather than in a private capacity.

Links to follow up

www.civilservant.org.uk — independent site detailing the work of the civil service.

Reforms since 1988

Significant reforms of the civil service have been introduced since the 1988 *Next Steps* report. It argued that the civil service was too big, lacked innovation and was not providing quality policy advice or effective policy delivery. The main reforms have been:

➤ **Executive agencies.** The policy-making and policy implementation roles of the civil service were separated. Civil servants working in **Whitehall** continue to advise ministers, but policy implementation functions and the delivery of public services were transferred to executive agencies (e.g. HM Prison Service). These operate at arm's length from government departments. A chief executive is responsible for their day-to-day operations.

➤ **Marketisation.** Many activities of government departments and executive agencies were contracted out to the private sector, which, it was claimed, would provide cheaper and more efficient services. Private sector finance has been used to fund public projects through the Private Finance Initiative.

Key terms

➤ **Executive agency** An agency responsible for the delivery of government policy that is subordinate to a government department but enjoys significant autonomy in its day-to-day operations.

➤ **Whitehall** The UK civil service and government departments, named after the area of London in which many departments are based.

➤ **Marketisation** The extension of market mechanisms into government and the public sector: for example, by the transfer of the provision of public services to the private sector.

➤ **Managerial culture.** Private sector management techniques have been introduced into departments and executive agencies. These include efficiency drives, performance measures and changes to working conditions. The size of the civil service has been cut (from 732,000 in 1979 to 453,000 full-time equivalent basis in 2011) and jobs relocated outside London.

➤ **Recruitment.** More outsiders have been recruited, particularly those with experience in the private sector or with specialist skills (e.g. in IT or communications).

➤ **Diversity.** Senior ranks of the civil service were, into the 1980s, largely made up of white, middle-class men who had a public school and Oxbridge education. By 2011 women made up 35% of the senior civil service and ethnic minorities 5%.

Concerns about the reforms

These radical changes to the structure, functions and character of the civil service have prompted concerns that the principles of impartiality, anonymity and permanence are under threat. The main concerns are:

➤ **Fragmentation.** The separation of the policy advice and service delivery functions of the civil service has brought fragmentation and problems of control and coordination.

➤ **Markets and agencies.** Critics argue that market forces and new managerial practices have eroded the public service ethos of the civil service. Although executive agencies have brought greater efficiency and improved service delivery, there have been some notable failures (e.g. the Child Support Agency).

➤ **Accountability.** The creation of executive agencies has blurred the lines of accountability. It is not clear whether agency chief executives or government ministers should be held ultimately responsible for policy failures. Ministers use the distinction between policy and operations to escape direct responsibility for policy delivery problems.

➤ **Politicisation.** Governments have been criticised for exerting too much political pressure on the civil service. The use of special advisers, the role that civil servants play in promoting government policy, and senior appointments based in part on political considerations are said to have undermined impartiality.

Links to follow up

www.instituteforgovernment.org.uk — think tank focusing on the civil service and government departments.

Viewpoint **Does the civil service play a crucial role in policy-making?**

 YES

● Senior civil servants hold the key roles in government departments, which often develop their own policy ethos.
● Civil servants have expertise, resources and relationships with outside groups that are not available to ministers and special advisers.
● Civil servants shape government policy by defining which options are workable and affordable.
● Civil servants are key actors in policy implementation, which is critical to the success of a policy.

 NO

● Ministers increasingly turn to special advisers, appointed from outside Whitehall, for policy advice.
● Senior civil servants spend more time on departmental management, and seven out of ten civil servants work in operational delivery.
● The coalition government aims to obtain more policy advice from outside the civil service.
● Ministers are accountable for policy decisions, but not for operational ones.

What you should know

◗ The prime minister is the predominant actor within the executive branch. He or she has significant institutional resources. The prime minister appoints and dismisses members of the government; chairs the cabinet and directs discussion within it; and is supported by the Prime Minister's Office and Cabinet Office. Leadership of the largest party in the House of Commons brings additional authority.

◗ However, the powers of a prime minister are tempered by constraints: for example, the need to placate senior colleagues and the party when appointing the cabinet. The prime minister has the potential to exercise leadership, but this depends upon effective use of these institutional resources, a favourable context (e.g. policy success) and the prime minister's own leadership skills.

❖ The position of the prime minister has been strengthened in recent decades, with some scholars claiming that we have seen its presidentialisation. Leadership has become personalised, and prime ministers turn to their inner circle of ministers and advisers rather than to the formal institutions of the cabinet system.

❖ But no prime minister can monopolise power. They can lead but not command, and direct rather than control policy. Other individuals (e.g. cabinet ministers) and institutions (government departments) also have resources. The cabinet discusses major issues but tends to ratify decisions that are made elsewhere. Nonetheless, to achieve his or her goals, the prime minister needs the support of senior cabinet ministers.

❖ Coalition government constrains the prime minister's patronage and policy-making powers. Cabinet has been revived under the coalition government, but key decisions are taken in meetings between Cameron and Clegg or in the 'Quad'.

UK/US comparison

The prime minister and the president

➤ The US president is head of state as well as head of government. Many of the powers of the president are set out in the US Constitution. It places significant limits on presidential power. The queen is head of state in the UK. The powers of the prime minister are not set out in statute law.

➤ The US president is directly elected and can claim a personal mandate. Fixed-term elections take place every 4 years. The prime minister is not directly elected; he or she is leader of the largest party in the House of Commons.

➤ In the USA, the separation of powers means that the executive does not dominate the legislature. The president cannot force Congress to accept his will, although he does have some powers to veto legislation. The legislature cannot dismiss the president. In the UK, the executive exercises significant control over the legislature. But the government must resign if it loses a vote of confidence in the Commons.

➤ The US executive branch serves the president. The US cabinet is an advisory body subordinate to the president; it does not share executive power with him. The Executive Office of the President provides strong institutional support. Presidents also appoint many of the officials working within their administration. The prime minister is the predominant figure in the executive, but needs the support of senior cabinet colleagues. The British civil service is impartial and is not politically appointed.

➤ The US president's nominees for key posts, such as cabinet members and Supreme Court judges, are subject to approval by the legislature. Many appointments made by the prime minister are not subject to parliamentary approval.

➤ The US president is head of his political party, but parties are loose organisations whose members often act independently. The prime minister is also leader of his or her party, but enjoys much greater control over it.

Further reading

Foley, M. (2009) 'The presidential controversy in Britain', *Politics Review*, Vol. 18, No. 3, pp. 20–22.

Hazell, R. and Yong, B. (2012) *The Politics of Coalition: How the Conservative-Lib Dem Coalition Works*, Hart.

Heffernan, R. (2008) 'Prime-ministerial predominance', *Politics Review*, Vol. 17, No. 3, pp. 2–5.

Heffernan, R. (2010) 'Gordon Brown as prime minister', *Politics Review*, Vol. 20, No. 1.

Theakston, K. (2013) 'David Cameron: how powerful is a coalition prime minister?', *Politics Review*, Vol. 22, No. 3, pp. 18–21.

Exam focus

Short response questions (around 5–6 minutes each)

1 Define the term *primus inter pares*?
2 What is the cabinet office?
3 What are cabinet committees?
4 Give *three* examples of how prime ministers can control their cabinets.
5 Define the term royal prerogative.

Mid-length response questions (around 10–12 minutes each)

1 Distinguish between collective responsibility and individual ministerial responsibility.
2 What are the advantages and disadvantages of a coalition government?
3 Explain the view that cabinet government no longer exists.
4 Outline and explain *three* reasons why ministers resign.
5 Outline and explain *three* characteristics of the UK civil service.

Mini-essay questions (around 25–30 minutes each)

1 Critically assess the view that the UK prime minister has become too powerful.
2 To what extent has the UK prime minister effectively become a president?
3 'Cabinet government no longer exists in the UK.' Discuss.
4 'More master than servant.' To what extent is this an accurate statement on the power of the UK civil service?

 Extra resources to help you revise and consolidate your knowledge for this chapter are provided online at **www.hodderplus.co.uk/philipallan**. These include a revision PowerPoint, extension tasks and up-to-date weblinks.

Chapter 9

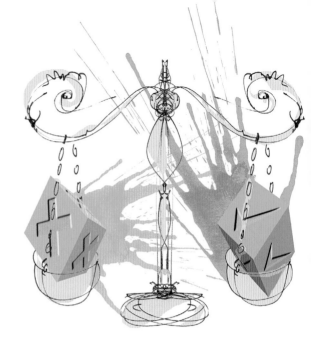

Judges and civil liberties

Key questions answered in this chapter

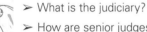

➤ What is the judiciary?

➤ How are senior judges appointed?

➤ How powerful is the UK judiciary?

➤ How has the creation of a UK Supreme Court changed things?

➤ What are civil liberties?

➤ How effectively are civil liberties protected in the UK?

➤ Does the UK need a Bill of Rights?

What is the judiciary?

In its simplest sense, the term 'judiciary' refers collectively to all UK judges, from lay magistrates and those serving on tribunals right up to the 12 senior justices sitting in the UK Supreme Court. Indeed, in a wider sense the term might even be seen as encompassing all of those who are directly involved in the administration and application of justice.

It is important to remember that the UK judiciary does not exist as a single body — Scotland and Northern Ireland operate under different legal arrangements than those in place in respect of England and Wales. The one feature common to all three systems is the part played by the UK Supreme Court, which acts as the highest court of appeal from the High Court of Justiciary and Court of Session in Scotland, the Court of Judicature in Northern Ireland and the Court of Appeal in England and Wales.

Although the judiciary in all three territories is broadly hierarchical in structure (see Figure 9.1, for example), the picture is in fact a good deal more complicated than it might appear to be at first sight. This complexity results, in part at least, from the fact that there are different legal pathways for cases involving different types of dispute, with the most obvious division coming between those cases brought under **criminal law** and those rooted in **civil law**.

The system of courts operating in England and Wales, our primary focus in this chapter, is shown in detail in Figure 9.2.

Links to follow up

www.judiciary.gov.uk — the Judiciary of England and Wales site.

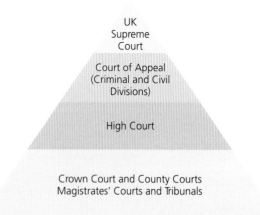

UK
Supreme
Court

Court of Appeal
(Criminal and Civil
Divisions)

High Court

Crown Court and County Courts
Magistrates' Courts and Tribunals

Figure 9.1 An outline of the judiciary in England and Wales

Criminal and civil law

Distinguish between

Criminal law

➢ Criminal law deals with crimes by an individual or group against the state (e.g. violent behaviour, serious fraud or burglary). Such cases are normally brought by the state and can lead to fines and imprisonment.

Civil law

➢ Civil law is concerned with interrelationships between different individuals and groups. Civil cases generally involve matters such as wills or contracts. Cases under civil law are generally brought by individuals rather than the state and they tend to result in compensation awards as opposed to prison sentences.

What do judges actually do?

➢ Judges at all levels are involved in ensuring that justice is done and the law is properly applied.

➢ At the lower levels of the judiciary, the main role of judges is to preside over trials, give guidance to the jury and impose sentences.

➢ At the High Court level, judges hear more serious cases and can also hear cases on appeal from lower courts.

➢ At the Court of Appeal level and above, judges are generally concerned with clarifying the meaning of the law, rather than simply applying it. These courts can establish legal precedent (i.e. common law).

➢ Cases heard at the Court of Appeal normally result from confusion in the lower courts regarding the meaning of a law. The Court of Appeal also deals with major cases arising under the 1998 Human Rights Act (HRA).

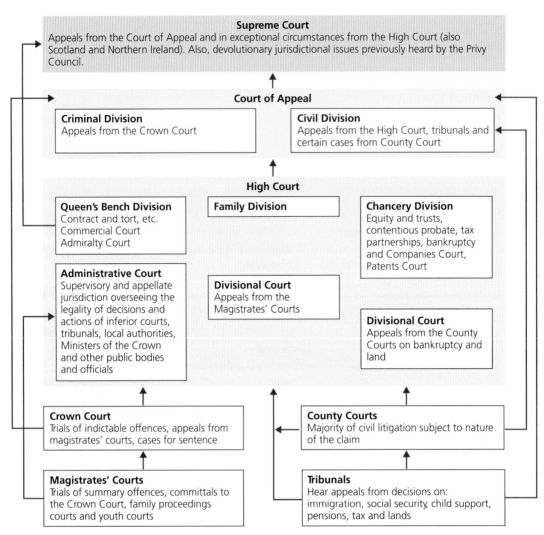

Figure 9.2 The judiciary in England and Wales in detail

> The UK Supreme Court — located in Middlesex Guildhall, Westminster — generally hears cases on appeal from the Appeals Court. In recent years, such disputes have often been brought under the HRA (1998) or under EU law.

While it is helpful to have an awareness of the judiciary in its broader sense, the higher levels of the judiciary (i.e. the top two tiers of our simplified pyramid) are of most concern to students of politics. This is because it is these higher tiers that have the power to set legal precedent establishing **common law** through their use of **judicial review**. In short, these higher courts clarify the meaning of the law as opposed to simply applying the letter of the law.

Key terms

➤ **Common law** The body of legal precedent resulting from the rulings of senior judges. Sometimes referred to as case law or judge-made law, it is an important source of the UK constitution.

➤ **Judicial review** The process by which judges review the actions of public officials or public bodies in order to determine whether or not they have acted in a manner that is lawful.

 Stretch and challenge

The changing character of judicial review in the UK

Judicial review often requires senior judges to clarify the legal meaning of a particular law or regulation. Judicial review may also involve reviewing on appeal cases heard previously at lower ('inferior') courts.

The doctrine of parliamentary sovereignty and supremacy of statute law means that judicial review in the UK is generally seen as being less significant than in the USA, where the US Supreme Court can strike down pieces of regular statute that are judged to have violated the provisions of the US Constitution.

In the UK, judicial review traditionally involved little more than judges determining whether or not a public official had operated beyond the authority granted to them under the law (i.e. acted ultra vires), as opposed to questioning the basis of the law itself.

However, the passing of the Human Rights Act (1998) and the power given to UK courts in respect of EU legislation in recent years have seen a change in the nature and scope of judicial review in the UK.

Questions

1 Explain why judicial review in the UK has traditionally been seen as being less significant than in the USA.

2 In what ways have recent developments in the UK prompted a change in the character of judicial review?

Judicial independence and judicial neutrality

Judges at all levels of the UK judiciary are expected to operate with a high level of independence and dispense justice with a degree of neutrality. However, it is important to draw a clear distinction between judicial independence and judicial neutrality. The absence of judicial independence will threaten judicial neutrality because, if judges are subject to external control, their impartiality will be compromised. However, judicial independence does not guarantee judicial neutrality because judges may still allow their personal views to influence their administering of justice.

Judicial independence and neutrality

Distinguish — between

Judicial independence

➤ Judicial independence is the principle that those in the judiciary should be free from political control. Such independence allows judges to 'do the right thing' and apply justice properly, without fear of the consequences.

Judicial neutrality

➤ Judicial neutrality is where judges operate impartially (i.e. without personal bias) in their administration of justice. Judicial neutrality is an essential requirement of the **rule of law**.

How is the independence of the judiciary maintained?

Judicial independence in the UK is based upon six main pillars:

➤ **The security of tenure enjoyed by judges.** Judges are appointed for an open-ended term, limited only by the requirement that they must retire by the age of 75. This

Key concepts

Rule of law A key principle of the UK constitution under which justice is guaranteed to all. A. V. Dicey saw the rule of law as one of the 'twin pillars' of the constitution; the other being parliamentary sovereignty.

According to Dicey the rule of law has three main strands:

➤ **No one can be punished without trial.** While this principle makes good sense in theory, it is not always maintained in practice. As we will see later in this chapter, terrorist suspects have been subject to a range of punishments without trial under measures passed since 2001, including indefinite detention, the imposition of control orders and the freezing of their assets.

➤ **No one is above the law and all are subject to the same justice.** Again, while this would appear to be a principle that would hold true in all liberal democracies, there have always been those who are effectively above the law in the UK: for example, the monarch, foreign ambassadors and MPs. In the case of the latter, a number of MPs even tried to use parliamentary privilege as a way of ending legal proceedings taken against them over their expenses.

➤ **The general principles of the constitution (e.g. personal freedoms) result from the judges' decisions rather than parliamentary statute.** While the decisions of judges (i.e. case law or common law) certainly have a part to play in defining the UK's constitutional arrangements, parliament remains sovereign and statute law reigns supreme: any legal precedent can be overturned by the means of a simple Act of Parliament.

Security of tenure It is extraordinarily hard for judges at High Court level and above (i.e. the 'senior judiciary') to be removed. Indeed, this can only take place as a result of impeachment proceedings requiring a vote in both houses of parliament. However, those in more junior ranks of the judiciary can be removed by the Lord Chancellor and the Lord Chief Justice. For example, two junior judges were dismissed for misconduct in 2005.

means that politicians cannot seek to bring influence to bear by threatening to sack or suspend them.

➤ **Guaranteed salaries paid from the Consolidated Fund.** The salaries of judges cannot be altered with the aim of putting pressure on them because control of judges' pay has been placed beyond everyday political control. As a result, judges are free to make decisions as they see fit without fear of financial penalty, and politicians are unable to offer judges financial inducements to make the decisions they want.

Key term

➤ **Consolidated Fund** A government bank account used to pay the salaries of judges and certain other officials. The fund, managed by the Bank of England, receives all government tax revenues. Judges' salaries are classified as 'standing services' and are therefore paid from the fund automatically. The fact that the payment of such salaries is not part of the regular budgetary planning process means that politicians are unable to manipulate judges' salaries as a way of controlling them.

➤ **The offence of contempt of court.** Under sub judice rules, the media, ministers and other individuals are prevented from publicly speaking out during legal proceedings. This requirement is designed to ensure that justice is administered fairly, without undue pressure being brought to bear by politicians or the public in general.

➤ **A growing separation of powers.** The downgrading of the post of Lord Chancellor and the creation of a new UK Supreme Court enhanced the separation between the senior judiciary and the other branches of government. Prior to these changes, the most senior judges, the Law Lords, sat in the House of Lords and the Lord Chancellor held significant roles in all three branches of government: executive, legislature and judiciary.

➤ **An independent appointments system.** The Constitutional Reform Act (2005) saw the creation of an independent Judicial Appointments Commission. This brought greater transparency to the process of judicial appointments and served to address concerns that the system in place previously had been open to political bias.

➤ **The training and experience of senior judges.** Most senior judges have served an 'apprenticeship' as barristers and come to the bench having achieved a certain status within their chosen profession. It is argued that such individuals take considerable pride in their legal standing and are therefore unlikely to defer to politicians or public opinion, where this would be seen to compromise their judicial integrity.

How is judicial neutrality guaranteed?

In simple terms, of course, it is impossible to guarantee judicial neutrality; judges are human, after all, and they will inevitably bring some degree of personal bias to their work. However, the promise of a universal application of the law under the doctrine of the rule of law requires that such bias is not allowed to colour judicial decisions.

There are four main ways in which this goal is achieved:

- **The relative 'anonymity' of senior judges.** Judges have traditionally operated away from the public eye. Until recently, judges rarely spoke out publicly on issues of law or public policy, and senior judges are still expected to avoid being drawn into open defence of their rulings, or criticism of those in government.
- **Restriction on political activity.** As with many senior civil servants, judges are not supposed to campaign on behalf of a political party or a pressure group. Although judges retain the right to vote, their political views or outlook should not become a matter of public record.
- **Legal justifications of judgments.** Senior judges are generally expected to offer an explanation of how their decisions are rooted in law. This requirement that decisions be clearly rooted in the law makes it less likely that senior judges will be guided be personal bias.

  Note that in the case of the UK Supreme Court, decisions are published in full on the court's official website, along with press summaries of significant cases.
- **Training.** Judges are part of a highly trained profession, regulated by the Law Society. Senior judges have commonly served for many years as barristers before taking to the bench, and their elevation to the higher ranks of the judiciary would normally reflect a belief that they are able to put any personal bias they might hold to one side when administering justice. Although the security of tenure enjoyed by senior judges makes it difficult to remove those whose neutrality is open to question, additional guidance and training can be required in such cases, and individual judges might also be moved away from more serious cases while their performance is monitored.

Threats to judicial neutrality

The main question mark over judicial neutrality comes from the narrow recruiting pool from which senior judges have traditionally been drawn, with most of those appointed to the higher tiers of the judiciary being privately schooled, Oxbridge-educated, white, middle-class men, who are beyond middle age. How, it is argued, can judges be truly neutral when their own life-experiences are so very different from most of those who are brought before them? As we will see later in this chapter, the creation of the Judicial Appointments Commission appears to have done little to address this problem, and the composition of the UK Supreme Court, although determined under entirely different procedures, is similarly unrepresentative.

Critics also point to the way in which senior judges have been drawn into the political fray in recent years, the suggestion being that the passage of measures such as the Human Rights Act (1998) has resulted in a **politicisation** of the judiciary. However, while some see this growing public profile and increased conflict between senior judges and politicians as posing a threat to judicial neutrality, it could just as easily be seen as evidence of growing independence and neutrality — not least because senior judges appear increasingly willing to take on the political establishment in defence of civil liberties.

Key concept

> **Politicisation.** The process by which individuals traditionally regarded as being beyond the party political fray are drawn into it. Politicisation of the judiciary is said to result from appointments being made on political grounds as opposed to being truly meritocratic. The way in which the UK judiciary was drawn into areas of political controversy in the wake of the Human Rights Act (1998) was also seen by some as evidence of politicisation.

Viewpoint Has the UK judiciary become more politicised in recent years?

 YES

- Politicians have often broken with convention by publicly criticising rulings handed down by senior judges.
- Measures such as the Human Rights Act (1998) have drawn senior judges into the political arena by requiring them to rule on the 'merit' of individual pieces of statute law as opposed to their 'application'.
- The *Factortame* case (1990) showed that UK courts are able to 'suspend' Acts of Parliament where they are found to contradict EU law.
- The decision to transform the Law Lords into justices of the Supreme Court and locate the new court in Middlesex Guildhall has brought the most senior UK judges into the public arena for the first time, subjecting them to greater scrutiny by the media and the general public.

 NO

- The process by which senior judges are appointed in the UK has been made more transparent and less open to accusations of political interference — in part as a result of the creation of an independent Judicial Appointments Commission.
- Whereas the concept of 'politicisation' is often associated with a loss of judicial independence, the UK senior judiciary has in fact become more independent in the wake of the Constitutional Reform Act (2005), not least with the 'downgrading' of the role of Lord Chancellor.
- Increased conflict between judges and politicians is a 'good' sign, as it shows that the courts are challenging the government when it appears to be encroaching upon our civil liberties.
- The fact that senior judges still benefit from security of tenure and guaranteed salaries affords them a degree of 'insulation' from political pressure.

Appointments to the senior judiciary

Appointments to the **senior judiciary** were traditionally made by the monarch on the advice of the prime minister and the Lord Chancellor. The Lord Chancellor customarily consulted serving senior judges through a process known as **secret soundings**. Although lower-level vacancies in the senior judiciary (e.g. for High Court judges) were advertised from the 1990s, the Lord Chancellor was under no obligation to fill vacancies by selecting his appointees from the ranks of those who had formally applied. It was said that this system lacked transparency, compromised the separation of powers, and resulted in a senior judiciary drawn almost exclusively from a very narrow social circle: public school and Oxbridge educated, white, male and beyond middle age.

Key terms

➤ **Senior judiciary** The senior judiciary comprise justices of the Supreme Court (formerly the Lords of Appeal in Ordinary, or Law Lords); heads of divisions; Lords Justices of Appeal; High Court judges; and deputy High Court judges.

➤ **Secret soundings** The informal and secretive way in which most senior UK judges were once appointed. The phrase described the way in which the Lord Chancellor consulted in secret with close associates and those already serving in the senior judiciary. The resulting lack of transparency in appointments led to accusations of elitism.

Reform of the process under New Labour

The Constitutional Reform Act (2005) reduced the power of the Lord Chancellor and placed most senior judicial appointments into the hands of a new, independent Judicial Appointments Commission (JAC). It was hoped that this change would enhance the separation of powers and result in a senior judiciary that was more socially representative of the broader population. In spite of this second stated desire, early indications based upon the work of the JAC suggested that the process of creating a judiciary that 'looked like the UK' might take longer than originally anticipated.

On 28 January 2008, the *Guardian* reported that the new JAC had approved 21 individuals to become High Court judges, with ten of those approved having been appointed to positions on the High Court. Of these ten appointees:

➤ All were white, male, former barristers.
➤ Six of the nine who were educated in the UK went to leading independent schools.

The JAC has maintained that it is committed to appointing 'on merit and merit alone [using] selection processes that are open and fair to all applicants, regardless of their gender, race or background', in a defence that echoes the commission's self-proclaimed guiding principle in making appointments: 'diversity in the field, merit in the selection'. However, according to government figures, only 4 of the 161 senior level judges in post on 1 April 2011 were known to be from a BME (Black and Ethnic Minority) background; with 123 from a 'White background' and 34 having no recorded ethnicity.

Appointments to the UK Supreme Court

Founding members of the UK Supreme Court

Justices of the UK Supreme Court are appointed under a different system from that used in respect of all other appointments to the senior judiciary. The founding justices of the new Supreme Court were those active Law Lords in-post on 1 October 2009 (see Table 9.1). Under the Constitutional Reform Act (2005) the most senior of the 12 at that time, Lord Phillips of Worth Matravers, took on the role of president of the court, with the second most senior, Lord Hope of Craighead, assuming the role of deputy president.

Although these former Law Lords themselves remained members of the House of Lords, they were barred from sitting and voting in the upper chamber for as long as they remained

Table 9.1 The make-up of the first UK Supreme Court (October 2009)

Justice	Date of birth	University	Retires
Lord Phillips of Worth Matravers President of the Supreme Court	21/01/1938	Kings College, Cambridge	2013
Lord Hope of Craighead Deputy president	27/06/1938	St John's College, Cambridge University of Edinburgh	2013
Lord Saville of Newdigate Justice of the Supreme Court	20/03/1936	Brasenose College, Oxford	2011
Lord Rodger of Earlsferry Justice of the Supreme Court	18/09/1944	New College, Oxford University of Glasgow	2019
Lord Walker of Gestingthorpe Justice of the Supreme Court	17/03/1938	Trinity College, Cambridge	2013
Baroness Hale of Richmond Justice of the Supreme Court	31/03/1947	Girton College, Cambridge	2022
Lord Brown of Eaton-under-Heywood Justice of the Supreme Court	09/04/1937	Worcester College, Oxford	2012
Lord Mance Justice of the Supreme Court	06/06/1943	University College, Oxford	2018
Lord Collins of Mapesbury Justice of the Supreme Court	07/05/1941	Downing College, Cambridge Columbia Law School, New York	2011
Lord Kerr of Tonaghmore Justice of the Supreme Court	22/02/1948	Queen's University, Belfast	2023
Lord Clarke of Stone-cum-Ebony Justice of the Supreme Court	13/05/1943	King's College, Cambridge	2018
Lord Neuberger of Abbotsbury	10/01/1948	Christ Church, Oxford	2009

Justices of the Supreme Court. Under the Constitutional Reform Act (2005) those appointed to the court subsequently are not automatically awarded peerages.

Note that at the time that it began its work on 1 October 2009, only 11 of the 12 places on the UK Supreme Court were filled. This was because one of the former Law Lords, Lord Neuberger of Abbotsbury, had taken up the position of Master of the Rolls in preference to making the move across Parliament Square to Middlesex Guildhall.

Profile of justices

Although one would hardly expect a superior court such as the UK Supreme Court to be socially representative of the broader population, the membership of the new court left it open to accusations of elitism that were not dispelled by appointments made to the court between 2009 and 2013 (see Table 9.2).

Table 9.2 The changing profile of Supreme Court justices

	2009 (October)	2013 (May)
Number of Justices in post	11	12
Number who attended an independent secondary school	10	11
Number who attended Oxford or Cambridge	10	10
Number of women	1	1
Average age	67.8	66.3

Qualifying to sit in the UK Supreme Court

In order to be considered for appointment as a justice of the Supreme Court, candidates must have either:

- ➤ held high judicial office for at least 2 years, or
- ➤ been a **qualifying practitioner** for a period of 15 years

Selection commission

Vacancies in the court are filled by an ad hoc selection commission as opposed to the JAC. According to Schedule 8, part 1 of the Constitutional Reform Act (2005), this five-member commission comprises:

- ➤ the president of the Supreme Court
- ➤ the deputy president of the Supreme Court
- ➤ one member of the Judicial Appointments Commission (JAC)
- ➤ one member of the Judicial Appointments Board for Scotland
- ➤ one member of the Northern Ireland Judicial Appointments Commission

Appointments process

Although the appointments process (see Figure 9.3) still involves the minister who formally retains the title of Lord Chancellor (i.e. the justice minister), his role is greatly reduced as he or she is not permitted repeatedly to reject names put forward by the selection commission.

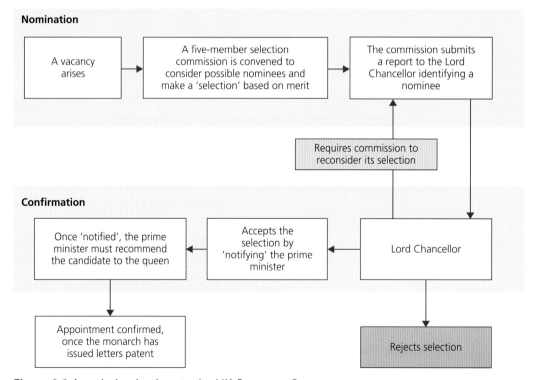

Figure 9.3 Appointing justices to the UK Supreme Court

Key term

➢ **Qualifying practitioner** Someone who: has a senior courts qualification; is an
advocate in Scotland or a solicitor entitled to appear in the Scottish Court of Session
and the High Court of Justiciary; or is a member of the Bar of Northern Ireland or a
solicitor of the Court of Judicature of Northern Ireland.

The power of the UK judiciary

Whereas the US Supreme Court can declare Acts of Congress unconstitutional, thereby
striking them down, UK courts have no such power in respect of parliamentary statute. This
is because statute law remains the supreme source of constitutional law in the UK. Despite
this reality, however, senior courts in the UK still wield considerable power when reviewing
the actions of the government or government officials.

Ultra vires cases

Traditionally the most significant cases were those where senior courts reviewed the actions of
government officials in order to decide whether or not they have acted unlawfully or **ultra vires**.

In recent years, however, the power of the UK judiciary has been enhanced by two key
developments: the growing importance of EU Law; and the impact of the Human Rights Act (1998).

Key term

➢ **Ultra vires** From the Latin, meaning 'beyond the authority' or 'beyond one's powers'. The
process of judicial review can be used to determine whether or not a minister or other
government officer has acted ultra vires: that is, beyond the authority granted to them in law.

EU membership and judicial power

Under the European Communities Act (1972), the UK incorporated the Treaty of Rome
into UK law. The effect of this simple change was to give European laws precedence over
conflicting UK statutes, whether past or present. For many years this simply meant that the
UK government could be called to account at the European Court of Justice. However, in the
wake of the *Factortame* case (1990), UK courts have also been able to 'suspend' UK statutes
that appear to be in violation of EU law.

Key concept

➢ *Factortame.* A case in which the European Court of Justice established the precedent
that UK courts can suspend UK statute law where it appears to violate EU law, at
least until the European Court of Justice is able to make a final determination as
to the legality of the statute in question. The case took its name from a Spanish-
owned fishing company, Factortame Limited, which had challenged the legality of the
Merchant Shipping Act (1988) under European law.

The Human Rights Act and judicial power

Before 1998 cases brought under the European Convention on Human Rights were heard at the European Court of Human Rights in Strasbourg. Under the Human Rights Act (HRA, 1998), the convention was incorporated into UK law, meaning that UK citizens can now have their cases heard in UK courts. Under the HRA, UK courts are able to issue a declaration of incompatibility where a parliamentary statute appears to violate the rights guaranteed. Crucially, however, parliament is not obliged to amend the offending statute. Note that the scope and extent of power afforded to the judiciary under the HRA will be dealt with in more detail later in the chapter when considering the protection of civil liberties.

How has the UK Supreme Court changed things?

Why was the court established?

The UK Supreme Court was established under the Constitutional Reform Act (2005) in response to a number of longstanding concerns:

➢ concerns over the incomplete separation of power — or 'fusion of powers' — present in the UK system: specifically, the position of the Lord Chancellor and the presence of the Law Lords in the upper chamber of the legislature

➢ criticisms of the opaque system under which senior judges such as the Law Lords were appointed

➢ widespread confusion over the work of the Law Lords — specifically, a widespread failure to understand the distinction between the House of Lords' legislative and judicial functions

Powers assigned to the UK Supreme Court

Under the Constitutional Reform Act (CRA, 2005) the new UK Supreme Court simply took on most of those roles previously performed by the Law Lords:

➢ acting as the final court of appeal in England, Wales and Northern Ireland

➢ hearing appeals on issues of public importance surrounding arguable points of law

➢ hearing appeals from civil cases in England, Wales, Northern Ireland and Scotland

➢ hearing appeals from criminal cases in England, Wales and Northern Ireland (with the High Court of Justiciary retaining jurisdiction over criminal cases in Scotland)

Early cases before the court

The sense that the creation of a new UK Supreme Court was more a change in form than in substance was reinforced by the early cases heard by the new court, few of which represented a significant departure from what the Law Lords had done hitherto. For example, the court's ruling in the case of those suspected terrorists who had had their assets seized without trial under the new anti-terror regime (see case study) was not so very different in tone or scope from those handed down previously in respect of the indefinite detention of terrorist suspects at Belmarsh under the Anti-terrorism Crime and Security Act (2001) or the use of control orders introduced under the Prevention of Terrorism Act (2005).

<table>
</table>

Case study	**The Supreme Court finds against the Treasury's seizure of the assets of suspected terrorists**

On 27 January 2010, the Supreme Court ruled that the UK Treasury had acted ultra vires when implementing parts of the Terrorism (United Nations Measures) Order 2006 (TO) and the Al-Qaida and Taliban (United Nations Measures) Order 2006 (AQO).

These measures had been introduced by the Treasury as 'Orders in Council' (laws passed without parliament) as a way of fulfilling the UK's commitments under United Nations Security Council resolutions.

Under the TO, an individual's assets could be frozen if there was a 'reasonable suspicion' that they were involved in terrorist activities. Under the AQO, individuals whose names appeared on the UN Security Council's 'Consolidated List' were to have their assets frozen automatically. In both cases, those whose assets were frozen would have no real right to reply. The Supreme Court ruled that the Treasury's use of such Orders in Council encroached upon fundamental rights and was beyond the authority granted it under statute.

In simple terms, therefore, the court was doing little more than using those powers that had been available to the Law Lords previously in respect of ultra vires rulings, declarations of incompatibility and disputes arising under EU law.

Impact of the UK Supreme Court

The UK Supreme Court is still in its infancy and any conclusions we offer at this stage must therefore be tentative.

Already apparent

➤ **Appointments and composition.** The process by which justices are appointed to the Supreme Court is significantly more independent and less opaque than the system under which Law Lords were appointed previously. This may, in time, have a knock-on effect on the composition of the court.

➤ **Power.** The move across Parliament Square to Middlesex Guildhall has not been accompanied by any change in the roles or power of the court.

➤ **Judicial independence.** On the face of it, judicial independence has been enhanced, not least as a result of a clearer separation of powers. However, evidence of increasing friction between the judiciary and leading politicians in the years before the creation of the new court would suggest that the highest tier in the UK judiciary was already functionally independent.

Less tangible

➤ **Importance of a physical separation.** The move to Middlesex Guildhall had a significance beyond simply taking the active Law Lords out of the Palace of Westminster. Giving the new court its own building raised its profile, engendered greater public interest in the court and allowed it to develop a distinctive identity and character.

> **Lifting of restrictions on television cameras.** The likelihood of regular televised sessions should demystify the senior judiciary and might well result in the emergence of a new relationship between the media and senior judges.
> **Changes in the way rulings are delivered.** The Supreme Court's website carries downloadable texts of its rulings along with press summaries of many judgments. This allows for greater public scrutiny of the workings of the court and those it finds against.
> **Relations between the court and government.** The changes outlined above may well have affected the way in which the other branches of government view the new court and their relationship with it.

Links to follow up

www.supremecourt.gov.uk — the official site of the UK Supreme Court.

Civil liberties in the UK

Often seen as synonymous with the term **rights**, **civil liberties** are those fundamental freedoms enjoyed by citizens under the style of limited government practised in liberal democracies such as the UK and the USA. As Paul Floyd has noted, such liberties may 'concern the freedom to do or to have something, such as the right to assemble, to privacy, to ownership of property or to a fair trial', or instead 'be about freedom from things, such as oppression, arbitrary arrest, slavery or imprisonment without trial'. In theory, at least, government should only encroach upon — or 'abrogate' — such liberties in time of war or when facing other emergencies.

Key terms
> **Rights** Legal or moral entitlements to have something or behave in a particular way.
> **Civil liberties** The fundamental freedoms enjoyed by citizens in a liberal democracy, properly limited only by those laws established for the common good.

What civil liberties are protected in the UK?

The main liberties available to UK citizens are no different from those afforded to citizens living under other western liberal democratic systems of government: the right to life; freedom of expression; freedom of religion and conscience; freedom of movement; freedom of association; the right of protest; freedom from arbitrary arrest; freedom from torture; the right to fair trial; political rights, such as the right to vote (the franchise); and property rights.

Where are civil liberties set out in the UK?

The uncodified nature of the UK's constitutional arrangements has traditionally made it hard to determine precisely 'where' civil liberties are set out. Historically, the UK has had neither a codified constitution, nor — prior to 1998 at least — anything analogous to the US Bill of Rights. The constitution and the statutory framework have instead evolved over time, with

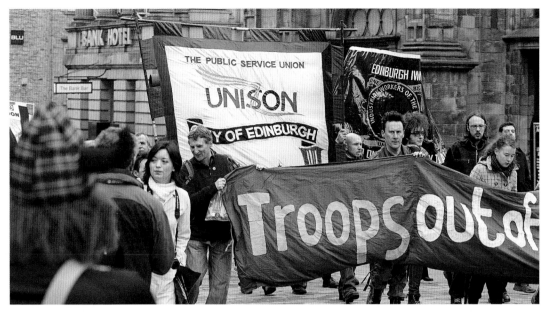

Demonstrators during a May Day rally in Edinburgh in 2010, protesting about the war in Afghanistan and cuts to public services

citizens remaining free to do anything that is not prohibited in statute; a system characterised by **negative rights** as opposed to **positive rights**.

Positive and negative rights

> **Distinguish between**

Positive rights
> Those explicitly assigned to citizens, often being entrenched as a part of a codified constitutional settlement — as is the case in the USA.

Negative rights
> Those liberties that are not explicitly set out, but exist in the absence of any law forbidding individuals from exercising them.

According to the nineteenth-century constitutional lawyer A. V. Dicey, such freedoms are protected:

> through the actions of a sovereign, independent and robust parliament, which will act quickly to address perceived injustices
> by the fact that public opinion will not stand for encroachment on longstanding freedoms
> through the laying down of judge-made case law — often called common law or ordinary law

These three factors combined created a system under which the rights of UK citizens were protected by an overlapping web of provisions, some rooted in convention, some afforded statutory footing and others resulting from legal precedents established in the courts. This

can be seen, for example, in the protection afforded to the 'right to life'. Long established in common law, the right to life has also been recognised in parliamentary statutes such as the Offences Against the Persons Act (1861), the Murder (Abolition of Death Penalty) Act (1965) and the Crime and Disorder Act (1998), as well as a number of international treaties and conventions — for example, Protocol 13 (2002) of the European Convention on Human Rights and the United Nations Convention on the Rights of the Child (1989).

The UK's new 'rights culture'

It was the absence of a clear and authoritative summary of the rights available to UK citizens that prompted New Labour to bring three new pieces of legislation to the statute books following its return to office in 1997: the Human Rights Act (1998), the Freedom of Information Act (2000) and the Data Protection Act (DPA 1998), the first two measures having been included in the party's manifesto at the 1997 general election:

> We will by statute incorporate the European Convention on Human Rights into UK law.

> [This] will establish a floor, not a ceiling for human rights. Parliament will remain free to enhance these rights, for example by a Freedom of Information Act.

Some commentators argue that the passage of these measures has resulted in the emergence of a new culture of positive rights in the UK — something more akin to that embedded in US political culture.

Human Rights Act (1998)

The Human Rights Act (HRA) came into force in October 2000. It incorporated most of the articles of the **European Convention on Human Rights** (ECHR) into UK law, thereby allowing citizens to pursue cases under the ECHR through UK courts as opposed to having to go directly to the European Court of Human Rights in Strasbourg.

Key term

> **European Convention on Human Rights (ECHR, 1950)** The ECHR was established by the Council of Europe, an intergovernmental body that is separate from the European Union and not to be confused with the EU's Council of Ministers or European Council. Alleged violations of the ECHR are investigated by the European Commission on Human Rights and tried in the European Court of Human Rights, based in Strasbourg. Again these bodies are not to be confused with the EU's European Commission and European Court of Justice.

As the HRA is based on the Council of Europe's ECHR, rather than on EU law, it is not superior to parliamentary statute, as EU laws are under the Treaty of Rome. That said, the HRA (like the ECHR) has a 'persuasive authority' that has enhanced the protection of individual rights in the UK (see Box 9.1).

Distinguish between

European Court of Human Rights and European Court of Justice

European Court of Human Rights

➤ The European Court of Human Rights was established by the Council of Europe

➤ It hears cases brought under the European Convention on Human Rights.

➤ It is based in Strasbourg but is not an EU institution.

European Court of Justice

➤ The European Court of Justice is the 'supreme court' of the European Union.

➤ It hears cases arising under EU law

➤ It is based in Luxembourg.

Box 9.1 The scope of the HRA

The HRA (1998) came into force in October 2000. It incorporated the 18 Articles of the European Convention on Human Rights (1950) into UK law.

Article 1   commits all signatories to protecting the rights included in the convention.

Article 2   protects the right to life.

Article 3   prohibits torture and degrading or inhuman treatment.

Article 4   outlaws slavery and involuntary servitude.

Article 5   secures liberty and security of the individual against arbitrary arrest and imprisonment.

Article 6   guarantees a fair trial.

Article 7   prevents legislation that criminalises acts retrospectively.

Article 8   promotes respect for the individual's private and family life.

Article 9   protects the freedom of thought, conscience and religion.

Article 10   enshrines the right to freedom of expression.

Article 11   protects the rights of association and assembly: for example, the right to form a trade union.

Article 12   protects the right of men and women to marry and start a family.

Article 13   allows for the redress of grievances where convention rights have been violated.

Article 14   prohibits discrimination in the application of rights guaranteed in the convention.

Article 15   allows for suspension or 'derogation' of some of the rights guaranteed by the convention in times of national emergency.

Article 16   permits restrictions on the political rights of foreign nationals.

Article 17   prevents rights protected in the convention from being used to limit other convention rights.

Article 18   holds that the 'get out clauses' included in some articles of the convention should not be abused as a way of limiting those rights protected in more general terms.

Freedom of Information Act (2000)

New Labour's manifesto at the 1997 general election included an explicit commitment to introduce freedom of information legislation — a response both to the allegations of sleaze that had affected the dog-days of John Major's Conservative administration and to a more widespread perception that there needed to be greater transparency in government.

The Freedom of Information Act (FOI) received the royal assent on 30 November 2000, but did not come into force until 1 January 2005 (see Box 9.2). This delay in implementation was supposed to provide public authorities an opportunity to prepare for the anticipated avalanche of requests for information.

Box 9.2 **The Freedom of Information Act in outline**

➢ The FOI (2000) came into force in January 2005.
➢ It gave citizens a right to access information held by public authorities.
➢ It required public bodies seeking to deny requests for information to show that the public interest warrants an exemption under the Act.
➢ It established a new Information Commissioner and Information Tribunal.
➢ It required public authorities to adopt a scheme for the publication of information.

Data Protection Act (1998)

The Data Protection Act (DPA), though often overshadowed by the HRA (1998) and the FOI (2000), nonetheless provides some significant guarantees.

➢ It places restrictions on the storage of personal data.
➢ It limits the sharing of such data between different organisations.
➢ It requires that information is held securely.
➢ It gives individuals the right to see any information that relates to them and to have factual inaccuracies corrected.

The status of rights in the UK

As we have seen, UK courts cannot declare an Act of Parliament unconstitutional as a result of the supremacy of statute law. The power of senior judges is therefore limited to declaring that a government official has acted beyond the authority given to them under statute (ultra vires), suspending UK statutes where they appear to violate EU law (since the *Factortame* case) or issuing a declaration of incompatibility where the measures in question appear to violate the HRA (1998).

The HRA in action

As we have seen, the HRA does not have the same legal status as EU law or the US Bill of Rights, with the latter being both entrenched and superior to regular statute. As a regular piece of statute, the HRA can be amended, 'suspended' (**derogated**) — in its entirety or in part — or simply repealed, like any Act.

Key concept

➢ **Derogation** A process by which a country is exempted, perhaps temporarily, from observing a law or regulation it has previously agreed to abide by. Under Article 15 of the European Convention on Human Rights (ECHR), national governments are permitted to derogate some of the convention's articles in times of national crisis.

While the courts cannot strike down parliamentary statute under the HRA, they can make a declaration of incompatibility and invite parliament to reconsider the offending statute. Furthermore, where statute is silent or unclear, the courts can make even greater use of the HRA by using its provision to establish legal precedent in common law. In addition, we should remember that the HRA also has a hidden influence through the process by which draft legislation is now examined by parliament's Joint Committee on Human Rights in order to ensure that it is HRA compatible.

The coverage of early cases brought under the HRA was fairly comprehensive, taking in the full range of rights protected (see Box 9.3). However, recent years focus far more on the way in which the HRA sits with the government's efforts to protect UK citizens from the threat of terrorism (see case study overleaf).

Box 9.3 Early cases under the HRA

➢ **The killers of James Bulger.** The court imposed a lifetime ban on revealing the new identities of Thompson and Venables, the two boys convicted of killing toddler James Bulger in 1993. The ban was granted on the grounds that identifying them might threaten their right to life (Article 2) and could also result in their being subjected to inhuman and degrading treatment (Article 3). The court also held that such a ban might protect the boys' right to private and family life (Article 8). Newspapers had argued that the freedom of expression protected under Article 10 gave them the right to publish detail; the court disagreed. In April 2013, two men who published pictures online that were said to show Thompson and Venables were given 9-month suspended prison sentences for being found in contempt of court.

➢ **The 1997 'two strikes and you're out' legislation.** A case was brought by four men imprisoned for life under legislation requiring mandatory life sentences for those convicted of serious offences for a second time. The men argued that the legislation violated their right to liberty (Article 5), was inhuman and degrading (Article 3) and fell foul of the Article 7 ban on making laws retrospective. The Court of Appeal ruled that judges should be able to use their discretion when sentencing — as they had done prior to the Act being passed — rather than being forced to impose a life sentence in such cases.

➢ **Treatment of mental patients.** A paranoid schizophrenic killer detained at Broadmoor argued that the Mental Health Act (1983) reversed the burden of proof by requiring him to prove that he was cured before he could be considered for release. The Court of Appeal ruled that the Act violated both Article 5 and Article 6 of the convention.

➢ **Right to remain silent.** A woman charged after admitting being drunk in charge of a vehicle argued that section 172 of the Road Traffic Act (1988) had violated her right to silence (Article 6) by making it an offence for her to refuse to name the driver of a vehicle. Section 172 also applied to vehicles caught on speed cameras. Scotland's High Court threw out the prosecution against her on the grounds that the Act undermined her right to a fair trial (Article 6).

Case study | The Courts, the HRA and the detention of terrorist suspects

Part 4 of the UK's Anti-Terrorism Crime and Security Act (2001), which allowed the indefinite detention of foreign terrorist suspects, was only passed into law after the government chose to derogate Article 5 of the European Convention on Human Rights on the grounds that there was a 'public emergency threatening the life of the nation'. This was the form of words required to meet the requirements for derogation under Article 15 of the European Convention on Human Rights.

In the landmark case *A and Others* v *Secretary of State for the Home Department* (2004), an appellate committee of nine Law Lords ruled (8:1) that the **indefinite detention** of suspects under the Anti-terrorism, Crime and Security Act (2001) was incompatible with Articles 5 and 14 of the HRA.

In June and August 2006, the High Court found that the use of **control orders** allowed under the Prevention of Terrorism Act (2005) also violated Article 5, as such restrictive measures amounted to imprisonment without trial.

Key terms

➤ **Indefinite detention** The right to hold foreign terrorist suspects indefinitely without trial, as authorised by the Anti-terrorism, Crime and Security Act (2001). Suspects were famously held at Belmarsh Prison in London. Indefinite detention was ruled incompatible with the Human Rights Act (1998) in the case *A and Others* v *Secretary of State for the Home Department* (2004).

➤ **Control order** A form of close house arrest allowed under the Prevention of Terrorism Act (2005). It was introduced after the indefinite detention of foreign terrorist suspects, which was sanctioned under the Anti-terrorism, Crime and Security Act (2001), was declared incompatible with the ECHR incorporated into UK law under the Human Rights Act (1998). In 2011, control orders were re-branded as terrorism prevention and investigation measures.

The FOI in action

In much the same way as the HRA (1998) initially failed to live up to its billing, the FOI (2000) did not lead to the anticipated avalanche of requests for information. Public authorities ranging from government departments to local police and fire authorities had spent 5 years preparing for 'information D-day' on 1 January 2005. Indeed, in many cases additional staff had been taken on specifically to deal with requests from the public.

Most early requests for information under the Act came not from individual citizens but from media organisations that saw the Act either as a means of tying up loose ends on earlier stories or as an additional tool when engaged in investigative journalism. By 2013, however, the FOI was being used more widely and was increasingly seen as an effective means by which the government and elected officials could be held to account.

In no area was the use of the FOI more apparent than in the case of the furore over MPs' expenses. Although this scandal entered the broader public consciousness as a result of the *Daily Telegraph*'s decision to publish leaked details of MPs' expenses verbatim, we should remember that the chain of events that led to these disclosures began with a request by the Anglo-American journalist Heather Brooke made under the FOI.

The DPA in action

Although the DPA (1998) was designed to enhance the privacy of citizens in an information age, it has failed to deliver in a number of key areas. First, the Act has not prevented the emergence of massive national databases. Second, there is mounting concern regarding the way in which information is shared between state institutions. Third, there have been numerous losses of personal data. Such problems were highlighted in a 2008 survey conducted by the Rowntree Trust which found that:

➤ a quarter of all the largest public database projects breached data protection and rights laws
➤ a half had problems with privacy and could fall foul of a legal challenge
➤ only 6 of the 46 database schemes got 'the green light'

Importance of political culture

One should not underestimate the part played by **political culture** when assessing the extent to which a government is able to encroach upon individual liberties unchallenged.

It was unrealistic to think that UK political culture would be transformed overnight as a result of the passage of measures such as the HRA (1998) and the FOI (2000). It takes time for such Acts to enter the public consciousness and longer still

 Key term

➤ **Political culture** The opinions, attitudes and values that shape political behaviour. A nation's political culture consists of the citizens' collectively held attitudes towards the political system and their place in it.

before significant numbers of ordinary citizens are moved to employ those rights in legal action. Thus, whereas early cases saw the HRA being used largely by celebrities as a means of protecting their privacy — rather than by 'ordinary citizens' protecting their civil liberties — recent years have seen more widespread and ground-breaking use of the Act.

The prevailing political culture is also shaped by factors beyond the control of government and parliament, such as the state of emergency that followed the attacks of 9/11 (2001) and 7/7 (2005). These events saw most if not all UK citizens accept restrictions on their civil liberties that would previously have been considered unthinkable. Such a willingness to defer to the government in a crisis should come as no great surprise; even the philosopher John Locke (1632–1704) acknowledged that in times of emergency, 'responsible leaders could resort to exceptional power'. However, it is equally significant that as the immediate terrorist threat appeared to recede after 2008, the opposition to government measures that threatened individual civil liberties grew. This can be clearly seen in the battle over New Labour's plans for a national ID card scheme.

Threats to civil liberties post-9/11

The lack of entrenchment afforded to civil liberties in the UK has been underlined by the extent to which individual liberties were eroded in the face of the increased terrorist threat perceived after 9/11.

Caught between the need to protect the lives of UK citizens and a desire to protect other civil liberties, the government's legislative programme often appeared to prioritise the former over the latter (see Table 9.3).

Table 9.3 Civil liberties under threat in the decade that followed 9/11

Act	Year	Key provisions
Anti-terrorism, Crime and Security Act	2001	Allowed the indefinite detention of foreign terrorist suspects.
Proceeds of Crime Act	2002	Allowed the confiscation of the assets of suspected terrorists without prosecution.
Regulation of Investigatory Powers Act	2002	Empowered the police and local authorities to undertake covert surveillance.
Criminal Justice Act	2003	Limited the right to trial by jury in some cases.
Anti-social Behaviour Act	2003	Allowed the imposition of curfews.
Prevention of Terrorism Act	2005	Introduced control orders.
Serious Organised Crime and Police Act	2005	Restricted protests in the vicinity of parliament.
Identity Card Act	2006	Provided for the phased introduction of a compulsory national biometric ID card scheme.
Terrorism Act	2006	Made it an offence to 'glorify' acts of terrorism.
Counter-terrorism Act	2008	Allowed the police to restrict photography in public places as well as extending the rights of policy to take DNA evidence and monitor those suspected of involvement in terrorist activity.
Coroners and Justice Act	2009	Allowed inquests into deaths relating to terrorist activities to be held in secret.

It is perhaps inevitable that citizens will defer to government in times of national emergency: accepting restrictions on their civil liberties that they would surely never countenance in the normal course of events. Once passed into law, however, it is largely up to the authorities to determine precisely how such powers are applied and when (if ever) they are rescinded. The open-ended nature of many of those measures which have found their way on to the statute books in recent years presents a clear and present danger to civil liberties in the UK. As the American cryptographer and computer expert Bruce Schneier noted in the *Guardian*, 'It is poor civic hygiene to install technologies that could some day facilitate a police state.'

The remains of a double-decker bus after the terrorist attack in London, July 2005

Does the UK need a formal Bill of Rights?

Controversy over the Human Rights Act (1998)

Supporters of the HRA argue that it simply brings into British law those freedoms and rights previously available to British citizens under the European Convention on Human Rights. However, the application of these guarantees since the HRA came into force in October 2000 has given cause for concern. A particular bone of contention has been the extent to which the Act has been used by those who engender little public sympathy; specifically criminals and foreign nationals facing deportation. The case of the Afghan hijackers in 2006 provides a clear illustration of this point. Originally arrested and charged with a range of offences in connection with the hijacking of a passenger airliner, nine Afghans who claimed to have fled from the Taliban were ultimately allowed to remain in the UK and seek employment after the government was found to have denied them their rights under the HRA.

The reaction of many politicians and the broader public to cases such as this, while being entirely understandable, strikes at the very heart of what the HRA is supposed to do in terms of making fundamental rights available universally. The whole point of codifying such rights in this way is to protect those who might be denied their liberty under a more arbitrary set of arrangements.

It is true that the HRA has seen the senior judiciary coming into conflict with government ministers more regularly than was previously the case in the UK, but this is an inevitable consequence of an emergent rights culture. Although the anti-terror legislation that came in the wake of the attacks on 9/11 and 7/7 has raised serious questions regarding the proper relationship between the judiciary and politicians, the key function of an independent judiciary is to protect citizens from a government that seeks to encroach upon their rights and freedoms.

This observation is particularly true of the judicial criticism of indefinite detention without trial of terrorist suspects under the Anti-terrorism, Crime and Security Act (2001) and the imposition of control orders under the Prevention of Terrorism Act (2005). Both measures struck at the heart of the presumption of innocence, the right to a free and fair trial, and freedom from arbitrary arrest and imprisonment. While the belief of successive Labour home secretaries that the judges 'don't get it', as John Reid put it, or are 'confused on rights', as Charles Clarke claimed, reflected their genuine concern and frustration, it also betrayed a failure to see the bigger picture. The same criticism might be levelled at Theresa May, the coalition's home secretary, in her pursuit of the deportation of the suspected Al-Qaida terrorist Abu Qatada — a man who had never faced trial in Britain yet had, nonetheless, spent much of the period 2002–13 in prison.

Ultimately, of course, the government is not required to give way under pressure from judges. Declarations of incompatibility issued under the HRA only invite parliament to reconsider its position, allowing a 'freedom to differ' that was apparent over control orders. The UK government can also apply to derogate those guarantees enshrined in the ECHR in times of national emergency.

Calls for a UK Bill of Rights

Long-standing concern over the operation of the HRA among leading conservatives was reflected in the fact that the party entered the 2010 general election campaign promising a rather different approach to the protection of rights and liberties than the other two main UK parties (see Table 9.4).

Table 9.4 2010 manifesto positions on the HRA

Conservative	Labour	Lib Dem
To protect our freedoms from state encroachment and encourage greater social responsibility, we will replace the Human Rights Act with a UK Bill of Rights.	We are proud to have brought in the Human Rights Act, enabling British citizens to take action in British courts rather than having to wait years to seek redress in Strasbourg. We will not repeal or resile from it.	Liberal Democrats will ensure that everyone has the same protections under the law by protecting the Human Rights Act.

In opposition, the Conservative leader, David Cameron, had consistently maintained the position he had initially set out in 2006 (see Box 9.4).

Under the 2010 Coalition Agreement, however, the Conservatives and the Lib Dems adopted a form of words that could not have been more ideally suited to the task of kicking the issue into the long grass (see Box 9.5) — a view likely to be supported by any reading of the report of the Commission on a Bill of Rights, which was finally published in December 2012 (see case study).

Box 9.4 Cameron on the case for a new UK Bill of Rights

We need a new approach:

The Human Rights Act has made it harder to protect our security;

It is hampering our fight against crime and terrorism;

It has done little to protect our liberties; and

It has helped create rights without responsibilities.

Source: David Cameron, 'Balancing freedom and security — a modern
British Bill of Rights', 26 June 2006.

Box 9.5 The Coalition Agreement on the HRA

We need a new approach. We will establish a Commission to investigate the creation of a British
Bill of Rights that incorporates and builds on all our obligations under the European Convention
on Human Rights, ensures that these rights continue to be enshrined in British law, and protects
and extends British liberties. We will seek to promote a better understanding of the true scope of
these obligations and liberties.

Case study The report of the Commission on a Bill of Rights

The Commission on a Bill of Rights delivered its report to the government in December 2012. It
did not offer a strong or unanimous way forward.

On the central issue, seven of the commission's nine members came down in favour of a UK Bill
of Rights. Such a bill would incorporate and build on all the UK's obligations under the European
Convention on Human Rights (ECHR), and would provide no less protection than is contained in
the current Human Rights Act and the devolution settlements.

The minority were concerned that a premature move to a UK Bill of Rights would be contentious
and possibly even dangerous, with unintended consequences.

Nothing further is likely to happen in this Parliament. The government remains divided, with the
Conservatives critical of the Human Rights Act, and the Liberal Democrats staunch defenders of it.

In the run-up to the next election the parties will differentiate on the issue, with the
Conservatives repeating their commitment (first announced by Cameron in 2006) to repeal
the Human Rights Act and replace it with a UK Bill of Rights; and Labour and the Lib Dems
committed to its retention.

Source: Constitution Unit *Monitor 53*, February 2013

Problems in establishing a new UK Bill of Rights

What should be included in the new bill?

The US Bill of Rights — the first ten amendments to the US Constitution — is often championed
as a model of how fundamental rights can be codified and protected. In reality, however, it
is a rather disparate document that combines guarantees of basic freedoms such as those

outlined in the First Amendment (see Box 9.6) with other measures that today appear at best anachronistic (e.g. the Third Amendment) and at worst rather unhelpful (e.g. the Second Amendment). Moreover, the US Bill of Rights did not prohibit slavery (only added with the Thirteenth Amendment) or give a guarantee of equal protection under the law (later included in the Fourteenth Amendment).

Box 9.6 Extracts from the US Bill of Rights (1791)

First Amendment
Congress shall make no law respecting an establishment of religion, or prohibiting the free exercise thereof; or abridging the freedom of speech, or of the press, or the right of the people peaceably to assemble, and to petition the Government for a redress of grievances.

Second Amendment
A well regulated Militia, being necessary to the security of a free State, the right of the people to keep and bear Arms, shall not be infringed.

Third Amendment
No Soldier shall, in time of peace be quartered in any house, without the consent of the Owner, nor in time of war, but in a manner to be prescribed by law.

The question of precisely what should be included in a new UK Bill of Rights is likely to prove similarly difficult to resolve. The beauty of the UK's Human Rights Act was that it effectively sidestepped the need for a discussion over the fundamentals of what should and should not be included simply by bringing a pre-existing list of rights and liberties — the European Convention on Human Rights — into UK law.

How will the broader public be consulted on the proposals?
In the past, both major parties have suggested a kind of 'national conversation' or, as Labour put it, 'a dialogue with the British public'. Quite what this would mean in practice is unclear in a nation of over 60 million souls. A formal consultation along the lines that normally accompanies a Green Paper would surely fall way short of the kind of popular engagement and participation that both parties have looked to encourage, as such processes are invariably dominated by organised interests. The alternative, some kind of democratically appointed constitutional convention of the type employed at Philadelphia in 1787, appears equally improbable.

How will a new Bill of Rights square with UK commitments under the ECHR?
The repeal of the HRA would not, of course, deny UK citizens access to the rights it guarantees, because these rights are enshrined in the European Convention on Human Rights (ECHR), on which the HRA was based and to which the UK has been a signatory since 1950. Repealing the HRA would do little more than turn the clock back a decade to a time when UK citizens had no option but to take their grievances to the European Court of

Human Rights in Strasbourg. Although there is nothing to prevent the UK from withdrawing from the ECHR entirely, such a course of action would be problematic, for while remaining a party to the ECHR is not a legal requirement of EU membership, all 28 EU member states are signatories to it.

The issue of entrenchment

As a regular piece of statute law, the HRA can be amended or repealed like any other. As we have seen, national governments can also apply to derogate some or all of the convention's articles in times of national emergency.

Although the creation of a new UK Bill of Rights might remove the second problem, as it would be entirely separate from the ECHR, the first problem would remain under the doctrine of parliamentary sovereignty. In the absence of the kind of 'higher law' provided by a properly codified and entrenched constitution, parliament would always be free to alter or suspend the freedoms and liberties set out in any new Bill of Rights. Back in 2006, David Cameron suggested that a degree of entrenchment might be achieved by adding a Bill of Rights to the list of measures that the House of Commons cannot force through the House of Lords under the authority of the Parliament Act. While such a move would not prevent a government from encroaching upon the rights of citizens, it might at least offer an additional level of protection.

Some commentators take a different line entirely, arguing that concerns over a lack of entrenchment are largely unfounded. This view is generally rooted in a belief that the House of Commons will be reluctant to encroach upon citizens' rights for fear of provoking a public backlash. In this way, the new Bill of Rights might in time become so embedded in the public consciousness that no government would dare to tamper with it, even though parliament would ultimately retain the authority to do so. Although some argue that this line of reasoning relies rather too heavily on the Commons checking themselves, evidence of this kind of 'governmental restraint' has been seen previously in the New Labour government's willingness to defer to the courts over indefinite detention — and to the Lords over the proposed 42-day detention of terrorist suspects.

Viewpoint   Does the UK need a formal Bill of Rights?

YES

- A properly entrenched Bill of Rights would give enhanced constitutional protection to those rights considered fundamental.
- A Bill of Rights would serve to limit the power of the state.
- A UK Bill of Rights would reinforce the Rule of Law.
- A Bill of Rights could build upon rather than replace the guarantees offered under the HRA (1998).
- The presence of a formal Bill of Rights would help to raise public awareness of rights, thus contributing to the emergence of a rights culture.
- A Bill of Rights could link the concept of rights to the responsibilities and duties of UK citizens.

NO

● A Bill of Rights is unnecessary given the protection already afforded under the ECHR, common law and regular parliamentary statute.

● Entrenching rights would undermine the doctrine of parliamentary sovereignty.

● It would be difficult to entrench the Bill of Rights properly in the absence of a codified and entrenched constitution.

● It would be difficult to decide what to include and what to leave out.

● A codified and entrenched document might serve to undermine other rights set out elsewhere but not included in the new Bill of Rights.

● Some supporters of a UK Bill of Rights are motivated more by a desire to weaken the guarantees provided under the HRA (1998) than by a commitment to protecting civil liberties.

What you should know

❯ The term 'judiciary' refers collectively to all judges in the UK, from lay magistrates all the way up to justices of the UK Supreme Court. However, students of politics are primarily concerned with the senior judiciary.

❯ The senior judiciary comprises justices of the Supreme Court (formerly known as Lords of Appeal in Ordinary or 'Law Lords'); heads of divisions; Lords Justices of Appeal; High Court judges; and deputy High Court judges.

❯ Judges at the Appeals Court level and above have the power to establish legally binding precedent or 'common law' using the power of judicial review. This role is particularly significant where statute law is ambiguous or unclear, or where the laws passed by parliament conflict with European law or are deemed incompatible with the Human Rights Act (1998).

❯ Under the doctrine of the rule of law, UK judges are expected to operate under the twin principles of judicial independence and judicial neutrality. Judicial independence requires that judges are able to apply the law as they see fit, free from external political controls. Judicial neutrality demands that justices set aside personal bias when applying the law.

❯ In recent years, the independence of the UK judiciary has been enhanced as a result of reforms to the judicial appointments process and the greater separation of powers achieved following reforms to the role of the Lord Chancellor, and the creation of a new UK Supreme Court.

❯ The Supreme Court is likely to grow in status and authority in the coming years, although it was not afforded any significant powers beyond those held by the Appellate Committee of the House of Lords, which it replaced in October 2009.

❯ Civil liberties are those fundamental freedoms enjoyed by citizens in a liberal democracy, limited only by those laws established for the common good. They include the right to life and liberty, and the freedom of speech.

❯ Traditionally, the UK was said to be characterised by the concept of negative rights — that citizens were free to do all that was not prohibited in law. In recent years there has been a move towards the setting out of positive rights, such as those included in the Freedom of Information Act (2000) and the guarantees incorporated into UK law under the Human Rights Act (1998).

❯ The courts can defend the rights of citizens by making ultra vires rulings where government officials have acted beyond their authority, by finding that UK law violates EU law, or by issuing a declaration of incompatibility under the Human Rights Act.

◗ The lack of a codified and entrenched constitutional settlement makes the rights of UK citizens vulnerable to change. This fact and the controversy surrounding the application of the Human Rights Act have led to calls for a UK Bill of Rights.

UK/US comparison

Judiciary and rights in the USA

➤ Under the US Constitution, the 50 US states are free to organise their own state-level judiciary largely as they see fit. As a result, UK/US comparisons tend to focus on the higher levels of the US federal judiciary in the USA and the senior judiciary in the UK.

➤ The US judiciary, like the UK judiciary, is broadly hierarchical in structure. The US Supreme Court sits above 13 US Federal Circuit Courts of Appeal, with US District Courts, the US Claims Court and the US Court of International Trade at the lowest tier.

➤ Whereas the UK Supreme Court comprises 12 members (the president of the court, the deputy president of the court and 10 justices of the court), the US Supreme Court has numbered 9 justices since 1869 (with one chief justice and 8 associate justices).

➤ The role and powers of the US Supreme Court are set out in Article 3 of the US Constitution, but the court's main power — that of judicial review — is not clearly enumerated. This power was instead 'discovered' by the court in the case of *Marbury* v *Madison* (1803) and extended in a number of landmark cases thereafter.

➤ The power of judicial review allows the US Supreme Court to strike down regular Acts of Congress where they violate constitutional provisions. This makes the US Supreme Court significantly more powerful than its UK counterpart — which has the doctrine of parliamentary sovereignty and the supremacy of statute law to contend with.

➤ US courts, like their UK counterparts, are expected to operate with high levels of judicial independence and judicial neutrality. Judges on both sides of the Atlantic must rely on other state institutions to enforce their judgments.

➤ Whereas the UK has traditionally operated under a system of negative rights, the USA has a long-established rights culture based upon explicit guarantees. The first ten amendments to the constitution, known collectively as the Bill of Rights (1791), offer entrenched protection to a range of fundamental freedoms and rights.

➤ The US Bill of Rights is far harder to change or ignore than the UK Human Rights Act (1998), which can easily be repealed or derogated in times of national emergency. Subsequent amendments to the US Constitution have offered citizens further guarantees: for example, the Thirteenth Amendment (1865) prohibits slavery and the Fourteenth Amendment (1868) guarantees equal protection under the law.

➤ As in the UK, the rights of US citizens are also protected under regular law, e.g. the US Civil Rights Act (1964) and the US Freedom of Information Act (1966), and through legal precedents established by judicial interpretation e.g. *Brown* v *Board of Education* (1954), which outlawed racial segregation in schools, and *Roe* v *Wade* (1973), which prevented states from banning abortion outright.

Further reading

Garnett, M. (2011) 'Supreme Justice? The US and UK Supreme Courts', *Political Insight*, Vol. 2, No. 1, pp. 26–28.

McNaughton, N. (2012) 'UK judges: too powerful or not powerful enough?', *Politics Review*, Vol. 21, No. 3, pp. 28–31.

McNaughton, N. (2013) 'Judges: do they protect civil liberties?', *Politics Review*, Vol. 22, No. 4, pp. 2–5.

McNaughton, N., Fairclough, P. and Magee, E. (2012) 'A new UK Bill of Rights: a pointless exercise?', in *UK Government and Politics Annual Update 2012*, pp. 57–62, Philip Allan Updates.

McNaughton, N., Fairclough, P. and Magee, E. (2013) 'Freedom of Information: is it under threat?', in *UK Government and Politics Annual Update 2013*, pp. 57–63, Philip Allan Updates.

Exam focus

Short response questions (around 5–6 minutes each)

1 What is judicial review?
2 Define the term ultra vires.
3 What is the Human Rights Act?
4 What is *Factortame*?
5 What is the Judicial Appointments Commission (JAC)?

Mid-length response questions (around 10–12 minutes each)

1 Distinguish between judicial independence and judicial neutrality.
2 Assess the impact of *three* recent reforms to the UK judiciary.
3 What are the advantages and disadvantages of a British Bill of Rights?
4 Outline and explain the role of the UK Supreme Court.
5 How has the Human Rights Act affected the administration of justice in the UK?

Mini-essay questions (around 25–30 minutes each)

1 'Neither neutral nor independent.' To what extent is this an accurate statement on the senior judiciary in the UK?
2 How and to what extent have judicial reforms shifted the relationship between judicial, executive and legislative branches?
3 Are judges effective guardians of civil liberties in the UK?
4 'Politicians wearing wigs.' To what extent would you accept this view of the senior judiciary in the UK?

 Extra resources to help you revise and consolidate your knowledge for this chapter are provided online at **www.hodderplus.co.uk/philipallan**. These include a revision PowerPoint, extension tasks and up-to-date weblinks.

Chapter 10

Devolution and local government

Key questions answered in this chapter
- ➤ Why did demands for devolution emerge?
- ➤ What powers do the devolved bodies have?
- ➤ What are the implications of devolution for British politics?
- ➤ What functions does local government have?

The UK is a multinational state made up of four nations: England, Scotland, Wales and Northern Ireland. For all but the final year of the twentieth century, the UK was one of the most centralised states in western Europe. Labour's 1997 general election victory, however, brought major changes to the territorial politics of the UK as power was devolved to new institutions in Scotland, Wales and Northern Ireland in 1999. **Devolution** has brought significant changes to the politics of these nations and to the wider UK political system.

 Key term
- ➤ **Devolution** The transfer of political power from central government to subnational government.

The Union

The official title of the British state is the 'United Kingdom of Great Britain and Northern Ireland'. Great Britain consists of three nations: England, Scotland and Wales.

England is the largest of the UK's four nations with a population of 53.0 million (83.9% of the UK population). It is also the wealthiest and is home of the capital city, London. Scotland has a population of 5.3 million, Wales 3.1 million and Northern Ireland 1.8 million.

The nations of the UK joined a union with England at different times and in different circumstances.

- Wales entered the Union in 1536 when England completed its conquest of the principality. It was governed from London but retained a distinctive culture despite Anglicisation. The 2011 census reported that 19% of people in Wales are able to speak the Welsh language.
- Scotland was an independent state with its own parliament until the 1707 Act of Union. This international treaty saw Scotland join the Union but retain its legal system, education system and local government. Scottish identity continues to draw upon the history of independent statehood and a robust civil society.
- The six counties of Northern Ireland chose to remain part of the UK when the rest of the island of Ireland formed the Irish Free State in 1922. Ireland had joined the Union in 1800 through an Act of Union. The Union was a troubled one with the 'Irish Question' a long-running and difficult issue in British politics. Demands for home rule eventually led to the partition of Ireland in 1922. The Irish Free State became the Republic of Ireland, an independent state, in 1949.

Unitary or union state?

Prior to devolution, the United Kingdom was usually described as a **unitary state**. A unitary state is a centralised state in which political power is located at the centre in national institutions. There is a high degree of centralisation and homogeneity — all parts of the state are governed in the same way. In the UK, parliamentary sovereignty means that Westminster can make law on any subject of its choosing and this law cannot be overturned by any higher institution. Aside from the Stormont Parliament (1922–72) in Northern Ireland, the other parts of the UK did not have their own parliaments.

Unitary, union and federal states

Distinguish between

Unitary state
- A unitary state is a highly centralised state in which political power is concentrated at the centre.
- Central government has ultimate authority over subnational institutions.
- The centre dominates the political, economic and cultural life of the state.
- All areas of the state are governed in the same way and there is a very high degree of administrative standardisation.

Union state
- A union state is a state whose component parts have come together through a union of crowns or by treaty.
- There is a high degree of administrative standardisation, but the component nations retain some of their pre-union features (e.g. separate churches or legal systems).
- Political power is concentrated at the centre, but the component nations have some degree of autonomy (e.g. through devolution).

Federal state
- A federal state is a state in which the constitution divides decision-making authority between national (federal) and regional (state) tiers of government.
- The different tiers of government are protected by the constitution: one tier cannot abolish the other.
- The regions within the state have a distinctive political, and often cultural, identity.

The centralisation found in a unitary state contrasts with the division of powers that characterises **federal** systems. In federal states such as the USA and Germany, power is divided between the national government (the federal government) and regional (state) governments. The constitutions of federal states allocate policy competences to the different tiers and give the states protected status.

Not all political scientists accept the description of the UK as a unitary state. James Mitchell views the UK as a **union state** or a 'state of unions'. In a union state, important political and cultural differences remain after union. Although there is a relatively high degree of administrative standardisation, differences in the way that parts of the state are governed persist.

Key terms
➢ **Unitary state** A homogeneous state in which power is concentrated at the political centre and all parts of the state are governed in the same way.
➢ **Federalism** The sharing of power, enshrined in a constitution, between national (federal) and regional (state) authorities.
➢ **Union state** A state in which there are cultural differences and where, despite a strong centre, different parts of the state are governed in slightly different ways.

Administrative and legislative devolution

Two types of devolution have been found in the UK:
➢ **Administrative devolution.** Political power is concentrated at the centre, but special arrangements are made to take account of distinctive regional interests and identities. Prior to 1999, Scottish and Welsh interests were catered for through distinctive procedures at Whitehall and Westminster, but Scotland and Wales did not have their own parliaments.
➢ **Legislative devolution.** This involves the creation of separate parliaments with legislative powers. It existed in Northern Ireland during the Stormont period (1922–72). In 1999, power was devolved from Westminster to new legislative assemblies in Scotland, Wales and Northern Ireland.

Key concepts
➢ **Administrative devolution** A form of devolution in which political power is concentrated at the centre but special arrangements are found in the executive and legislature to take account of the distinctive interests and identities of various nations or regions. These nations and regions do not, however, have their own assemblies.
➢ **Legislative devolution** A form of devolution in which separate parliaments are established in the nations or regions of a state. Policy-making powers are transferred from the centre to the devolved assemblies, but the state-wide legislature retains ultimate authority and can overrule or abolish the devolved bodies.

Administrative devolution

Before 1999, a number of special arrangements existed for the government of Scotland and Wales:

> **Territorial ministries in UK central government.** The Scottish Office (established in 1885) and the Welsh Office (1964) were responsible for a range of government activities — e.g. agriculture, education and health — in their respective nations. A secretary of state sat in the UK cabinet. The territorial ministries represented the interests of their nations in central government, but were also responsible for implementing UK government policy.

> **Over-representation at Westminster.** Scotland and Wales were over-represented in the Commons, having more MPs per head of population than England. A Scottish Grand Committee and Welsh Grand Committee discussed matters in those countries. They consisted of all MPs representing Scottish and Welsh constituencies respectively.

> **A preferential formula for public spending.** The **Barnett formula**, agreed in 1978, translates changes in public spending in England into equivalent changes in the block grants for Scotland, Wales and Northern Ireland, calculated on the basis of population. Under the formula, Scotland, Wales and Northern Ireland had higher public spending per person than England.

 Key term

> **Barnett formula** A formula devised by Joel Barnett MP in 1978 which determines relative levels of public spending in England, Scotland, Wales and Northern Ireland.

Towards legislative devolution

Demands for legislative devolution have a long history. In the early twentieth century, the 'Irish Question' prompted interest in 'Home Rule all round' under which each **nation** would have had its own parliament in a federal state. **Nationalism** found political expression in the Welsh nationalist party Plaid Cymru, founded in 1925, and the Scottish Nationalist Party

Key concepts

> **Nation** A group of people who inhabit a historic territory, share common traditions and culture, and regard themselves as a distinctive political community. A nation may also share a common language or religion.

> **Nationalism** A political ideology or movement that regards the nation as the main form of political community, and believes that humanity is divided into distinctive nations and that nations should be self-governing. National self-determination is the right of the nation to govern itself and have its own independent state. Two variants of nationalism are commonly identified: civic or political nationalism, which views the nation as the citizens of a territory who share a political culture, and upholds the rights of nations to govern themselves; and ethnic or cultural nationalism, which defines the nation in terms of ethnic descent and shared culture, and is often chauvinist or aggressive in character.

(SNP), founded in 1934. They campaigned for independence and the recognition of their national cultures. The nationalists made electoral breakthroughs at Westminster in the 1960s and 1970s, helped by dissatisfaction with the British political system and a popular revival of Scottish and Welsh identities.

The Conservatives responded to the nationalists' success by briefly supporting a Scottish Assembly, but opposed legislative devolution from the mid-1970s. Opponents of devolution in the Labour Party feared that it would undermine the equitable provision of public services and make the break-up of the UK more likely. But supporters of devolution argued that it would cement support for Labour and reduce the nationalists' appeal.

The 1979 referendums

The Labour government of James Callaghan (1976–79) introduced bills to establish legislative assemblies in Scotland and Wales. They would not, however, come into force unless devolution was supported in referendums in Wales and Scotland. It was also stipulated that the Scottish Assembly had to gain the support of 40% of the total Scottish electorate.

The 1979 Welsh referendum produced a decisive 'no' when only 20% of those who voted backed an assembly. In Scotland, 52% of those who voted supported devolution, but the 40% threshold was not reached as only 33% of the total electorate voted 'yes'.

Demands for legislative devolution gathered momentum in the 1980s. They were fuelled by general elections won by the Conservatives despite their low (and declining) support in Scotland and Wales. A further concentration of power in Whitehall and the perceived insensitivity of the Thatcher government to Scottish distinctiveness also increased support for devolution. Labour's conversion to devolution under John Smith (1992–94), was crucial. Devolution was seen as the optimal way of preserving the Union, and was part of a wider constitutional reform agenda. A Scottish Constitutional Convention set up in 1989 proposed a Scottish Parliament with legislative and tax-raising powers.

The 1997 referendums

Tony Blair insisted that referendums be held in Scotland and Wales to approve devolution. In Scotland, the 1997 referendum asked voters whether they supported (1) a Scottish Parliament and (2) tax-varying powers for the parliament — 74.3% supported a Scottish Parliament and 63.5% tax-varying powers. In Wales, 50.3% voted 'yes' to a Welsh Assembly and 49.7% 'no' on a turnout of 50.1%. Much of western Wales, which has a higher proportion of Welsh speakers, supported the assembly but eastern Wales did not.

Devolution in Scotland and Wales

The Scottish Parliament and Welsh Assembly began work after elections to the new institutions in May 1999. Labour's devolution settlement was one of **asymmetric devolution**: that is, each of the devolved institutions has different powers and

Key term
➤ **Asymmetric devolution**
A form of devolution in which the political arrangements are not uniform, but differ from region to region.

distinctive features. The Scottish Parliament has legislative and tax-varying powers and is solely responsible for law-making in devolved matters. The Welsh Assembly initially had only executive powers, determining how Westminster legislation was implemented in Wales. After the 2011 referendum, the Welsh Assembly gained primary legislative authority in devolved matters.

The Scottish Parliament

The Scottish Parliament has 129 members (MSPs) elected by the additional member system. Seventy-three MSPs (57% of the total) are elected in single-member constituencies using the first-past-the-post system; the remaining 56 MSPs (43%) are 'additional members' chosen from party lists. They are elected in eight multi-member regions, each of which elects seven members using the list system of proportional representation. These seats are allocated to parties on a corrective basis so that the distribution of seats reflects the share of the vote won by the parties (see Chapter 2). Elections are held every 4 years, although the next elections to the Scottish Parliament will be held in 2016 to avoid a clash with the UK general election.

It has primary legislative powers in a range of policy areas, including law and order, health, education, transport, the environment and economic development (see Table 10.1). Westminster no longer makes law for Scotland on these matters. The Scottish Parliament also has tax-varying powers: it can raise or lower the rate of income tax in Scotland by up to 3% (i.e. 3p in the pound), but has not used this power. The Scotland Act (2012) gave the Scottish Parliament the power, from 2016, to set a Scottish rate of income tax higher or lower than that in the UK. Funding comes from a Treasury block grant (£27 billion in 2012) determined by the Barnett formula.

The Scotland Act (1998) sets limits on the Scottish Parliament's legislative powers. It specifies several policy areas in which the Scottish Parliament has no legislative authority. These 'reserved powers' remain the sole responsibility of Westminster. They include the UK constitution, economic policy, foreign policy and relations with the European Union. The Act also states that Westminster remains sovereign in all matters, but has chosen to exercise its sovereignty by devolving legislative responsibility to a Scottish Parliament without diminishing its own powers. Westminster retains the right to override the Scottish Parliament in areas where legislative powers have been devolved. It may also legislate to abolish the Scottish Parliament, although an attempt to do so would be hugely controversial.

The Scottish government, known as the Scottish executive before 2007, draws up policy proposals and implements legislation passed by the parliament. The first minister, usually the leader of the largest party at Holyrood, heads the Scottish government and appoints the cabinet. Alex Salmond has been first minister since 2007.

Links to follow up

www.scottish.parliament.uk and www.scotland.gov.uk — the Scottish Parliament and Scottish government.

The Scottish Parliament buildings at Holyrood, Edinburgh

The Welsh Assembly

The National Assembly for Wales, commonly known as the Welsh Assembly, has 60 members elected by the additional member system. Forty members are elected in single-member constituencies using the first-past-the-post system, and 20 in five multi-member regions using the list system. Elections are held every 4 years but the next contest will be in 2016 to avoid a clash with the UK general election.

The Government of Wales Act (1998) specified the devolved policy areas. These include education, health, transport, the environment and economic development (see Table 10.1). The Assembly initially had only executive and secondary legislative powers, determining how legislation passed by Westminster on a range of Welsh issues should be implemented. If Westminster left significant scope for interpretation, the assembly could play an important role in determining policy in Wales. But if Westminster legislation was tightly drawn, the prospects for assembly initiative were reduced. Following a 'yes' vote in the 2011 referendum on extending the powers of the Welsh Assembly, it assumed primary legislative authority over devolved matters.

Funding comes from a Treasury block grant (£15 billion in 2012) determined by the Barnett formula. The assembly decides how to allocate this money and can alter the basis of local taxation, but does not have tax-varying powers.

The Welsh government, known as the Welsh Assembly government before 2011, formulates and implements policy. The first minister, who is normally the leader of the largest party in the assembly, heads the Welsh government and appoints the cabinet. Carwyn Jones became first minister in 2009.

The Senedd, National Assembly for Wales building on Cardiff Bay waterfront

Links to follow up

www.assemblywales.org and **www.wales.gov.uk** — the Welsh Assembly and the Welsh government.

Table 10.1 Major powers of the devolved administrations and reserved powers, 2013

Scottish Parliament	Welsh Assembly	Northern Ireland Assembly	Powers reserved to Westminster
Law and home affairs	Economic development	Law and order	UK constitution
Economic development	Agriculture and fisheries	Economic development	Defence and national security
Agriculture and fisheries	Education and training	Agriculture and fisheries	Foreign policy, including relations with the EU
Education and training	Local government	Education and training	Fiscal, economic and monetary systems
Local government	Health	Local government	Common market for British goods and services
Health	Housing	Health	Employment legislation
Housing	Environment	Housing	Social security
Environment	Transport	Environment	Media
Transport and road safety	Culture, the Welsh language and sport	Transport	Protection of borders
Culture and sport		Culture and sport	
Tax-varying powers of 3p in the pound			

Further powers

The creation of the devolved assemblies marked a beginning not an end. Former secretary of state for Wales, Ron Davies, recognised that devolution is a 'process not an event'. The Scottish Parliament and Welsh Assembly have both gained further powers since 1999.

The Government of Wales Act (2006) enabled the Welsh Assembly to ask Westminster to transfer additional competences, bringing an incremental extension of devolution. It also paved the way for the assembly to gain primary legislative powers if this was supported in the assembly, at Westminster and in a referendum. The main parties supported further powers for the assembly and the March 2011 referendum produced a 63.5% 'yes' vote. The assembly duly gained the power to make primary legislation in the 20 devolved areas.

Debate on further devolution continues. The coalition government established the independent Silk Commission to examine the case for the further transfer of powers. In its first report in 2012 the commission proposed that, subject to approval in a referendum, the assembly should, by 2020, have the power to vary income tax. It would be responsible for raising around a quarter of its budget, and would also gain powers to borrow money. The UK government broadly favours the status quo whereas the Welsh government proposes that issues such as policing, criminal justice and road safety should be devolved. The Silk Commission's final report is expected in 2014. Opinion polls show little support for Welsh independence.

Links to follow up

http://devolutionmatters.wordpress.com — blog examining devolution developments by the academic Alan Trench.

Scotland: more devolution or independence?

The UK government and the other main parties in the Scottish Parliament set up the Calman Commission to consider further devolution — but not independence. The 2009 Calman Report recommended that the Scottish Parliament should be given greater tax-varying powers, responsibility for some other taxes and duties, and for policy on issues such as drink-driving and speed limits.

The main parties at Westminster accepted most of Calman's recommendations. The Conservative–Liberal Democrat coalition government enacted them in the Scotland Act (2012). Its key provisions are:

➤ **Scottish rate of income tax.** The Scottish Parliament will, from 2016, have the power to set a Scottish rate of income tax. The income tax paid by Scottish taxpayers will be calculated by reducing the UK rate by 10 pence then adding the new Scottish rate, which the Scottish Parliament will be able set at a higher or lower rate than that in the rest of the UK. On current rates, this could raise £5.6 billion for the Scottish government.

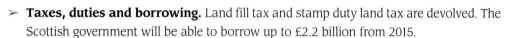

- **Taxes, duties and borrowing.** Land fill tax and stamp duty land tax are devolved. The Scottish government will be able to borrow up to £2.2 billion from 2015.
- **Devolution of further powers.** Powers on policy on air guns, misuse of drugs, drink-driving limits, speed limits on roads, and the administration of Scottish Parliament elections are devolved.
- **Return of powers.** Responsibility for regulation of activities in Antarctica becomes a reserved matter. The Scottish Parliament had never exercised its competence in this area.

The election of an SNP government in 2007 gave momentum to the issue of Scottish independence. It set out three options:

- **Further devolution.** The devolution of further powers, as proposed by Calman.
- **Full devolution ('devo max').** The Scottish Parliament would be responsible for all taxes, duties, spending and laws, except for defence, foreign policy, monetary policy and the UK currency which would remain with the UK government.
- **Independence.** The Scottish Parliament and government would take full responsibility for all reserved areas, ending the UK Parliament's power to legislate for Scotland and the UK government's competence for executive action in Scotland. This is the SNP's preferred option.

Independence referendum, 2014

The SNP won a majority of seats in the 2011 Scottish Parliament elections and pledged to hold a referendum on independence. This raised the spectre of a major dispute between the Scottish government and UK government because the constitution is a reserved power (i.e. the responsibility of Westminster). However, in October 2012, David Cameron and Alex Salmond signed the Edinburgh Agreement. Its key provisions are:

- **Legal referendum.** The UK government will give temporary powers to the Scottish Parliament, under Section 30 of the Scotland Act (1998) to hold a referendum in 2014. The date of the referendum was subsequently announced as 18 September 2014.
- **Single question.** The referendum will have a single question. The SNP had suggested that voters might choose between the status quo, further devolution and independence. The UK government opposed this. The SNP proposed that the referendum question should be: 'Do you agree that Scotland should be an independent country?'. However, the Scottish government subsequently accepted the Electoral Commission's recommendation that the referendum ask: 'Should Scotland be an independent country?'.
- **Electoral Commission.** As well as advising on the wording of the question, the Electoral Commission will regulate the referendum campaign and campaign spending.
- **Franchise.** The voting age will be lowered from 18 to 16 for the referendum only. The franchise will include UK citizens resident in Scotland but not the 800,000 Scots resident in other parts of the UK.

The referendum campaign groups were launched in 2012. The campaign in favour of independence, Yes Scotland, is supported by the SNP and Greens. It argues that the people of

Scottish First Minister Alex Salmond and Deputy First Minister Nicola Sturgeon walk past a sign outside the Scottish Parliament showing the date for the Scottish independence referendum

Scotland are best placed to make decisions that affect Scotland. The Scottish government will publish details of its model of an independent Scotland in late 2013. The pro-Union campaign, Better Together, is supported by Labour, the Conservatives and Liberal Democrats. It argues that Scotland enjoys the best of both worlds in the UK — extensive devolution and the economic, political and cultural benefits of the Union. The UK government will produce its assessments of the benefits of the Union and costs of independence in the run-up to the referendum.

Since devolution, opinion polls have reported that between a quarter and a third of Scots support independence. Greater self-government within the Union is the preferred choice of a plurality. However, this will not be an option in the 2014 referendum. Better Together will need to persuade supporters of 'devo max' that a 'no' vote will not preclude further devolution.

Links to follow up

www.yesscotland.net — the pro-independence referendum campaign group.

www.bettertogether.net — the pro-Union referendum campaign group.

⟷ Stretch and challenge

An independent Scotland?

The SNP suggests that, if there is a 'yes' vote in the 2014 referendum, Scotland could be independent by 2016. This appears ambitious given the complex issues that would have to be settled during the transition period. These include:

- **Economic relations.** The SNP plans to keep the pound sterling, but monetary policy, trade, social security and Scotland's share of the UK national debt would have to be settled in negotiations between the Scottish and UK governments.
- **European Union.** European Commission president Jose Manuel Barroso stated that an independent Scotland would not automatically join the EU, but would have to apply for membership.
- **Defence.** NATO membership and the siting of nuclear weapons in Scotland are key issues here.

Scottish independence would have important implications for politics in the rest of the UK. MPs from Scottish constituencies would no longer sit at Westminster. If Scotland became independent in 2016, one scenario would see a Labour government deprived of its parliamentary majority. After Scottish independence, Labour would find it more difficult to win power at Westminster. In 2010, the Conservatives won 298 seats in England to Labour's 191, whereas they won one seat in Scotland compared to Labour's 41.

Questions

Follow the debate in the Scottish independence referendum campaign and consider the following:

1 What would an independent Scotland look like?
2 If Scotland voted for independence, how would this change the government and politics of the UK?

The impact of devolution

Devolution has had a significant impact on politics in Scotland and Wales, and on the UK political system. This section examines:

- ➢ a new politics
- ➢ multi-party politics
- ➢ minority and coalition governments
- ➢ policy divergence
- ➢ funding
- ➢ intergovernmental relations
- ➢ Westminster and the English Question
- ➢ Britishness

A new politics

Hopes were high in Scotland and Wales that legislative devolution would usher in a different style of politics. Whereas Westminster politics was seen as adversarial and elitist, the hope was that post-devolution politics would be consensual and more democratic. This was always likely to prove over-optimistic, and the new institutions have not been free of scandal.

But there is a different atmosphere in the Scottish Parliament and Welsh Assembly. Two examples are:

➢ **Representation of a broader range of society.** Women constitute a higher proportion of the Scottish Parliament (35%) and Welsh Assembly (40%) than is the case at Westminster (22%).

➢ **Greater opportunity for public participation in the legislative process.** A petition helped persuade MSPs to ban smoking in public places.

Multi-party politics

A casual observer might be forgiven for thinking that elections in Scotland and Wales are not very competitive. Labour won 41 of 59 seats (69.5%) in Scotland and 26 of 40 (65%) in Wales at the 2010 general election, but on 42% and 36% of the vote respectively. Elections to the devolved bodies provide a more accurate reflection of multi-party politics. The additional member system produces more proportional outcomes than are found at Westminster. Nationalist parties perform better in these elections than in Westminster elections, while support for Labour is lower. The Scottish and Welsh Labour, Conservative and Liberal Democrat parties try to distance themselves from their Westminster counterparts.

Minority and coalition governments

Elections to the Scottish Parliament and Welsh Assembly have produced different types of government. Scottish Parliament elections led to:

➢ Labour–Liberal Democrat coalition following the 1999 and 2003 elections. These were based on formal policy agreements and a division of ministerial posts between the parties.

➢ A minority SNP government after the 2007 election. It relied on support from smaller parties to get key measures through the parliament.

➢ A majority SNP government formed after its resounding victory in 2011 (see Table 10.2).

Welsh Assembly elections have produced complex outcomes:

➢ Labour formed a minority government after the 1999 election, then a 'partnership' with the Liberal Democrats in 2000.

➢ Labour won 30 of the 60 seats in the assembly in 2003 but had a technical majority because the Presiding Officer and his deputy were from other parties. This disappeared in 2005 when Peter Law left Labour to sit as an independent.

➢ Following a month of minority Labour government, Labour and Plaid Cymru formed a coalition after the 2007 election.

➢ Labour currently governs alone after winning 30 of the 60 seats in the 2011 election (see Table 10.3), but has sought support from other parties on key issues.

Policy divergence

Devolution has allowed governments in Scotland, Wales and Northern Ireland to adopt policies which differ from those pursued by the UK government in England. Policy divergence was evident in health and education before devolution, and has become more pronounced since (see Table 10.4). The Scottish government introduced free long-term personal care for

Table 10.2 Elections to the Scottish Parliament, 2011

	Constituency contests			Regional lists			Total seats	
	Share of vote (%)		Seats won		Share of vote (%)		Seats won		Total seats
Con	13.9	(−2.7)	3	(−1)	12.4	(−1.5)	12	(−1)	15	(−2)
Lab	31.7	(−0.5)	15	(−22)	26.3	(−2.9)	22	(+13)	37	(−9)
Lib Dem	7.9	(−8.3)	2	(−9)	5.2	(−6.1)	3	(−2)	5	(−11)
SNP	45.4	(+12.5)	53	(+32)	44.0	(+13.0)	16	(−10)	69	(+22)
Green	0	(−0.2)	0	(+0)	4.4	(+0.3)	2	(+0)	2	(+0)
Others	1.1	(−0.9)	0	(−0)	7.7	(−2.9)	1	(+0)	1	(+0)

Note: figures in brackets refer to change since 2007.

Table 10.3 Elections to the Welsh Assembly, 2011

	Constituency contests			Regional lists			Total seats	
	Share of vote (%)		Seats won		Share of vote (%)		Seats won		Total seats
Con	25.0	(+2.6)	6	(+1)	22.5	(+1.1)	8	(+1)	14	(+2)
Lab	42.3	(+10.1)	28	(+4)	36.9	(+7.2)	2	(+0)	30	(+4)
Lib Dem	10.6	(−4.2)	1	(−2)	8.0	(−3.7)	4	(+1)	5	(−1)
Plaid Cymru	19.3	(−3.1)	5	(−2)	17.9	(−3.1)	6	(−2)	11	(−4)
Others	2.8	(−5.5)	0	(−1)	14.7	(−1.6)	0	(+0)	0	(−1)

Note: figures in brackets refer to change since 2007.

Table 10.4 Examples of policy divergence (health and education)

Scotland	Wales	Northern Ireland
Abolition of prescription charges	Abolition of prescription charges	Abolition of prescription charges
Restructuring of NHS; abolition of NHS internal market	Restructuring of NHS; higher waiting times than in England	Restructuring of NHS
Free long-term personal care for the elderly	Free school milk for children under 7	Free fares for the elderly
Ban on smoking in public places takes effect before ban elsewhere in UK	Abolition of testing for 7, 11 and 14 year olds	Abolition of school league tables
Abolition of up-front tuition fees for students at Scottish universities; abolition of student payment.	Introduction of Welsh Baccalaureatte	Establishment of Children's Commissioner
Minimum price for alcohol	Establishment of Children's Commissioner	

the elderly, and prescription charges have been abolished in Scotland and Wales. Policies on university tuition fees and testing in schools differ across the UK.

Policy differences can be seen as a positive development because the devolved bodies reacted to the concerns of their electorate. Policies developed in Scotland and Wales — such as the ban on smoking in public places in Scotland — were taken up subsequently by the UK government. However, policy divergence may undermine the principle of equal rights for UK citizens if it widens disparities in welfare provision.

The UK civil service and EU law promote policy convergence, and the limited budgets of the devolved institutions do not allow them to increase public spending greatly. There have been few major disputes between the UK governments and the devolved administrations. The most controversial issue was the decision by the Scottish executive in 2009 to free the Lockerbie bomber Abdelbaset Ali Al-Megrahi from a Scottish prison.

Funding

The devolved administrations are funded by block grants from the UK Treasury, the size of which is settled by the Barnett formula. Agreed in 1978, it translates changes in public spending in England into equivalent changes in the block grants for Scotland, Wales and Northern Ireland, calculated on the basis of population. Scotland, Wales and Northern Ireland receive more public spending per head of population than England. For 2008/09, if the UK level was taken as 100, then government funding for England would be 97, for Wales 111, for Scotland 116, and for Northern Ireland 122. In other words, government funding per head of population was 16% higher in Scotland than in the UK as a whole.

Critics claim that this amounts to an English subsidy of the rest of the UK. However, Scotland and Wales have seen their share of public spending squeezed. The Holtham Committee (2009), which reviewed the formula in Wales, recommended a new needs-based funding system.

Intergovernmental relations

The Scotland Office, Wales Office and Northern Ireland Office represent the interests of their respective nations in Whitehall. Secretaries of state for Scotland, Wales and Northern Ireland sit in the cabinet, although the holders of the first two posts have sometimes also held other portfolios.

New mechanisms to handle relations between the UK government and the devolved bodies (i.e. **intergovernmental relations**) have been established to foster cooperation and resolve disputes:

Key term
➢ **Intergovernmental relations**
Relations between the UK government and devolved administrations.

➢ **Concordats.** Concordats set out the rules governing the relationship between UK government departments and the devolved administrations.
➢ **Joint Ministerial Committee.** Meetings are held between UK ministers and those from the devolved administrations to discuss policy and resolve disputes.
➢ **Supreme Court.** This is the final arbiter in cases where disputes about the competences of the devolved administrations arise. In its first key decision in this area, the Supreme Court ruled in 2012 that the Welsh Assembly had not exceeded its powers in its Local Government Bye-Laws Bill.

➤ **British–Irish Council.** Created by the Good Friday Agreement, this promotes the sharing of ideas between the UK and Irish governments, the devolved administrations in Scotland, Wales and Northern Ireland, plus the Isle of Man, Jersey and Guernsey.

However, coordination has been characterised by pragmatism and ad hoc arrangements rather than clear rules of the game.

Westminster and the English Question

Devolution required procedural changes at Westminster. MPs at Westminster can no longer ask parliamentary questions on solely devolved matters. Legislative consent motions ('Sewel motions') enable the Scottish Parliament to delegate responsibility for legislating on devolved matters back to Westminster on a case-by-case basis. By 2012, more than 100 had been passed.

The **West Lothian Question** asks why MPs representing Scottish constituencies at Westminster should be permitted to vote on purely English matters (e.g. local government in England) when English MPs have no say over matters devolved to the Scottish Parliament. It was named after Tam Dalyell, MP for West Lothian, who raised it during debates on devolution in the 1970s. Legislation on foundation hospitals and university tuition fees in England in 2003–04 would not have passed without the votes of Labour MPs from Scotland. The reduction in the number of Scottish MPs from 72 to 59 in 2005 was a partial response to the question.

Key term

➤ **West Lothian Question.** Why should Scottish MPs be able to vote on English matters at Westminster when English MPs cannot vote on matters devolved to the Scottish Parliament?

The West Lothian Question would be more pressing if the governing party at Westminster had a majority of seats in the UK as a whole but not a majority of seats in England. Labour polled fewer votes in England than the Conservatives in 2005 but won 92 more seats.

These issues are part of a broader 'English Question' about how England should be governed within the post-devolution Union. Underpinning it is a sense that English interests and identity are not recognised explicitly. Four main solutions have emerged:

➤ **Elected regional assemblies in England.** The Blair governments proposed that directly elected regional assemblies with limited executive functions be created in the eight English regions outside London. The policy was scrapped after a 'no' vote in a referendum on a regional assembly for northeast England in 2004. Regional Development Agencies, created in 1999 to promote economic development, were abolished by the Conservative–Liberal Democrat coalition in 2012. Few English regions have a strong sense of identity.

➤ **Regional select committees at Westminster.** The Brown government established regional select committees for the nine English regions in 2009. But Conservative and Liberal Democrat MPs did not attend and the committees ceased work in 2010.

➤ **English votes for English laws**. The Conservatives propose a system in which MPs representing Scottish constituencies would not be permitted to amend or vote on bills on English matters. However, this would create two classes of MPs and public spending decisions in England impact on Scotland and Wales through the Barnett formula. The Conservative–Liberal Democrat coalition established the McKay Commission to examine the issue. It recommended in 2013 that decisions 'with a separate and distinct effect for England' should normally require the consent of a majority of MPs representing English constituencies. The House of Commons as a whole would retain the right to make the final decision. The commission rejected proposals that MPs from outside England should be prevented from voting on English matters. Instead, procedures would be adapted to allow the expression of views from England (e.g. in English public bill committees or report committees).

➤ **An English parliament.** This would have powers, similar to those of the Scottish Parliament, over domestic English issues. There is limited elite and public support for this option.

All these solutions have problems. The status quo thus emerges as a fifth option because the 'answer' to the English Question may be as problematic as the question.

Links to follow up

> **http://tmc.independent.gov.uk** — the McKay commission on the consequences of devolution for the House of Commons.

Britishness

Britishness is an umbrella identity that provides a common bond between the peoples of the UK, but which also enables them to retain their distinctive national (i.e. English, Welsh, Scottish and Northern Irish) identities. British identity has been built around symbols of the British state, such as the monarchy, parliament and the National Health Service.

The number of people describing themselves as exclusively Scottish, Welsh or English has risen slightly since 1997, but most people still feel British to some extent.

A quasi-federal UK

Devolution has created a new relationship between the UK's component nations. It provides institutional recognition of the distinctiveness of these nations while reflecting their desire to remain part of the Union. The post-devolution UK no longer fits the criteria of a highly centralised unitary state, but nor is it a federal state with power constitutionally divided between autonomous institutions.

Professor Vernon Bogdanor characterises the UK as a **quasi-federal** state that has some federal characteristics but retains some of the features of a unitary state. When William Gladstone sought to recognise the multinational character of the UK by devolving power to a legislative assembly in Ireland in the late nineteenth century, constitutional theorist A. V. Dicey argued that there could be no halfway house between parliamentary sovereignty and

Key concept

> **Quasi-federal** A quasi-federal state is one in which the central government of a unitary state devolves some of its powers to subnational governments. It has some of the features of a unitary state and some of a federal state. Legally, there is a supreme legal authority located at the centre, as in a unitary state. But in practice, the centre no longer makes domestic policy for some parts of the state and it would find it difficult politically to abolish the subnational tier of government.

separatism. A century later, Labour's devolution settlement took the UK into this middle ground. The main features of quasi-federalism are:

> **Parliamentary sovereignty is limited.** In legal terms, Westminster remains sovereign because it can overrule or abolish the devolved bodies. In practice, however, Westminster is no longer sovereign over domestic matters in Scotland, Wales and Northern Ireland — it does not have unlimited power. Although sovereignty has been formally delegated rather than devolved, Westminster has accepted that it will not impose legislation in devolved areas. A UK government that sought to abolish the Scottish Parliament or Welsh Assembly without holding a referendum would provoke a constitutional crisis.

> **Westminster is a quasi-federal parliament.** Westminster operates as an English parliament in the sense that it makes domestic law in England, and is a federal parliament for Scotland, Wales and Northern Ireland because it retains reserved powers on major UK-wide matters. MPs from Scotland, Wales and Northern Ireland have few constituency responsibilities and deal mainly with economic and foreign affairs issues in the House of Commons.

> **Supreme Court.** The Supreme Court resolves disputes over competences by determining if the devolved bodies have acted within their powers.

Viewpoint Has devolution weakened the union?

YES

- The piecemeal approach to devolution has meant that problems (e.g. the West Lothian Question and the future of the Barnett formula) have not been addressed effectively.
- Insufficient attention has been paid to the purpose and benefits of the Union and Britishness in the post-devolution UK.
- The rules of the game on policy coordination and dispute resolution are not clear enough.
- Policy divergence has undermined the idea of common welfare rights in the UK.
- The SNP has gained power, leading to a referendum on Scottish independence.
- There is unease in England about the perceived unfairness of the devolution settlement.

NO

- Devolution has answered Scottish, Welsh and Northern Irish demands for greater autonomy, bringing decision making closer to the people.
- Devolution has proceeded smoothly, without major disputes between the British government and the devolved bodies.
- Policy divergence reflects the different interests of the nations of the UK and has allowed initiatives that have proved successful in one nation to be adopted elsewhere.
- Most people in the UK still feel British to some degree, and only a minority in each nation favour independence.
- The prospects for peace and power sharing in Northern Ireland are stronger than ever before.

Northern Ireland

From 1922 to 1972, the Stormont Parliament and executive were responsible for the government of Northern Ireland. It was dominated by unionist politicians who represented the Protestant majority and pursued policies that discriminated against the Catholic minority. The civil rights movement and the Irish Republican Army (IRA) took up Catholic grievances in the 1960s. British troops were sent to the province in 1969, but as 'the Troubles' escalated, Edward Heath's Conservative government suspended the Stormont Parliament in 1972. **Direct rule** from London was imposed: UK government ministers and Northern Ireland Office officials took policy decisions, not local politicians. Subsequent British governments introduced a series of unsuccessful initiatives to bring about **power-sharing devolution**, but the IRA's terrorist campaign continued. The Good Friday Agreement of 1998 proved a significant breakthrough.

Key terms

➢ **Direct rule** The government of Northern Ireland from London, through special procedures at Westminster.

➢ **Power-sharing devolution** A form of devolution in which special arrangements are put in place to ensure that both communities in a divided society are represented in the executive and that they assent to legislation on sensitive issues.

Stormont Castle, Belfast was the home of the Stormont Parliament from 1922 to 1972. Now the Northern Ireland Assembly sits here

A place apart

British governments have treated Northern Ireland as 'a place apart' in UK territorial politics. Special circumstances have applied to Northern Ireland:

> **Conditional status.** Northern Ireland's status as a part of the UK is conditional on a majority of its population wishing to remain within the UK. At present, a majority support the constitutional status quo. The UK government depicts itself as a neutral broker in the search for a peaceful solution.

> **Separate administration.** Northern Ireland has been governed differently from the rest of the UK. Between 1922 and 1972, it was the only part of the UK to have its own parliament with legislative and executive powers. After 1972, under direct rule, the secretary of state for Northern Ireland had greater policy-making powers than the secretaries of state for Scotland and Wales. Policy was made through Orders in Council rather than primary legislation at Westminster. Devolution in Northern Ireland has also been distinctive because it has been designed so that unionist and nationalist parties share power.

> **The 'Irish dimension'.** Since the 1980s, the UK government and the government of the Republic of Ireland have worked together to find a peaceful settlement in Northern Ireland. The Anglo-Irish Agreement (1985) gave the Republic a formal role in the search for a settlement.

> **Communal conflict.** The main political divide in Northern Ireland is that between **unionists** and **nationalists**. Unionists want Northern Ireland to remain part of the UK. Nationalists favour constitutional change, such as a united Ireland or a greater role for the Irish republic in the affairs of Northern Ireland. Unionists identify with the British state and tend to be Protestant, whereas nationalists identify themselves as Irish and tend to be Catholic. Catholics made up 45% of the Northern Ireland population in 2011.

Key terms

> **Unionist** An adherent of a political position in Northern Ireland that supports the continued union between Great Britain and Northern Ireland.

> **Nationalist** An adherent of a political position in Northern Ireland that supports constitutional means of achieving improved rights for Catholics, and the eventual incorporation of the six counties of Northern Ireland into the Republic of Ireland.

> **Distinctive party system.** Communal divisions shape Northern Irish politics. Elections are contested between unionist and nationalist parties; the main electoral issue is the constitutional status of Northern Ireland. The main UK parties have tended not to field candidates in Northern Ireland elections, but the Conservatives formed an alliance with the Ulster Unionist Party for the 2010 general election.

> **Security.** Terrorist campaigns by republican and loyalist paramilitary organisations posed security problems. British soldiers patrolled the streets for several decades. The IRA

has been on ceasefire for much of the period since 1995, but the breakaway Real IRA — which killed 29 people in the 1998 Omagh bombing — remains active.

The Good Friday Agreement

Years of negotiations between the UK and Irish government, and (some of) the Northern Irish political parties, resulted in the 1998 Good Friday Agreement (the 'Belfast Agreement'). It created a number of institutions:

> **Northern Ireland Assembly.** The assembly consists of 108 members, elected by the single transferable vote system of proportional representation (see Chapter 2). It has primary legislative powers in a range of policy areas, but does not have tax-raising power (see Table 10.1, page 298). Some measures require cross-community support from both unionist and nationalist parties.

> **Northern Ireland executive.** This is led by a first minister and deputy first minister. The first minister is the leader of the largest party in the assembly, and the deputy first minister is drawn from the second largest party. Ministerial posts are allocated on a proportional basis according to party strength in the assembly. The agreement thus ensures power sharing, with both unionists and nationalists represented in government.

> **North–South Ministerial Council.** In this body, the Northern Ireland executive and Republic of Ireland government cooperate on cross-border issues.

> **British–Irish Council.** Here the UK and Irish governments, the devolved administrations in Scotland, Wales and Northern Ireland, plus the Isle of Man and Channel Islands, exchange policy ideas.

> **British–Irish Intergovernmental Conference.** In which the UK and Irish governments discuss the situation in Northern Ireland.

The agreement also required the UK and Irish governments to amend their constitutions to clarify the status of Northern Ireland. It paved the way for a new Police Service of Northern Ireland and the early release of prisoners.

However, the UK suspended the devolved institutions and reimposed direct rule on four occasions as the lack of trust between the two communities continued. Parades by the Protestant Orange Order, paramilitary activity, policing issues and, most importantly, decommissioning all threatened to derail the peace process. The IRA, the main **republican** paramilitary body, did not fully decommission its arms or declare explicitly that its conflict was over until 2005. Most **loyalist** paramilitary groups have also disarmed.

Key terms

> **Republican** An adherent to a variant of Irish nationalism that has supported the use of political violence to end British rule in Northern Ireland.
> **Loyalist** An adherent to a variant of unionism that has supported the use of political violence to defend the union between Great Britain and Northern Ireland.

The pro-Agreement centre 'hollowed out' as unionists lost faith in the peace process. The Ulster Unionist Party (UUP) and Social Democratic and Labour Party (SDLP) had been key players in the agreement and shared the top positions in the Northern Ireland executive. But by the 2003 assembly elections, they had been overtaken by their rivals. The Democratic Unionist Party (DUP), which had initially opposed the agreement, became the main representative of the unionist community. Sinn Fein, a republican party with strong ties to the IRA, became the main voice of nationalists.

In a remarkable turn of events, the DUP and Sinn Fein agreed to work together. Former enemies Ian Paisley, dubbed 'Dr No' for his refusal to share power with Sinn Fein, and Martin McGuinness, one time IRA commander in Derry, became first minister and deputy first minister in 2007. Paisley retired the following year and was succeeded by Peter Robinson. Responsibility for law and order was devolved in 2010.

Case study Community relations in Northern Ireland

There has been substantial progress in Northern Ireland since the Good Friday Agreement. Former enemies work together in government; the number of conflict-related deaths has fallen significantly; and polling for the Northern Ireland Life and Times Survey (**www.ark.ac.uk/nilt**) shows that a majority believe that relations between Protestants and Catholics have improved.

However, political and cultural identities remain deeply embedded. Peace lines separating Protestant and Catholic neighbourhoods in Belfast are a potent symbol of the communal divide. Public housing and education are largely segregated. The violent protests that followed Belfast city council's decision to limit the number of days on which the Union flag would be flown from city hall also illustrated the continued tensions.

Links to follow up

www.niassembly.gov.uk and **www.northernireland.gov.uk** — the Northern Ireland Assembly and the Northern Ireland executive.

Local government

The UK has moved away from a system of centralised government to one of **multi-level governance**. Central government remains the single most important actor, but it does not monopolise decision making because a number of bodies operating at different levels have policy competences. These include:

➤ supranational level: the European Union (see Chapter 11)
➤ UK level: the Westminster Parliament and UK government
➤ regional level: the devolved institutions, the mayor of London and the London Assembly
➤ local level: elected local authorities and local **quangos**

Local authorities are the lowest level of government in the UK, and in England are the only elected branch of government below central government. **Local government** is not protected by the uncodified constitution, allowing central government to change its structure and functions. The last 30 years have seen two main trends that have brought about a decline in the power of local government:

➢ **Centralisation.** Central government has taken over or redistributed some of the functions of local authorities, and has exercised a tight grip on their finance. However, the Localism Act (2011) allows ministers to delegate some responsibilities (e.g. over aspects of housing or transport policy) to local authorities.

➢ **Local governance.** Rather than local authorities providing most local services directly, there is now a system of local governance in which a range of bodies are involved in decision making at local level.

Key terms

➢ **Multi-level governance** A system of decision making in which policy competences are shared between local, regional, national and supranational institutions.

➢ **Quangos** Quasi-autonomous non-governmental organisations; unelected public bodies responsible for the funding or regulation of certain areas of public policy.

➢ **Local government** A system in which elected local authorities provide many local services directly, and are accountable to voters at local elections.

➢ **Local governance** A system in which a range of bodies and networks are involved in the provision of local services.

Structure

The 1974 reorganisation of local government in England established a uniform two-tier structure in which the provision of local services in an area was divided between two authorities. This became more complex in the 1990s with the creation of unitary authorities (i.e. a single tier of local government) in some parts of England. Scotland and Wales moved to a uniform system of unitary authorities. In 2013, the structure of local government in England was:

➢ 55 unitary authorities, responsible for a full range of local services
➢ 27 county councils, responsible for some local services (e.g. education, social services, policing and transport) in the shires
➢ 201 district councils, responsible for some local services (e.g. housing, leisure and refuse collection) in the shires
➢ 36 metropolitan borough councils, responsible for a full range of local services in urban areas

Different arrangements apply in London, where the Greater London Authority has strategic responsibility for economic development, transport, planning and policing. It consists of a directly elected mayor and a 25-member London Assembly. The mayor sets the budget and determines policy. The main initiative taken by the mayor was the congestion charge introduced in 2003.

The Blair government and the Conservative–Liberal Democrat coalition hoped the directly elected mayor model would be adopted elsewhere. However, by 2013, only 15 local authorities had directly elected mayors. Voters in 34 areas have voted against adopting the system, with nine of ten referendums held in 2012 producing 'no' votes. Most local authorities have an indirectly elected leader who heads a cabinet of councillors.

Links to follow up

www.gwydir.demon.co.uk/uklocalgov — click on 'Council Political Compositions' for information on the political composition of local authorities and links to council websites.

Funding and functions

Local government expenditure accounts for over a quarter of all public spending in England. Funding comes from three main sources:

> **Grants from central government.** This makes up 55% of local authority income, but central government determines what proportion of this funding can be spent on individual services.

> **Local taxation on domestic properties.** The council tax accounts for 25% of local authority income. Levels are set by local authorities but are subject to capping by central government. The council tax is based on the value of a property, with a 25% discount for single householders. It replaced the community charge, commonly known as the poll tax, in 1993. This was paid by most citizens at a flat rate.

> **Local taxation on business properties.** The national non-domestic rate accounts for 20% of local authority income. It is set and collected by central government.

Local authorities are responsible for many of the services used by citizens on a day-to-day basis, including:

> education (e.g. primary and secondary schools)
> social services (e.g. residential care and care in the community)
> housing (e.g. public housing)
> roads (e.g. maintenance and regulation of smaller roads) and public transport (e.g. bus services)
> planning (e.g. decisions on planning applications)
> environmental health (e.g. refuse collection and recycling)
> leisure services (e.g. libraries and leisure centres)

Local authorities do not provide all of these services directly. Instead, they have been transformed into **enabling authorities** that oversee the provision of services by other bodies. Rather than providing services directly, local authorities now organise, supervise, regulate and fund the provision of services by others. Services such as refuse

Key term
> **Enabling authorities**
Local authorities that set the framework in which other bodies provide local services, but do not provide all these services themselves.

collection are often provided by private companies. Other services that used to be provided by local authorities are now delivered by housing associations, health trusts and academy schools.

The three main parties propose further localism, with local community bodies given a greater role in shaping priorities and delivering programmes (e.g. to tackle poverty and crime). With turnout in local elections low, this offers an alternative model of **local democracy** in which local authorities are required to promote democracy by fostering participation in community groups.

Links to follow up

www.local.gov.uk — website of the Local Government Association, with information on the role and structure of local government.

Viewpoint Is local government still important?

- Local government has overall responsibility for many of the local services that people use on a regular basis.
- Local authorities are responsible for 25% of public spending.
- Local authorities are major players in local governance, shaping policy and enabling others to provide effective service delivery.
- Local authorities play a leadership role in promoting community action and participation.
- Elected local authorities are directly accountable to voters.

- Local government has lost much of its autonomy in the last three decades and its structure has been changed frequently.
- Central government determines how local authorities raise and spend most of their money.
- Local services that used to be delivered by local authorities (e.g. education and housing) are now delivered by other bodies.
- Turnout in local elections is low, and those who do vote often do so on national rather than local issues.
- Local government operates in a system of multi-level governance in which more decisions are now taken at regional or EU level.

🔑 Key concept

➤ **Local democracy** The traditional perspective on local democracy is that elected local authorities should be responsible for the provision of local services. They are held accountable to voters in local elections. But this model became problematic because of low turnout in local elections and the reduction in the power of local authorities to collect and spend money. The enabling authority model sees local citizens as consumers of services. Service providers are held accountable through contracts and regulatory frameworks, leaving local councillors responsible for strategic decisions. Local authorities have a statutory duty to promote democracy by encouraging, for example, participation in community groups.

What you should know

- The UK was a highly centralised state for most of the twentieth century. A system of administrative devolution provided some recognition at the centre for the distinctive interests of Scotland and Wales. But Northern Ireland (1922–72) was the only part of the UK to have its own assembly.

- The Labour government elected in 1997 implemented legislative devolution in which policy-making powers were transferred from Westminster to a Scottish Parliament, Welsh Assembly and Northern Ireland Assembly. These began work in 1999. The new system is asymmetric: the devolved bodies have different powers and institutional arrangements. Devolution is also an ongoing process, with additional powers transferred to the devolved bodies since 1999. A referendum on Scottish independence will be held in 2014.

- Devolution has brought about significant changes in UK territorial politics. Elections to the devolved bodies have produced minority and coalition governments, which have introduced policies that differ from those pursued by the UK government in England. It has also posed questions about the government of England which have yet to be answered fully.

- Devolution is an important element in the emergence of multi-level governance in the UK, with policy-making competences held by institutions at supranational, national, regional and local levels. Local government is relatively weak and has lost functions to both central government and unelected local bodies. However, local authorities remain responsible for many of the services used by citizens on a daily basis.

UK/US comparison

Federalism in the USA

- The USA is a federal state in which law-making power is divided between two tiers of government: the federal government (located in Washington DC) and the governments of the 50 states of the USA. The UK is a unitary state, but since devolution it has taken on quasi-federal features.

- The two tiers of government in the USA are protected by the constitution. Their powers are inalienable. One tier of government cannot abolish the other tier of government. The division of powers can only be altered by amendment to the constitution, which requires special procedures. In the UK, Westminster retains parliamentary sovereignty and can overrule or abolish the devolved bodies. In practice, parliament has recognised that it no longer has authority over devolved policies.

- Powers that are reserved to the US federal government include defence, foreign policy, the US currency and the US single market. Relatively few powers are reserved exclusively to the states (e.g. local taxes), but power is shared between the federal and state governments in many areas (e.g. criminal and civil law, health and education). Westminster also has reserved powers over issues such as defence, foreign policy, the constitution and the UK currency.

- There is significant policy divergence between the 50 states of the USA (e.g. on the death penalty and drug laws). Devolution has produced limited policy divergence between the four nations of the UK.

➤ The US Supreme Court makes binding judgments where disputes arise about the distribution of powers between federal and state governments. The UK Supreme Court can pronounce on whether the devolved bodies have acted within their powers, but it cannot strike down an Act of the Westminster Parliament.

➤ The nature of US federalism has changed over time, with the USA becoming a more centralised nation than was envisaged in the Constitution. The policy-making scope of the federal government expanded, notably with the 1930s New Deal and 1960s Great Society programmes, and it exercised more control over state funding. Some policy responsibilities were returned to the states under the Reagan administration in the 1980s, but funding was also cut. The UK was highly centralised for much of the twentieth century, but power was devolved to new institutions in three of its component nations in 1999, creating a quasi-federal system.

Further reading

Bogdanor, V. (2010) 'Sovereignty and devolution: quasi-federalism?', *Politics Review*, Vol. 19, No. 3, pp. 12–15.

Jeffrey, C. (2009) 'Devolution in the UK: what's wrong with the status quo?', *Politics Review*, Vol. 18, No. 4, pp. 14–16.

Mitchell, J. (2011) 'The 2011 Scottish elections: why did the SNP win?', *Politics Review*, Vol. 21, No. 1, pp.18–20.

Scully, R. and Wyn Jones, R. 'Territorial politics in post-devolution Britain', in R. Heffernan, P. Cowley and C. Hay (eds.), *Developments in British Politics 9*, Palgrave Macmillan.

Tonge, J. (2011) 'The 2011 devolved elections in the UK', *Political Insight*, Vol. 2, No. 2, pp. 7–10.

Trench, A. (2010) 'Devolution since 2007', *Politics Review*, Vol. 20, No. 2, pp. 12–14.

Exam focus

Short response questions (around 5–6 minutes each)

1 What is the West Lothian Question?
2 What is asymmetrical devolution?
3 What is federal government?
4 Define the term multi-level governance.
5 Define the term local government.

Mid-length response questions (around 10–12 minutes each)

1 Outline and explain *three* differences between devolution and federalism.
2 Distinguish between primary legislative powers and secondary legislative powers.
3 Outline and explain the arguments in favour of the case for 'English votes for English laws'.
4 Outline and explain *three* functions of local government.
5 In what ways does central government control local government?

Mini-essay questions (around 25–30 minutes each)

1 To what extent has devolution turned the UK into a quasi-federal state?
2 How accurate is it to say that Scotland's devolved powers are greater than those of Wales?
3 'New Labour's programme of devolution has left England under-represented.' Discuss.
4 'The UK has effectively discarded local government.' To what extent do you agree with this statement?

 Extra resources to help you revise and consolidate your knowledge for this chapter are provided online at **www.hodderplus.co.uk/philipallan**. These include a revision PowerPoint, extension tasks and up-to-date weblinks.

Chapter 11

The European Union

Key questions answered in this chapter

➢ How has the European Union developed?

➢ What are the roles and powers of the European Union institutions?

➢ What policies have British governments pursued in the European Union?

➢ How has membership of the European Union affected the British political system?

The United Kingdom joined the European Economic Community (EEC) — later to become the European Union (EU) — in 1973. Since then, the EU has enlarged to 28 member states and taken on more policy responsibility. Membership of the EU has had a significant impact on the British political system, and the UK's relationship with the EU is an important issue in contemporary politics.

Links to follow up

http://europa.eu — website of the European Union.

Development of the European Union

The origins of the European Union lie in the aftermath of the Second World War (1939–45) when six western European states sought closer economic cooperation. They were France, West Germany, Italy, Belgium, the Netherlands and Luxembourg ('the Six'). The 1950 Schuman Plan proposed a European Coal and Steel Community (ECSC). Set up in 1952, this was a **supranational** body with its own policy-making authority, budget and laws. It differed from **intergovernmental** bodies in which states cooperated voluntarily and could veto proposals.

Key concept

> **Supranational** A supranational organisation is one in which nation states transfer sovereignty to institutions which then have their own independent authority to create laws that take precedence over national laws. The EU has a number of supranational features. It has exclusive competence in some policy areas (e.g. competition policy). EU law takes priority over national law, and is interpreted by the Court of Justice. The European Commission acts in the interests of the EU as a whole rather than that of individual member states. The European Parliament is directly elected by EU citizens. In many policy areas, national governments do not have a veto.

Intergovernmental and supranational organisations

Distinguish between

Intergovernmental organisations

> National governments are the dominant actors in decision making.
> Nation states retain sovereignty, cooperating on a voluntary basis.
> Decisions are taken by unanimity — states have the right to veto proposals.

Supranational organisations

> Nation states transfer decision-making authority to a higher body whose institutions have authority independent of their member states.
> Nation states pool their sovereignty and accept supranational laws that take priority over national law.
> Decisions are taken by majority or qualified majority votes — states do not have veto rights.

In 1957 the Six signed the Treaties of Rome, establishing the supranational European Economic Community (EEC) and European Atomic Energy Community (EURATOM). They began operating in 1958. The EEC agreed a Common Agricultural Policy (CAP) in 1962 and completed a customs union in 1968 by removing internal tariff barriers and establishing a common external tariff. The 1965 Merger Treaty brought together the existing bodies to form the European Community (EC).

The pace of **integration** slowed in the mid-1960s as French president Charles de Gaulle blocked plans to strengthen the EC's supranational elements. He also twice vetoed British membership of the EC. The 1970s brought only limited policy advances. The most significant was the creation in 1979 of the European Monetary System. It included the exchange rate mechanism (ERM), a currency grid in which the values of currencies were fixed against each other. The EC expanded to nine members when the UK, Ireland and Denmark joined in 1973. Three further states joined in the 1980s: Greece (1981), Spain and Portugal (both 1986).

Key term

> **Integration** The process of coordinating the activities of different states through common institutions and policies.

Box 11.1   The European Union: a chronology

1950   Schuman Plan proposes a European Coal and Steel Community (ECSC).

1952   ECSC is established.

1957   Treaty of Rome, establishing the European Economic Community (EEC), is signed by Belgium, France, West Germany, Italy, Luxembourg and the Netherlands.

1958   EEC is established.

1960   Seven states, including the UK, establish the European Free Trade Association (EFTA).

1961   UK applies for EEC membership (vetoed by France in 1963).

1965   Merger Treaty establishes the European Community (EC).

1967   UK reapplies for EEC membership — vetoed by France again.

1973   UK, Ireland and Denmark join the EEC.

1979   European Monetary System established. First direct elections to the European Parliament.

1981   Greece joins the EEC.

1985   Single European Act agreed (comes into force in 1987).

1986   Spain and Portugal join the EEC.

1989   Collapse of Communist regimes in central and eastern Europe.

1990   German unification.

1991   Maastricht Treaty agreed (comes into force in 1993).

1992   UK leaves the exchange rate mechanism.

1993   European Union (EU) is established.

1995   Austria, Finland and Switzerland join the EU.

1997   Amsterdam Treaty agreed (comes into force in 1999).

1999   Stage III of Economic and Monetary Union begins with 11 member states.

2000   Treaty of Nice agreed (comes into force in 2003).

2004   Cyprus, Czech Republic, Estonia, Hungary, Latvia, Lithuania, Malta, Poland, Slovakia and Slovenia join the EU.

2005   EU Constitutional Treaty shelved after 'no' votes in French and Dutch referendums.

2007   Bulgaria and Romania join the EU. Lisbon Treaty is agreed (comes into force in 2009).

2010   Eurozone crisis begins in Greece.

2012   25 member states, but not the UK, agree the fiscal compact.

2013   Croatia joins the EU.

Single market to single currency

The Single European Act (SEA), which was agreed in 1985 and came into effect in 1987, revived European integration. It created a single European market by the end of 1992. This is 'an area without internal frontiers in which the free movement of goods, services, persons and capital is ensured'. Three main barriers were removed:

➢ **Physical barriers**: customs checks at borders were scaled back.

➤ **Technical barriers**: under a system of 'mutual recognition', goods that met minimum standards in one member state could be freely traded in another. Professional qualifications would also be accepted across the EU.

➤ **Fiscal barriers**: new VAT procedures were introduced.

The single market led to a greater EC role in social and regional policy. France, Germany and the European Commission pushed for **economic and monetary union** (EMU) and further political union, but the UK opposed them. The Maastricht Treaty was agreed in 1991 and came into force in 1993. Its key features were:

Key term

➤ **Economic and monetary union** The creation of a single currency, central bank and common monetary policy.

➤ the creation of the European Union, comprising of three pillars: the existing EC; an intergovernmental pillar on Common Foreign and Security Policy (CFSP); and an intergovernmental pillar on Justice and Home Affairs (JHA)

➤ EMU, with a single currency to be established by 1999 for those member states meeting specified 'convergence criteria'

➤ the principle of **subsidiarity**, under which the EU should act only where member states are unable to do so effectively

Key concept

➤ **Subsidiarity** The principle that decisions should be taken as close as possible to the citizen. It has been a principle of EU law since the Maastricht Treaty — the EU should not act unless it can do so more effectively than national, regional or local government. Actions should not go beyond what is required to achieve the policy objective: decisions should be proportional.

The British government won two exemptions:

➤ an **opt-out** from EMU — the UK did not have to join the single currency; parliament was free to decide whether or not to participate at a future date

➤ an opt-out from the social chapter which extended cooperation in social policy — although the UK would accept the social chapter in 1997

Key term

➤ **Opt-out** An exemption negotiated by a state, and set out in a treaty or law, which means that it does not have to take part in a specific policy.

Deepening and widening

Since Maastricht, the EU has been engaged in both 'deepening' (further integration) and 'widening' (**enlargement**). Developments occurred in three main areas:

➤ economic and monetary union

➤ eastward enlargement

➤ treaty reform

Key term

➤ **Enlargement** The expansion of the EU to include new member states.

Economic and monetary union

The Eurozone included 17 states by 2013. Eleven states — Austria, Belgium, Finland, France, Germany, Ireland, Italy, Luxembourg, the Netherlands, Spain and Portugal — formed the 'first wave' at the launch of the single currency in 1999. The UK, Denmark and Sweden opted out. Greece joined in 2001, followed by Slovenia (2007), Cyprus and Malta (2008), Slovakia (2009) and Estonia (2011). Latvia joins in 2014. The values of the currencies of states adopting the euro were fixed. Their national currencies were then abolished and replaced by the euro.

EMU brings a number of benefits, including an end to exchange rate uncertainty and the elimination of transaction costs on cross-border trade. But it also involves a loss of monetary sovereignty. Interest rates in the Eurozone are set by the independent European Central Bank. Rules designed to ensure budgetary discipline and prevent excessive deficit and debt levels were not fully implemented. Some states ran up large debts, prompting a crisis in the Eurozone. Greece, Ireland, Portugal, Spain and Cyprus received bailouts from new EU funds and introduced austerity measures. The 2012 fiscal compact treaty established stricter rules and sanctions on budget deficits. It was signed by all member states except the UK and Czech Republic. The fiscal compact is an intergovernmental treaty outside the EU legal framework.

Links to follow up

http://ec.europa.eu/economy_finance — information on the euro.

Eastward enlargement

Austria, Finland and Sweden joined the EU in 1995. But the accession of 12 former Communist states from central and eastern Europe was the most ambitious and difficult in the EU's history. In the early 1990s, these states were slowly developing into liberal democracies with market economies — key criteria for EU membership. Each had to adopt existing EU law in its entirety.

Ten states became EU members in 2004: Cyprus, the Czech Republic, Estonia, Hungary, Latvia, Lithuania, Malta, Poland, Slovakia and Slovenia. Bulgaria and Romania joined in 2007, then Croatia in 2013. Five states — Iceland, Macedonia, Montenegro, Serbia and Turkey — are official candidates for membership. Albania, Bosnia-Herzegovina and Kosovo have also applied to join.

Links to follow up

http://ec.europa.eu/enlargement — information on EU enlargement.

Treaty reform

The EU's institutions and policies had to be reformed for an enlarged Union to function effectively. Since 1993, four new EU treaties have been agreed — Amsterdam, Nice, the Constitutional Treaty (which never came into force) and Lisbon:

> **Amsterdam Treaty.** The Amsterdam Treaty was agreed in 1997 and came into force in 1999. It transferred many policies from the intergovernmental Justice and Home Affairs

Figure 11.1 Map of the European Union

pillar to a supranational 'area of freedom, security and justice'. The UK gained opt-outs or opt-ins for some of these policies. Flexibility clauses allow a majority of member states to pursue further integration without the need for all states to participate.

➤ **Nice Treaty.** The Nice Treaty (agreed in 2001, came into force in 2003) created a European Security and Defence Policy under which the EU would develop a common defence policy and undertake limited military action. Nice also signalled post-enlargement changes to the EU institutions.

➤ **Constitutional Treaty.** The Treaty establishing a Constitution for Europe — often called the Constitutional Treaty or 'EU Constitution' — was signed in 2004 and included major institutional reforms. After 'no' votes in referendums in France and the Netherlands in 2005, the treaty was abandoned. However, many of its key features were enacted in the Lisbon Treaty.

> **Lisbon Treaty.** The Lisbon Treaty was agreed in 2007 and came into force in 2009, having initially been rejected in a referendum in Ireland. Rather than creating a constitution for the EU, it amended existing treaties. Lisbon brought about:
>   – the merging of the different pillars into one legal entity, the European Union
>   – a full-time president for the European Council, serving a 2½-year term
>   – a High Representative of the Union for Foreign Affairs and Security Policy
>   – a 'team presidency' system for the Council of the European Union
>   – a 'dual majority' system of **qualified majority voting**
>   – the extension of qualified majority voting and co-decision
>   – a clearer definition of the competences of the EU and its member states
>   – procedures that allow a move from **unanimity** to qualified majority voting without a treaty amendment

Key terms

> **Qualified majority voting** A voting arrangement in which proposals must win a set number of votes (more than 50%) to be approved.
> **Unanimity** A voting arrangement in which states can veto proposals.

Links to follow up

http://europa.eu/eu-law/treaties — guides to the EU treaties.

BBC 'Inside Europe' site, **http://news.bbc.co.uk** — news and analysis of developments in the EU.

The institutions of the European Union

The EU's institutional architecture is unique. It includes intergovernmental bodies in which national governments meet (the Council of the European Union and European Council) and supranational bodies with their own authority (the European Commission, the European Parliament and European Court of Justice).

European Commission

The European Commission is the executive body of the EU. It is based in Brussels. As a supranational body, it acts in the general interests of the Union and is independent of member states. The president of the commission and the College of Commissioners are its political face. But the commission also acts as a civil service for the EU, employing some 23,000 officials — far smaller than most national bureaucracies.

Key parts of the European Commission

> **President of the European Commission**. The commission president is nominated by a qualified majority vote in the European Council, and then elected by the European Parliament. The president and other commissioners serve a 5-year term. Jose Manuel

Barroso became president in 2004. His second term expires in 2014. The president allocates portfolios within the College of Commissioners, can reshuffle posts and demand the resignation of a commissioner. He or she provides leadership within the commission, but needs support from member states to lead the EU.

- **College of Commissioners.** Commissioners meet in the college to finalise legislative proposals and discuss developments. There are 28 commissioners, one nominated by each national government. But commissioners are not national representatives and must swear an oath of independence. The European Parliament votes to approve the college as a whole. After expressing concerns about some nominees, it forced changes in 2004 and 2010. Each commissioner has a portfolio covering an area of EU activity. The British national in the 2009–14 college is Catherine Ashton, who is High Representative of the Union for Foreign Affairs and Security Policy.
- **Directorates-general.** The commission is divided into administrative units called directorates-general, which cover particular policy areas (e.g. agriculture) or services (e.g. translation). There are 33 policy and external relations directorates-general.

Functions and powers

The European Commission has a number of powers. It:

- has the sole right to initiate draft legislation in most areas of EU activity (except common foreign and security policy)
- executes and administers EU legislation and programmes
- administers EU expenditure and collects revenue
- acts as a 'guardian of the treaties', ensuring that EU law is applied properly
- represents the EU on the world stage, notably in international trade negotiations

The commission has both a bureaucratic and a political role. Much of its work involves technical and administrative tasks similar to those performed by a national civil service. But it relies on national bureaucracies to monitor the implementation of **European Union law** and on the Court of Justice to punish transgressors.

Key term

- **European Union law** The laws of the European Union, contained in treaties, secondary legislation and decisions of the Court of Justice.

The commission played a significant agenda-setting role under Jacques Delors. But its standing was damaged by the allegations of fraud that led to the resignation *en masse* of the Santer Commission in 1999. Barroso has a high profile but his influence has been limited by the predominance of large member states in decisions concerning the Eurozone crisis.

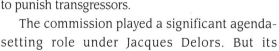
Links to follow up

http://ec.europa.eu — website of the European Commission.

Council of the European Union

The Council of the European Union is the main decision-making body of the EU. It is sometimes still referred to as the 'Council of Ministers' or the 'Council'. Based in Brussels, the Council of the European Union is the institution in which government ministers from the 28 member states take key decisions on EU legislation. It is the scene for intensive bargaining and negotiation.

The council consists of ten sectoral councils dealing with specific areas of EU activity. The most important are:

➢ **General Affairs.** Made up of national foreign ministers, it deals with issues that cut across policy areas (e.g. enlargement).

➢ **Foreign Affairs.** Made up of national foreign ministers and chaired by the High Representative, this deals with foreign, security and defence policy.

➢ **Economic and Finance Affairs (Ecofin).** Made up of national finance ministers, this covers budgetary and financial matters. An informal group of ministers from Eurozone states discusses Eurozone matters.

➢ **Agriculture and Fisheries.** This deals with the largest area of EU expenditure.

➢ **Justice and Home Affairs.** This deals with issues such as policing, crime and immigration.

Preparatory work is done by national delegations, headed by a Permanent Representative. They hold weekly meetings in the Committee of Permanent Representatives (COREPER), which takes decisions on technical issues.

The presidency of the Council of the European Union is held by member states. The Lisbon Treaty created a 'team presidency' system in which groups of three states cooperate for 18 months, with one of them formally holding it for a 6-month period. The UK will next hold the presidency in 2017. The state holding the presidency chairs council meetings but should not push its own interests at the expense of consensus.

Functions and powers

The Council of the European Union has a number of functions. It:

➢ is part of the EU legislature, although it shares legislative power with the European Parliament and legislative proposals must originate from the European Commission

➢ coordinates the broad economic policies of member states

➢ develops the common foreign and security policy

Many decisions in the council are made by consensus, but votes are also held regularly. Voting procedures vary from policy to policy. There are three main procedures:

➢ **Unanimity.** Here a proposal will fail if at least one member state vetoes it. An abstention does not count as a veto. Unanimity now applies only for major or sensitive policies.

➢ **Simple majority.** This applies to a limited number of technical decisions.

➢ **Qualified majority voting (QMV).** QMV now applies to most areas of EU activity. Each member state is allocated a set number of votes roughly according to their population (see Table 11.1). To be approved, a proposal must be backed, first, by a majority of member states, and second, by 260 votes from a total of 352. Under the Lisbon Treaty, weighted votes will from 1 November 2014 be replaced by a 'double majority' system in which a qualified majority is reached when at least 55% of member states, representing at least 65% of the population of the EU, vote for a proposal. In addition to not meeting these criteria, a blocking minority also requires at least four states.

QMV is an efficient way of taking decisions in a 28-member EU. But problems arise if states are forced to adopt policies they opposed. The Council of the European Union thus seeks consensus where possible.

Links to follow up

www.consilium.europa.eu — website of the Council of the European Union.

European Council

Set up in 1974, the European Council is the meeting place of the heads of government (or, in the cases of France and Finland, the heads of state) and foreign ministers of member states. The president of the European Council and the president of the European Commission also attend. The European Council is a political rather than legislative body. It was formally separated from the Council of the European Union by the Lisbon Treaty.

The European Council meets at least four times per year. The Lisbon Treaty created a permanent post of president of the European Council, held by an individual selected by the European Council for a renewable 2½-year term. Belgian prime minister Herman von Rompuy is the first to hold the post. His role has largely been one of preparing and chairing meetings. Leaders of the large states did not want the president of the European Council to become a rival who could determine the political direction of the EU. Lack of clarity about the relationship between the presidents of the European Council and European Commission has caused tensions.

Table 11.1 Votes allocated to member states under QMV (2003–14)

Member state	QMV votes	Population (millions)
Germany	29	82.2
France	29	63.8
United Kingdom	29	61.1
Italy	29	59.6
Spain	27	45.3
Poland	27	38.1
Romania	14	21.5
Netherlands	13	16.4
Greece	12	11.2
Portugal	12	10.6
Belgium	12	10.6
Czech Republic	12	10.3
Hungary	12	10.0
Sweden	10	9.1
Austria	10	8.3
Bulgaria	10	7.6
Denmark	7	5.5
Slovakia	7	5.4
Finland	7	5.3
Croatia	7	4.5
Ireland	7	4.4
Lithuania	7	3.4
Latvia	4	2.2
Slovenia	4	2.0
Estonia	4	1.3
Cyprus	4	0.8
Luxembourg	4	0.5
Malta	3	0.4

The functions of the European Council include:

➢ discussing major issues in the EU and in international affairs
➢ setting the agenda and political direction for the EU
➢ making key decisions on foreign policy and on the economic situation in the EU
➢ launching new policy initiatives and agreeing treaty change

The European Council has established itself as the EU's key strategic body, enhancing the power of member states and reducing the political influence of the European Commission.

Links to follow up

www.european-council.europa.eu — website of the European Council.

European Parliament

The European Parliament is the EU's only directly elected institution. The first direct elections were held in 1979. They take place at fixed 5-year intervals. Each member state uses a version of proportional representation. Turnout in European Parliament elections is lower than for general elections.

Seats in the European Parliament are allocated to member states roughly according to their population. After the accession of Croatia, there are 766 MEPs — 73 from the UK. This may be reduced as the Lisbon Treaty set a limit of 751.

A meeting of the European Parliament in Strasbourg

MEPs sit in transnational party groups based on ideology rather than nationality. Group membership brings funding and access to important posts within the European Parliament. The centre-right European People's Party (EPP) is the largest group. The Conservatives were members of the EPP from 1992 to 2009, but were uncomfortable with its federalist ethos. They formed the smaller European Conservatives and Reformists group in 2009. Labour and the Liberal Democrats sit in the social democratic and liberal groups respectively.

The European Parliament has three locations: Strasbourg (where most plenary sessions are held), Brussels (where committee meetings and some plenary sessions are held) and Luxembourg (where the Secretariat is based).

Functions and powers

The European Parliament has a number of powers:

➤ **Legislative power.** The European Parliament shares legislative power with the Council of the European Union. It cannot, however, initiate legislation. The influence of the European Parliament varies according to the legislative process being used. There are three main legislative routes for EU legislation:

– **Ordinary legislative procedure (formerly the co-decision procedure).** The European Parliament's power is greatest here, as it can both amend and block proposed legislation. It is now used for most areas of EU activity.

– **Consultation procedure.** The European Parliament is asked for its opinion on a legislative proposal, but the Council of the European Union and the European Commission are not obliged to take account of it. Before the Single European Act, this was the main legislative procedure. It is now used only in limited policy areas (e.g. competition law).

– **Consent procedure (formerly the assent procedure).** The European Parliament holds a simple majority vote. It is used to approve the accession of new EU members.

➤ **Budgetary authority.** The European Parliament shares budgetary authority with the Council of the European Union and can influence EU spending. It can request amendments to the draft budget and veto the final budget. Parliament's refusal to approve the budget contributed to the resignation of the Santer Commission in 1999.

➤ **Democratic supervision.** The European Parliament oversees the activities of the European Commission. Following nomination by the European Council, it elects the president of the European Commission. It holds hearings for nominees for the College of Commissioners, and forced the withdrawal of two nominees in 2004 and one in 2010. The European Parliament has not used its power to censure the commission. However, its investigations of financial mismanagement brought about the resignation of the Santer Commission. The European Parliament questions commissioners and members of the Council of the European Union. It also holds committees of inquiry (e.g. on the extraordinary rendition of terrorist suspects by the US Central Intelligence Agency in 2006).

Links to follow up

www.europarl.europa.eu — website of the European Parliament.

Is the European Parliament a 'real' parliament?

Parliaments perform a number of functions in national political systems, including:

● making laws
● holding the executive accountable and scrutinising its work
● representing the people
● legitimising the political system

The powers of the European Parliament have been extended in recent years, but they are not equivalent to those of national parliaments. It shares legislative power with the Council of the European Union and its powers to hold the European Commission accountable are limited. Low turnout in elections to the European Parliament limits its legitimacy and the representative role of MEPs. Public support for the European Parliament is weak and MEPs have low public profiles.

Questions

1 Compare the functions of the Westminster Parliament and the European Parliament.

2 Should the European Parliament be given powers similar to those of national parliaments in order to address the EU's democratic deficit, or should national parliaments be given a greater role in decision making in the EU?

Court of Justice

The Court of Justice of the European Union, located in Luxembourg, is the EU's judicial body. It consists of three courts:

➢ the Court of Justice
➢ the General Court (formerly the Court of First Instance)
➢ the Civil Service Tribunal

The first of these is the most significant. It has one judge from each member state, although most cases are heard by three or five judges. The Court of Justice upholds EU law, ensuring that it is applied uniformly and effectively. It decides cases involving member states, EU institutions, businesses and individuals. National courts ask the Court of Justice for preliminary rulings on matters of EU law.

Decisions by the court have extended the EU's competences and strengthened its institutions. In *Costa* v *ENEL* (1964) it ruled that Community law could not be overridden by national law. In *Cassis de Dijon* (1979), the court ruled that goods that are lawful in one member state — in this instance, French blackcurrant liqueur — cannot be prohibited by another. This established the principle of mutual recognition and paved the way for the single European market.

The Court of Justice should not be confused with the European Court of Human Rights in Strasbourg. The latter is associated with the Council of Europe, an intergovernmental organisation set up in 1949, and is not an EU institution.

Links to follow up

http://curia.europa.eu — website of the European Court of Justice.

The EU political system

It is difficult to fit the EU's institutions neatly into the categories of executive, legislature and judiciary because they tend to differ from national institutions. But we can broadly classify them by their function (see Figure 11.2). The Court of Justice is the EU's independent judicial branch. Much EU activity concerns economic and related policies (e.g. the single European market, agriculture). Here the EU legislative branch has the equivalent of two 'houses'. The Council of the European Union is the equivalent of an upper house where national governments are represented, and the European Parliament the equivalent of a lower house with member states represented roughly according to their population.

The European Commission can be seen as the executive branch of the EU. It does not have the power of national cabinets, but it resembles them in that each commissioner is responsible for a particular policy portfolio. It is also like an executive in that it makes proposals to the legislative branch and is responsible for implementing laws. But the Council of the European Union also performs some executive functions (e.g. influencing the EU's strategic direction).

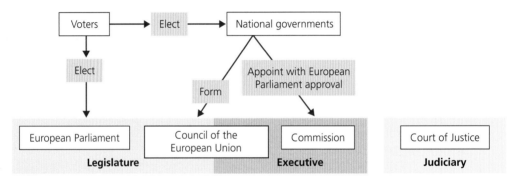

Figure 11.2 The EU system of government

Where does power lie?

It is helpful to distinguish between two different types of EU activity:

➤ 'history-making decisions' (e.g. treaty changes), which are the result of bargains between the EU's most powerful member states and are decided in the European Council

➤ 'day-to-day decisions' (e.g. single market legislation on mobile phone charges), where the European Commission, Council of the European Union and European Parliament are the major actors in decision making

The democratic deficit

The **democratic deficit** refers to the transfer of policy competences from national governments, which are accountable to national legislatures and electorates, to the EU, where decision-makers are less accountable to voters or elected bodies. National parliaments have been weakened because they cannot hold the European Commission accountable and

> ### Key concept
> ➤ **Democratic deficit** The erosion of democratic accountability that occurs when decision-making authority is transferred from institutions that are directly accountable to ones that are not. National parliaments and voters are less able to hold decision-makers accountable. The democratic deficit also refers to the perceived distance between the EU and its citizens. Citizens do not identify with or fully understand the EU, and have opposed important developments in the integration process.

national ministers may ignore domestic legislature or find themselves outvoted in the Council of the European Union.

The main executive body of the EU, the European Commission, is not directly elected. However, commissioners are nominated by national governments and the commission is accountable to the European Parliament. The European Parliament enjoys greater power than in the past and shares legislative power with the Council of the European Union in many policy areas, but it cannot propose legislation. The sharing of power between the EU institutions ensures that there are checks and balances.

The EU is also regarded as complex and remote from its citizens. Few citizens understand how the EU works. Decision making is often secretive, particularly negotiations in the Council of the European Union. When citizens have delivered a negative verdict on integration in referendums on EU treaties, the EU has often responded by stepping up its communications efforts ahead of a second vote. It is worth noting, though, that the EU's supranational institutions have most autonomy in technical areas which operate at arm's length from the democratic process in nation states as well. Decisions on interest rates, for example, are made by the European Central Bank in the EU and by the Bank of England in the UK. The EU has little power over taxation and spending, and its budget is relatively small. It also relies on national governments to implement EU policy.

Addressing the democratic deficit

Direct election of the president of the European Commission and a strengthening of the European Parliament are sometimes proposed as solutions to the democratic deficit. But critics argue that the model of the democratic nation state cannot be transposed to the European level. Democracy remains rooted within the nation state; relatively few citizens identify with the EU or, indeed, with Europe. The European Parliament enjoys neither the authority nor legitimacy of national parliaments. Turnout in European Parliament elections is low, falling to 43% across the EU in 2009, and campaigns are dominated by national issues.

The Lisbon Treaty included measures to address the democratic deficit:

➤ The power of the European Parliament increased, with co-decision extended to a further 40 areas and established as the standard legislative procedure.

➤ If one-third of national parliaments believe that a proposal from the European Commission breaches the principle of subsidiarity, they can ask it to reconsider.

➤ More decisions taken in the Council of the European Union are made public.
➤ Under the 'Citizens' Initiative', 1 million citizens from across the EU can call on the European Commission to launch a policy proposal.
➤ A secession clause sets out how a member state can leave the EU.

Links to follow up

www.votewatch.eu — details and analysis of voting in the European Parliament and Council of the European Union.

Viewpoint Is there a democratic deficit in the EU?

YES
● Legislation is initiated by the European Commission, which is not directly elected.
● National governments can be outvoted under qualified majority voting, and this may mean that the will of the electorate is thwarted.
● The directly elected European Parliament is not sufficiently powerful.
● Elections to the European Parliament are dominated by national issues and turnout is low.
● Citizens do not understand or identify with the EU — it is too distant and complex — and have opposed key developments (e.g. the Constitutional Treaty).

NO
● The European Commission is accountable to the European Parliament, and its key personnel are nominated by national governments.
● The EU's supranational institutions have greatest autonomy in technical matters (e.g. competition policy, central banking).
● National governments are represented in the Council of the European Union and the European Council, where bargaining is the norm.
● The European Parliament shares legislative power with the Council of the European Union in most policy areas — a system of checks and balances operates in the EU.
● The EU does not have power in key areas of national life, such as taxation, social security and education.

Understanding European integration

The EU has some of the characteristics of an international organisation and some of a federal state, but cannot be described accurately as either. Classic international organisations (e.g. the United Nations) and regional trade bodies (e.g. the North American Free Trade Area) are intergovernmental organisations in which nation states are the primary decision-makers. States cooperate voluntarily and retain the right to veto decisions they oppose: they retain sovereignty. But the EU has important supranational elements. The European Commission has independent authority and EU law is binding upon member states. States pool sovereignty when joining the EU: they give up some sovereignty but share in the greater capacity to act that this delivers.

Federalism

The EU is often compared to a federal system. **Federalism** is a political system in which the constitution divides power between two autonomous tiers of government: a federal (i.e. national) government and state (i.e. subnational) governments. Federalist ideas inspired

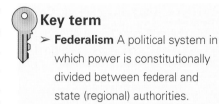

the pioneers of European integration in the postwar period, while some commentators also speak of the contemporary EU in terms of federalism. In the UK, Euro-federalism is often associated with the creation of a supranational EU 'state', whereas in continental Europe it refers to a constitutional sharing of power between the EU and its member states.

> **Key term**
> ➤ **Federalism** A political system in which power is constitutionally divided between federal and state (regional) authorities.

The EU has some of the features of a federal system:
➤ The EU treaties set out the powers held by different levels of government.
➤ EU law has primacy over national law.
➤ It has authority in many areas of public policy, including trade, monetary policy and agriculture.
➤ It has its own budget.
➤ It has its own currency, the euro.
➤ The European Commission negotiates trade treaties on behalf of member states.
➤ EU citizens are directly represented in the European Parliament.

To be a fully fledged federal system, however, the EU would have to be equivalent to a federal government, while the governments of member states would have powers equivalent to regional governments. This is not the case:
➤ States retain their distinctive political systems.
➤ Citizens primarily identify with their nation states and European identity is weak.
➤ Except for the European Parliament, the EU's major institutions derive their authority from national governments. The European Council and Council of the European Union are run by national governments; the key figures in the Commission and Court of Justice are appointed by them.
➤ The EU does not have substantial authority over areas such as taxation, health and defence policy.

Integration theory

Different theories have been put forward to explain the European integration process. The most significant are:
➤ neo-functionalism
➤ intergovernmentalism
➤ supranationalism
➤ multi-level governance

Neo-functionalism

Neo-functionalism was the prevalent theory of European integration in the 1950s and 1960s. It claims that interest groups and supranational bodies are the most important actors in the integration process. Integration is a dynamic process, with cooperation in one area (e.g. coal and steel) producing 'spillover' into others (e.g. trade). Neo-functionalism assumed that political and economic elites would then transfer their loyalties to supranational bodies.

The theory fell out of favour in the 1970s when national governments reasserted their authority. But it was revived in the 1980s by scholars who argued that the European Commission and business interests were responsible for pushing for the single European market and EMU. Critics argue that it ignores the power of national governments in 'history-making decisions'.

Intergovernmentalism

Intergovernmentalism claims that national governments are the most important actors in the EU. They determine the EU's development by agreeing to cooperate in areas of mutual benefit but defending their sovereignty in other areas. This perspective argues that EMU came about because the most powerful member states saw it as being in their national interest, and the details were thrashed out in bargaining between them. A variant of this approach, liberal intergovernmentalism, notes that prior to EU negotiations, governments form their policies in response to pressures from groups and institutions in the national arena. Critics argue that intergovernmentalism downplays the influence of supranational bodies and is more suitable in explaining 'history-making decisions' than routine policy formation.

Supranationalism

The theory of supranationalism (which is distinct from the concept of a supranational organisation) claims that major developments in the EU come about as a result of the formation of supranational coalitions. In the case of the Single European Act, it points to the importance of commission president Delors and lobbying by multinational corporations that were concerned by the relatively poor performance of the European economy compared to Japan and the USA.

Multi-level governance

The EU is a system of **multi-level governance** in which a range of actors are involved in decision making. National governments remain the most important actors: they have authority in the major policy areas and are the key players in big decisions in the EU (e.g. treaty change and common foreign and security policy). But national governments do not monopolise decision making. Supranational actors such as the European Commission have their own authority and are the most important actors in technical areas of policy (e.g. single market rules). Subnational governments such as the Scottish government also have policy-making powers.

Key term

➤ **Multi-level governance**
A system of decision making in which subnational, national and supranational institutions all have policy competences.

A system of multi-level governance operates in the UK, with decisions taken at different levels of government:

➤ the EU (e.g. the operation of the single European market)
➤ central government (e.g. income tax and social security)
➤ subnational government — the devolved bodies (e.g. education in Scotland)
➤ local government (e.g. local transport)

The UK and the European Union

The UK did not join the EEC at the outset, as the government feared the loss of sovereignty that would result from membership. It saw Britain operating in 'three circles': the Commonwealth, the 'special relationship' with the USA, and intergovernmental cooperation in Europe. The UK supported free trade rather than a customs union and joined the European Free Trade Association (EFTA) in 1960.

Harold Macmillan's Conservative government applied for EEC membership in 1961. The change in policy was a result of:

➤ the declining political and trading importance of the Commonwealth
➤ the UK's declining influence in world affairs, illustrated by the 1956 Suez crisis
➤ the successful development of the EEC, which prompted fears that the UK would be left behind
➤ pressure for British entry from the US government

The UK opposed supranationalism but hoped to defend its sovereignty within the EEC. But French president de Gaulle vetoed the application in 1963 and did so again in 1967 when Labour's Harold Wilson applied for entry.

Membership negotiations proved successful under Edward Heath's Conservative government and the UK joined the EEC on 1 January 1973. In 1975, the Labour government called a referendum which produced a two-to-one vote in favour of continued membership.

The Thatcher and Major governments (1979–97)

In its early years, Margaret Thatcher's Conservative government sought to reduce British contributions to the EEC budget. It then became a leading supporter of the single European market, which dovetailed with the Thatcherite commitment to the free market. But by the late 1980s, Thatcher was a staunch opponent of further European integration, particularly the Social Charter and EMU. Cabinet divisions on Europe contributed to Thatcher's downfall in 1990.

John Major had been instrumental in taking the UK into the ERM in the final weeks of Thatcher's premiership. He saw the Maastricht Treaty as a good deal for the UK, given the opt-outs on EMU and the social chapter. But **Eurosceptics** argued that it meant an unacceptable loss of sovereignty and opposed EMU, particularly after sterling's exit from the ERM in 1992. Major maintained his non-committal 'wait and see' policy on EMU, but struggled to hold the Eurosceptic and **pro-European** wings of the Conservative Party

Key terms

➤ **Eurosceptic** Concerned about the extension of supranational authority in the EU and hostile to further integration.
➤ **Pro-European** Supportive of further European integration and a leading role for the UK in the EU.

together. Policy became more Eurosceptic, notably the 'non-cooperation' policy pursued after the EU banned British beef exports during the BSE crisis.

The Blair and Brown governments (1997–2010)

The Blair government agreed the Amsterdam Treaty in 1997, signing the social chapter and framing an EU employment strategy that balanced labour market flexibility with social protection. In the Amsterdam, Nice and Lisbon treaties, Blair accepted an extension of QMV but preserved the veto on issues of 'vital national interest', such as taxation, treaty change and defence.

Conflict in Kosovo persuaded Blair that the EU must develop a more effective defence and security role. The UK was a pivotal player in the creation of a European Security and Defence Policy. The government maintained British border controls but supported EU action on organised crime, illegal immigration and asylum.

The Blair government supported British membership of the Eurozone if the economic conditions were right. It would hold a referendum if the cabinet decided to join. Chancellor Gordon Brown set out five 'economic tests' against which entry would be judged:

➢ sustainable convergence between the UK economy and the Eurozone
➢ sufficient economic flexibility
➢ the impact on investment in the UK
➢ the impact on financial services
➢ the impact on employment

Brown announced in 2003 that only one of the tests (financial services) had been met. This ended the prospect of the UK joining the euro in the medium term, and an issue that had dominated British politics for a decade fell off the agenda.

The government had promised to hold a referendum on the abandoned Constitutional Treaty, but did not hold a referendum on the Lisbon Treaty. Climate change, competitiveness and economic reform were key priorities in the final years of Labour's period in office.

Blair had hoped to increase British influence in, and domestic support for, the EU. On defence, internal security and economic reform, the UK played an active role in the EU. But the invasion of Iraq and non-participation in EMU limited British influence. Domestically, Labour was unable to turn back the tide of Eurosceptic opinion.

The Conservative–Liberal Democrat coalition (2010–)

In coalition negotiations, the Conservatives dropped demands for repatriation of powers (e.g. on social and employment policy) and safeguards on the Lisbon Treaty (e.g. on criminal justice and the Charter of Fundamental Rights). The Liberal Democrats accepted that there would be no further transfers of power to the EU under the coalition. Like its predecessors, the coalition supports the single market and deregulation, advocates further enlargement and seeks reform of the EU budget. Ministers have suggested that the UK will exercise its right under the Lisbon Treaty to opt-out of some 130 EU measures on crime and justice in 2014, before opting-in to a limited number of these measures.

The Eurozone crisis prompted the EU to create bailout funds and move towards fiscal union. In the Euro Plus Pact (2011) and fiscal compact (2013), most member states agreed tougher rules on budget deficits and public debt, and greater coordination of their tax systems. However, the UK did not sign these and Cameron vetoed plans for an EU treaty

David Cameron speaking at a European Council press conference in Brussels in 2011

on fiscal union in 2012, before 25 member states signed the fiscal compact. The coalition has agreed that some member states should develop European economic governance as a way of saving the euro (which it regards as in Britain's national interest) in return for assurances that the UK would not participate. This raises the prospect of the UK being outside the inner core of a two-speed Europe. However, the government launched a legal challenge against the Financial Transactions Tax which was agreed by eleven states under the EU's flexibility provisions.

Domestically, the coalition introduced the European Union Act (2011) which requires any treaty transferring powers from the UK to the EU to be put to a referendum. It also launched a review of EU competences and how they affect the UK.

Links to follow up

www.gov.uk/government/topics/europe — details of the government's EU policy.

An awkward partner

Professor Stephen George described the UK as an 'awkward partner' within the EU. This does not imply that the UK is the only country to oppose further integration or fight for its national interest. But it is less enthusiastic about European integration than most other member states. Factors contributing to British 'awkwardness' include:

➢ **A distinctive history and culture.** The UK's historical development differs from that of continental Europe. It has had a global outlook and close relationship with the USA, and has not experienced the major political upheavals seen in other European states.

> **Wariness of further integration.** British governments have tended to be less enthusiastic about (and often hostile to) further integration. The UK has supported intergovernmental cooperation rather than extensive supranational authority; a single market rather than EMU. Great importance has been attached to the defence of **national sovereignty**.

 Key term

> **National sovereignty** Ultimate decision-making authority is located in the nation state.

> **Limited influence in EU negotiations.** On some key EU policies (e.g. EMU), British governments have not set the agenda but have reacted to proposals from others by attempting to slow the pace of integration or limit its impact. The UK has often been in a minority of states opposed to change and has not developed durable alliances to rival the Franco-German partnership. But it has been influential on some issues, notably the single market and defence.

> **Weak elite consensus.** The UK does not have the strong elite consensus on the benefits of the EU found in many other member states. Labour and the Conservatives have often taken adversarial positions on Europe, and the issue has also caused divisions within the main parties. Euroscepticism is prominent in the Conservative Party and the UK Independence Party (UKIP).

> **Limited popular support.** Levels of public support for EU membership and integration are lower in the UK than in most other member states (see Table 11.2). UK citizens are also less knowledgeable about the EU and less likely to feel European. Sovereignty issues are prominent in the British debate and many newspapers take populist Eurosceptic positions.

Table 11.2 UK public opinion and EU membership

Question: 'If there were a referendum now on whether Britain should stay in or get out of the European Union, how would you vote?'

Year	Stay in (%)	Get out (%)
1977	47	42
1980	26	65
1983	36	55
1987	48	39
1990	62	28
1991	60	29
1992	52	35
1993	46	39
1994	52	36
1996	44	40
1997	49	35
1998	47	40
1999	51	41
2000	49	44
2001	48	43
2003	49	41
2007	51	39
2011	41	49
2012	44	48

Source: Ipsos MORI, www.ipsos-mori.com.

The EU and British politics

Membership of the EU has had a significant impact upon the British political system. The EU is the main actor in many areas of public policy (see Table 11.3). Much legislation in policy fields such as agriculture and the standards of goods and services emanates from the EU.

Table 11.3 Policy competences of the EU (selected)

Areas where the EU has exclusive competence	Areas where the EU and member states share competence	Areas where member states retain competence
Customs union	Single European market	Taxation
Competition policy	Social and employment policy	Social security
Monetary policy (in the Eurozone)	Regional policy	Education
Trade	Agriculture	Health
Fisheries	Freedom, security and justice	Defence

Sovereignty and the EU

An institution is generally understood to be sovereign if it has final legislative authority and can act without undue external constraint. The term 'sovereignty' is used in different ways in the debates on Europe, for example:

➤ **national sovereignty** — the idea that final decision-making authority should reside within the nation state, with the national government determining law for its own territory

➤ **parliamentary sovereignty** — the doctrine that the Westminster Parliament is the supreme legislative body within the UK

➤ **popular sovereignty** — the idea that the electorate should choose decision-makers

➤ **economic sovereignty** — the idea that national governments should have the authority to determine economic and monetary policy

Key term

➤ **Parliamentary sovereignty** Parliament is the supreme law-making body.

Eurosceptics and pro-Europeans offer different interpretations of sovereignty and the implications of EU membership. Eurosceptics tend to define sovereignty in absolute terms, seeing it as ultimate decision-making authority. They argue that the supranational EU has undermined British sovereignty.

Eurosceptics differ on how 'lost' sovereignty can be regained. Most favour a referendum on EU membership. 'Soft Eurosceptics' want UK opt-outs on policies on issues such as policing and crime, and the repatriation (i.e. the return to national governments) of some EU powers (e.g. employment policy). 'Hard Eurosceptics' regard either withdrawal from the EU or a fundamental renegotiation of British membership as the best means of restoring sovereignty.

Instead of viewing sovereignty as a legal concept concerned with ultimate law-making authority, pro-Europeans define sovereignty in terms of effective influence and a practical capacity to act. The UK has not lost sovereignty; rather it has *pooled sovereignty* — it has shared sovereignty with other EU member states in order to increase its influence and capacity to act.

Viewpoint Has EU membership eroded British sovereignty?

YES
- EU law has primacy over national law, meaning that UK law can be overturned.
- The UK has lost its right of veto in policy areas where qualified majority voting is used.
- The EU has extended its competences into crucial areas such as immigration, defence and monetary policy.
- Parliament and voters have few opportunities to hold EU decision-makers accountable.

NO
- By pooling sovereignty, the UK has achieved policy objectives (e.g. the single market) that it could not have achieved alone.
- The UK has more influence in European and world affairs as a member of a strong EU.
- **Globalisation** means that no state can act independently on issues such as the environment, migration and economic policy.
- The UK Parliament can repeal the European Communities Act, and the Lisbon Treaty sets out how a state could leave the EU if it chooses.

Key term
> **Globalisation** The process by which states and peoples become more interdependent and interconnected.

Parliamentary sovereignty

The doctrine of parliamentary sovereignty is a central element of the British constitution. It has three elements:

➤ Legislation made by parliament cannot be overturned by any higher authority.
➤ Parliament can legislate on any subject of its choosing.
➤ No parliament can bind its successors.

But EU law has primacy: in cases of conflict between national law and EU law, the latter takes priority. The European Communities Act (1972) gave future EU law legal force in the UK and denied effectiveness to national legislation which conflicts with it. This was illustrated in the 1990 *Factortame* case. The Merchant Shipping Act (1988) had prevented non-British citizens from registering boats as British in order to qualify for the UK's quota under the Common Fisheries Policy. But the House of Lords, following a ruling from the European Court of Justice, decided that the Act was incompatible with Community (now EU) law and should be 'disapplied'. Compensation was subsequently paid to the Spanish fishermen who brought the case.

This would appear to undermine parliamentary sovereignty, as parliament cannot legislate on any subject of its choosing and laws made by parliament can be overturned by another authority. However, we cannot say that parliamentary sovereignty is now meaningless. *Factortame* concerned legislation that was not intended as a deliberate breach of EU law. In *Thoburn* v *Sunderland City Council* (2002), the Law Lords ruled that there was a hierarchy of Acts of Parliament: 'ordinary' statutes and 'constitutional' statutes. Constitutional statutes such as the European Communities Act (1972) should only be repealed when parliament does so by express provisions, rather than as an unintended consequence of a new law. Ultimately, parliament still retains ultimate legislative authority, as it has the right to repeal the European Communities Act.

Section 18 of the European Union Act (2011) restates the sovereignty of parliament, but does not alter the relationship between the UK and EU. The Act also provides a 'referendum lock' under which any future treaty transferring powers from the UK to the EU must be put to a binding referendum. A referendum must also be held if, for example, the government seeks to joins the euro or give up the national veto.

Parliamentary scrutiny

National parliaments find it difficult to hold ministers accountable for decisions made in the EU and scrutinise EU activity. Under the scrutiny reserve, UK ministers cannot agree to EU legislation which has not been debated in the House of Commons or cleared by the House of Commons European Scrutiny Committee. It receives some 1,100 documents per year. The House of Lords EU Select Committee holds inquiries on key developments.

The prime minister gives statements to the Commons after European Council meetings. Parliament is also an important arena for debate on Britain's relationship with the EU. EU treaties must be ratified by parliament and, under the European Union Act (2011), parliamentary approval is required for specified decisions (e.g. adopting qualified majority voting).

Policy making

The lead actors in British policy towards the EU are the prime minister, the Cabinet Office and the Foreign and Commonwealth Office. The prime minister shapes the key policy objectives and attends European Council meetings. In this respect, EU membership has strengthened the position of the prime minister. But cabinet divisions on Europe undermined the authority of Thatcher and Major, Blair ceded responsibility for policy on EMU to the Treasury, and Cameron's soft Euroscepticism is constrained by coalition with the pro-European Liberal Democrats.

Within the cabinet system, a cabinet committee undertakes detailed policy work. The prime minister's European adviser leads the Europe and Global Issues Secretariat. It is based in the Cabinet Office and coordinates policy so that departments fall in line with the agreed negotiating position. The Foreign and Commonwealth Office also coordinates policy and takes the lead in EU negotiations.

Government departments and local authorities implement EU legislation, and the UK courts enforce EU law. Some local authorities have benefited from money available to poorer regions through the EU Structural Funds. The EU has policy competence in many areas (e.g. agriculture) devolved to the Scottish Parliament, Welsh Assembly and Northern Ireland Assembly. But responsibility for the UK's relations with the EU is 'reserved' to the UK Parliament. The devolved administrations are consulted on UK policy in the EU, but once the UK government's single negotiating line has been settled, they are bound by it.

Political parties and the EU

The UK's role in the EU is an issue that political parties have found difficult to handle. Reasons for this include: changes in the positions of the main parties, internal divisions and the difficulties of exploiting the issue for electoral advantage.

Policy change

The two main parties have swapped positions on Europe. The Conservatives were the more pro-European from the 1960s to the late 1980s. But Euroscepticism escalated after Maastricht and became the dominant creed in the party in the 1990s. Many Conservatives saw further European integration as a threat to national sovereignty and their free market policies. The Conservatives are now a soft Eurosceptic party — they support a limited renegotiation of EU membership and repatriation of some policies.

Labour opposed EEC membership in 1961, applied for entry in 1967, then opposed the membership terms agreed by the Conservatives in 1971–72. It called for withdrawal from the European Community in its 1983 manifesto. A pro-European conversion began in the late 1980s when Labour supported the Community's social and regional policy agenda. Labour has been the more pro-European of the main parties since then, particularly under Blair. He believed that, in an era of globalisation, economic and social reforms had to be pursued at European as well as national level.

Internal divisions

Differences on Europe have also been found *within* the two main parties. Heath's Conservative government only secured parliamentary backing for EEC entry when 69 Labour MPs defied the whip to support it. Labour's policy of withdrawal from the European Community was an important factor in the defection of pro-European MPs to the Social Democratic Party in 1981. During the ratification of the Maastricht Treaty, 20% of Conservative MPs rebelled. In coalition, Cameron has faced backbench rebellions from 'hard' Eurosceptic Conservatives and criticism from pro-European Liberal Democrats over EU policy.

Party leaders try to quell dissent by lowering the prominence of the issue, postponing difficult decisions and pledging referendums. Wilson held a referendum on continued membership of the EEC in 1975 in which ministers were permitted to take opposing sides. Major maintained a 'wait and see' policy on EMU and promised a referendum should Britain seek to join the euro. Blair promised referendums on the single currency and Constitutional Treaty. Cameron has promised a renegotiation of Britain's relationship followed by an 'in-out' referendum should the Conservatives win the next general election.

Party competition

Debates on Europe have often been characterised by adversarial politics in which the two main parties take opposing positions. This has sometimes resulted from pronounced differences between the parties, such as at the 1983 and 2001 elections. However, the Conservatives and Labour broadly supported the Maastricht Treaty, but Labour voted against it because the government had not signed the social chapter.

Since the 2001 election, when the Conservative campaign to 'save the pound' did not bring them great electoral reward, Labour and the Conservatives have downplayed the issue of European integration. Europe has not been one of the most important issues for voters. But it has a higher profile in European Parliament elections. The UK Independence Party (UKIP), which wants withdrawal from the EU, won 16% of the vote in the 2009 European Parliament elections but has fared less well in general elections. However, opinion polls in 2013 put support for UKIP above 10% — the party is attracting support from former Conservative and Labour voters.

What you should know

❯ The European Union has changed significantly since the UK joined the EEC in 1973. It now has 28 members and has extended its policy competence into areas such as economic, internal security and foreign policy. The EU's supranational institutions have also grown in importance. The EU, then, looks less like an organisation of sovereign nation states than the EEC did, but nor is it a fully fledged federal state. Nation states shape the EU's development and retain significant powers in major policy areas, such as taxation, social security and defence.

❯ The UK is regarded as an 'awkward partner' in the EU. Successive governments have sought to defend national sovereignty and opted out of major EU policy developments such as EMU. The Blair governments were more pro-European in outlook than the Thatcher and Major governments, but did not join the euro. The coalition government has not participated in the EU's measures to tackle the Eurozone crisis. British governments have, however, also been influential agenda setters in areas such as the single European market.

❯ EU membership has had a significant impact on British politics. Many areas of public policy are now determined in the EU. EU law takes priority over national law. Political parties have changed positions on Europe and experienced damaging internal divisions. Euroscepticism is more prevalent in the British party system, public opinion and the media than in many other EU member states.

UK/US comparison

Federalism in the USA and EU

➤ The USA is a federal state in which law-making power is divided between two tiers of government: the federal government (located in Washington DC) and the governments of the 50 states of the USA. The European Union has some of the characteristics of a federal system, but is a hybrid of intergovernmental and supranational elements.

➤ The US federal system is enshrined in the US Constitution. The 13 original states initially agreed the Articles of Confederation (1777) which created a union of sovereign states. These were replaced by the Constitution of the United States in 1787. The Tenth Amendment states that powers that are not delegated to the federal government nor prohibited to the states are reserved to the states or to the people. The division of powers can only be altered by amendment to the constitution. The EU was created by international treaty and its member states remain sovereign under international law. The distribution of powers between the EU and its member states is set out in the EU treaties, which can be amended with the unanimous support of the member states.

➤ A clear separation of powers exists between the executive, legislative and judicial branches of the US federal government. In the European Union, there is no clear distinction between executive, legislative and judicial functions. The EU's major decision-making institutions, the Council of the European Union and European Council, derive their authority from national governments.

➤ Powers reserved to the US federal government include defence, foreign policy, the US currency and the US single market. Few powers are reserved exclusively to the states (e.g. local taxes), but power is shared between the federal and state governments in many areas (e.g. criminal and civil law, health, education). The EU has substantial power in areas such as trade, but lacks power over taxation, social security and defence.

➤ The US Constitution does not contain a secession clause: there is no automatic right for a state to leave the USA. Eleven southern states declared secession in 1860–61 but were defeated in the American Civil War. The Treaty of Lisbon includes a secession clause that sets out how a member state might leave the EU.

Further reading

Cini, M. (2011) 'Where does power lie in the EU?', *Political Insight,* Vol. 2, No. 1, pp. 13–15.

Geddes, A. (2013) *Britain and the European Union*, Palgrave Macmillan.

Lynch, P. (2012) 'The coalition and the European Union', *Politics Review*, Vol. 21, No. 3, pp. 8–11.

McCormick, J. (2011) *Understanding the European Union*, 5th edn, Palgrave Macmillan.

Moxon, K. and MacEwan, I. (2012) 'Debate: should the UK remain within the EU?', *Politics Review*, Vol. 22, No. 1, pp. 16–17.

Whitaker, R. and Lynch, P. (2009) 'Where does power lie in the European Union?', *Politics Review*, Vol. 18, No. 1, pp. 10–13.

Exam focus

Short response questions (around 5–6 minutes each)

1 What is supranationalism?
2 What is qualified majority voting (QMV)?
3 What is meant by the term subsidiarity?
4 What is a Eurosceptic?
5 Define the term 'democratic deficit'.

Mid-length response questions (around 10–12 minutes each)

1 Distinguish between supranationalism and intergovernmentalism.
2 What is the significance of the European Commission within the EU?
3 Outline and explain two advantages and two disadvantages of the European Single Currency (the 'euro')?
4 Identify and explain *three* arguments against further European integration.
5 How has European Union membership affected parliamentary sovereignty?

Mini-essay questions (around 25–30 minutes each)

1 To what extent is it accurate to say that there is little real difference between the three main parties on the question of UK relations with the European Union?
2 'The European Union has effectively become a federal superstate.' To what extent do you agree with this statement?
3 'Those EU institutions that hold the most power are those which are the least democratically accountable.' Discuss.
4 Critically assess the view that the twin processes of EU integration and enlargement have gone too far.

Extra resources to help you revise and consolidate your knowledge for this chapter are provided online at **www.hodderplus.co.uk/philipallan**. These include a revision PowerPoint, extension tasks and up-to-date weblinks.

Index

Page numbers in red type refer to key terms and concepts